Street by Stree

LEICESTER MARKET HARBOROUGH

LUTTERWORTH, OADBY, SYSTON, WIGSTON

Anstey, Birstall, Blaby, Broughton Astley, Cosby, Countesthorpe, Earl Shilton, Enderby, Fleckney, Groby, Kibworth Beauchamp, Markfield, Narborough, Ratby, Stoney Stanton

2nd edition December 2005

Original edition printed August 2003

Published by AA Publishing (a trading name of Automobile Association Developments Limited, whose registered office is Fanum House, Basing View, Basingstoke, Hampshire RG21 4EA. Registered number 1878835).

Mapping produced by the Cartography Department of The Automobile Association. (A02549)

A CIP Catalogue record for this book is available from the British Library.

Printed by Oriental Press in Dubai

 The publishers would welcome information to correct any errors or omissions and to keep this atlas up to date. Please write to Publishing, The Automobile Association, Fanum House (FH12), Basing View, Basingstoke, Hampshire, RG21 4EA.

Ref: ML225z

Key to map pages ii-iii

Key to map symbols iv-1

Enlarged map pages 2-3

Main map pages 4-81

Index – towns & villages 82

Index – streets 83-99

Index – featured places 99-101

Acknowledgements 101

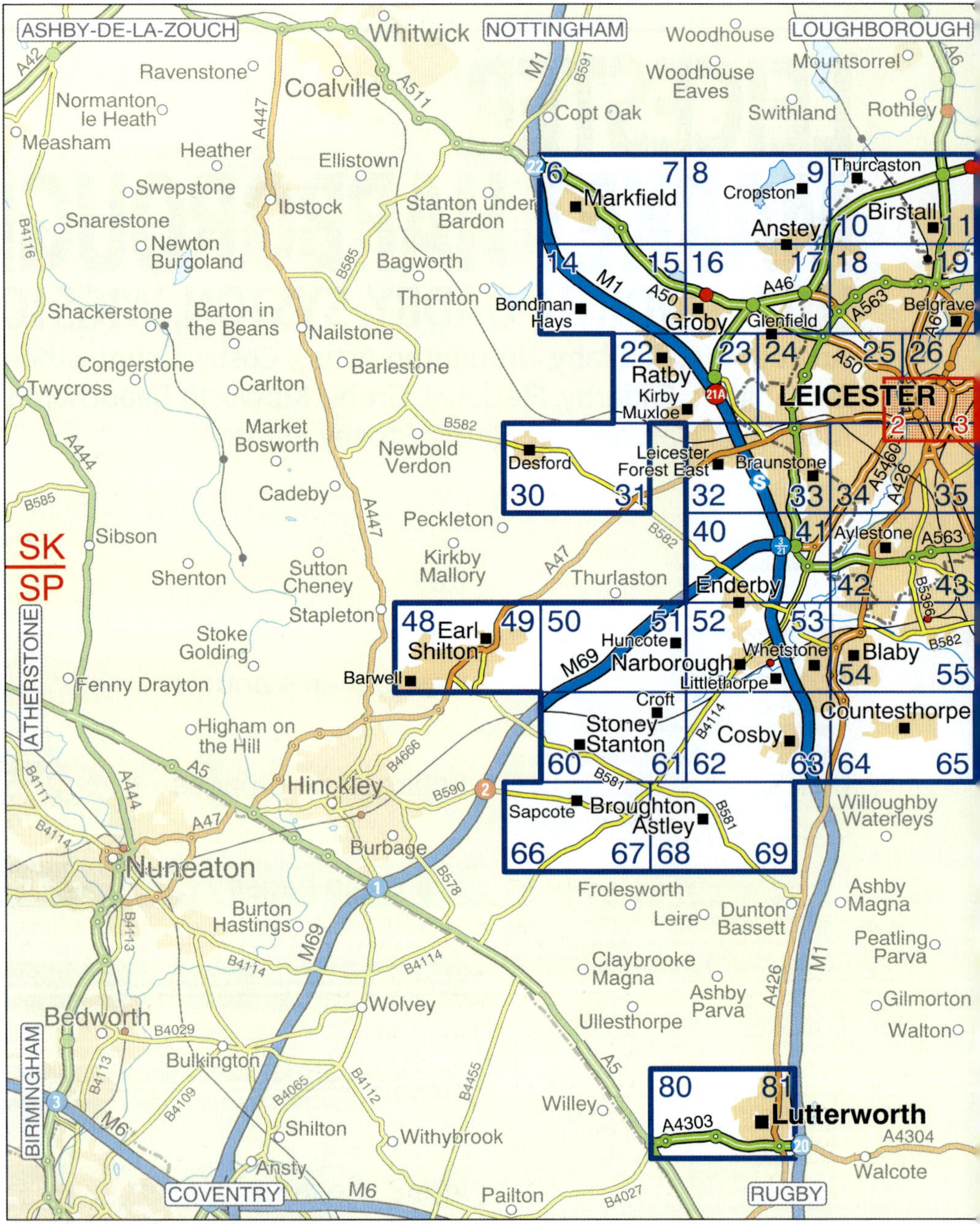

Scale of enlarged map pages 1:10,000 6.3 inches to 1 mile

0 1/4 miles 1/2

0 1/4 1/2 kilometres 3/4 1

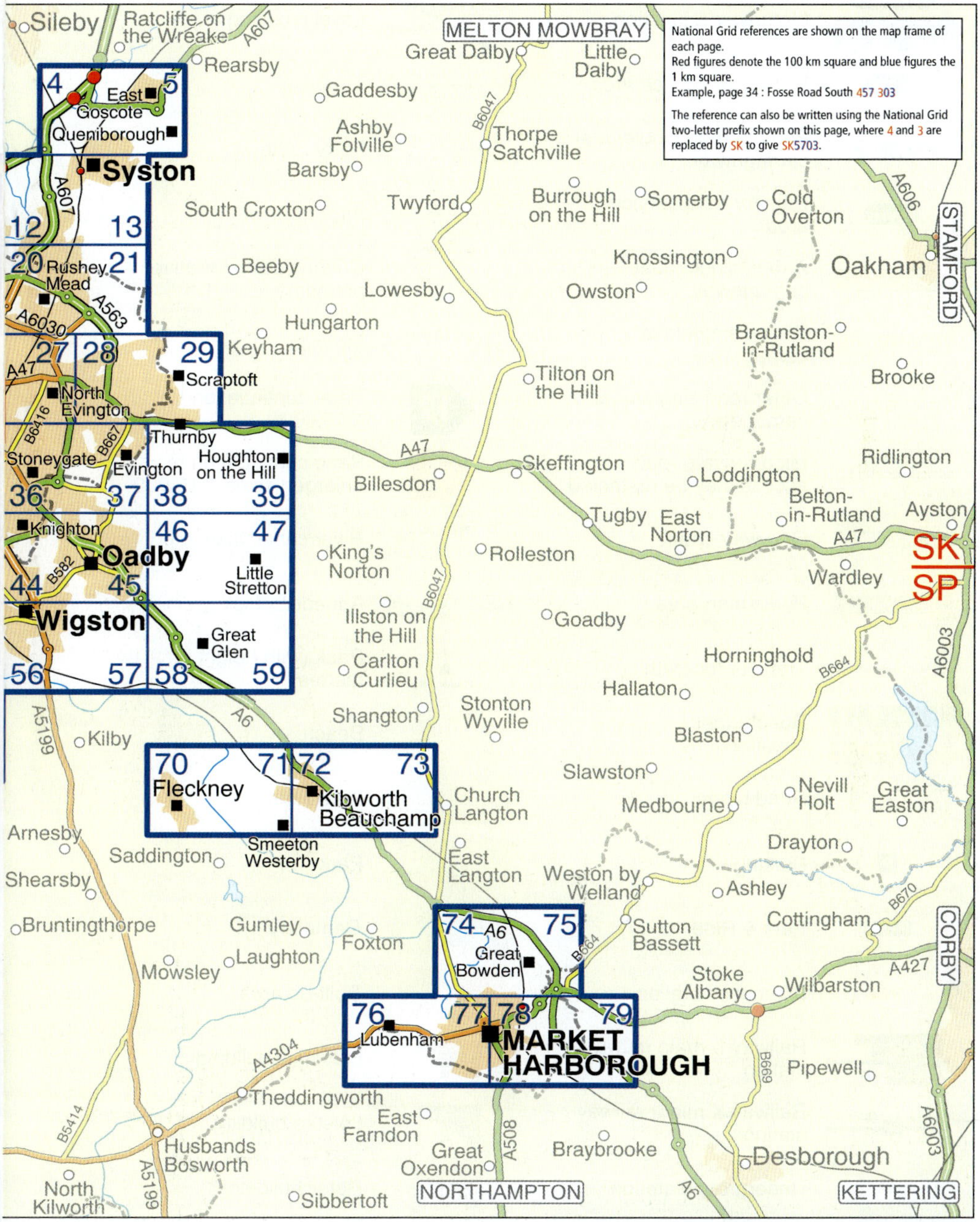

National Grid references are shown on the map frame of each page.
Red figures denote the 100 km square and blue figures the 1 km square.
Example, page 34 : Fosse Road South 457 303

The reference can also be written using the National Grid two-letter prefix shown on this page, where 4 and 3 are replaced by SK to give SK5703.

4.2 inches to 1 mile **Scale of main map pages** **1:15,000**

0 1/4 miles 1/2 3/4 1

0 1/4 1/2 kilometres 3/4 1 1 1/4 1 1/2

- [Junction 9] Motorway & junction
- [Services] Motorway service area
- Primary road single/dual carriageway
- [Services] Primary road service area
- A road single/dual carriageway
- B road single/dual carriageway
- Other road single/dual carriageway
- Minor/private road, access may be restricted
- One-way street
- Pedestrian area
- Track or footpath
- Road under construction
- Road tunnel
- Parking
- Park & Ride
- Bus/coach station
- Railway & main railway station
- Railway & minor railway station
- Underground station
- Light railway & station
- Preserved private railway
- [LC] Level crossing
- Tramway
- Ferry route
- Airport runway
- County, administrative boundary
- Mounds
- [17] Page continuation 1:15,000
- [3] Page continuation to enlarged scale 1:10,000
- River/canal, lake, pier
- Aqueduct, lock, weir
- [465 Winter Hill] Peak (with height in metres)
- Beach
- Woodland
- Park
- Cemetery
- Built-up area
- Industrial building
- Leisure building
- Retail building
- Other building

Symbol	Meaning	Symbol	Meaning
	City wall		Castle
A&E	Hospital with 24-hour A&E department		Historic house or building
PO	Post Office	Wakehurst Place NT	National Trust property
	Public library		Museum or art gallery
	Tourist Information Centre		Roman antiquity
	Seasonal Tourist Information Centre		Ancient site, battlefield or monument
	Petrol station, 24 hour Major suppliers only		Industrial interest
	Church/chapel		Garden
	Public toilets		Garden Centre Garden Centre Association Member
	Toilet with disabled facilities		Garden Centre Wyevale Garden Centre
PH	Public house AA recommended		Arboretum
	Restaurant AA inspected		Farm or animal centre
Madeira Hotel	Hotel AA inspected		Zoological or wildlife collection
	Theatre or performing arts centre		Bird collection
	Cinema		Nature reserve
	Golf course		Aquarium
	Camping AA inspected	V	Visitor or heritage centre
	Caravan site AA inspected		Country park
	Camping & caravan site AA inspected		Cave
	Theme park		Windmill
	Abbey, cathedral or priory		Distillery, brewery or vineyard

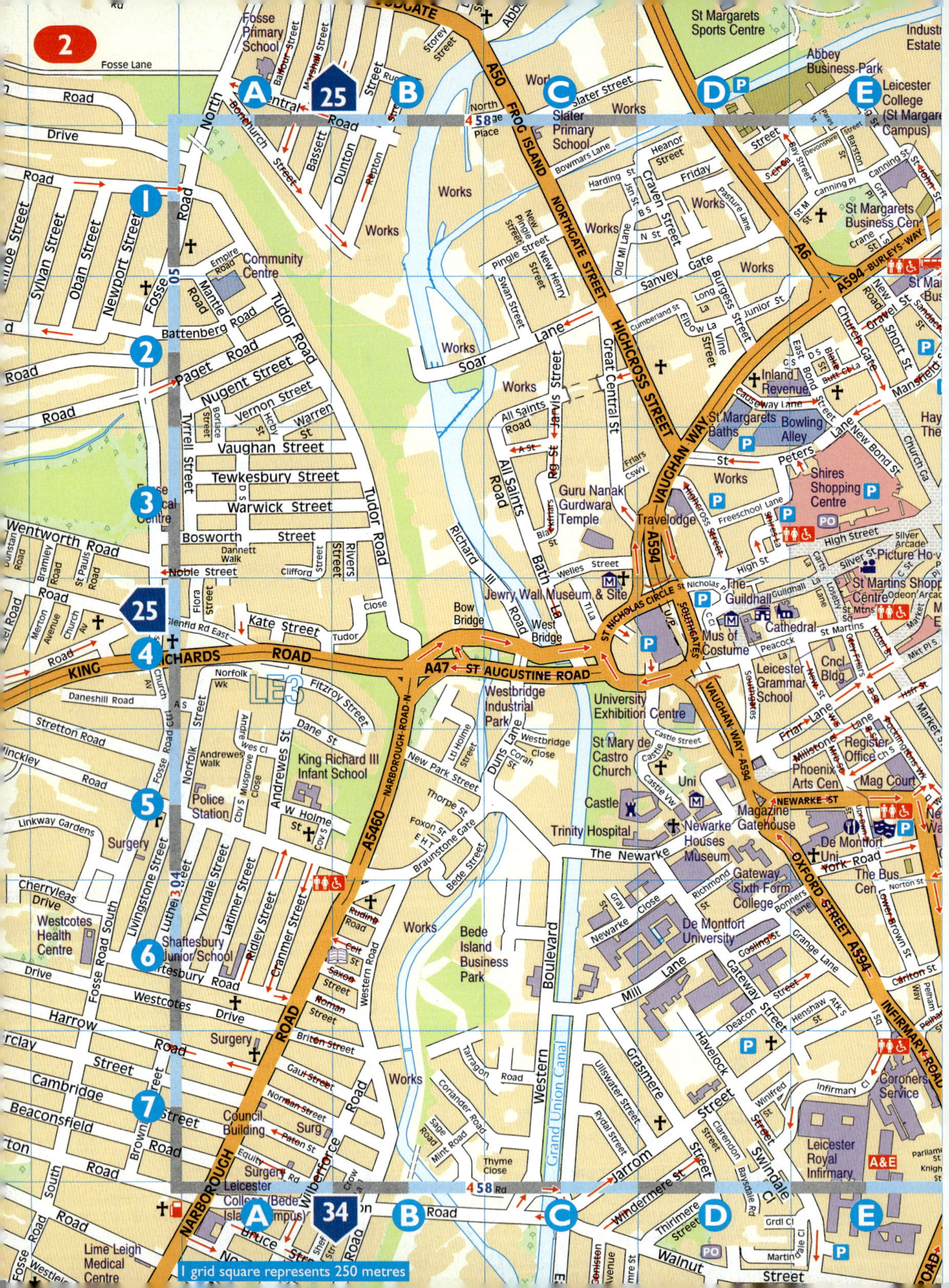

1 grid square represents 250 metres

26
27
35
59
60
F
G
H
J
K
I
2
3
4
5
6
7
LEICESTER
Highfields
LE1
Burleys Flyover
St Matthews Way
A594
A47
Humberstone
St Georges Way
London Road A6
Waterloo Way
Welford Road
A594 Tigers Way
Belgrave Gate
Haymarket Shopping Centre
Clock Tower
Kemble Square
Shonki Business Centre
St Matthews Business Cen
Campanile Hotel
Days Inn
Piccadilly
Gilbros Bus Cen
Lee Circle
Hindu Temple
Leicester Exhibition Centre
Med Cen
Haramead Business Centre
St Mathews Sports Hall
Cncl Bldg
Taylor Rd Primary School
St George's Retail Park
Trading Estate
Charnwood Primary School
Vulcan Business Centre
Shenton Primary School
Leicester Markazi Mosque
Surgery
The Temple
Moat Community College
Council Building
Gulzar-e-Madina Mosque
Highfields Medical Centre
Islamic Girls School
Highfields Primary School
Uplands Junior School
Leicester Central Mosque
St Peters Health Cen
Sparkenhoe Community Prim Sch
Sparkenhoe Community Primary School
Hotel Ibis
Leicester Station
Police Station
City Gallery
Town Hall
Ramada Hotel
The Little Thtr
YMCA
Crown & County Courts
New Walk Museum & Art Gal
HM Prison
De Montfort Mews
Belmont House Hotel
University of Leicester
Medway Community Primary Sch
Medway Infants Sch
Dar-es-Salam Mosque
Irwin College
Leicester Montessori Sixth Form College
Leicester Montessori Grammar School
Nelson Mandela Park
Fire Station
De Montfort Hall
Queen Street
Southampton Street
Humberstone Rd
Charles Street
Rutland Street
Granby Street
Belvoir Street
Wellington Street
King Street
Princess Road West
Regent Road
New Walk
Upper New Walk
Lancaster Rd
University Road
Salisbury Road
Granville Rd
Evington Road
St Peters Road
Melbourne Road
Sherrard Road
Mount Road
Grove Road
Frederick Rd
Cecil Road
Kent Street
Sussex Street
Nedham Street
Christow St
Ottawa Road
Manitoba Road
Kamloops Crescent
Montreal Road
Vancouver Road
Kashmir Road
Chester Close
Cobden Street
Syston Street East
Dunlin Rd
Farnham St
Hart Road
Vulcan Road
Maynard Rd
Skipworth St
Hamilton St
Myrtle Road
Cedar Road
Bartholomew St
Tennyson Street
Twycross Street
Worthington Street
Donnington Street
Diseworth Street
Derwent Street
Dale Street
Ashbourne St
Duffield Street
Beckingham Rd
Oxford Avenue
Abingdon Rd

LC
Glebe Lodge Farm
Humble Lane
Blackberry Lane
A
B
C
D
461
62
14
13
312
1
2
3
4
5
Fisher Close
Humble Lane
Lane
Back Lane
Middlefield Road
Home Farm
Wreake House Farm
River Wreake
A607 SYSTON ROAD
COSSINGTON LANE
A607
Chestnut Farm
Lewin Bridge
A46
Works
Meadow Lane
Meadow Lane
Grand Union Canal
St Peter & St Paul CE Primary School
Clumber Close
Badminton Road
Shirley Dr
Wy Dr
Avery Drive
Beatty Road
Parks
Ind Est
Works
Lower Church St
Church Street
Upper Church Street
Church Cl
Northfields
High Street
The Half Croft
Industrial Estate
Turn St
Harcourt Close
Brook St
Chapel Cl
Chapel St
School Street
Walkers Way
Bath St
V Cl
Works
PO
Syston Health Centre
The Stiles
Works
Glebe Way
Wren Close
Teal Way
Prtrd Cl
Kn Cl
Swallow Drive
Mallard Drive
K C
H W
Martin Drive
Swift Close
St Columba Way
Cygnet Cl
S Wy
Moorland Rd
Glebe Way
C Cl
Blackthorn
H C
Iona R
West St
North St
Brookside
Brksd
Brookfield St
Albion St
Necton St
Brdw
St Peter's Street
Broad Street
12
Priory Close
Lindisfarne Road
Fosse Way
Abbotts Cl
Wolsey Way
Syston Station
Wanlip Road
Wanlip
S C
Sedgeh Dri
Heath Avenue
Willow Walk
Gorse Lane
Glebe Way
Cranmer Dr
Hardwick Crs
Chatsworth Dr
Taylor Cl
Melton Road
Sandf
Works
Albert Street
Wellington St
Victoria St
Cross St
Trinity Cl
University Close
Barkby Road
Brookfield Av
1 grid square represents 500 metres

Priory Farm
Broome Lane
LC
New Avenue
Weston Close
Grange Avenue
Westfield Close
East Goscote
Golf Course
Badger's Corner
Huntsman's Dale
Fx H
The Chase
Countryman's Way
Squirrel's Corner
Broome Lane
MELTON ROAD
A607
Headlands
The Meadows
Greensward
Wayfarer Dr
Broome Avenue
Furrow
Long Ride
Squire's Ride
Yeoman's Dale
Freeman's Way
Bracken Dale
T W
Ling Dale
Foxglove Close
Tinker's Dell
Beedles Lake Golf Centre
Industrial Estate
Honeysuckle Close
Meadow View
Lilac Wy
Ln F
PO
Cncl Bldg
Broomfield Primary Sch
Chestnut Way
Cooper's Nook
Way
T Cnr
Woodman's Chase
Fletchers' Way
Ploughman's Lea
Brm
Watergate
Farriers' Way
Keepers' Croft
Saddlers' Close
Long Furrow
The Warren
The Warren
Craftsman's Way
A607
New Zealand Lane
Michael Close
Rupert Crs
Ervin Way
Rearsby Road
Bluebell
F C
William Close
The Ringway
Primrose Way
Wetherby Cl
Syston Road
The Ringway
Coppice Lane
Bourden Farm
Dobney Avenue
Curzon Cl
Marsden Avenue
Avn Cl
Wt Av
New Street
Queniborough Road
Queniborough CE Primary School
Works
Link Road
Beechwood Avenue
Nursery Close
Gascoigne Avenue
Peggs Lane
Chestnut Close
The Ridings
Avenue Road
Glebe Road
The Banks
Wreake Valley Community College
Melton Road
Queniborough Industrial Estate
Main Street
Hall Farm Close
Queniborough Hall
Queniborough
School Lane
Mere Lane
Naylor Road
Works
Millstone Lane
Brighton Avenue
Tentercroft Avenue
Mostyn Avenue
Gloucester Avenue
Central Avenue
Ridgemere Close
Avenue
Belvoir Dr
East
Mowbray Drive
Barkby Road
Oxford Court
Oxford
Close
Lodge Street
Cambridge Close
Hungarton Drive
Cemetery
Beeby Cl
Ridgemere Lane
Bd Cl
E
F
G
H
1
2
3
4
5
63
64
65
14
13
12
13

6
Ulverscroft Grange
Chitterman Hill Farm
Lea Lane
Priory Lane
A
B
C
D
448
49
Shaw Lane
1
Junction 22
Cottage Lane
Whitwick Road
Ulverscroft Cottage Farm
Altar Stones La
Altar Stones Lane
M1
A50
2
Cliffe Lane
Hill La Cl
Hill La
Hill Lane Industrial Estate
Ashby Road
Leicester Road
Markfield
Hill Lane
Upland Drive
Avery Dr
Main Street
Dandees Cl
The Paddock
Park Av
Li Cl
Cft
Ulvers T Rs
Meadow La
Cem
3
Stoney Lane
Mill Hill La
St M Cl
Rectory Road
Beacon Cl
Bradgate Road
Bradgate Rd
W C
Hillside
The Green
Bracken Wy
Roecliff Cl
Janes Way
Chambers Cl
Forest Road
Queen St
Poplar Av
Warren Cl
Linford Crs
Wesley Wy
Lane
Dabey Cl
Church Drive
Surg
Neville Dr
Walnut Cl
Mayflower Cl
Htntsmns Close
Woodland
Oakfield Avenue
Surgery
PO
LEICESTER ROAD
4
Mercenfeld Primary School
Chitterman Way
The Chase
Countryman
Launde Road
Link Ri
Leicestershire Round
Croftway
Birchfield Avenue
London Road
Beech Cl
Valley Rd
Robinson
Jacqueline Road
Turnpike Wy
Pinfold
Field Head
Lane
5
Ratby
Al aqsa Primary School
309
14
Pinewood Dr
Birch Cl
Chestnut Wk
The Blossoms
1 grid square represents 500 metres

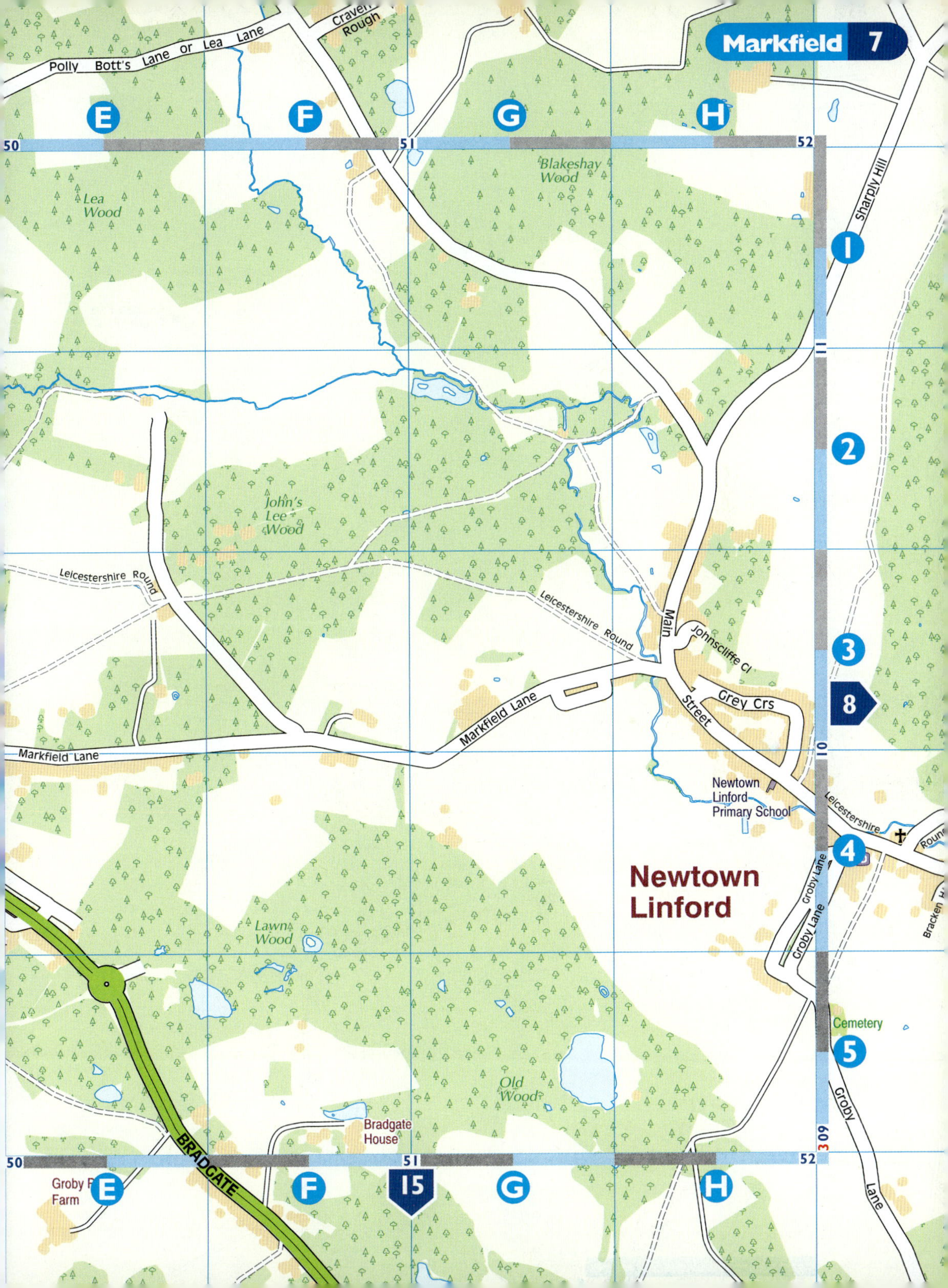
Polly Bott's Lane or Lea Lane
Craven Rough
Blakeshay Wood
Lea Wood
Sharply Hill
John's Lee Wood
Leicestershire Round
Main Street
Johnscliffe Cl
Grey Crs
Markfield Lane
Newtown Linford Primary School
Newtown Linford
Groby Lane
Lawn Wood
Old Wood
Cemetery
Bradgate House
BRADGATE
Farm
E
F
G
H
1
2
3
4
5
8
15
50
51
52
11
10
309

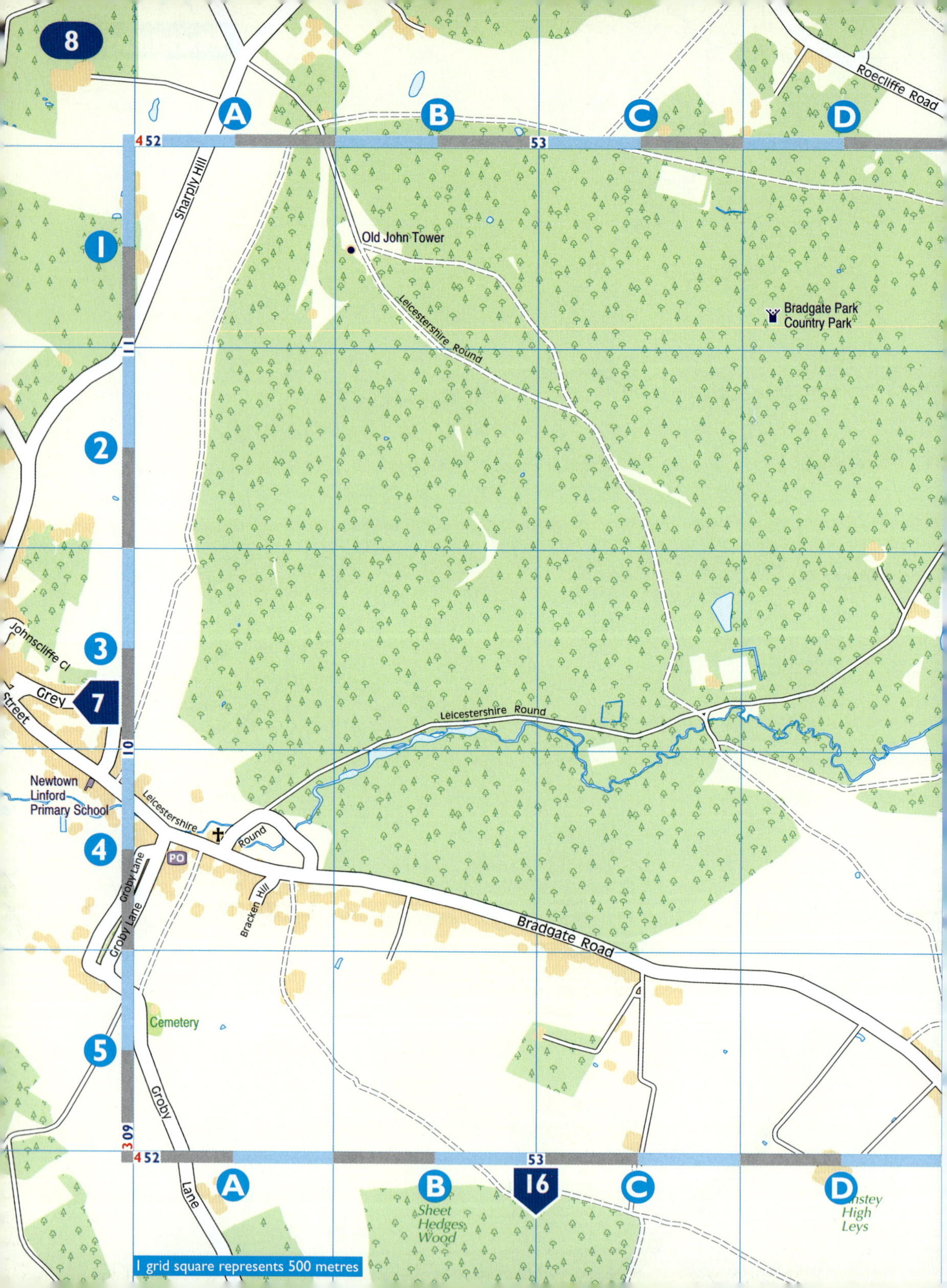
8
A
B
C
D
Roecliffe Road
4 52
53
Sharpley Hill
1
Old John Tower
Leicestershire Round
Bradgate Park Country Park
2
3
Johnscliffe Cl
Grey
7
Street
Leicestershire Round
10
Newtown Linford Primary School
Leicestershire
Round
4
PO
Groby Lane
Groby Lane
Bracken Hill
Bradgate Road
Cemetery
5
Groby
309
4 52
53
Lane
A
B
16
C
D
Sheet Hedges Wood
High Leys
1 grid square represents 500 metres

E
F
G
H
54
55
56
Swithland Road
Road
Station Road
Bradgate Rd
Bradgate
Lodge La
Reservoir
Road
Cropston
Reservoir
Leices
Cemetery
Sandham Br
Rd
Guild
Cl
Caudle
Cl
Latimer
Road
Thistle Cl
Stamford Drive
Waterfield
Rd
Outfields
Dr
Waterfield Road
Ridley
Cl
PO
Cropston
Thur
Causeway Lane
Lychgate
Cl
Cropston Road
11
10
09
1
2
3
4
5
10
Anstey
Lane
A46
Leicestershire County
City of Leicester
Fairhaven Rd
Woolden
Hill CP
School
Holgate
Cl
Martin
High
School
Netherfield Rd
Broadway
Furlong
Sutherington Way
Wooldale
Cl
Cropston Road
Link Road
Balladine
Rd
Broughton
Cl
D Cl
The
Close
Charnwood
Rd
Street
Rosebery Rd
Andrew Road
Charles Drive
KWW
Anstey
Nomads
FC
Link Road
Dalby
Road
James St
Kitchener Road
Bradgate Road
Birkdale
Rd
Hazelhead Rd
Forest Gate
Ellis
St
Hollow Road
Stadon
Road
Woodgon Rd
George St
Bencro
Close
17
Albion Street
Highfield St
Princes
Cl
Andrew
Rd
stone St
Dr
Charles
Cropston Road
Paper Ml
Cl
Graysswood Dr
Sharpley Dr
Beacon
Close
Blackthorn
Dr
Osprey Rd
Ipswich Cl

A
B
C
D
456
57
1
2
3
4
5
9
11
10
309
Station Road
Thurcaston Lane
Leicester Road
Cemetery
Lanesborough Close
Lanesborough Dr
Vinehouse Cl
Chapel Cl
Mill Road
Wallis Cl
Sandham Br Rd
Caudle Cl
Latimer Road
Thistle Cl
Drive
Cropston
Thurcaston
Richard Hill CE Primary School
Memorial Hall
Hall Farm Rd
All Saints Rd
Anstey Lane
Rectory Lane
Leicestershire County
City of Leicester
Great Central Railway
A46
Hogarth Rd
R Cl
Lawrence Cl
Bevan Road
Monk's Crs
Deanery Crescent
Glebelands Rd
Glebelands Primary School
Chancel Rd
Deacon Rd
Anstey Lane
Beaumont Leys Lane
Thurcaston Road
Cherrybrook Cl
Castle Hill Country Park
St Mellion Close
Kingsbridge Crs
Surgery
Taverners Road
Durban Rd
Benskins Oval
Bevan Road
Lords Av
Trent Av
Croft Rd
Ed Cl
Grayswood Dr
Parkside Cl
Sharpley Dr
Beacon Close
Astill Lodge Road
Plover Crs
Swallowdale Dr
Chaffinch Cl
Halley Close
Osprey Rd
Peregrine Rl
Blackthorn Dr
The Poppins
Beaumont Lodge Rd
Threadgold Cl
Laithwaite Cl
Phillips Cl
Bennion Road
PO
Beaumont Primary
18
Bennion Rd
Madeline Rd
Knights Rd
Beaumont Leys La
Hoods Close
1 grid square represents 500 metres

E
F
G
H
58
59
60
Council Building
Wanlip Hill
A6
I
Fillingate
A46
Road
Rectory
Rectory Rd
Church Road
2
Wanli
A46
A6 LOUGHBOROUGH ROAD
Wanlip Lane
3
Longslade Community College
Stonehill High School
Russ Way
Melba Wy
12
Allington Dr
Worcester Av
Malling Cl
Myrtle Av
Birch Tree Av
Lime Tree Av
Holly Tree Av
Rose Tree Av
Sycamore Rd
Bentley Rd
Hawthorn
Acacia Av
Dalby Av
Allington Drive
Worcester Av
Kswc Cl
Road
Blenheim Road
4
Windmill Av
Stonehill Avenue
Iris Av
Gwendolin Avenue
Laxton Cl
Nfield Av
Paget Av
Hill Rise
The Meadway
Colindale Av
Harrowgate Drive
Highgate Av
Briargate Dr
Queensgate Dr
Westgate Av
Woodgate Drive
Moorgate Av
Ryegate Crs
Denegate Avenue
Ambergate Dr
Sandgate Av
Lyngate Av
Saltersgate Drive
Wellgate Avenue
Brdg Cl
Castlegate Av
PO
Kingsgate Avenue
Heathgate
Fieldgate Crs
Greengate Medical Centre
L Rd
Greengate Lane
Greengate Lane
Cem
Highcliffe Primary School
Hallam Av
Walnut Av
Spinney Rise
Poplar Av
Avenue
Elmfield
Cliffwood Avenue
Oakfield Av
Cedar Av
Fielding
Sibson Rd
The Wayne Wy
PO
Wanlip Avenue
Wanlip Lane
Meadow Lane
Lambourne Rd
Bramley Road
Orchard Road
The Crossways
Riverside Community Primary School
5
Lawn Av
Firfield Av
Beechfield Av
Council Building
Farm Cl
Whiles La
Johnson Road
BIRSTALL
Copeland R
19
Cliffe Road
Henson Cl
Goscote
Walker Road
Park Road
LOUGHBOROUGH ROAD
School Lane
Curzon
Council Building
Front St
Church Hl
Mill Cl
Netherhall
The Drive
Golf Course
309
310
311

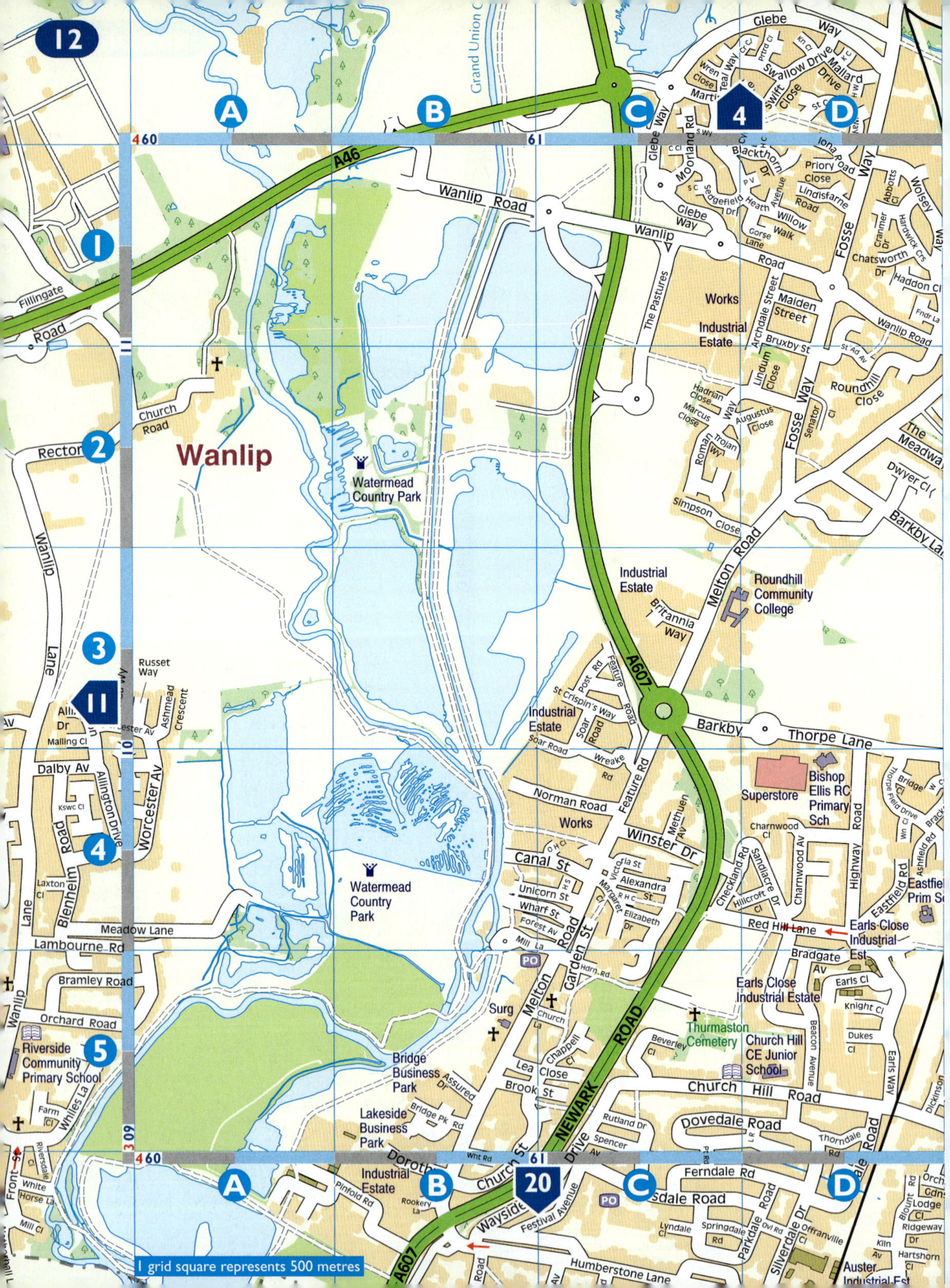
Wanlip
Watermead Country Park
Watermead Country Park
Grand Union Canal
A46
A607
NEWARK ROAD
Wanlip Road
Wanlip Road
Fillingate
Church Road
Rectory
Wanlip Lane
Russet Way
Ashmead Crescent
Worcester Av
Allington Drive
Malling Cl
Dalby Av
Blenheim Road
Laxton Cl
Meadow Lane
Lambourne Rd
Bramley Road
Orchard Road
Riverside Community Primary School
Farm Cl
Whiles La
Riverside
White Horse La
Mill Cl
Front St
Glebe Way
Wren Close
Teal Way
Swallow Drive
Mallard Drive
Swift Close
Moorland Rd
Blackthorn Dr
Seagefield Dr
Heath Avenue
Willow Walk
Gorse Lane
Priory Close
Lindisfarne Road
Iona Road
Fosse Way
Abbotts Cl
Wolsey Way
Cranmer Dr
Hardwick Crs
Chatsworth Dr
Haddon Cl
Works
Industrial Estate
The Pastures
Archdale Street
Maiden Street
Bruxby St
Wanlip Road
Lindum Close
Hadrian Close
Marcus Close
Augustus Close
Roman Way
Trojan Wy
Senator Cl
Roundhill Close
The Meadway
Dwyer Cl
Barkby La
Simpson Close
Melton Road
Industrial Estate
Britannia Way
Roundhill Community College
Feature Road
Post Rd
St Crispin's Way
Soar Road
Industrial Estate
Soar Road
Wreake Rd
Barkby Thorpe Lane
Superstore
Bishop Ellis RC Primary Sch
Thorpe Field Drive
Bridge
Ashfield Rd
Eastfield Rd
Eastfield Prim Sch
Norman Road
Works
Feature Rd
Methuen Av
Winster Dr
Canal St
Victoria St
Alexandra St
Unicorn St
Wharf St
Forest Av
Mill La
Margaret Cl
Elizabeth Dr
Garden St
Charnwood Cl
Checkland Rd
Sandiacre Dr
Hillcroft Cl
Charnwood Av
Highway Road
Red Hill Lane
Earls Close Industrial Est
Bradgate Av
Earls Close Industrial Estate
Earls Cl
Knight Cl
Dukes Cl
Earls Way
Beacon Avenue
PO
Surg
Melton Road
Church La
Chappell Cl
Thurmaston Cemetery
Beverley Cl
Church Hill CE Junior School
Bridge Business Park
Assured Dr
Lea Close
Brook St
Church Hill Road
Lakeside Business Park
Bridge Pk Rd
Rutland Dr
Spencer Av
Dovedale Road
Thorndale Rd
Dickinson
Dorothy
Industrial Estate
Rookery La
Pinfold Rd
Church St
Wayside
Festival Avenue
Drive
Ferndale Rd
sdale Road
Lyndale Rd
Springdale Rd
Parkdale Road
Silverdale Dr
Offranville Cl
Humberstone Lane
Kiln Cl
Hartshorn Cl
Ridgeway Dr
Lodge Cl
Orch
Auster Industrial Est
A
B
C
D
1
2
3
4
5
4
11
20
460
61
309
1 grid square represents 500 metres

SYSTON
Barkby
Thurmaston
Barkby Thorpe
Industrial Estate
Street
Brook St
Chapel St
Turn St
Harcourt Close
Brookside
West St
North St
Upper
Syston Health Centre
Works
PO
The Stiles
Mostyn Avenue
Gloucester Avenue
Central Avenue
East Avenue
Belvoir Dr
Ridgemere Close
Oxford Court
Oxford Close
Lodge Close
Street
Cambridge Close
Hungarton Drive
Necton St
Halford St
Syston Station
Broad Street
St Peter's Street
Melton Road
Works
Victoria St
Albert Street
Wellington St
Cross St
Nelson street
Brookfield St
Brookfield Av
Albion St
Barkby Road
Trinity Cl
University Close
College Road
Keble Drive
Oriel Dr
Cemetery
Quenby Crs
Orchard Way
Beeby Cl
Ridgemere
Taylor Cl
Works
Sandford Road
PO
Goode's Lane
Holmdale Rd
Station Rd
Millers Close
St Paul's Drive
Coplow Crescent
Goode's Av
Merton Av
Plumtree Way
Southfield Av
Montague Av
Dalley Cl
St John's Avenue
Pembroke Avenue
Balliol Av
Lincoln Dr
St Annes Close
Ruskin Avenue
St Hildas Close
Barkby Road
Syston Grange
The Firs
Pine Drive
Ash Dr
Beech Dr
Oak Drive
Cherry Drive
Cedar Dr
Lime Dr
The Merton Primary School
Barkby Lane
Barkby Lodge
Cemetery
Queniborough Road
The Hall
PO
Main Street
Barkby Holt Lane
Barkby Thorpe Lane
Thorpe Lane
School La
Vicarage La
Pochin Primary School
Beeby Road
Queen St
Gregory Cl
Field Vw
Price Way
Ap Rd
The Coppice
Shenton Cl
Everett Close
Elliott Dr
Hollybrook Cl
Cresswell Close
Colby Drive
Barkby Thorpe Road
King Street
E
F
G
H
1
2
3
4
5
62
63
64
11
10
309
5
21

A
B
6
C
D
4 48
49
09
08
3 07
1
2
3
4
5
Ratby
Primary School
The Laurels
Pinewood Dr
Birch Cl
Chestnut Wk
The Blossoms
Ratby Lane
The Oaks
Thornton Lane
M1
Whittington Grange
Markfield Road
New Hayes Farm
Great Wood
Bondman Hays
Thornton Lane
Markfield Road
Cow Lane
Markfield Lane
Forest Hill Golf Club
Old Hays Farm
Ratby Burroughs
1 grid square represents 500 metres

Cemetery
Old Wood
Groby Park Farm
BRADGATE HILL
A50
Groby Lane
Lady Hay Wood
Elsalene Dr
Lena Drive
Wallace Dr
Bradgate Home Farm
Groby Pool
Dowry F
Wildlife
Groby Lodge Farm
LE6
MARKFIELD ROAD
Markfield
Martinshaw Primary School
Forest Vw
Woodlands Dr
Fern Crs
Woodlands Drive
Parklands Av
Forest Ri
Forest Cl
Lawnwood Rd
Farr Wd Cl
Shaw Wd Cl
Wnd Ri
Fir Tree La
Stephenson Wy
Poplars Cl
Martinshaw Road
Martinshaw Wood
Hilary Crs
Carmen Cv
The Orch
Woodbank Rd
Ratby
Oaktree Cl
Spinnys Cl
Highfie
Groby Community College
Brookvale High School
Spinney Cl
Buckingham Cl
Oakme
Greys Dr
Garendon Wy
Qr Ri
Warrington Dr
Laundon
M1
Markfield Road
Road
Cem
Bevington
Ash Cl
Bradgate Dr
Wolsey Dr
Whittin
Saxo
Groby
Sacheverell W
Burroughs
E
F
G
H
I
2
3
4
5
7
16
22
50
51
52
07
08
09

Cemetery
Groby Lane
A
B
8
C
D
452
53
09
08
307
Sheet Hedges Wood
Anstey High Leys
Groby Pool
Newtown Linford Lane
Dowry Furlong Wildlife Area
P
MARKFIELD ROAD
Martins Primary School
15
Groby Trading Estate
Groby
MARKFIELD ROAD A50
Markfield Road
Parkside
Greyland Paddock
Grey Cl
Rookery
PO
Leicester Road
Daisy Cl
Bluebell Drive
Primrose Close
Foxglove Dr
Foxglove Drive
Poppy Cl
Anstey Lane
Branting Hl
Leicester Road
A50
Leicester Rd
Field Ct Road
Dalby Drive
Marston Dr
Jonathan Cl
Marina Drive
Castell Drive
Groby Road
Groby Rd
Overdale Avenue
Glen Park Avenue
Glendale Av
Branting Hill Av
Overdale Cl
Sacheverell Way
A46
Forest Vw
Farr Wd Cl
Shaw Wd Cl
Fir Tree La
Stephenson Wy
Poplars Cl
Surgery
Rookery Lane
Crane
Ley Road
Chapel Hl
Ferrers Ri
Parklands Av
Forest Ri
Forest Cl
Lawnwood Rd
Martinshaw La
Holmes Cl
Hilary Cl
The Orch
Carmen Gv
Woodbank Road
Mallard Av
Flaxfield Cl
Lane
Pymm Ley Cl
Mdw Ct
Rd
Meadow Wy
Glebe Road
Oaktree Cl
Ratby Road
White House Cl
Road
Hawthorn Ri
Sycamore Cl
Slate Brook Cl
Old Hall Cl
Sycamore Drive
Larchwood Av
Spinneys
Highfield
The Elizabeth Woodville Primary School
Spinney
Cedar Ct
Elm Cl
Chestnut Wk
Beaumont Gn
Timberwood Dr
Beacon Cl
Pymm
Buckingham Cl
Oakmeadow Wy
Queensmead Cl
Lady Jane Grey Primary School
Pine Tree Avenue
Wolsey Cl
Laundon Cl
Bedford Dr
Stamford Drive
Greys Dr
Garendon Wy
Way
Castle Ri
Victoria Dr
Lancaster Ct
Windsor Av
Kings Wy
Warrington Dr
Laundon
Ash Ct
Lime
Louise Av
Willow Dr
Beech Av
Tudor Gv
Brookvale High School
Road
Cem
Sachev Way
23
Superstore
Mill Lane
1 grid square represents 500 metres

Anstey
Anstey Nomads FC
School
Link Road
The Close
Bradgate Road
Forest Gate
Hollow Road
Hazelhead Rd
Birkdale Rd
Ellis St
Bencroft Close
Woodgon Rd
George St
Stadon Road
Paper Ml Cl
Church La
Caters Cl
PO
Edward
Highfield St
The Nook
Albion Street
Princes Cl
Andrew Rd
Gladstone St
Charles Dr
Charles Drive
Cropston Road
Melody Av
Coronet Cl
Rosebery Rd
Broughton Cl
Kitchener Road
Street
Balladine Rd
Latimer St
Latimer Primary School
Leicester Road
Gorse Hill
Gynsill Close
Falcon Road
Burgin Rd
Cherrytree Cl
Ashfield Dr
Millfield Cl
Peartree Cl
Park Rd
Groby Road
A46
Anstey Lane
A5630
Gorse Hill Hospital
Gynsill Lane
Rothley Brook
Stelle Way
Premier Travel Inn
County Hall
Council Building
Surgery
Willow Brook Close
Oakfield Avenue
Glenville Avenue
Leicester Road
A50
Groby Road
Glenfield Hospital
Leicester Frith Hospital
Thorntree Cl
Tyburn Cl
End Cl
Lyn Cl
Lady Hay Rd
Whittington Rd
Broombriggs Rd
Glenfrith Cl
Glenfrith Way
A563
Krefeld
Heatherbrook Primary School
Heatherbrook Rd
Astill Lodge Rd
Maplewell Dr
Manor Dr
Stoneywell Road
Barnsdale Rd
Blackthorn Dr
Pitchens Cl
Blue Gates Rd
Bennion Rd
Castle Flds
Pinewood
Clematis Cl
Works
Boston Rd
Sheene Road
Bennion Road
Gilroes Cemetery
Gilroes Cres
Station Road
West St
Stephenson Ct
Newquay Dr
Loxley Rd
Bude Dr
Dorset Avenue
Sandown Road
Saintbury Rd
Fairfield Crescent
Wellesbourne Dr
Steyning Crs
Callimore Cl
Cedar Cl
Kemp Rd
Amhurst Cl
Allerton
E F G H I
9 18 24
54 55 56
2 3 4 5
07 08 09

18
10
17
25
Castle Hill Country Park
St Mellion Close
Beaumont Lodge Primary School
Heatherbrook Primary School
Barrington Park Industrial Estate
Leicester Leys Leisure Centre
Council Building
Police Station
Gilmour Cl
Works
Gorse Hill Hospital
Mowmacre Hill Primary School
Beaumont Leys
Buswells Lodge Prim Sch
Babington Community Technology College
Barley Croft Prim Sch
Beaumont Leys Health Cen
Stock Farm
Council Building
Beaumont Leys School
Leicester Frith Hospital
Gilroes Crematorium
Gilroes Cemetery
A46
A563 RED HILL WAY
A563 KREFELD WAY
A5630
B5327 ANSTEY LANE
Bennion Road
Beaumont Leys Lane
Thurcaston Road
Hoods Close
Belgrave Bvd
Strasbourg Drive
Heacham Drive
Somerset Avenue
Lodge
Surgery
PO
1 grid square represents 500 metres

BIRSTALL
Mowmacre Hill
Belgrave
LE4
LOUGHBOROUGH ROAD
RED HILL A6
RED HILL WAY
WATERMEAD WAY
A563
A6030
LOUGHBOROUGH ROAD
CHECKETTS ROAD
A607
ABBEY LANE
River Soar
Golf Course
Mowmacre Community & Sports Centre
Birstall Golf Club
Belgrave & Birstall Station
Belgrave Cemetery
Belgrave RFC
Belgrave St Peters CE Primary School
Belgrave Hall & Gardens
Mellor Primary School
Woodstock Primary School
Wolsey House Primary School
Rushey Mead School
Council Building
Leics Museum of Technology
Abbey Pumping Station
National Space Centre
BUSM Business Park
Husseini Mosque
Belgrave Ind Ctr
Rana Academy
St Patricks RC Primary School
Cossington Street Sports
Primary School
Elmfield
Oakfield Avenue
Cliffwood Av
Cedar Av
Firfield Av
Beechfield Av
Orchard Road
Copeland Road
Cliffe Road
Henson Cl
Goscote Hall Rd
Went Road
Walker Road
Park Road
School Lane
Curzon Avenue
Birstall Road
Church Hl
Front St
Netherhall La
Mill Cl
White Horse La
Riversdale Cl
The Drive
Tempest Rd
Station Rd
Clarke Gv
Holt Road
Acorn Cl
Parkhouse Cl
Kedleston Av
Kilby Av
Birstall Rd
Roman Road
Freehold Rd
Perseverance Rd
East Rd
Thurcaston Road
Galway Rd
Hadrian Rd
David Av
Oakenshaw Cl
Mowmacre Hl
Millwood Cl
Bridlespur Wy
Astill Dr
Belgrave Bvd
Woodstock Rd
Pamela Pl
Helena Crs
Barnwell Av
Mortisford Rd
Marwell Cl
Millbrook Cl
Grovebury Rd
Kingsthorpe Cl
Langley Av
Packwood Rd
Halifax Drive
Rainsford Crs
Chilcombe Cl
Canonsleigh Rd
Robertsbridge Av
Billington Cl
Beaumont Leys Lane
Hobson Road
Orton Road
Robert Hall St
Drummond Rd
Thurcaston Road
Wesley St
Whitefield Rd
Beaumanor Road
Anchor St
Corporation Road
Carnarvon St
Sudeley Av
Downham Av
Welbeck Av
Belle Vue Av
Egerton Av
Eileen Av
Byford Road
Chale Rd
Exploration Dr
Wallingford Rd
Meadows
Stadium Pl
Menzies
Parker Drive
Works
Industrial Estate
Swithland Av
Bath St
Elsadene Av
Pauline Av
Berridge Lane
Lanesborough Road
Wavertree Drive
Sandringham Av
Woodbridge Road
Clarke St
Cameron Av
Payne St
Linford St
Claremont St
Vicarage Lane
Victoria Rd N
Belgrave Av
Elmdale St
Shirley St
Jackson St
Laundry La
St Bernard St
Bernards St
Checketts Cl
Windsor Av
Holden St
Herbert Av
Asha Margh
Shaftesbury Av
Lexham St
Ulverscroft Rd
The Greenway
Portsmouth Rd
Canon Street
Ellis Av
Down Street
Halkin Street
Doncaster Road
Cossington St
Cross St
Coral St
Wand St
Cooper St
Law St
Walk
Stafford St
Lancashire St
St Michaels Av
Marfitt St
Gipsy Road
Moores Road
Flax Road
Arbor Road
Leire St
Acorn St
Jermyn St
Glen St
Agar St
Scarborough Rd
Penrith Rd
Yorkshire Road
Shetland Road
Purley Road
Harrison Rd
Temple
Uxbridge Rd
Melton Rd
Oakland Avenue
Alan Cl
Surgery
PO
58
59
60
07
08
09
E
F
G
H
1
2
3
4
5
20
26

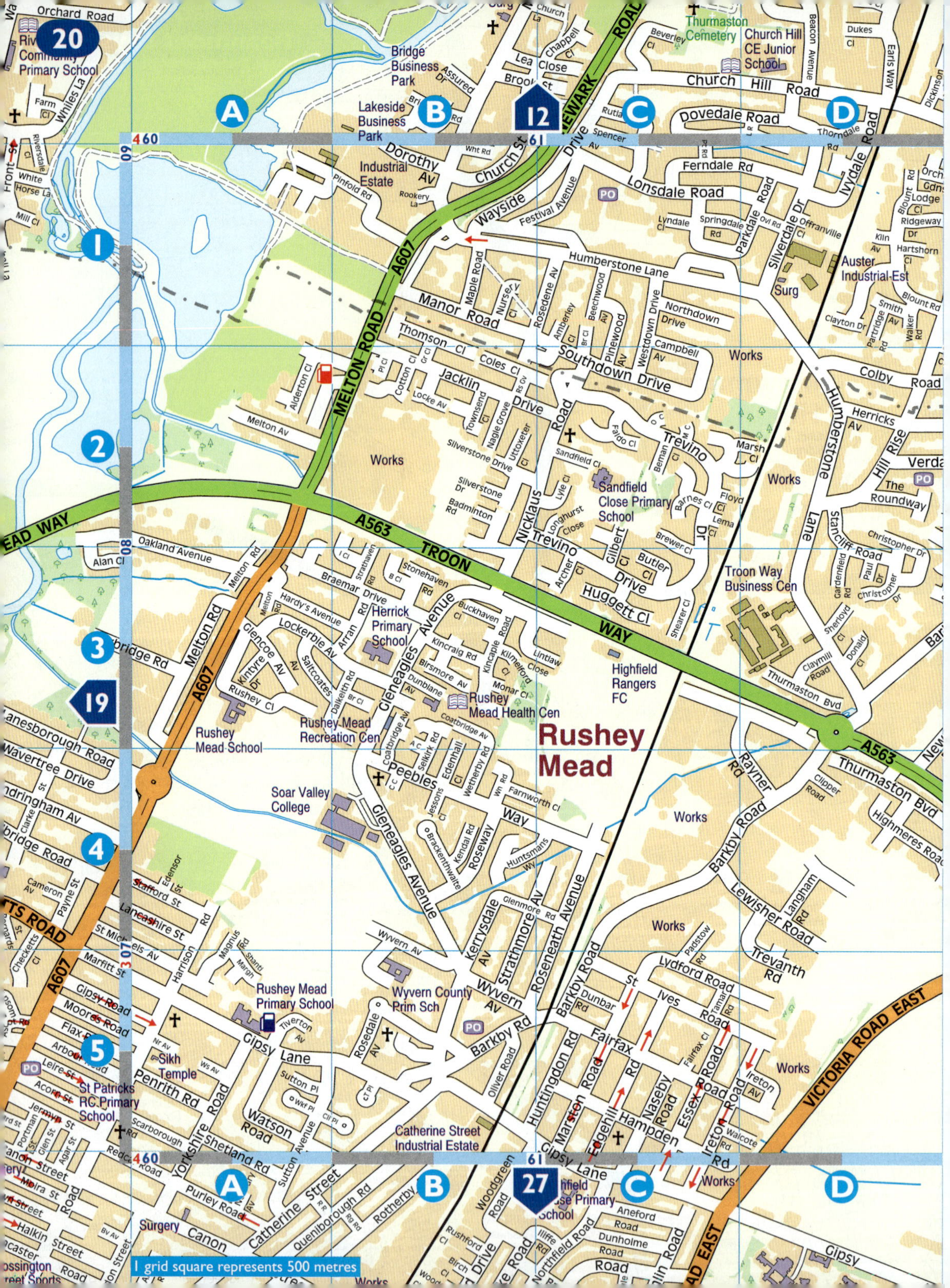
20
12
19
27
A
B
C
D
1
2
3
4
5
Rushey Mead
Melton Road
A607
A563
Troon Way
Thurmaston Bvd
Victoria Road East
Humberstone Lane
Gleneagles Avenue
Barkby Road
Gipsy Lane
Church Hill Road
Lonsdale Road
Dovedale Road
Humberstone Lane
Southdown Drive
Manor Road
Jacklin Drive
Nicklaus Road
Trevino Drive
Huggett Cl
Rayner Rd
Lewisher Road
Trevanth Rd
Lydford Road
Ives Road
Fairfax Rd
Hampden Road
Essex Road
Ireton Road
Naseby Road
Marston Road
Huntingdon Rd
Roseneath Avenue
Strathmore Av
Kerrysdale Av
Wyvern Av
Peebles Way
Rushey Mead School
Soar Valley College
Rushey Mead Recreation Cen
Rushey Mead Health Cen
Herrick Primary School
Sandfield Close Primary School
Highfield Rangers FC
Troon Way Business Cen
Auster Industrial Est
Lakeside Business Park
Bridge Business Park
Industrial Estate
Thurmaston Cemetery
Church Hill CE Junior School
Rushey Mead Primary School
Wyvern County Prim Sch
Sikh Temple
St Patricks RC Primary School
Catherine Street Industrial Estate
Highfield House Primary School
Works
Surg
PO
Oakland Avenue
Braemar Drive
Lockerbie Av
Hardy's Avenue
Wavertree Drive
Gipsy Road
Moores Road
Penrith Rd
Shetland Rd
Yorkshire Road
Watson Road
Catherine Street
Canon Street
Melton Av
Wayside Drive
Festival Avenue
Colby Road
Herricks Av
Hill Rise
The Roundway
Stancliff Road
Ivydale Road
Silverdale Dr
1 grid square represents 500 metres

Barkby Thorpe
Queen St
Barkbythorpe Road
King Street
Field Vw
Gregory Cl
The Coppice
Shenton Cl
Everett Close
Elliott Dr
Hollybrook Cl
Colby Drive
Cresswell Close
Griffin Close
June Avenue
Cookson Rd
Warren Av
Warren Dr
Tilbury Crs
Staythorpe Rd
Manston Cl
Coleford Rd
Newham Cl
Cheney Rd
Stanier Dr
Mountain Rd
Valley Rd
Waterside Road
Hilltop Road
Troon Industrial Estate
Wenlock Way
Cannock St
Tuxford Rd
Hamilton Business Park
Waterside Rd
Highcliffe Rd
Progress Way
THURMASTON LANE
A6030
THURMASTON LA A563 HAMILTON WAY
Sandhills Av
Sandhills Avenue
Lakeview Cha
Speedwell Dr
Columbine Rd
Jasmine Cl
Larkspur Cl
Orpine Rd
Edgfld Cl
Bellflower Road
Harebell Cl
Mallow
Cloverdale Rd
Oakridge Cl
Holly Bank Cl
Wintergreen Close
Wainwright Av
Celandine Rd
Bryony Rd
Charlock Rd
Burdock Cl
Coltsfoot Rd
Ramson Cl
Sundew Rd
Maidenwell Av
Ashtree Rd
Foxglove Rd
Hazeldene Rd
Hollowtree Rd
Elmtree Cl
Trefoil Cl
Sorrel Rd
Willowtree Cl
Kestral Lane
Kestrels Field Primary School
Keyham Lodge School
Burnet Cl
City of Leicester
Leicestershire County
Nether Hall
Hamilton - site Medieval Villag
Hamilton Community College
Golf Course
Humberstone Heights Golf Club
Thurmaston Lane
Police Station
Keyham Lane
Preston Ri
Fern Ri
Chestnut Av
Barry Road
Selby Av
Limehurst Road
Greenbank Rd
Ivychurch Crs
Maplin Road
Rayleigh Gr
Briarfield Dri
13
28
62
63
64
E
F
G
H
1
2
3
4
5

High School
M1
Markfield Rd
15
A
B
C
D
Road
Cem
Bevington Cl
Charnwood
Ash Cl
Bradgate Dr
Wolsey Dr
Whittington Dr
Saxons Ri
Groby
Burroughs Road
Stamford Street
Cottage Cl
Ratby Primary School
Main St
Nook Cl
Overfield Cl
Woodley Rd
Church La
Dane Hill
Ferndale Drive
Six Acre Cl
Cooper La
Middlebrook
Berry's La
Ingle Dr
PO
Chapel La
Dane Hl
Wesley Cl
Bell Cl
Lee Ri
Meadow Cl
Gillbank Dr
Cardinal Cl
Grange Cl
Tyler Road
Ratby Sports Club
Desford Lane
Nicholas Drive
Lockley Cl
The Pinfold
Dane Hl
Heathbrook Dr
Windmill Cl
Ratby
Brook Dr
Station Road
Cuffling Cl
Mill Dr
Barton Cl
Surg
Works
Park Road
Taverner
Desford La
Kirby Muxloe
Cemetery
Desford Lane
Desford Road
The Huntings
Barns Cl
Hedgerow Lane
Ladysmith Rd
Pretoria Rd
Fox Lane
Main St
Castle Rd
Church Rd
Barons Close
Barwell Rd
Gullet Lane
Links Road
Lime Gv
Wilshere Cl
Station Road
Princess Dr
31
Elms Farm
1 grid square represents 500 metres

Buckingham Cl
Lady Jane Grey Primary School
Oakmeadow Wy
Queensmead
Pine Tree Avenue
Wolsey Cl
Launde Cl
Bedford Dr
Stamford Drive
Garendon Wy
Greys Dr
Windsor Av
Castle Rl
Kings Wy
Warrington Dr
Laundon Cl
Lime Av
Louise Av
Willow Dr
Beech Av
Tudor Gv
Sacheverell Way
16
52
53
54
E
F
G
H
West St
Station Road
Dorset
Ilmington Cl
Superstore
Sandown Road
Piers Road
The Maltings
The Square
The Balk
Main St
Church Rd
PO
The Av
Mill Lane Industrial Estate
A46
The Mill Lane
Kirby Road
Bramley Ct
Grange Cl
Millers Cl
St Peter's Cl
Glenfield Primary School
Stamford Street
Ashleigh Rd
Chestnut Road
Elm Tree Av
Forge Cl
Crofters Cl
Glebe Cl
The Oasis
Saddlers Cl
Foresters Cl
Bowmans Wy
Hayfield Cl
Wollaton Cl
Slate Cl
Park Dr
Ellis Cl
Dominion Road
Fairestone Av
Jordan Cl
Harrison Cl
Manor Gdns
Glenfield Crs
Barley Cl
Jubilee Dr
Blackthorn Rd
Somerset Drive
Winterfield Cl
Manor Farm Way
Wheatfield Close
Prince
Spring Fld
Oakmeadow
Peartree Cl
Utah Cl
Normandy Cl
Swords Cl
Surgery
24
Astill Cl
Geary Cl
Preston Cl
Kirby Rd
B5380
M1
Ratby Lane
Vicarage Cl
Vicarage Lane
Glenfield Lane
Farley Way
Primrose Way
B5380 RATBY LANE
Leicestershire County
City of Leicester
Golf Course
Mulberry Av
Kirby Muxloe Sports Club
Castle Hotel
Kirby Muxloe Castle
Junction 21a
Western Golf Club
Ganton Rd
Ryder Rd
Ferndown
St Davids Cl
Cherry Hills Rd
Street
Armson Av
Garfit Rd
Oakcroft Avenue
Court Cl
Scudamore Road
Wanstead Road
Wanstead Industrial Park
Wembley Road
Elland Rd
Carrow Road
Braunstone Frith Industrial Estate
Murrayfield
RATBY LANE
Kirby Muxloe Primary School
Portland Rd
Roundhill
Holmewood Dr
The Fairway
Hastings Road
Forest Drive
Rosedene Cl
32
Sunningdale
Sunningdale Industrial Park
Oak Spinney Pk
Stamford Road
Station Cl
Walton
Avenue
Kirby
1
2
3
4
5
06
05
04

Glenfield
New Parks
Western Park
Western Park
LE3
Golf Course
Western Golf Club
Leicester Road
A50
Groby Road
A563
New Parks Way
Hinckley Road
County Hall
Council Building
Glenfield Hospital
Leicester Frith Hospital
Surgery
Superstore
The Maltings
The Square
Main St
Glenfield Primary School
Stamford Street
Station Road
West St
Dorset Avenue
Sandown Road
Loxley Rd
Glenfield Frith Dr
Salcombe Drive
Clovelly Road
Sports Road
Victor Rd
Olympic Cl
Dominion Road
Unity Road
Triumph Road
Tournament Road
Liberty Road
Treaty Road
Prince Albert Dr
Dupont Gdns
Tatlow Road
Chestnut Road
Pine Road
Park Dr
Glenfield Crs
Wheatfield Close
Somerset Drive
Hayfield Cl
Wellesbourne Dr
Fairefield Crescent
Frith
Glenfield
Tysoe Hill
Saintbury Rd
Gallimore Cl
Cedar Cl
The Hall Primary School
Holmwood Drive
Kemp Rd
Towle Road
Bland Road
Keightley Road
New Parks Blvd
Battersbee Road
Falconer Crs
Speers Road
Pickwell Cl
Hassal Rd
Charnor Road
Forest Lodge Primary School
Musson Rd
New Parks Leisure Cen
St Oswalds Road
Greencoat Rd
New College Leicester
Glenfield Road
Emily Fortey School
Western Park School
Council Building
Surgery
Elgin Av
Alkman
Dillon Rd
Hackett Rd
Bringhurst Road
Kerrial Road
Drayton Road
Frolesworth Rd
Allexton Gdns
Sacheverel Road
Braunstone Frith J&I School
Cokayne Rd
Cuffling Dr
Brookdale Rd
Chevin Av
Scudamore Road
Fulford Rd
Ryder Road
Ganton Rd
Mulberry Av
Yew Tree Dr
Council Building
Park Rise
Green Wk
Wessex Dr
Industrial Estate
Oswin Road
The Meads
Braunstone Frith Industrial Estate
Murrayfield Road
Radar Rd
Golf Course La
Foxholes Road
Hockley
Winforde Cr
Crescent Junior School
Wellinger Way
Webster R
Erdyngton Road
Wembley Road
Sunninga
A B C D
17
23
33
1 2 3 4 5
454 55
1 grid square represents 500 metres

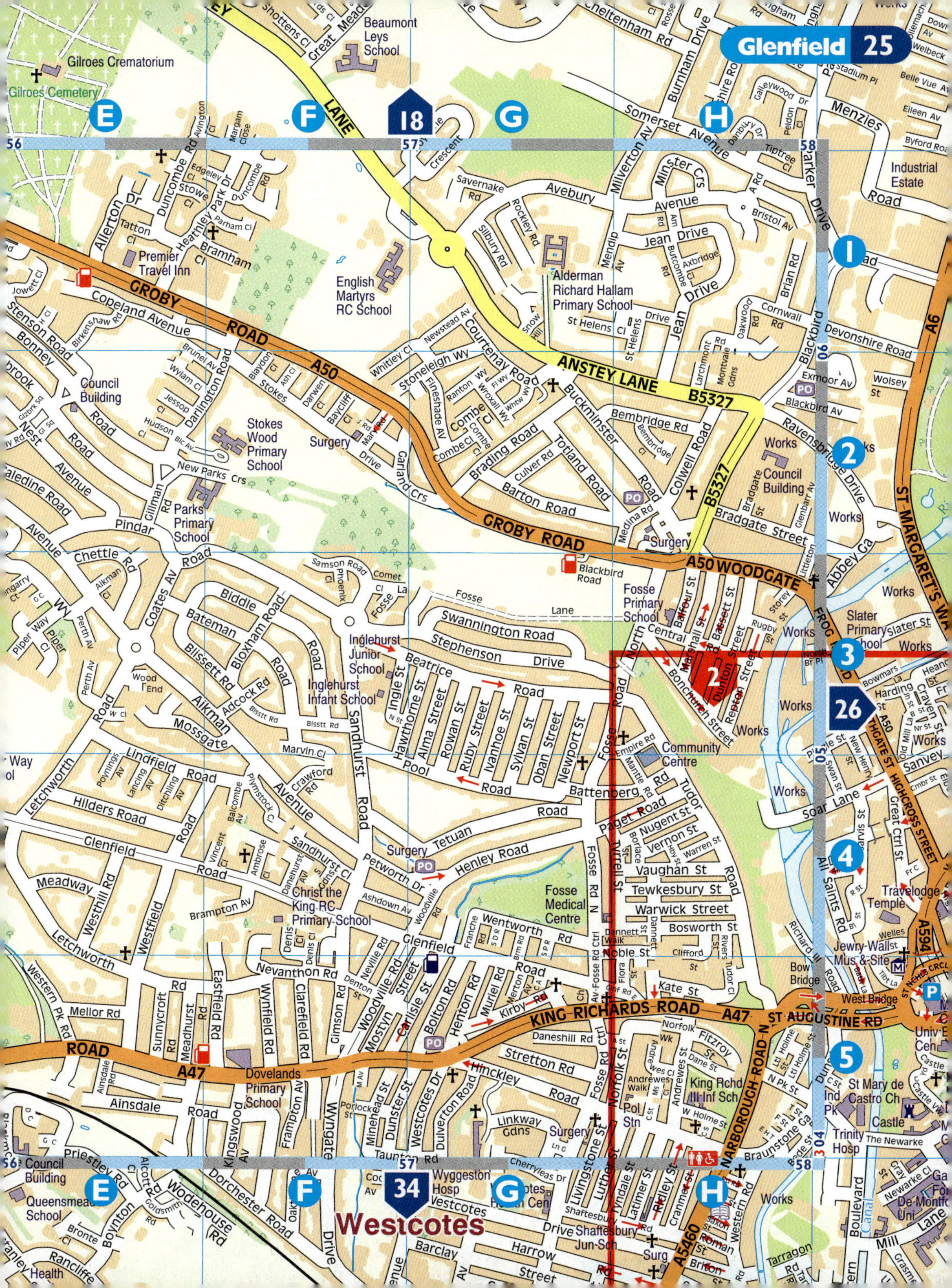
Glenfield 25
18
26
34
Westcotes
Gilroes Crematorium
Gilroes Cemetery
Beaumont Leys School
English Martyrs RC School
Alderman Richard Hallam Primary School
Premier Travel Inn
Council Building
Stokes Wood Primary School
Parks Primary School
Surgery
Inglehurst Junior School
Inglehurst Infant School
Fosse Primary School
Community Centre
Christ the King RC Primary School
Fosse Medical Centre
Dovelands Primary School
King Rchd III Inf Sch
Slater Primary School
Travelodge
Temple
Jewry Wall Mus & Site
St Mary de Castro Ch
Castle
Trinity Hosp
The Newarke
Industrial Estate
Wyggeston Hosp
Westcotes Health Cen
Shaftesbury Jun Sch
Queensmead School
Works
GROBY ROAD
A50
ANSTEY LANE
B5327
A50 WOODGATE
FROG ISLAND
A6
ST MARGARET'S WAY
A50 NORTHGATE ST
HIGHCROSS STREET
A594
KING RICHARDS ROAD
A47
ST AUGUSTINE RD
NARBOROUGH ROAD N
A5460
West Bridge
Bow Bridge
Soar Lane
Groby Road
Copeland Avenue
Glenfield Road
Hinckley Road
Fosse Road North
Tudor Road
Blackbird Road
Parker Drive
Somerset Avenue
Avebury Avenue
Jean Drive
Stephenson Drive
Swannington Road
Beatrice Road
Battenberg Road
Tetuan Road
Henley Road
Wentworth Road
Letchworth Road
Hilders Road
Ainsdale Road
Dorchester Road
Wodehouse Rd
Westcotes Drive
Harrow Road
Ravensbridge Drive
Bradgate Street
Abbey Ga
Devonshire Road
Cornwall Rd
Buckminster Road
Brading Road
Barton Road
Totland Road
Colwell Road
Sandhurst Road
Pindar Road
Chettle Rd
Bloxham Road
Bateman Road
Biddle Road
Aikman Avenue
Mossgate
Lindfield Road
Coates Av
Westfield Road
Meadway
Westhill Rd
Mellor Rd
Eastfield Rd
Wynfield Rd
Clarefield Rd
Woodville Rd
Bolton Rd
Henton Rd
Muriel Rd
Kirby Rd
Stretton Rd
Daneshill Rd
Tewkesbury St
Warwick Street
Bosworth St
Vaughan St
Nugent St
Vernon St
Paget Road
Kate St
Noble St
Fosse Lane
Menzies Road
Byford Road
Wolsey St
Exmoor Av
Bembridge Rd
Culver Rd
Courtenay Road
Stoneleigh Wy
Fineshade Av
Combe Cl
Garland Crs
Stokes Drive
New Parks Crs
Darlington Road
Allerton Dr
Duncombe Rd
Heathley Park Dr
Bramham Cl
Tatton Cl
Stenson Road
Bonney Road
Gilliman Rd
Perth Av
Piper Way
Crawford Rd
Marvin Cl
Plymstock Cl
Brampton Av
Nevanthon Rd
Gimson Rd
Mostyn Street
Carlisle St
Frampton Av
Wyngate Drive
Kingswood Av
Priestley Rd
Boynton Rd
Ranclife
Barclay St
Braunstone Ga
Western Rd
Tarragon Rd
Boulevard
Newarke Cl
Mill Lane

26
19
25
35
A
B
C
D
1
2
3
4
5
Belgrave
LEICESTER
Abbey Park
River Soar
Abbey Park Road
ABBEY
A6
ST MARGARET'S WAY
BELGRAVE ROAD
BELGRAVE GA A607
BURLEYS F/O
ST MATTHEWS WAY
A594
ST GEORGES WAY
VAUGHAN WAY
NORTHGATE ST HIGHCROSS STREET
FROG ISLAND
A50 WOODGATE
B5327
A47 ST AUGUSTINE RD
NARBOROUGH ROAD N
NEWARKE ST
OXFORD ST
INFIRMARY
WELFORD ROAD
LONDON
WATERLOO WY
Corporation Road
Leics Museum of Technology
Abbey Pumping Station
National Space Centre
Council Building
Exploration Dr
Byford Road
Industrial Estate
Works
Abbey Meadows
BUSM Business Park
Swithland Av
Abbey Community Primary Sch
Rana Academy
Belgrave Ind Ctr
Holden St
Husseini Mosque
Darul Uloom Sch
Loughborough Rd
Leire St
Arbor Road
Flax Road
St Patrick's RC Primary School
Canon Street
Cossington Street Sports Cen
Melrose Street
Doncaster Road
Harrison
Burfield St
Catherine Junior School
Catherine Infant School
Brandon Street
Devonshire Road
Blackbird Av
Exmoor Av
Ravensbridge Drive
Bradgate Street
Council Building
Parker Drive
Abbey Ga
St Margarets Sports Centre
Leicester College (Abbey Park Campus)
Abbey Business Park
Shonki Business Centre
Leicester College (St Margaret's Campus)
Slater Primary School
Syston St W
Dysart Way
Taylor Rd Primary Sch
Haramead Business Ctr
Manitoba Road
Ottawa Rd
St Matthews Bus Cen
St Mathews Sports Hall
Charnwood Primary School
Kent Street
Med Cen
St Margarets Bus Stn
Pasture
Sanvey Gate
Soar Lane
Bowling Alley
Baths
St Peters La
Shires Shop Cen
Clock Twr
Haymkt Shop Cen
Haymkt Thtr
Humberstone Gate
Humberstone Rd
Hindu Temple
Leics Exhib Cen
Business Cen
St George's Retail Park
Trading Estate
Mosque
LE1
Jewry Wall Mus & Site
Travelodge Temple
Bow Bridge
West Bridge
The Guildhall
Cath
Mus of Costume
Univ Exhibition Cen
Picture Ho
Mkts & Corn Exchange
Town Hall
Ramada Hotel
Granby St
City Gal
Police Stn
Hotel Ibis
Leicester Stn
Central Health Cen
Moat Comm Coll
Highfields Prim Sch
Castle
Newarke Houses
Magazine Gatehouse
Trinity Hosp
The Newarke
St Mary de Castro Ch
King Rchd III Int Sch
Reg Off
Mag Court
New Walk Cen
Co Bldg
Mosque
Little Thtr
YMCA
Gateway 6th Form Coll
De Montfort Uni
Courts
New Walk Mus & Art Gal
De Montfort Mews
Belmont House Hotel
Dar-es-Salam Mosque
Com Prim Sch
Braunstone Ga
Western Rd
Tarragon Rd
Mill Lane
Regent Rd
Phoenix
1 grid square represents 500 metres

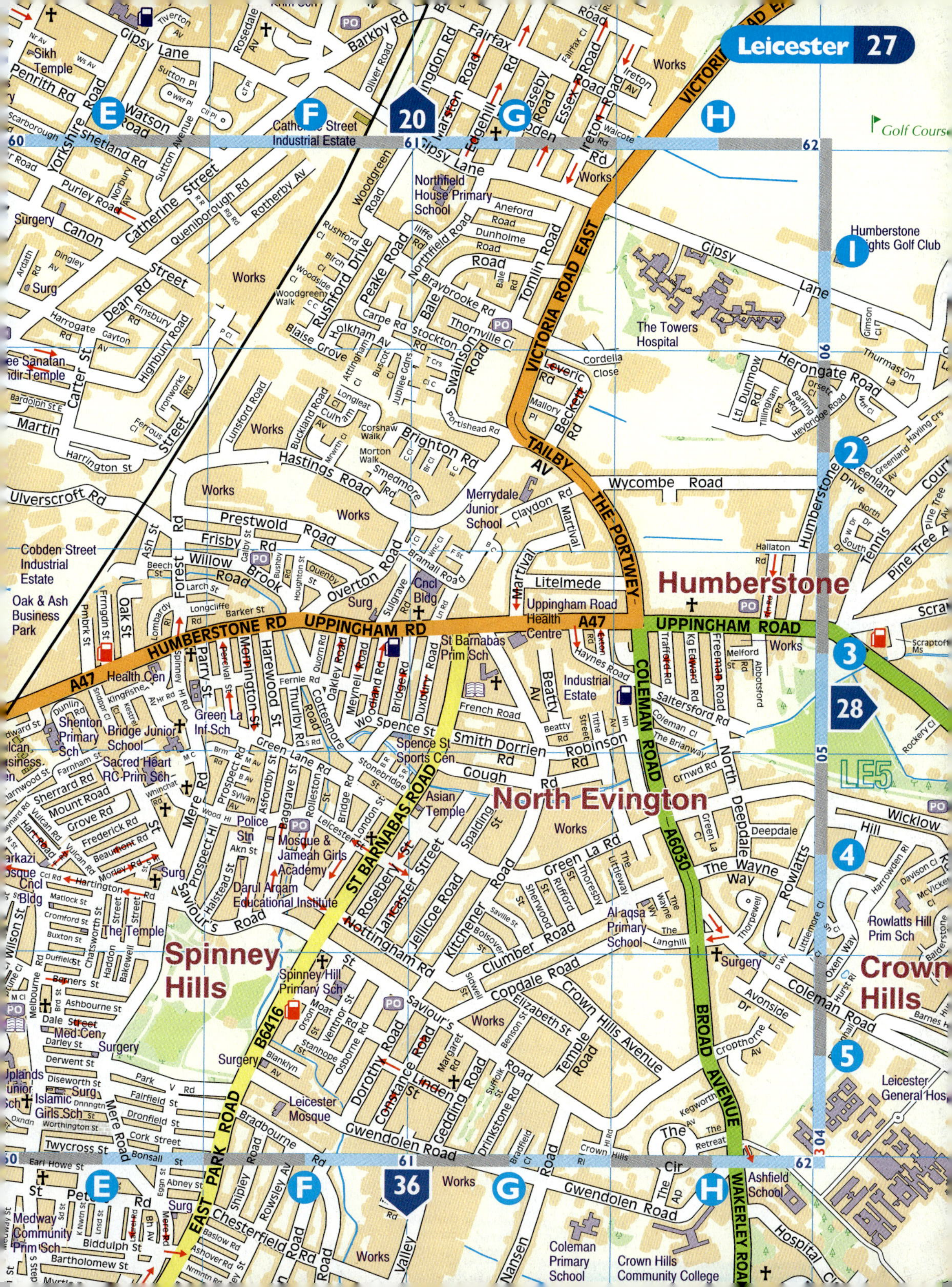
Humberstone
North Evington
Spinney Hills
Crown Hills
The Towers Hospital
Humberstone Heights Golf Club
Golf Course
Leicester General Hospital
Cobden Street Industrial Estate
Oak & Ash Business Park
Catherine Street Industrial Estate
Northfield House Primary School
Merrydale Junior School
Uppingham Road Health Centre
Industrial Estate
St Barnabas Prim Sch
Shenton Primary Sch
Bridge Junior School
Sacred Heart RC Prim Sch
Green La Inf Sch
Spence St Sports Cen
Asian Temple
Mosque & Jameah Girls Academy
Darul Arqam Educational Institute
Police Stn
Spinney Hill Primary Sch
Leicester Mosque
Al aqsa Primary School
Rowlatts Hill Prim Sch
Islamic Girls Sch
Medway Community Prim Sch
Ashfield School
Coleman Primary School
Crown Hills Community College
Sikh Temple
Works
Surgery
Med Cen
The Temple
Cncl Bldg
Health Cen
VICTORIA ROAD EAST
TAILBY AV
THE PORTWAY
HUMBERSTONE RD
UPPINGHAM RD
UPPINGHAM ROAD
A47
COLEMAN ROAD
A6030
BROAD AVENUE
WAKERLEY ROAD
ST BARNABAS ROAD
EAST PARK ROAD
B6416
Gipsy Lane
Humberstone Drive
Wycombe Road
Hastings Road
Prestwold Road
Nottingham Rd
Gwendolen Road
Crown Hills Avenue
Coleman Road
Herongate Road
Clumber Road
Copdale Road
Smith Dorrien Rd
Gough Rd
Green Lane Rd
Saltersford Rd
Wicklow
LE5
E
F
G
H
I
2
3
4
5
20
28
36
60
61
62
05
06
304

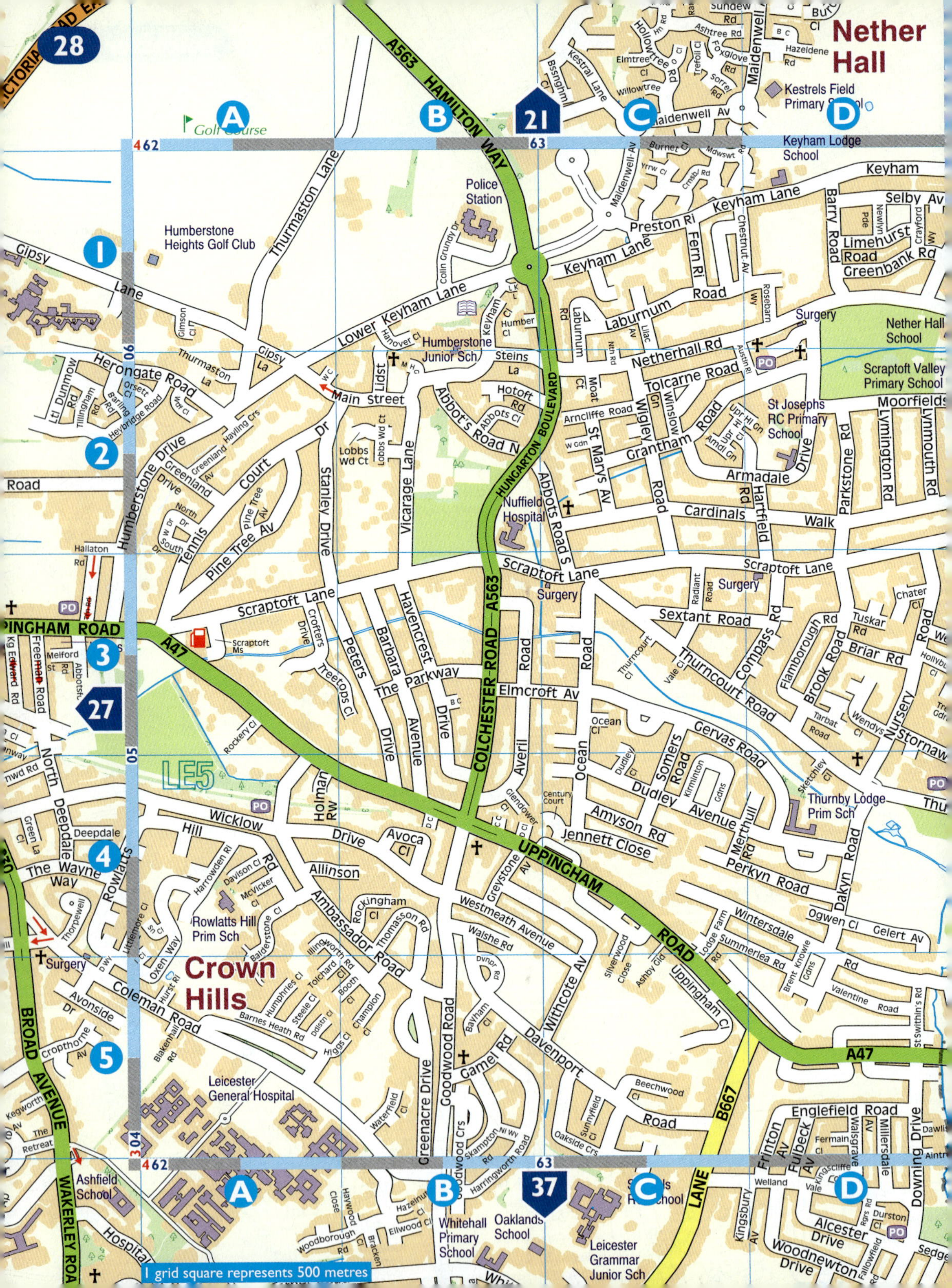
28
21
27
37
Nether Hall
Crown Hills
LE5
Golf Course
Humberstone Heights Golf Club
Police Station
Humberstone Junior Sch
Kestrels Field Primary School
Keyham Lodge School
Nether Hall School
Scraptoft Valley Primary School
St Josephs RC Primary School
Nuffield Hospital
Surgery
Thurnby Lodge Prim Sch
Rowlatts Hill Prim Sch
Leicester General Hospital
Ashfield School
Whitehall Primary School
Oaklands School
Leicester Grammar Junior Sch
A563 HAMILTON WAY
HUNGARTON BOULEVARD
COLCHESTER ROAD A563
A47
UPPINGHAM ROAD
B667
LANE
BROAD AVENUE
WAKERLEY ROA
Gipsy Lane
Thurmaston Lane
Lower Keyham Lane
Keyham Lane
Preston Ri
Maidenwell Av
Laburnum Road
Netherhall Rd
Tolcarne Road
Grantham Road
Armadale Drive
Cardinals Walk
Scraptoft Lane
Sextant Road
Thurncourt Road
Gervas Road
Dudley Avenue
Perkyn Road
Wintersdale
Main Street
Herongate Road
Humberstone Drive
Greenland Drive
Tennis Court
Pine Tree Av
Stanley Drive
Vicarage Lane
Abbot's Road N
Abbots Road S
Hotoft Rd
Barbara Drive
Havencrest Drive
The Parkway
Peters
Elmcroft Av
Averil Road
Ocean Road
Wicklow Drive
Avoca Cl
Allinson
Ambassador Road
Rowlatts Hill
Coleman Road
Westmeath Avenue
Davenport Road
Withcote Av
Goodwood Road
Greenacre Drive
Englefield Road
Downing Drive
Alcester Drive
Woodnewton Drive
Deepdale
The Wayne Way
Avonside Dr
Jennett Close
Amyson Rd
Barry Road
Limehurst Road
Greenbank Rd
Selby Av
Moorfields
Lymington Rd
Lynmouth Rd
Parkstone Rd
Flamborough Rd
Brook Road
Briar Rd
Nursery
Stornaway
Ogwen Cl
Gelert Av
Valentine Road
Dakyn Road
Uppingham Cl
Hartfield Rd
Compass Rd
Hospital
462
63
1 grid square represents 500 metres

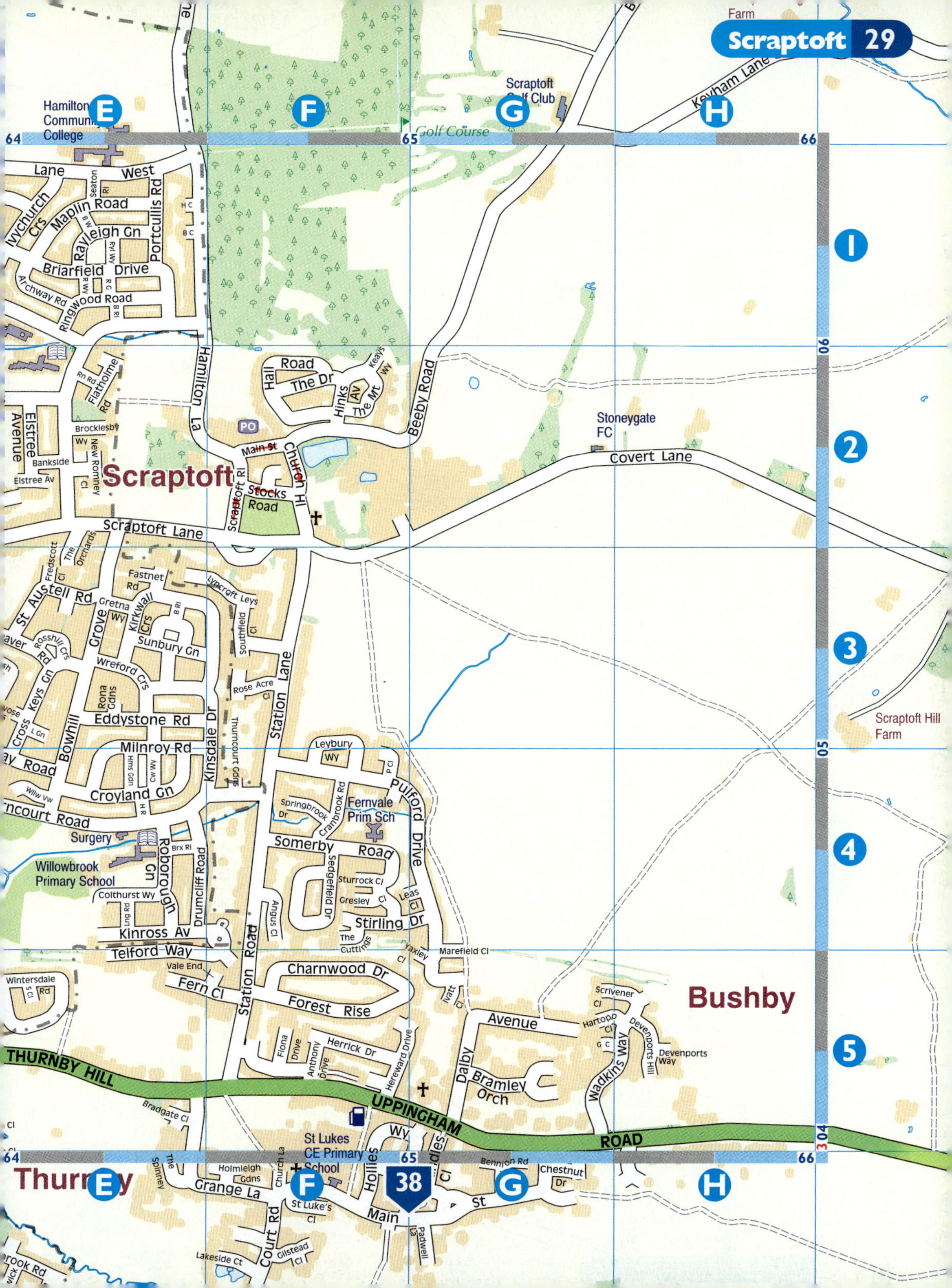
Scraptoft
Bushby
Thurnby
Hamilton Community College
Scraptoft Golf Club
Golf Course
Keyham Lane
Farm
Stoneygate FC
Covert Lane
Scraptoft Hill Farm
Lane West
Maplin Road
Ivychurch Crs
Rayleigh Gn
Portcullis Rd
Seaton Ri
Briarfield Drive
Archway Rd
Ringwood Road
Flatholme Rd
Rn Rd
Elstree Avenue
Brocklesby Wy
New Romney Cl
Bankside
Elstree Av
Hamilton La
Hall Road
The Dr
Hinks Av
The Mt
Keays Wy
Beeby Road
PO
Main St
Church Hl
Scraptoft Ri
Stocks Road
Scraptoft Lane
Fredscott Cl
The Orchards
Fastnet Rd
Lyncroft Leys
St Austell Rd
Gretna Wy
Kirkwall Crs
B Ri
Southfield Cl
Rosshill Crs
Grove Rd
Sunbury Gn
Wreford Crs
Rose Acre Cl
Station Lane
Keys Gn
Rona Gdns
Cross L Gn
Bowhill
Eddystone Rd
Kinsdale Dr
Thurncourt Gdns
Milnroy Rd
Hms Gdn
Mw Wy
Croyland Gn
H R
Wllw Vw
Thurncourt Road
Leybury Wy
P Cl
Pulford Drive
Springbrook Dr
Cranbrook Rd
Fernvale Prim Sch
Surgery
Willowbrook Primary School
Roborough Gn
Brx Ri
Drumcliff Road
Somerby Road
Sedgefield Dr
Sturrock Cl
Gresley Cl
Leas Cl
Colthurst Wy
Lng Rd
Kinross Av
Angus Cl
Stirling Dr
The Cuttings
Telford Way
Station Road
Yaxley Cl
Marefield Cl
Vale End
Charnwood Dr
Wintersdale Rd
S Cl
Fern Cl
Forest Rise
Watt Cl
Scrivener Cl
Avenue
Hartopp Cl
Devenports Hill
Devenports Way
G C
Wadkins Way
Flona Drive
Anthony Drive
Herrick Dr
Hereward Drive
Dalby
Bramley Orch
THURNBY HILL
UPPINGHAM ROAD
Bradgate Cl
St Lukes CE Primary School
Wy
Hollies
The Spinney
Holmleigh Gdns
Church La
Grange La
Bennion Rd
Chestnut Dr
St Luke's Cl
Main St
Padwell La
Court Rd
Gilstead Cl
Lakeside Ct
Brook Rd
38
64
65
66
06
05
04
3
E
F
G
H
1
2
3
4
5

Unthank
Lindridge Wood Farm
Lindridge Lane
LC
A
B
C
D
4 47
48
04
03
3 02
1
2
3
4
5
Tropical Birdland
Lindridge Lane
Station Road
Little Lane
Cemetery
Cottage La
Chapel La
Main Street
Grange Court
Church La
Station Road
Barns Wy
Fuller Close
B582
Manor Gdns
Stewards Cl
MANOR ROAD B582
HIGH STREET
Maple Way
Martin's Dr
St
Holmfield Road
High St
PO
Roman Cl
Drovers Way
Forest Rise
Bosworth Community College
Desford
Oak Road
Bch Wy
The Gv
Lynwood Cl
Peckleton Lane
Rngwd Cl
Hayes End
Grace Road
Bambrook Cl
Willow St
Hamble Cl
Burley Cl
Oxford Rd
Hazel St
Warwick Cl
Cambridge Dr
Belvoir Cl
Bedford Cl
Parkstone Road
Lncs Cl
Peckleton Vw
Meadow Wy
LEICESTER
Desford Primary School
Norfolk Road
Suffolk Way
Beaufort Cl
Richmnd Cl
Shericles Farm
Lane
Peckleton
Broomhills Farm
Works
Lane
Desford
Peckleton Common
Hill
Dan's
1 grid square represents 500 metres

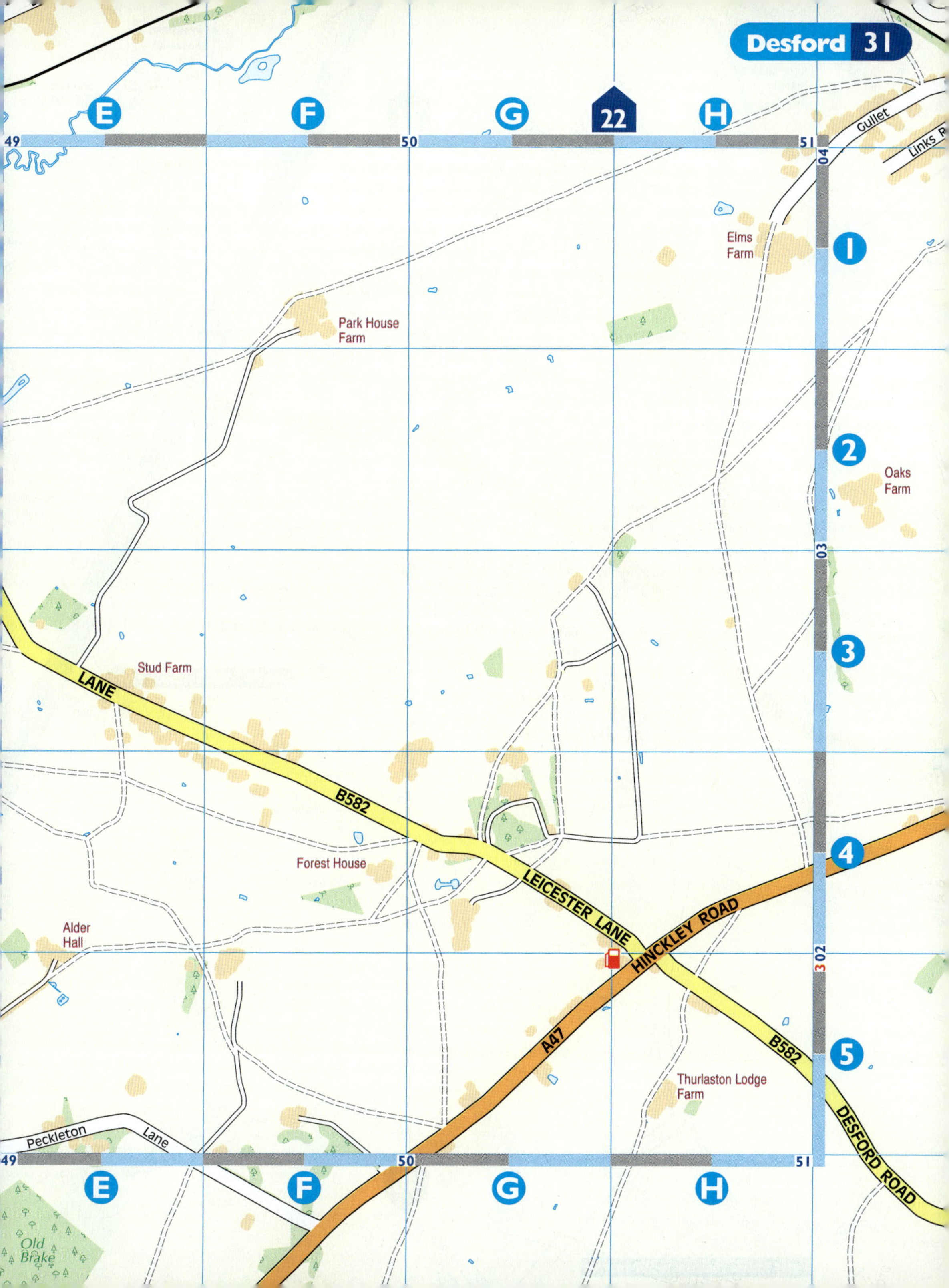
E
F
G
22
H
49
50
51
04
Gullet
Links R
Elms Farm
Park House Farm
1
2
Oaks Farm
03
3
Stud Farm
LANE
B582
Forest House
LEICESTER LANE
HINCKLEY ROAD
4
Alder Hall
302
A47
B582
5
Thurlaston Lodge Farm
DESFORD ROAD
Peckleton
Lane
Old Brake

1 grid square represents 500 metres

Scudamore Road
Elsham Cl
Mu eld Road
Braunstone Fr Industrial Estate
Radar Rd
NEW WAY
24
Green Wk
Park Rise
Trescoe Ri
The Meads
Industrial Estate
Oswin Road
HINCKLEY ROAD
54
55
56
E
F
G
H
Sunningdale Industrial Park
Golf Course La
Foxholes Road
HINCKLEY ROAD
A47
P+
Hockley Farm Rd
Wyatt Cl
Surgery
Hockley
Winforde Crs
Worrall Rd
Worrall Cl
Avery Hl
Heyford Road
Gunthorpe Rd
Meadwell Rd
Gallards
Cantrell Rd
Wilmore Crs
Cowdall Rd
Bendbow Rise
BRAUNSTONE WAY A563
Farm
Road
Crescent Junior School
Wellinger Way
Webster Rd
PO
Hollins Rd
Gallards Hill
Hill
Morcote Rd
Pollard Rd
Didsbury St
Cort
Bendbow Ri
Limber Crs
Council Building
Crs
Pilkington Rd
Corfield Rise
Edale Cl
Linacres Rd
Cort Crs
Woodshawe Rise
Woodshawe Ri
Hamelin Road
Erdyngton Road
Rose Farm Cl
Camville Rd
Gooding Avenue
Aylmer Rd
Winstanley Dr
Overpark Av
Council Building
Queensmead School
Priestley Rd
Health Centre
Rancliffe Crs
Bronte Cl
Drive
Wynthorpe Ri
Gooding Av
Redmarle Rd
Braunstone Park
1
2
3
4
5
04
03
02
Holmfield Av E
Drive
Walk
Park
St Mary's Ct
St Mary's Avenue
Radford Drive
Braunstone La
Maple Av
Richard Cl
Larch Grove
Beech Drive
Woodland Drive
Ch Ct
Sun Wy
Thornton Cl
Bendbow Rise Infant School
Hand Av
Hand
Dunstall Avenue
Valley Drive
Valley Dr
Hardie Crs
Braunstone Lane
Neal Av
Evelyn Road
Withington
Westover Road
LUBBESTHORPE WAY
Kingsway
Bidford Road
Bidford Cl
Avon Road
Balmoral Dr
Main Street
Herle Av
Odam Cl
Cort Crescent
Braunstone Av
Police S
34
Reynolds Pl
Hillary Place
New Fields
Crescent
Vyner Cl
Goodheart Wy
Bolus Rd
Haskell Cl
Clare Gv
Marshall Cl
Jewsbury Wy
Bromwich Cl
Tom Paine Cl
Smart Cl
Morris Cl
Littlefare
Tillett Rd
Cooke Cl
Collins Cl
Wilson Cl
Gavin Cl
Lakin Dr
Hilcot Gn
Royce Cl
Darien Rd
Seaton Rd
Hilcot
Way
Yeats Cl
Seacole Cl
Ferrars Cl
The Way
Withers Way
Heawood Wy
Kingsway Primary School
Winstanley High School
Braunstone
Shakespeare Dr
Hathaway Av
Shottery Av
Arden Av
Stratford Rd
Wilnicott Rd
Henley Crs
Caldecote Community Primary School
Braunstone
Attenborough Cl
Ltl Masons Cl
Sherrard Way
Hastings
Foxon Wy
Nether Fld Wy
Isobella Rd
Murby Way
Burchnall Rd
Rivers Cl
Meadow Cl
Own Cl
Owen Cl
Withers Wy
Priestman Rd
Darwin Cl
Tilley Cl
Meridian Wy
Meridian Wy
Meridian Leisure Park
Warner Village
Lubbesthorpe Bridle Rd
Shakespeare Cl
Charlecote Av
Burdet Cl
Welcombe Av
Council Building
Stonehurst Rd
Ravenhurst Rd
Ravenhurst Primary School
Bramble Wy
Claybrook Av
Cleveland Avenue
Vitruvius Wy
Premier Travel Inn
Legion Wy
Dominus Wy
Centurion Way
Tiber Way
Meridian East
LUBBESTHORPE
Mossdale Road
Chislehurst Av
Kingsway
Fernhurst Rd
Lyndale Rd
Turnbull
Rosamund Av
Rosamund Av
Hillrise Av
Una Av
Drive
Meridian Business Park
Staplehurst Av
Crowhurst Dr
Brockenhurst Drive
Edward
Kirkland Road
Millfield Community Primary School & C
Centurion
M1
41
Watergate Lane
Hat Rd
Freeboard Rd
Gayhurst Cl
Woodcote Road
Avenue
Francis Avenue
Monica Rd
Headley Rd
Pits Av
Fishpools
The Glade
The Chase
Surgery
The Poplars
ROAD

34
25
33
42
A
B
C
D
1
2
3
4
5
456
57
04
03
302
Westcotes
HINCKLEY ROAD
A47
KING RICHARDS ROAD
NARBOROUGH ROAD NORTH
NARBOROUGH ROAD
NARBOROUGH ROAD SOUTH
A5460
AYLESTONE ROAD
Dovelands Primary School
Council Building
Queensmead School
Health Centre
Wyggeston Hosp
Westcotes Health Cen
Shaftesbury Jun Sch
King Rchd III Inf Sch
Pol Stn
Surgery
Surg
Leicester College
Lime Leigh Medical Centre
Imperial Avenue Inf Sch
Fullhurst Community Coll
Folville Junior School
Ellesmere College
Leeson Clinic
Merridale Medical Centre
St Marys Fields Inf Sch
Marlow Road Industrial Estate
Faircharm Industrial Estate
River Soar
Works
Caldecote Community Primary School
Ravenhurst Primary School
Riverside Community College
Granby Prim Sch
Braunstone Park
Hamelin Road
Winstanley Drive
Gooding Avenue
Thurlington Road
Braunstone Avenue
Fullhurst Avenue
Imperial Avenue
Winchester Avenue
Fosse Road South
Hallam Crescent East
Ellesmere Road
Evesham Road
Collingham Road
Marlow Road
Rowley Fields Avenue
Harefield Av
Braunstone Lane
Braunstone Lane East
Turnbull Drive
Kirkland Avenue
Upperton Road
Westcotes Drive
Harrow Street
Cambridge St
Beaconsfield Rd
Barclay
Ashleigh
Sykefield Av
Wodehouse Rd
Dorchester Road
Kingswood Av
Priestley Rd
Taunton Rd
Ainsdale Road
Stretton Rd
Daneshill Rd
Braunstone Gate
Western Rd
Bruce St
Stuart St
Noel St
Walton St
Eastleigh Road
Bisley St
Raymond Rd
Danvers Rd
Wolverton Rd
Mountcastle Rd
Hopefield Rd
Haddenham Rd
Lambert Road
Heyworth Road
Dumbleton Road
Somerville Road
Meredith Rd
Lindsay Rd
Sybil Road
Alvaston Rd
Lyncote Rd
Rosamund Av
Hillrise Av
Una Av
Cleveley Avenue
Crossway
Close
Gwencole Crs
Canal St
Disraeli St
Duncan
Park Hill Av
Ravenhurst Rd
Lyndale Rd
Edward
Kingsway
Francis Avenue
Monica Rd
Headley Rd
Edenhurst Av
Stratford Rd
Arden Av
Shottery Av
Henley Crs
Odam Cl
Fairway
Hallam Crescent East
Reynolds Pl
Hillary Place
New Fields Avenue
Peverel Road
Caldecote Rd
Wyville Row
Beaufort Rd
Audley End
Mortimer Wy
Ayston Road
Camden Rd
Belton Rd
Claybrook Av
Bramble Wy
Blam Way
Cyril St
Percy St
Amy Street
1 grid square represents 500 metres

Knighton Fields
Clarendon Park
Aylestone Park
Knighton
Victoria Park
Cemetery
University of Leicester
Leicester Royal Infirmary
HM Prison
Leicester City FC (Walkers Stadium)
John Doran Gas Museum
Saffron Lane Stadium
Saffron Lane Sports Centre
Running Track
Cycle Track
Aylestone Leisure Centre
Knighton Fields Primary School
Millgate School
Wyggeston & Queen Elizabeth I College
Leicester Tigers RFC (Welford Road Ground)
Leicester College (Freemen's Park Campus)
Regent College
De Montfort Hall
War Memorial
Leicester Montessori Grammar School
Leicester Montessori Sixth Form College
St Crispins School
Victoria Clinic
Freemens Common Trading Estate
Council Building
Odeon Multiplex
Superstore
Police Station
St Thomas More Catholic School
St John the Baptist CE Prim Sch
Nelson Mandela Park
De Montfort Uni
Gateway 6th Form Coll
Magazine Gatehouse
Trinity Hosp
Leicestershire CC (Grace Road)
Sir Jonathan North Community College
AYLESTONE ROAD
WELFORD ROAD
SAFFRON LANE
VICTORIA PARK ROAD
LONDON ROAD
OXFORD ST
INFIRMARY ROAD
TIGERS WAY
WATERLOO WY
ALMOND ROAD
NEWARKE ST
ST GEORGES WY
A6
A426
A594
A5199
B568
B5366
26
36
43
E
F
G
H
1
2
3
4
5
58
59
60

36
27
35
44
A
B
C
D
1
2
3
4
5
460
61
04
03
02
Stoneygate
Knighton
South Knighton
Victoria Park
Leicester Montessori Sixth Form College
St Crispins School
Medway Community Prim Sch
Uplands Junior Sch
Islamic Girls Sch
Irwin College
Coleman Primary School
Crown Hills Community College
Mayflower Prim Sch
Ashfield School
Evington Valley Primary School
Medical Centre
Stoneygate School
Stoneygate College
St John the Baptist CE Prim Sch
Springfield Road Health Centre
Leicester Islamic Academy
Leicester Montessori School
The Synagogue
Regency Hotel
London Rd Private Hosp
St Thomas More Catholic School
University of Leicester
Leicester High School Junior Dept
University of Leicester Harold Martin Botanic Garden
Leicester Golf Club
Golf Course
Works
Surgery
Cncl Bldg
EAST PARK ROAD
PARK ROAD
MAYFIELD RD
BECKINGHAM RD
WAKERLEY ROAD
STOUGHTON DRIVE
EVINGTON LANE
CARTREE ROAD
STOUGHTON ROAD
Gwendolen Road
Evington Road
Evington Drive
Evington Lane
Bodnant Avenue
Homeway Road
Ethel Road
Chesterfield Road
Kimberley Road
Stanley Road
Elmfield Av
Ashfield Rd
Holmfield Road
St Johns Road
Clarendon Pk Rd
Springfield Road
Knighton Road
Knighton Grange Road
Knighton Rise
Morland Avenue
Shirley Road
Ratcliffe Road
Toller Road
Stoneygate Road
Broadway Road
Kingsway Road
Highway Road
Trueway Road
Romway Road
Portland Rd
Queens Road
Carisbrooke Gdns
Sackville Gdns
Barrington Rd
Freemantle Rd
Meadowcourt Rd
1 grid square represents 500 metres

Leicester General Hospital
Barnes Heath Rd
Higgs Cl
Waterfield Cl
Greenacre Drive
Goodwood Rd
Goodwood Crs
Gamel Rd
Davenport
Beechwood Cl
Sunnyfield Cl
Skampton Rd
Harringworth Rd
B667
St Pauls RC School
Leicester Grammar Junior Sch
Oaklands School
Whitehall Primary School
Hazelnut Cl
Ellwood Cl
Woodborough Rd
Haywood Close
Bracken Cl
Englefield Road
Frinton Av
Fulbeck Av
Millersdale
Downing Drive
Dawlish Cl
Welland Vale Road
Kingscliffe Crs
Kingsbury Av
Alcester Drive
Woodnewton Drive
Durston Cl
Fallowfield Rd
Chorley Wd
Sedgebrook Rd
Hardwick Rd
Delaware Rd
Bathurst Rd
Swinstead Rd
Earlswood Rd
Hemington Rd
Chatteris Av
Thurnby
City of Leicester School
Evington Pool
Surgery
Ethel Road
Whitehall Rd
Harwin Rd
Cordery Rd
Aldgate Av
Angela Dr
Judith Drive
Susan Av
Leicester Dyslexia Assoc
Mickleton Drive
Spencefield Dr
Ensbury Gdns
SPENCEFIELD LANE
Thurnview Road
Ingarsby Drive
Downing Drive
Barnstaple Rd
Kilverstone Av
Bideford Rd
Crantock Cl
Pevensey Av
Newhaven Road
Chalvington Cl
Yelverton Av
Drive
Marydene
Marydene Ct
Judgemeadow Community College
City of Leicester
Leicestershire County
Hextall Road
Blundell Rd
Headland Road
Grocot Rd
Linden Primary School
Hawthorne Dr
The Common
Cordery Road
Evington Ms
Denys Road
Goodwood Rd
Gifford Cl
MAIN ST
Biggin Hill Road
Frfd Av
Crwll Cl
CHURCH RD
High St
School La
Rectory Gdns
B667
Evington
Stoughton Lodge Farm
Stoughton Lane
SHADY LANE
B582
GARTREE ROAD
Farmworld
Stoughton Farm Park
Church La
Thurnby
Gaulby Lane
Gartree Road
Fairway
The Broadway
Ringer's Spinney
Ringers Cl
Manor Road
Manor Cl
Cranbourne Gdns
University of Leicester Sports Ground
Southmeads Road
Southmeads Cl
Blackthorn La
Quickthorns
Whitebeam
Hornbeam Close
Holly Ct
Manor Rd Extn
Oadby
E F G H I
28 38 45
62 63 64
2 3 4 5

38
THURNBY HILL
Crest Rise
Avenue
Hartopp Cl
Devenports Hill
Devenports Way
Wadkins Way
Herrick Dr
Flona Drive
Anthony Drive
Hereward Drive
Dalby
Bramley Orch
29
ROAD
Bradgate Cl
Dawlish Cl
Downing Drive
Millersdale
Walsgrave Av
A
B
C
D
464
65
04
Thurnby
St Lukes CE Primary School
The Spinney
Holmleigh Gdns
Church La
Grange La
Hollies
Randles Cl
Bennion Rd
Chestnut Dr
Main
St
St Luke's Cl
Padwell La
Court Rd
Gilstead Cl
Lakeside Ct
Durston Cl
PO
1
Edgebrook Rd
Hardwick Rd
Bathurst Rd
Fallowfield Rd
Earlswood Rd
Swinstead Rd
Delaware Rd
Hemington Rd
Chatteris Av
Road
2
Stoughton Road
Stoughton Lane
03
County
Stoughton Lodge Farm
3
37
Thurnby Lane
Houghton Lane
4
Church La
Stoughton
302
Gaulby Lane
5
Clarke's Bush
Gaulby Lane
46
Leicester Airport
1 grid square represents 500 metres

Houghton on the Hill
Redver's
E
F
G
H
66
67
68
04
03
302
A47
UPPINGHAM ROAD
Ingarsby Cl
Deane Gate Dr
Linwal Av
Thomas Cl
Scotland
Lane
Scotland La
The Ri
Winckley Cl
PO
North Wy
St Catharines Way
Chapel Cl
Elizabeth Close
Hollies Cl
Firs Cl
Home Cl
Rd
Field Cl
Weir Lane
Surg
Main Street
End Forsells
Freer Cl
School La
Stretton Lane
Houghton on the Hill CE Primary School
Bushby Spinney
Sunny Leys
Mere Farm
Houghton Lodge
Houghton Lane
Cotterill Farm
River Sen
I
2
3
4
5
47

32
A
B
C
D
452
53
Enderby Lodge
New House Farm
Lubbesthorpe Bridle Road
1
2
3
4
5
B582
DESFORD ROAD
Beggar's Lane
Forest Road
MILL HILL
M69
Feldspar Cl
Warren Park Way
Harolds Lane
Granite Cl
Froanes Cl
Works
Mill Hill Industrial Estate
Quarry La
Cook's Lodge
Seine Lane
Thurlaston Lane
HALL WALK
Conery Lane
Moores La
Pope Crs
Capers Cl
Drummond Rd
Chapel St
High St
Sloane Cl
Grays Ct
Blake Ct
Carter Cl
Jarrett Cl
Mitchell Rd
Alexander Av
Townsend Rd
Cross St
Brook St
Broad St
Works
End
Co-operation St
Bantlam La
PO
Coleridge Drive
Aquitaine Cl
Herrick Cl
Keats Cl
George St
Jacob Cl
Equity Road
Federation St
King St
Rawson St
Cornwall St
Shortridge La
John St
Mill Lane
Salt's Close
300
299
Hardwicke Lodge Farm
52
Coleridge
Shelley Rd
Byron Cl
Holyoake St
West Street
Enderby Danemill Primary School
The Pastures Primary School
Meadow Edge
Thornhills
Forest Road
Enderby Centre
I grid square represents 500 metres

Meridian Business Park
Centurion Way
Tiber Way
Meridian East
Staplehurst Av
Brockenhurst Drive
Millfield Community Primary School & Centre
Mossdale Rd
Chislehurst Av
Kingsway
Turnbull
Kirkland Road
Hat Rd
Freeboard Rd
Gayhurst Cl
Woodcote Road
Lubbesthorpe Rd
Pits Av
Watergate Lane
Fishpools
The Glade
The Chase
Pinfold
The Osiers
Grass Acres
Farmway
Lubbesthorpe Road
Millfield Crs
Cottage Farm Cl
Bloxams Cl
Edenhurst Av
Francis Avenue
Monica Rd
Headley Rd
Avenue
Hillrise Drive
Una Av
Gwencole
Surgery
The Poplars
Edith Av
Colbert Dr
Kingsway
Leyland Rd
Riddington Rd
Bilberry Cl
Hazel Drive
NARBOROUGH ROAD
A5460
Watergate Lane
Meridian N
Court
Centre
East Link
Abbey Farm
Meridian West
Industrial Estate
Meridian South
Harcourt Wy
Harcourt Way
The Osiers Business Centre
M1
A5460
Junction 3/21
A563
LUBBESTHORPE WAY
Fosse Park Av
Superstore
Fosse Park Shopping Centre
P
NARBOROUGH RD SOUTH
Everard Way
Brewery
Grove Way
Penman Wy
Thorpe Wy
Smith Way
SOAR VALLEY WAY
The Park
Leicester Lane
B4114
Leicestershire Police HQ
Ratby Meadow La
St Johns
Hill View
erby
Kirk Lane
Works
JOHNS ST
Gee's Lock
Glen Hills Primary
Blue Banks Avenue
Aldeby Cl
ROAD
BLABY RD B582
Fosse Cl
Hr Wy
Trinity Road
Brocking College
Leisure Golf Club
E
F
G
H
I
2
3
4
5
33
42
53
54
55
56
300
299

42
34
41
54
A
B
C
D
1
2
3
4
5
456
57
299
300
301
Riverside Community College
Harefield Av
Foxcroft Close
Rosamund Av
Biam Way
Avenue
Hillrise Av
Una Av
Turnbull
Drive
Edward
Kirkland
Road
Avenue
Edenhurst Av
Francis Avenue
Monica
Kingsway
Surgery
Percy St
Cyril St
Amy
Street
Gwencole Av
Gwencole Crs
The Poplars
Edith Av
Colbert Dr
Leyland Rd
Riddington Rd
Bilberry Cl
Hazel Drive
Narborough Road
South
City of Leicester
Leicestershire County
Aylestone La East
Canal St
Works
Disraeli St
Granby Rd
Granby Prim Sch
Hall La
Ward Cl
Church St
Aylestone Road
A426
Park Hill Av
Duncan
Hampshire Rd
Worcester Rd
Hereford Rd
Banks Road
Belmont St
Lorraine
Cheshire
Middlesex Rd
Shropshire Rd
Berkshire Rd
Aylestone Rd
St Anne's Drive
Paigle Rd
Aylestone
Riverside Dr
Middleton Street
Old Church St
PO
Narrow La
Croft Av
Sanvey La
Logan Av
Marsden Lane
Conaglen Road
Morban Rd
Franklyn Road
Belvoir Drive
Lutterworth Road
Cooper Cl
Holywell Rd
Paget St
Carl St
Montrose Rd
Plantation Avenue
Wigston Lane
Montrose Primary School
Belvoir Dr
Cranfield
Highgrove Crs
Buckingham Dr
Althrp Cl
Magnolia Cl
Monsell Drive
Alvecote Rd
Matts Cl
Montrose Rd
Seaford Rd
Winder's Wy
Eastwood Road
Cheriton Road
Sharpland
Springclose
Glenhills
Glenhills Wy
Valley Way
A563
Surgery
Fontwell Dr
Keenan Cl
Gilmorton Av
Gilmorton Cl
Holts Cl
Hopyard Cl
Aldeby Cl
Bridgemere Cl
Lockhouse Cl
Rushton Dr
Gilmorton Avenue
Amanda Rd
Nuthall Gv
Walnut Gv
The Bridle
Glen Ri
Greendale Road
Glenhills Bvd
Brettell Rd
Markland
The Slade Gns
Howden Rd
Whitteney Dr
Pawley Gdns
Lawford Rd
Simmins Crs
Camfield Ri
Bentinghouse Rd
Tovey Crs
Kepston Cl
Pasley Road
Victors Cl
Sturdee Gn
Sturdee Rd
Eyres Monsell Primary Sch
Hlth Cen
Red House Rd
Red House Ri
Roche Cl
Garnett Crs
Ford Ri
Ebchester Rd
Hesketh Av
Hesketh Cl
Epping Wy
Runcorn Rd
Kelso Gn
Strensall Rd
Ambleside
Autumn Rd
Caversham Rd
Oak Pool Gdns
Tadcaster Av
Scotswood Crs
Packhorse Road
Hillsborough Road
Ibsley Wy
Silsden Rise
Radcot Lawns
Hall Cl
Glen Parva
Leicester Road
Spinney Cl
Hewes Cl
Foxhill Dr
Parsons Dr
Nursery Hollow
Featherby Drive
Bellamy Close
Brook Gdns
Dorothy Avenue
West View Av
Bradshaw Av
Glen Hills Primary Sch
Iris Av
Howard Road
Orchard Av
Grange Drive
Blue Banks Avenue
Needham Av
Lane
Gee's Lock
Hillsborough Rd
Stuart Rd
Thurcroft Cl
Westdale Av
Cork
Court Rd
Glenville
Saxon Dl
Wensley Ri
Swinford Av
Twickenham Rd
Monmouth
Eden Wy
Hebden Cl
Primary School
Works
Wharf Way
1 grid square represents 500 metres

Aylestone Park
Knighton
Eyres Monsell
WIGSTO
Aylestone Leisure Centre
Leicestershire CCC (Grace Road)
Lane FC
Sir Jonathan North Community College
The Lancaster School
Millgate School
Overdale Junior Infant School
Marriott Primary School
Southfields Infant School
The Newry Junior School
Holy Cross Catholic Primary School
Saffron Hill Cemetery
Water Leys Primary School
The Fairfield Primary School
Council Building
Chartwell Dr Industrial Estate
Industrial Estate
South Leicestershire College
Leicester Stage Ho
The Record for Leicesters
Works
Surgery
Cncl Bldg
ATTLEE WAY
A563
ASQUITH WAY
ASQUITH WAY
STONESBY AVENUE
B5418
SAFFRON LANE
B5366
AYLESTONE LANE
WELFORD RD
LEICESTER
A5199
ROAD
Landsdowne Road
Lorrimer Rd
Knighton Lane
Clifton Rd
Grace Road
Copinger Road
Whittier Rd
Great Arler Road
Chapel Lane
Herrick Rd
Milford Rd
Houldiitch Rd
Northcote Rd
Pope St
Shelley St
Scott Street
Heather
Newmarket St
Carisbrooke Gdns
Balmoral Close
Kenwood
Meadvale Road
Welford Court
The Cedars
Brinsmead Road
Church La
Pendlebury Dr
Muston Gdns
Larchwood Cl
Chadderton Cl
Cheviot Road
Cairngorm Cl
Grampian Cl
Heathcott Rd
Bloomfield Road
Neston Rd
Neston Gdns
Cyprus Road
St Andrews Rd
Burgess Rd
Saffron Wy
Saffron Wy
Burnaston Rd
Bretby Rd
Alton Road
Bradston Rd
Hawkesbury Rd
Vernon Road
Percy Rd
Manners Rd
Handley St
Leeson St
Vaughan Rd
Hallaton St
Milligan Rd
Fayrhurst Rd
Marriott Rd
Broughton Road
The Crossway
Fairway
Elston Fields
Brookfield Ri
Stanton Row
Linwood La
Windley Road
Burnside Rd
Meadow Gdns
Babington Rw
Southfields Drive
Uplands Rd
Aspin Road
Woodcroft Av
Skelton Dr
Shrewsbury Av
Oakdene Rd
Lamborne Road
Fairholme Rd
Cairnsford Rd
Hylion Road
Northdene Road
Aberdale Road
Deancourt Rd
Asquith Blvd
Asquith Boulevard
Baldwin Road
Highgate Dr
Roehampton Dr
Westgate Rd
Kingsmead
Overdale Rd
Northfold Rd
Eastcourt Rd
Palmerston Blvd
Woodbank Rd
South Kings Roa
Hillcrest Rd
Ramsbury Rd
Heddington Way
Lynmouth Dr
Tythorn Dr
Brixham Drive
Shackerdale Rd
Bradgate Drive
Guildford Drive
Croft Dr
Dale Av
Kingston Av
Burleigh Ave
Westfield Av
Castleton Road
Bakewell Rd
Alfreton Road
Chellaston Rd
Carlton Drive
Willow Park Drive
Repton Rd
Exeter Rd
Northfield Av
Aylestone La
Brailsford Rd
Lyon Cl
Viking Rd
Wiltshire Rd
Warwick Rd
Dukes Close
Rollestone Road
Owston Drive
Orson Dr
Holmden Av
West Avenue
Chartwell Dr
Southfields Drive
Arnesby Crs
Belton Cl
Cottagers Cl
Farm Cl
Barfoot Road
Littlegarth
Highgate
Goldhill
Schoolgate
Newry
Crabtree Cnr
Trenant Road
Pen Cl
Sponne Rl
Stockland Rd
Tamerton Rd
Rydall Road
Spendlow Gdns
Allenwood Road
Saffron Lane
Rye Cl
Bluebell Dr
Poppy Cl
Glenborne Rd
Parvian Rd
Durham Drive
Dorset Avenue
Norfolk Road
Sussex Rd
Cheshire Drive
Cumberland Rd
Northumberland Rd
Gloucester Crescent
Anglesey Rd
Kent Crs
Oxford Dr
Kenilworth Road
Cardigan
Lincoln Dr
Stafford Dr
Radnor Rd
Cornwall Road
Hindoostan Avenue
Tigers Road
Moores Cl
Namur Rd
Aisne Rd
Central Avenue
Coronation Av
Cherry St
Manor St
Pullman Road
Clarkes Rd
Hansen Ct
Regent Rd
E
F
G
H
I
E
F
G
H
1
2
3
4
5
35
44
55
58
59
60
58
59
60
301
300
299

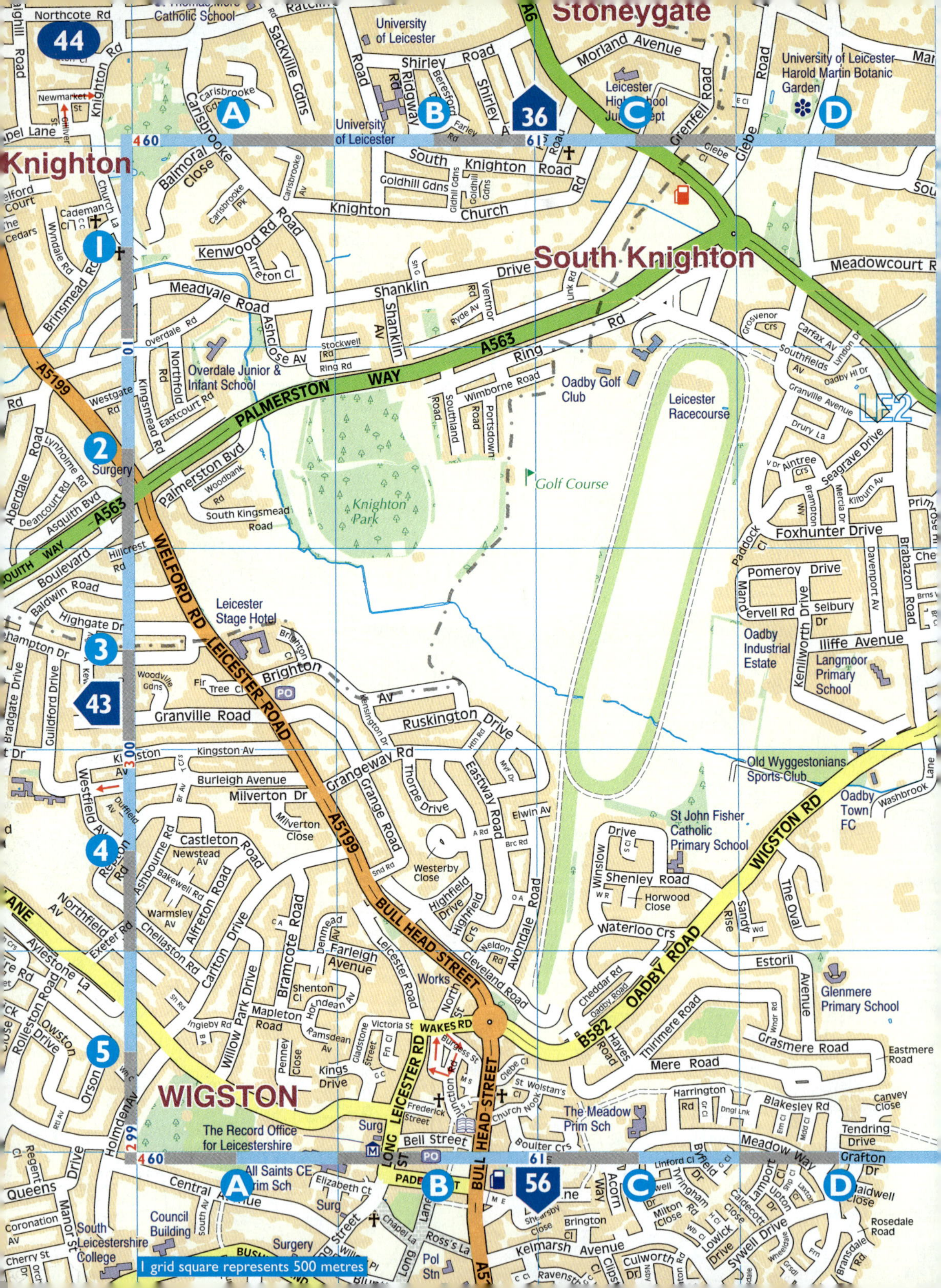
44
36
43
56
Stoneygate
Knighton
South Knighton
WIGSTON
LE2
University of Leicester
University of Leicester Harold Martin Botanic Garden
Leicester High School Junior Dept
Catholic School
Overdale Junior & Infant School
Oadby Golf Club
Leicester Racecourse
Golf Course
Knighton Park
Leicester Stage Hotel
Oadby Industrial Estate
Langmoor Primary School
Old Wyggestonians Sports Club
Oadby Town FC
St John Fisher Catholic Primary School
Glenmere Primary School
The Meadow Prim Sch
The Record Office for Leicestershire
All Saints CE Prim Sch
Council Building
South Leicestershire College
Surgery
Works
Pol Stn
Northcote Rd
Knighton Rd
Sackville Gdns
Carisbrooke Road
Shirley Road
Ridgway
Morland Avenue
Grenfell Road
Glebe Road
South Knighton Road
Knighton Church Rd
Balmoral Close
Kenwood Rd
Meadvale Road
Shanklin Drive
Meadowcourt Rd
Palmerston Way
A563
Ring Rd
Wimborne Road
Southland Road
Portsdown Road
Grosvenor Crs
Carfax Av
Southfields Av
Granville Avenue
Seagrave Drive
Foxhunter Drive
Pomeroy Drive
Kenilworth Drive
Iliffe Avenue
Brabazon Road
Welford Rd
Leicester Road
A5199
Palmerston Blvd
South Kingsmead Road
Asquith Blvd
Boulevard
Baldwin Road
Highgate Dr
Guildford Drive
Bradgate Drive
Granville Road
Brighton Av
Ruskington Drive
Kingston Av
Burleigh Avenue
Milverton Dr
Grangeway Rd
Grange Road
Thorpe Drive
Eastway Road
Castleton Road
Alfreton Road
Carlton Drive
Bramcote Road
Farleigh Avenue
Bull Head Street
Cleveland Road
Avondale Road
Wigston Rd
Oadby Road
B582
Shenley Road
Waterloo Crs
Estoril Avenue
Grasmere Road
Mere Road
Blakesley Rd
Meadow Way
Wakes Rd
Long Leicester Rd
Bell Street
Frederick Street
Paddock St
Central Avenue
Kelmarsh Avenue
Aylestone La
Rolleston Road
Owston Drive
Queens Drive
Northfield Av
Welford Road
1 grid square represents 500 metres

Oadby
37
46
57
E
F
G
H
62
63
64
01
00
2 99
1
2
3
4
5
University of Leicester Sports Ground
Manor Road
Southmeads Road
Southmeads Cl
Blackthorn La
Quickthorns
Manor Cl
Ringers Cl
Stoughton Road
B582
Manor Rd Extension
Brookside Primary School
Manor High School
Hornbeam Close
Holly Ct
Whitebeam Road
Wych Elm Rd
Dogwood Ct
Cross St
Regent Street
Pelham St
Beaumont St
Parkland Dr
Spencer Street
Stoughton Road
Sandhurst St
The Pde
South St
East St
PO
Brooksby Dr
High St
Church St
Surg
Health Cen
Leicester Road
Churchill Cl
Chapel St
Garden Cl
Cartwright Dr
Goddards Slang
Cem
B582 WIGSTON RD
Surgery
Holme Dr
Woodfield Road
Hall Dr
Leys Cl
Wyndham Cl
Launde Road
Copse Close
Woods Cl
Eden Road
Forest Rise
Frome Av
Swale Cl
Moon Half Crs
Covert Cl
Quiney Wy
Belleville Drive
Mosse Wy
Adlington Road
Bollington Rd
S Rd
Malton Dr
Dove Ri
Dove Rd
Hamble Rd
Ribble Av
Severn Road
St Pauls Close
Stour Cl
Waveney Rise
Isis Cl
Tamar Rd
Trent Cl
Windrush Drive
Dart Cl
Derwent Wk
Avon Cl
Nene Drive
Bourton Crs
Stoughton Cl
The Yews
Harvard Cl
Launde Primary School
Tudor Dr
Uplands Road
Martin Av
Queen Street
Fairfield Road
Wayside Dr
Kent Dr
Somerby Dr
Brookside Drive
Waldron Dr
NEW ST
A6
LONDON ROAD
B5403
King St
The Morwoods
Beech Rd
Greenbank Dr
Kendrick Dr
Rosemead Dr
Brocks Hl Dr
Elms Cl
Quinton Ri
Brambling Way
Rosemead Drive
Hidcote Road
Shipston Hill
Sibton La
Leys Drive
Briar Cl
Highcroft Av
Canon Cl
Medical Centre
Prince Dr
Edward Cl
Ann's Wy
Princess Av
Elizabeth Dr
Hursley Cl
Ullswater Dr
Ullswater Cl
Ludlow Cl
Meynell Close
Malham Wy
Pennine Cl
Hunters Way
Tynedale Cl
Berkeley Cl
Ledbury Cl
Thurlow Cl
Fitzwilliam Cl
Hayden Av
Eskdale Cl
Bonner Cl
Devonia Rd
Hawker Rd
Jackson Cl
Woodland Grange Prim Sch
Beaufort Way
Cooper Gdns
Wright Lane
Elliot Cl
Holbrook
James Gavin Way
Wragg Way
Smore Slade Hl
Boulton Court
Pipistrelle
Rawlings Ct
Hill Field
Gorse Lane
Belvoir Cl
Quorn Av
Fernie Cl
Cottesmore Avenue
Fox Hollow
Wickham Rd
Fairstone Hill
Turner Rise
Lowcroft Dr
Highcroft Av
Ash Tree Road
Ash Tree Close
Coombe Pl
Hill Way
Park Crescent
Glen Way
Glen Road
Orchard Close
Briar Walk
Pine Tree Cl
Vandyke Rd
Ridge Way
Howdon Road
Badgers Holt
Belper Close
Oxted Rise
Barnet Cl
Ashton Cl
Fenton Close
Broxfield Close
Briar Meads
Tilton Drive
Sutton Close
Brocks Hill Primary School
Gartree High Sch
The Beauchamp College
Brocks Hill Country Park
Richmond Way
Windsor Cl
Coombe Rise
Kew Dr
Whiteoaks Rd
Hyde Close
Laurel Dr
Highcroft Rd
Norman Ct
Raine Way
Mount Pleasant
Woodside Road
Gorse Lane
Glen Gorse Golf Club
LONDON ROAD
Mere Lane

46
38
45
58
A
B
C
D
1
2
3
4
5
464
65
01
00
300
299
Gaulby Lane
Leicester Airport
Manor High School
Gartree Road
Oadby Lodge Farm
Great Stretton
Windrush Drive
Frome Av
Swale Cl
Pennine Cl
Stvn Cl
Thurlow Cl
Rckb Rd
Eskdale Cl
Bonner Cl
Devonia Rd
Hawker Rd
Holbrook
James Gavin Way
Elliot Cl
Woodlands Ct
Celandine Cl
Willow Herb Cl
The Pastures
Pipistrelle Way
Florence Wragg Way
Boulton Court
Smore Slade Hl
Rawlings Ct
Woodland Grange Prim Sch
Beaufort Way
Wright Lane
Cooper Gdns
N Gdn
Hill Field
Mount Pleasant
Ellis Flds
Norman Ct
Raine Way
Highcroft Rd
Woodside Road
Gorse Lane
Glen Gorse
LONDON ROAD
Lane
Chestnut Drive
The Spinney
Chestnut Dr
The Av
Chestnut Drive
Stretton Hall (Hospital)
Sycamore Cl
Stretton Hall Drive
River Sence
1 grid square represents 500 metres

Little Stretton
Norton Gorse
Kings Norton Lodge
Gaulby Lane
Mere Road
Gartree Road
Gartree Road
Stretton Road
Stretton Road
Stackley House
The Cottage
39
59
E
F
G
H
1
2
3
4
5
66
67
68

A
B
C
D
1
2
3
4
5
44
45
99
98
97
Brockey Farm
Brooklands Farm
Kirkby Road
Barwell Fields Farm
Brockey Farm
White House Farm
The Brockey
Elwell Av
Apple Tree Cl
Yew Tree Cl
Pear Tree Cl
Bardon Road
Bradgate Road
Willow Tree Cl
Peckleton Gn
Ashleigh Gdns
Farm Road
The Drive
William Bradford Community College
Stapleton Lane
Glebe Farm
Charnwood Road
Heath Lane
Gartree Crescent
Heath Lane South
Barwell
Byron Street
Masefield Cl
Newlands Prim Sch
PO
Belle Vue Rd
Norton Rd
Field Way
HINCKLEY ROAD
A47
Howard Close
Cumberland Way
Cem
Moore Rd
Queensway
Newlands Rd
Frisby Rd
Chesterfield Wy
Heathfield High School
Doctors Fields
Regent St
Brockey Cl
Oxford St
Kingsfield Road
Hastings Rd
Meadow Rd
Mount Av
Shenton Rd
Mayfield Wy
Hazel Wy
Adrian Dr
Glyn Cl
Kirkby Road
George St
Red Hall Dr
Holly La
Greenhill Dr
Balmoral Rd
Coronation Rd
Oakdale Rd
Ash
Cedar
Russett Cl
Works
Kerry Cl
Russett Cl
Penny La
Faracre Road
Barwell Inf Sch
Bank Ter
East Gn
King St
Shilton Road
Elmsthorpe La
B581
ELMESTHORPE LANE
Hereford Close
Holloway Cl
Ayrshire Cl
Barwell Medical Centre
Angus Rd
The Barracks
Chapel Street
Queen St
Hill St
Dawson's Lane
Hawthorne Way
Stanley St
Works
Boston Wy
Washington Cl
Blackburn Rd
Street
Barwell CE Jun Sch
CARRS HILL
Inglenook
Elmdale Rd
Birch Cl
Maryland Close
Moat Way
Ind Est
Adct Cl
Croft Cl
Dovecote Wy
The Common
Church Lane
Elmsthorpe
A47
Moat Wy
High
St Mary's Court
Ivens Farm
Mill Street
Wensleydale Av
Waterfall Way
Waters End
Crabtree
LEICESTER ROAD
The Crs
Billington Road
1 grid square represents 500 metres

Earl Shilton
Leicester Road
A47
Hill Top
High Street
The Hollow
Wood Street
Church Street
Thurlaston Lane
Keats Lane
Green La
High Tor West
High Tor East
Shilton Road
Westfield Farm
Surgery
Park Road
Tower Rd
West St
Works
Almey's Lane
Alexander Avenue
Earl Street
Mill Lane
The Poplars
King Richard's Hill
Knights Link
St Peters RC Prim Sch
Weavers Close CE Prim Sch
Weaver Rd
Orton Rd
Astley Rd
Oaks Ind Est
Oaks Wy
Ivydene Cl
Peggs Cl
Candle La
Meadow Ct Rd
Lyndene Cl
East Equity Road
Equity Rd
Hurst Rd
Townlands CE Primary School
Station Road
B5364
B581
Breach Lane
The Breach Farm
Huit Farm
Melton St
New Street
Byron St
James St
Mona St
Jubilee Dr
Croft Road
Almond Wy
Wileman's Cl
The Grange
50

Farm
Moat Close
Earl Shilton Road
A
B
C
D
4 48
49
99
1
2
3
4
5
98
2 97
LE9
Normanton Turville
Earl Shilton Road
Lane
Dairy Farm
49
Mirfield Farm
Watery Gate Lane
Pingle Lane
Mill Lane
Huit Farm
M69
4 48
49
A
B
60
C
D
Potters Marston
1 grid square represents 500 metres

Thurlaston
Huncote
Thurlaston CE Primary School
PO
Enderby Road
Holt Crs
Desford Rd
Main Street
Tyers Cl
Church St
Normanton Cl
Nursery Cl
Croft Road
M69
Forest Road
Green's Lodge
Yennards Farm
Forest Rd
Thurlaston Brook
Huncote Leisure Centre
Huncote Cem
Sports Fld
La
Lodge Cl
Compton Dr
Denman
Critchlow Rd
Huncote Community Primary School
Cooper Cl
Chantry Cl
End
Cheney
Eunice Av
Mill Vw
Main St
Brook Street
Duncan Av
School La
The Gn
Fritchley Cl
Narborough Rd
St. James Cl
Carey Rd
Ratcliffe Drive
Sandpit Cotts
Croft
Lane
Thurlaston Lane
Hill Road
Croft
Stanton Lane
Huncote
E
F
G
H
1
2
3
4
5
50
51
52
99
98
297
52
61

52
40
51
62
A
B
C
D
1
2
3
4
5
452
53
99
98
297
NARBOROUGH
Red Hill
Huncote
Hardwicke Lodge Farm
Green's Lodge
The Pastures Primary School
Enderby Danemill Primary School
Enderby Centre
Red Hill Field Primary School
Woodlands Day Hospital
Council Building
Cncl Bldgs
Oaks Ind Est
Works
Elms Farm
Surg
PO
Forest Road
Forest Rd
Huncote Road
Copt Oak Road
Narborough Rd
Coventry Rd
Coventry Road
Desford Rd
West Street
Stewart Av
Hardwicke Rd
Woodhouse Rd
Coltbeck Avenue
Langham Drive
Red Hill Av
The Coppice
The Pastures
Kiplin Drive
Coleridge Drive
Equity Road
Mortimer Road
Finch Way
Burrows Close
Cutters Close
Robotham Cl
Chestnut Cl
Sycamore
Oak Rd
Poplar Rd
Beechwood Rd
B582
B4114
River Soar
1 grid square represents 500 metres

Kirk Lane
ROAD
BLABY RD B582
Brockington College
Leisure & Golf Club
Golf Course
M1
B4114
LEICESTER ROAD
ENDERBY ROAD
JOHNS
Works
Fosse Cl
Trinity Road
Heath Av
Packhorse Dr
Queens Dr
Sandhill Dr
Clarence Rd
Lime Tree Rd
Sparsis Gdns
Cumberwell Dr
Warren Rd
Abbey Road
Leicester Rd
Gee's Lock
Grand Union Canal
River Soar
Enderby Road Industrial Estate
Grange Business Park
Blaby Industrial Park
Glen Hills Primary
Blue Banks Avenue
KING EDWARD AVENUE
Carlton Av
Roy Cl
Alexandra St
Regent St
Princess St
Regent St Ind Est
Greystoke Primary School
Cem
Hlth Cen
Church Vw
Thornton Dr
Victoria St
Jubilee Crs
Bell La
Narborough Station
Station Road
Riverside Way
Cornfield Cl
Maple Cl
Field Cl
Tree Wk
The Paddocks
The Mdw
Haybarn Cl
Farm Cl
Waudby Cl
The Sq
Warwick Rd
Warwick Road
Littlethorpe
Biddle Road
Heighton Crs
Gurney Crs
Cosby Road
Ridgeway
Oak Rd
Hazel Way
Whetstone
Station St
Central Cl
Charnwood Av
Grange Dr
Victoria Rd
East Avenue
Trinity Road
Sunnyside Cl
Woodyard La
Daybell
Newby Cl
Vicarage La
Foulds La
Harrop Cl
B582
St Peters Dr
The Crestway
College
Cncl Bldg
St Peters CE Prim Sch
Church La
Cliffe House Ms
Spinney Halt
Fairview Av
Wale Road
King St
Shenton Cl
Broadbent Cl
Avon Dr
Elizabeth Gdns
High St
The Nook
Attfield Dr
The Dicken
Bridge Wy
Brook St
Grove Road
Brookside
Whittle Cl
Burnham Dr
Cambridge Road
Whetstone Brook
Works
Sanderson Close
BLABY-BY-PASS
A426
Westleigh RFC
Mill Hl Cl
Curtis Cl
Johnson Cl
Earle Smith Cl
Buxton Cl
Grove
Ridley
Coulson Cl
Phipps Cl
Worsley Wy
Kenny Cl
Cannam Cl
Laundon Wy
Hubbard Cl
Leveret Dr
Halford
Shaw Cl
Muntjack Rd
Fox Covert
Roebuck Cl
Badger Dr
Badgerbrook
Dog and Gun Lane
Alice Gdns
Bruce Wy
Industrial Estate
Whiteacres
Golf Course
Mawby Cl
E
F
G
H
I
2
3
4
5
41
54
63
55
56
98
99
297

BLABY
Gee's Lock
Glen Hills Primary Sch
Blue Banks Avenue
Featherby Drive
Bellamy Close
Brook Gdns
Hollow
Dorothy Avenue
West View Av
Iris
Howard Road
Lane
Needham Av
Westdale Av
Cork La
Court Rd
Glenville Av
Works
Wharf Way
LEICESTER
A426
Woodbank
Bradshaw Av
Ambleside
Autumn Rd
Caversham Rd
Copse
Grange Cl
Oak Pool
Gdns
Tadcaster Av
Scotswood Crs
Thurcroft Cl
Packhorse Road
Hillsborough Road
Ibsley Wy
Silsden Rise
Hillsborough Rd
Hillsborough Crs
Saxon Dl
Hebden Cl
Henray Av
Wensley Ri
Swinford Av
Twickenham Rd
Monmouth
Rolleston Primary School
Eden Wy
Sonning Way
Sonning Wy
Shield Crs
Salkeld Rd
Julian Rd
Wokingham Av
Queens Pk Wy
Featherstone Drive
HM Young Offender Institution & Remand (Glen Parva)
Grand Union Canal
New Bridge Rd
B582
LITTLE GLEN ROAD
River Sence
Blaby Industrial Park
Chelsea
Trafalgar Wy
Knightsbridge Rd
Grosvenor Cl
Regency Cl
Wstmnstr Dr
Nowell Cl
Kensington
The Ford
Winchester Avenue
Westleigh Business Park
West St
New St
James St
Lime Gv
Corus Hotel
Northfield Road
Surg
Home Cl
Chapel St
Manor Ct
Sycamore St
Wigston Rd
Church Street
Enderby Road
Leicester Rd
Holly Gv
Ash Gv
Lavender Cl
The Avenue
Park Road
Works
Auburn Road
Freer Cl
Welford Road
Cem
Mill Lane
Daybell
Woodyard La
Newby Cl
Sunnyside Cl
Vicarage La
Strudwick Wy
Foulds La
Harrop Cl
Victoria Rd
East Avenue
Albert Ct
St Peters Dr
Church La
St Peters CE Prim Sch
Mill Hl Cl
Curtis Cl
Johnson Cl
Earle Smith Cl
Buxton Cl
Wale Road
High St
King St
Shenton Cl
The Nook
Attfield
BLABY BY-PASS
Westleigh RFC
Queen's Road
The Elms
Lutterworth Road
Laurel Rd
Darley Rd
Dovedale
The Fairway
Thistly Meadow Primary School
The Crs
Western Drive
Beech Rd
Willow Road
Hospital La
Chester Road
Oaks Dr
Oakfield Crs
Hospital Lane
Grove Road
Heybrook Av
Keswick Rd
Cherry Rd
Avenue
Hwt Dr
Maple
Walnut Wy
Cedar Road
Wykeham Cl
Winchester Rd
Wynton Cl
Saville Road
Waverley Rd
Welbeck Cl
Cranmer Cl
Broadmead Rd
Latimer Cl
Ridley Cl
Ripon Dr
Dundee Rd
Salisbury Cl
Lichfield Drive
Lincoln Drive
Southway
Wareham Rd
Leamington Dr
Dorchester Cl
Brook St
Bridge Wy
Whittle Cl
Whetstone Brook
Sanderson Close
Chr Cl
Coulson Cl
Phipps Cl
Worsley Wy
Sn Cl
Rawley Cl
Kenny Cl
Council Building
Halford St
Leveret Dr
Shaw Cl
Muntjack Rd
Fox Covert
Otter Wy
Roebuck Cl
Badger Dr
Gun Lane
Badgerbrook
Cannam Cl
Laundon Wy
Hubbard
Paramore Cl
Mawby
Works
Keepers Farm
Willow Farm
42
53
64
A B C D
1 2 3 4 5
456 57
99 98 97
1 grid square represents 500 metres

Monsell
Cumberland Rd
Northumberland Rd
Norfolk Road
Essex Rd
Sussex Rd
Drive
The Fairfield Primary School
Council Building
Chartwell Dr Industrial Estate
Chartwell
Dukes Close
Rolleston Drive
Owston Drive
Avenue
Orson
Holmden Av
WIGSTON
The Record Office for Leicestershire
Aisne Rd
Namur
Gloucester Crescent
SAFFRON ROAD
Hindoostan Avenue
Kent Crs
Oxford Dr
Kenilworth Road
Anglesey Rd
Cardigan Dr
Lincoln Dr
Stafford Dr
Westmorland Av
Radnor Rd
Works
Regent Cl
Queens Drive
Central Avenue
South Av
Crete Av
Moores Cl
Glamorgan Av
Kent Crs
Worcester Dr
Cornwall Road
Chartwell Dr
Coronation Av
Manor St
South Leicestershire College
Council Building
Tigers Road
Tigers Cl
Waverley Rd
Marstown Av
Brecon Cl
Hansen Ct
Clarkes Road
Pullman Road
Cherry St
Orchards Dr
South Wigston Station
Bennett Wy
Works
STATION ROAD
Abington High School
Birkett House School and Hostel
Kirkdale Road
Jasmine Ct
Clifford St
Leopold St
Fairfield Street
Albion St
Glen Ga
Street
Station Street
South Wigston Hlth Cen
Cncl Bldg
Bushloe High Sch
Wigston Swim Pool
Guthlaxton College
Westleigh Rd
Aldri Rd
Oakleigh Av
Wilson Road
Industrial Estate
BLABY ROAD
Magna Road
Collaton Rd
Arnold Av
Florence Av
Chatsworth Av
Denacre Av
Buckfast Close
ST THOMAS ROAD
B582
PO
Curzon Av
Devonshire Av
Kenton Av
Cawsand Rd
B582
Windsor Av
South Wigston High School
Bassett St
Dunton St
Matlock Av
Baldwin Av
Penn Close
Richmond Drive
The Parkland Primary School
Timber Street
South Wigston
Cromford Av
Tansley Av
Harrison Close
Camborne
Little Hill Primary School
Lancaster Wy
York Cl
Edward Dr
Phillip Dr
Best Cl
Countesthorpe Road
Healey Street
Grove
Dr Av
D R Cl
Garden St
Canal St
Taylor's Br Rd
Clifton Dr
Blenheim Cl
Ellison Cl
Orange St
Irlam St
Hazelwood Rd
Barge Cl
Ervin's Lock
Laverstock Rd
Launceston
Park Road
Railway St
Lansdowne
Bush Lock Cl
Pochin's Br Rd
Britford Av
Pitton
Amesbury
Mill Cl
Works
Lane
Mill
Grand Union Canal
River Sence
Kilby Bridge Farm
Blaby Hill
Port Hill
Countesthorpe Road
Business Park
Rose Farm
Road
Foston Lodge Farm
E
F
G
H
I
2
3
4
5
43
56
65
58
59
60
99
98
297

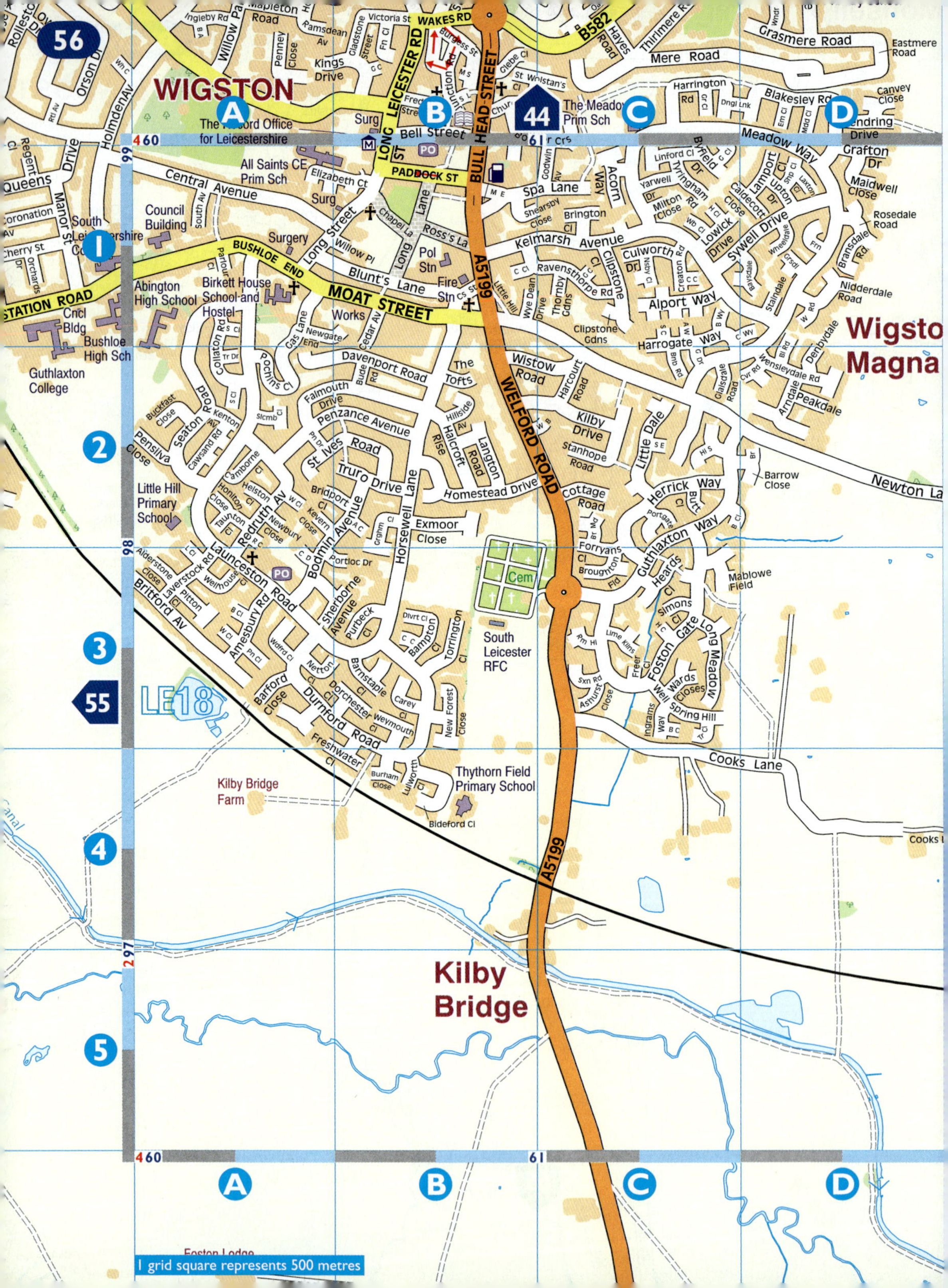
56
55
44
WIGSTON
Wigston Magna
Kilby Bridge
A
B
C
D
1
2
3
4
5
460
61
99
98
297
LE18
Wakes Rd
Long Leicester Rd
Long St
Bull Head Street
Welford Road
A5199
B582
Bell Street
Paddock St
Bushloe End
Moat Street
Station Road
Central Avenue
Long Street
Blunt's Lane
Chapel La
Ross's La
Spa Lane
Kelmarsh Avenue
Meadow Way
Mere Road
Grasmere Road
Thirlmere Rd
Eastmere Road
Harrington Rd
Blakesley Rd
Canvey Close
Endring Drive
Grafton Dr
Maidwell Close
Rosedale Road
Nidderdale Road
Denbydale
Peakdale
Arndale
Wensleydale Rd
Harrogate Way
Alport Way
Sywell Drive
Lowick Drive
Culworth Dr
Clipstone
Clipstone Gdns
Ravensthorpe Rd
Thornby Gdns
Acorn Way
Godwin Av
Brington Cl
Shearsby Close
Wistow Road
Harcourt Road
Kilby Drive
Little Dale
Stanhope Road
Herrick Way
Cottage Road
Barrow Close
Newton La
Guthlaxton Way
Heards Cl
Forryans Cl
Broughton Fld
Simons Cl
Foston Gate
Long Meadow
Mablowe Field
Wards Closes
Spring Hill
Well
Ingrams Way
Ashurst Close
Cooks Lane
Davenport Road
The Tofts
Falmouth Drive
Penzance Avenue
St Ives Road
Truro Drive
Bridport Cl
Bodmin Avenue
Horsewell Lane
Exmoor Close
Homestead Drive
Halcroft Rise
Langton Road
Hillside Av
Launceston Road
Redruth Av
Seaton Road
Pensilva Close
Buckfast Close
Kenton Av
Collaton Rd
Pochins Cl
Gas Lane
Newgate End
Cedar Av
Sherborne Avenue
Purbeck Cl
Bampton Cl
Torrington Cl
Barnstaple Cl
Dorchester Cl
Weymouth Cl
Durnford Road
Freshwater Cl
Netton Cl
Barford Close
Amesbury Rd
Britford Av
Alderstone Close
Laverstock Rd
Pitton Cl
Carey Cl
New Forest Close
Lulworth Cl
Burham Close
Bideford Cl
Holmsden Av
Queens Drive
Regent Cl
Manor St
Coronation Av
Cherry St
Orchards
Orson Dr
Rollestone
Willow Pk
Ingleby Rd
Mapleton Road
Ramsdean Av
Victoria St
Gladstone Street
Penney Close
Kings Drive
Burgess St
Glebe Cl
St Wolstan's Cl
Junction Rd
Elizabeth Ct
Willow Pl
The Record Office for Leicestershire
All Saints CE Prim Sch
Council Building
South Leicestershire Coll
Surgery
Surg
Abington High School
Birkett House School and Hostel
Cncl Bldg
Bushloe High Sch
Guthlaxton College
Little Hill Primary School
Pol Stn
Fire Stn
Works
PO
The Meadow Prim Sch
Cem
South Leicester RFC
Thythorn Field Primary School
Kilby Bridge Farm
Foston Lodge
Canal
1 grid square represents 500 metres

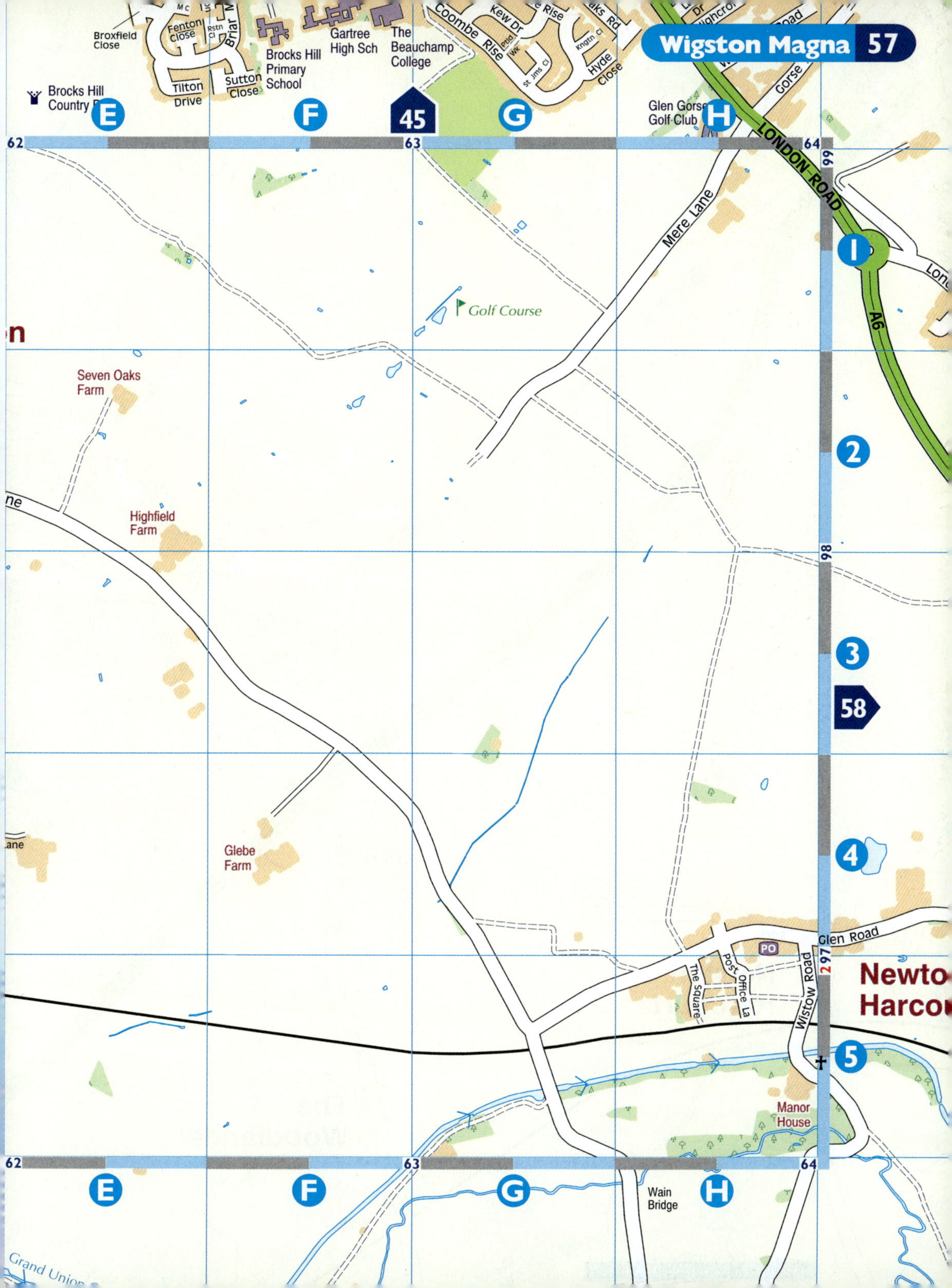
Broxfield Close
Fenton Close
Rstn Cl
Briar
Tilton Drive
Sutton Close
Brocks Hill Primary School
Gartree High Sch
The Beauchamp College
Coombe Rise
Kew Dr
Rise
Ptld Wk
St Jms Cl
Kngtn Cl
Hyde Close
Corse
Brocks Hill Country P
Glen Gorse Golf Club
LONDON ROAD
Mere Lane
Golf Course
A6
Seven Oaks Farm
Highfield Farm
Glebe Farm
Glen Road
PO
The Square
Post Office La
Wistow Road
Newto
Harco
Manor House
Wain Bridge
Grand Union
Lane
E
F
G
H
45
58
1
2
3
4
5
62
63
64
99
98
297

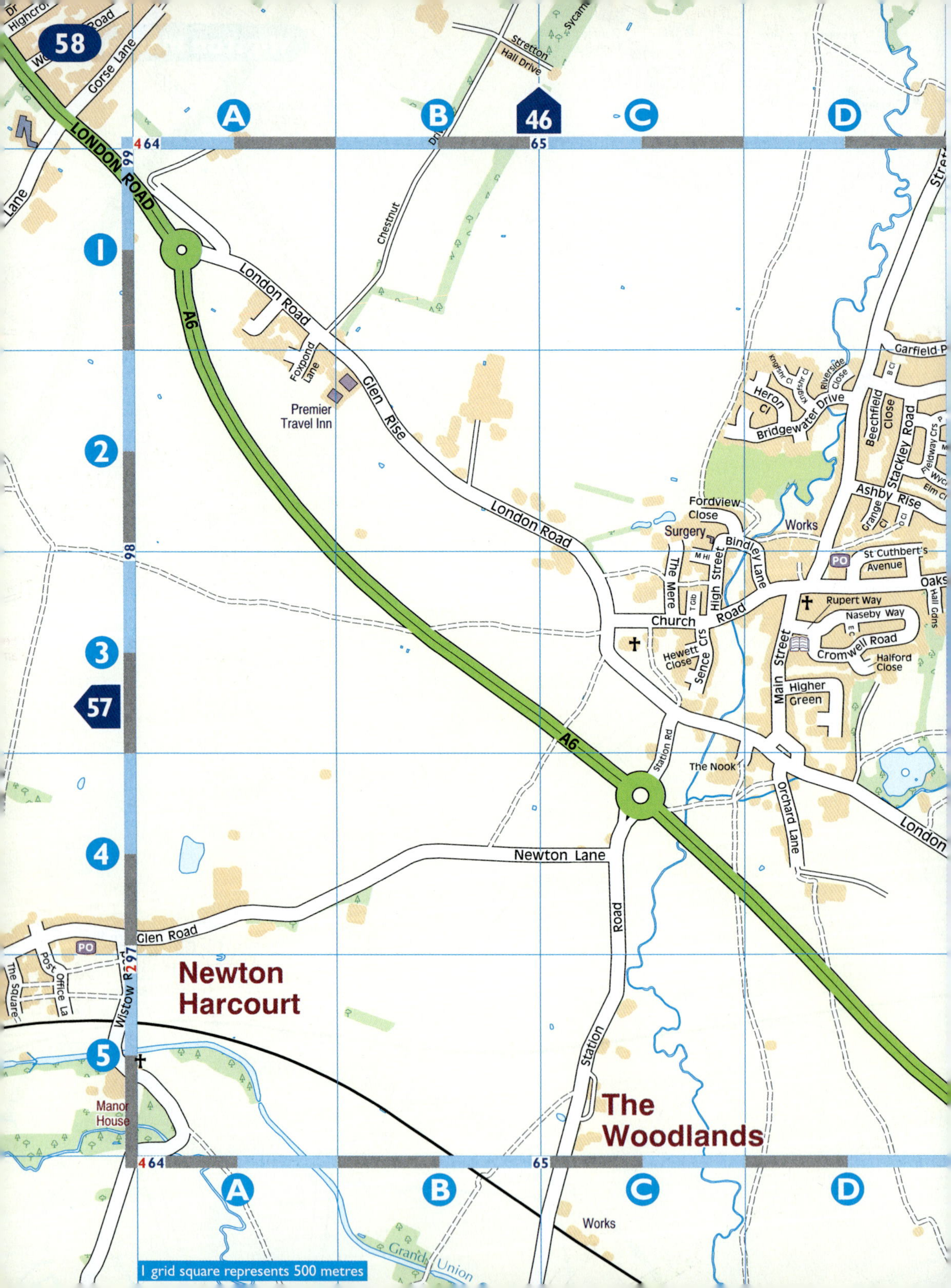

58
46
57
A
B
C
D
1
2
3
4
5
4 64
65
99
98
2 97
LONDON ROAD
A6
London Road
Gorse Lane
Lane
Stretton Hall Drive
Chestnut
Foxpond Lane
Premier Travel Inn
Glen Rise
Fordview Close
Surgery
Bindley Lane
High Street
The Mere
Church Road
Hewett Close
Sence Crs
Heron Cl
Bridgewater Drive
Riverside Close
Beechfield Close
Stackley Road
Ashby Rise
Grange Cl
Garfield
Fieldway Crs
Elm Cl
Works
PO
St Cuthbert's Avenue
Rupert Way
Naseby Way
Cromwell Road
Halford Close
Hall Gdns
Main Street
Higher Green
Station Rd
The Nook
Orchard Lane
Newton Lane
Road
Glen Road
Post Office La
The Square
Wistow Rd
Newton Harcourt
Manor House
Station
The Woodlands
Works
Grand Union
1 grid square represents 500 metres

Stackley House
The Cottage
Road
E
F
47
G
H
66
67
68
99
I
Scotland
Garfield Park
Park
Coverside Road
Spinney View
The Chase
Stonehill Drive
Fernie Dene
Woodbury Rise
St Cuthberts CE Prim Sch
Glen Oaks
Washbrook Lane
Elms Lane
2
Burton Overy
Baileys Lane
Main Street
Back La
PO
Bell La
Carlton Lane
98
Carlton
St Thomas's Road
Cherry Grove
Hilltop Avenue
Road
Great Glen
The Gravel
3
Works
Burton Brook
Road
Great Glen House
Burton Grange
Mayns Lane
4
297
5
London Road
A6
E
F
G
H

Hult Farm
60
M69
50
A
B
C
D
448
49
Potters Marston
Pingle Lane
Thorney Fields Farm
Works
96
Stanton Lane
Huncote Road
2
Stoney Stanton
3
N ROAD
B581
Drive
Cadles Close
Mays Farm
Ellison Cl
Knights Close
Huncote Road
John Bold Avenue
The Fleet
Achurch Close
Jms Str
George Hill Close
Wgh Cl
Highfield Street
Foxbank Industrial Estate
M B C
L Cl
Meadow Close
Clint Hill Drive
Oak Lodge Farm
Works
95
Long Street
Nock Verges
Cem
Rbrtsn Cl
T Cl
Fisher Close
Smithy Farm Dr
Manorfield CE Prim Sch
Church Street
Middleton Close
4
NEW ROAD
BROUGHTON ROAD
PO
Surgery
Disney Cl
Peter's Close
Farndon Drive
Webbs Way
Tansey Crescent
The Oval
The Orch
South Drive
Carey Hill Road
S C
Sapcote Road
Johnson Rise
Surgery
George Marriott Close
R C
Drive
Martin Close
Riley Close
Shadrack Close
Townsend Road
Underwood
Doudney Close
Howe Close
Lanes Hill Grove
5
Road
Stoney Cove
294
448
49
66
Lane
Stanton
Spa Drive
Sapcote
Grace Road
Harecroft Crescent
Underwood Crs
1 grid square represents 500 metres

Stanton Lane
Huncote Road
Marston Rd
The Green
Dovecote La
Dovecote Road
Hill Street
Cem
Works
Marion's Way
Station Rd
Shades Cl
Winston Av
Coniston Wy
Bala Rd
Windermere Dr
Arbor Road
Holliers Wy
Kendall's Av
Pochin St
PO
Salisbury Av
Petersfield Rd
Ash
Brookes Av
Bridle Cl
School Cl
Sparkenhoe
Sopers Rd
Croft
Croft Lodge
Broughton Road
B4114
COVENTRY ROAD
COVENTRY RD B4114
Port Hill Farm
Sutton Hill Farm
Leicester Road
B581
B581 COVENTRY ROAD
Sutton Hill Bridge
Stanton
Sutton the Elm
Riv
E
F
G
H
1
2
3
4
5
51
62
67
68
50
52
96
95
294

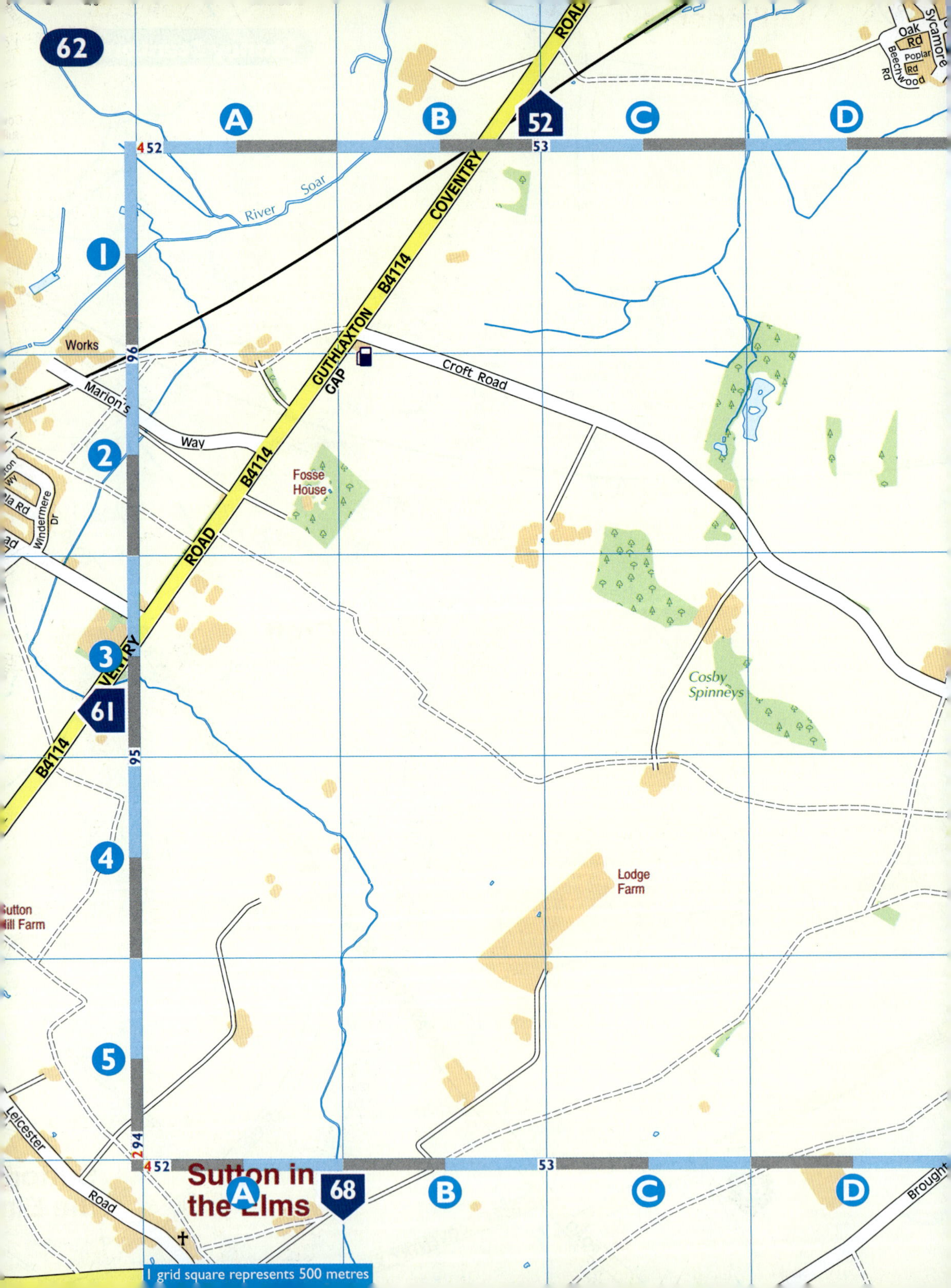
A
B
C
D
52
53
1
2
3
4
5
96
95
94
61
68
River Soar
COVENTRY ROAD
B4114
CUTHLAXTON GAP
Works
Marion's Way
Croft Road
Fosse House
Windermere Dr
Cosby Spinneys
Lodge Farm
Sutton Hill Farm
Leicester Road
Sutton in the Elms
Oak Rd
Sycamore
Poplar Rd
Beechwood Rd
Brought
1 grid square represents 500 metres

Littlethorpe
Cosby
M1
53
64
69
Works
Industrial Estate
Golf Course
Whetstone Golf Club
Cosby Primary School
Badgerbrook Primary School
Cosby Golf Club
Thorn Hill Farm
Cem
PO
Cosby Road
Narborough Road
Brooklands Rd
Cromford Rd
Ashover
Wavertree Cl
Andrew Av
Manor Rd
Jamesway
Portland St
Stevenson Gdns
Cambridge Rd
Cambridge Road
Starmer Cl
Mount Rd
Armston Rd
Gimson Av
Forrester Cl
White Barn Dr
Lady Leys
Park Road
Severn Cl
Linley Gn
Ash-Tree Rd
Hill Vw Dr
Farthingdale Close
Malvern Crs
Burley Cl
Bradbury Cl
Chiltern Av
Arnold Cl
Cambrian Cl
Croft Road
Richmond Cl
Elm Tree Rd
Kingsfield Road
Park Cl
The Nook
Main St
Walnut Leys
Bakery Cl
Forryan Cl
The Banks
Tudor Dr
Tudor Rd
Brierfield
Broughton Rd
Chapel La
Countesthorpe Road
Shuttleworth Lane
Whiteacres
Bruce Wy
Ashville Wy
Ashville Way
Dog and Gun Lane
Alice Gdns
Brown's Wy
Peacock Dr
Flamingo Dr
Franklin Wy
Shellduck Cl
Pintail Cl
Mandarin Wy
Grebe Wy
Eider Close
Humes Cl
Emperor Wy
Greylag Way
Upex Cl
Wright Cl
Elliot Cl
Springwell Lane
Fox Covert
Roebuck Cl
Otter Wy
Leveret Dr
Badger Dr
Halford Dr
Shaw Cl
Sandhurst
Coulson
Phipps Cl
Worsley Wy
Pawley Cl
Kenny Cl
Cannam Cl
Laundon Wy
Hubbard Cl
Paramore Cl
Wychwood Rd
Chr Wy
Coales Av
Bigg's Cl
Cosby Brook
Whetstone Brook
Ridley Cl
Ridgeway
Heighton Crs
Gurney Crs
Hazel Way
Oak Rd
LUTTERWORTH ROAD
A426
BY-PASS
Countesthorpe Road
Whetstone
E
F
G
H
1
2
3
4
5
54
55
56
95
96
94

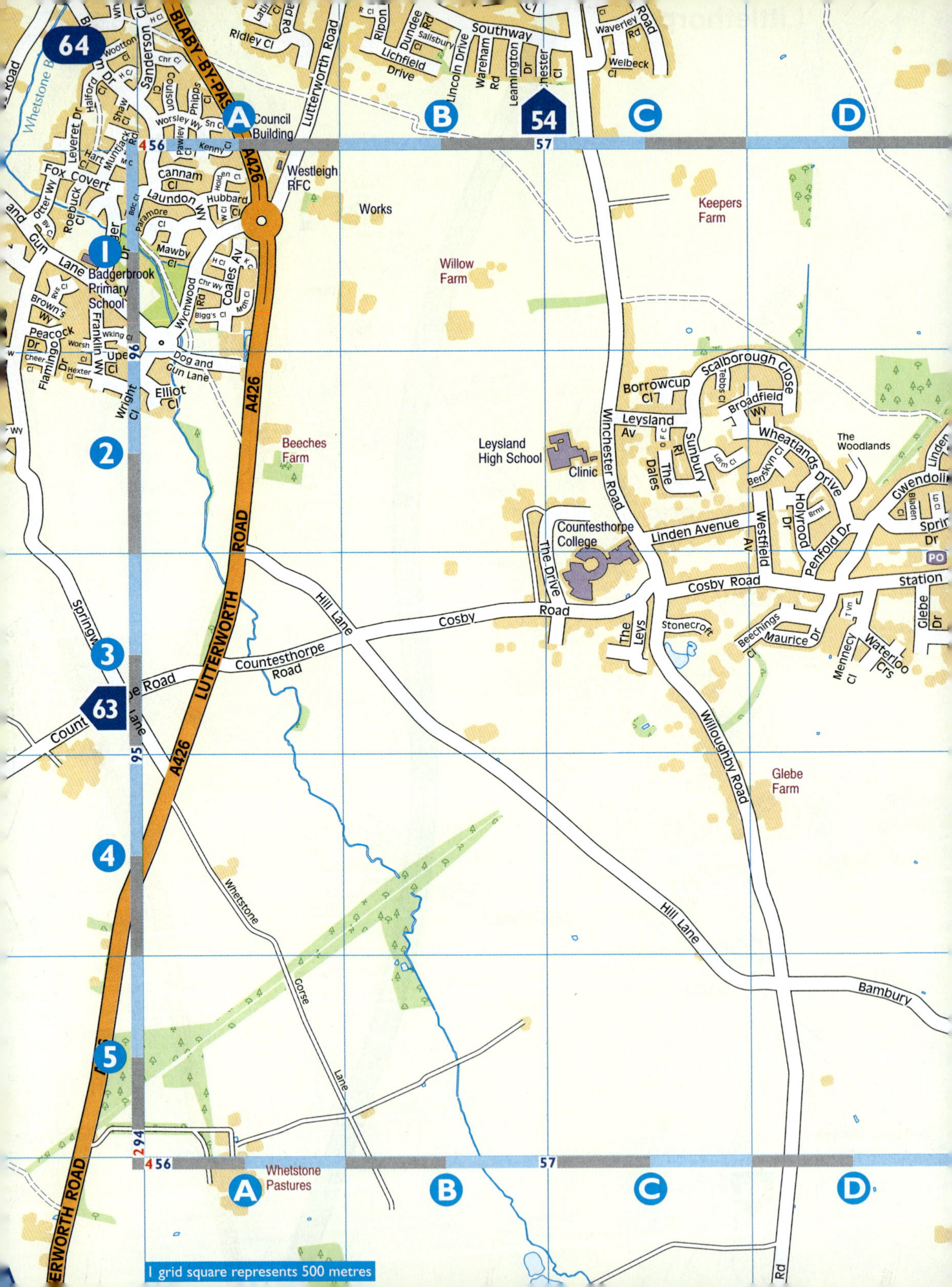

64
54
63
A
B
C
D
1
2
3
4
5
56
57
95
96
294
456
Council Building
Westleigh RFC
Works
Willow Farm
Keepers Farm
Beeches Farm
Glebe Farm
Whetstone Pastures
Badgerbrook Primary School
Leysland High School
Clinic
Countesthorpe College
The Woodlands
PO
BLABY-BY-PASS
A426
LUTTERWORTH ROAD
Lutterworth Road
Ridley Cl
Ripon
Dundee Rd
Salisbury
Lichfield Drive
Southway
Lincoln Drive
Wareham Rd
Leamington Dr
Waverley Rd
Road
Welbeck Cl
Wootton
Sanderson Cl
Chr Cl
Coulson
Phipps
Halford
Shaw Cl
Leveret Dr
Worsley Wy
Sn Cl
Pawley Cl
Kenny Cl
Muntjack Rd
Hart Cl
Fox Covert
Otter Wy
Roebuck Cl
Cannam Cl
Laundon Wy
Hubbard Cl
Paramore Cl
Mawby Cl
Coales Av
Gun Lane
Brown's Wy
Peacock Dr
Flamingo
Franklin Wy
Wychwood Rd
Chr Wy
Bigg's Cl
Dog and Gun Lane
Elliot Cl
Wright Cl
Springwell
Countesthorpe Road
Hill Lane
Cosby Road
The Drive
The Leys
Stonecroft
Winchester Road
Borrowcup Cl
Scalborough Close
Broadfield Wy
Leysland Av
The Dales
Sunbury
Wheatlands Drive
Benskyn Cl
Holyrood Dr
Penfold Dr
Westfield Av
Linden Avenue
Gwendolin
Station
Glebe Dr
Beechings Cl
Maurice Dr
Mennecy Cl
Waterloo Crs
Willoughby Road
Bambury
Whetstone
Gorse Lane
Whetstone Brook
Rd
1 grid square represents 500 metres

Business Park
Rose Farm
E
F
55
G
H
58
59
60
I
Foston Lodge Farm
96
2
3
95
4
5
294
Countesthorpe
Leicester Road
Foston Lane
Foston Lane
Foston La
Cem
Works
Hzlbnk Rd
Regent Rd
Rosebank Rd
New St
Kr Rd
Reedpool Close
Dale Acre
Shetland Wy
Brook Ct
Central St
Church
Scotland
Wigston St
Green La
Hlth Cen
The Sq
Main St
Mull Wy
Skye Wy
Arran Wy
Lewis Wy
Fairisle
Orkney Wy
Iona Wy
Heather
Orchard La
Way
Ladbroke Gv
Judith Dr
Buckingham Rd
Edgeley Rd
Spinney Av
Maple Avenue
Willow Drive
The Elms
Pinewood Cl
Fir Tree Av
The Rowans
Farm Drive
Almond Cl
Walnut Wy
Chestnuts
Cherrytree Cl
Laurel Dr
Greenfield Prim Sch
Barnley Cl
Poplar Aspen Av
Plantation Av
Paddock Cl
Road
Bassett Av
Hallcroft Av
Tophall Dr
Gillam Butts
Marston Crs
Peatling Road
Soars Lodge Farm
Red Pool Spinney
Barley Lane
Lane
Westdale Farm

Red Hill Farm
A
B
C
60
D
447
48
Brickyard Farm
94
B4669
HINCKLEY ROAD
1
2
3
4
5
Stanton Lane
Fields Farm
Spa Drive
Stanton Road
Hinckley Road
Frewen Drive
Penfold Close
Buckwell Rd
Mnr Rd
Kirby Close
Church St
PO
Livesey Drive
Neville Smith Close
Park Road
Castle Close
Bassett Lane
Cook's
All Saints CE Primary School
Cem
93
Springfield Farm
Road
Sharnford CE Primary School
Henson Way
Halls Crescent
Holyoak Dr
Park View
Brookfield
Halls Crs
Mill La
St Helen's Cl
B4114
Aston Lane
Park Vw
Works
Chapel La
Chapel St
Sharnbrook Gdns
Fx Hills
LEICESTER ROAD
PO
Ivy Bungalow Farm
School La
Works
Fosse Cl
Lees High
Sharnford
LE10
292
Mickle Hill Farm
447
48
A
B
C
D
1 grid square represents 500 metres

Grove
Road
Stoney Cove
E
F
G
H
61
B581
49
50
51
Su Hill Bridge
94
B581
COVEN
ROAD
Sapcote
Grace
Harecroft Crescent
Road
Underwood Crs
Mill Close
Tuckey Close
Brown's Close
Sapcote
Stanton Lodge
I
Works
COVENTRY
B4669
LEICESTER
ROAD
Wesley Cl
New Walk
Morley Rd
Calvert
Crescent
Lane
2
Pougher Close
Coventry Rd
93
Sharnford Road
B4114
ROAD
3
68
COVENTRY
Fosse Farm
Sutton Lodge
River Soar
4
292
Works
Lodge Farm
5
Lodge Cotta
49
50
51
E
F
G
H
The Homestead
Frolesworth Lodge
Bro

A
B
C
D
61
62
67
1
2
3
4
5
451
52
94
93
292
Sutton in the Elms
Primethorpe
Sutton Bridge
Works
B581 COVENTRY ROAD
BROUGHTON WAY
Coventry Road
Leicester Road
Warwick Road
Uppingham Dr
Whitby Cl
Melton Dr
Lichfield Avenue
Kite Cl
Kestrel Cl
Falcon Cl
Harrier Cl
Condor Cl
Osprey Cl
Eagle Cl
Peregrine Rd
Buzzard Cl
Montague Rd
Green Rd
Hobby Close
Main Street
Orchard Rd
Merton Cl
Whinham Av
The Av
Farleigh Cl
Malling Avenue
Baldwin Rl
Gorham Rl
Deniston Cl
Amsden Rl
Blenheim Crs
Estley Rd
Bramley Cl
Grange Rd
Glebe Rd
Jubilee Road
Cooke's Drive
Six Acres
Cosby Road
Orchard CE Primary School
Thomas Estley Community College
Old Mill Co Prim Sch
Station Road
St Marys Cl
Old Rectory Cl
Church Cl
Park Vw Cl
Old Mill Road
Frolesworth Road
Mill Farm
Cem
Lodge Farm
Sutton Lodge
Arkwright Cottages
The Fieldway
Millbook Dr
Burnside Rd
Bodycote Cl
Pickering Road
Fallow Cl
Harvest Wy
Glean Cl
Hallbrook Rd
Crowfoot Wy
Devitt Way
Murray Cl
Benford Cl
Hallbrook County Primary School
Leire Lane
The Bungalow
Lodge Farm
Lodge Farm Cottages
Broughton Road
Broughton La
1 grid square represents 500 metres

63
E
F
G
H
53
54
55
94
93
292
I
2
3
4
5
Broughton Road
Shuttleworth Lane
Golf Course
Cosby Road
Hill Field Farm
Broughton Astley
Cottage Lane Industrial Estate
Cottage Lane
Stanier Rd
Swannington Rd
Manton Cl
Croft
Trent Cl
Holbeck Dr
Cromford Way
Netherfield Cl
Aland Gdns
Kirtley Way
Willsmer Cl
New Inn Cl
Broctone Cl
Station Rd
The Meadow
Johnson Cl
Derby Cl
Chandler Way
Station Farm
Chestnut Cl
Lea Cl
Townsend Cl
Harris Cl
Cotton Cl
Crescent
Kiln Cl
Hall Fm Crescent
Knighton Cl
Talbott Cl
Thornton Cl
Machin Dr
Bell Cl
Plough Cl
Pinel Cl
Ceveze Way
Speedwell Drive
Trefoil Cl
T Cl
Orchid Pl
Muncaster Cl
Dunton Road
DUNTON ROAD
B581
PO
Holt House
LUTTERWORTH ROAD
26

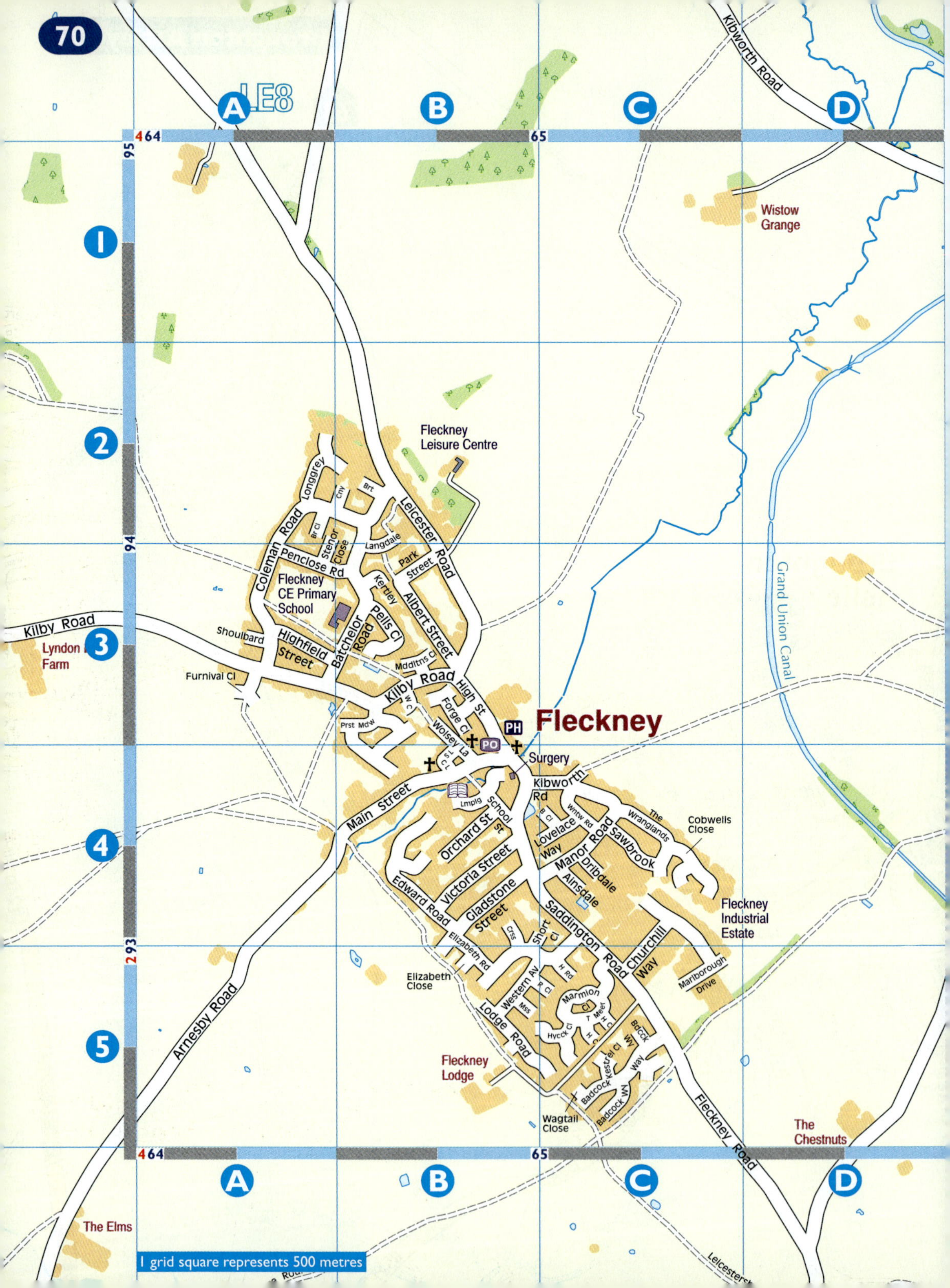

LE8
A
B
C
D
464
65
95
94
293
1
2
3
4
5
Kibworth Road
Wistow Grange
Fleckney Leisure Centre
Grand Union Canal
Kilby Road
Lyndon Farm
Longgrey
Cny
Brt
Leicester Road
Br Cl
Stenor Close
Langdale
Coleman Road
Penclose Rd
Park Street
Fleckney CE Primary School
Kertley
Albert Street
Pells Cl
Shoulbard
Highfield Street
Batchelor Road
Mddltns Cl
Furnival Cl
Kilby Road
High St
Forge Cl
Prst Mdw
Wolsey La
Fleckney
PH
PO
Surgery
Kibworth Rd
Main Street
Lmplg
School St
Orchard St
Lovelace Way
Manor Road
Sawbrook
The Wranglands
Cobwells Close
Victoria Street
Dribdale
Ainsdale
Edward Road
Gladstone Street
Saddington Road
Churchill Way
Fleckney Industrial Estate
Crss
Short Cl
Elizabeth Rd
Elizabeth Close
Western Av
H Rd
Marmion Cl
Marlborough Drive
Lodge Road
Mss
Hycck Cl
Badcock Wy
Kestrel Cl
Badcock Way
Badcock Wy
Fleckney Lodge
Wagtail Close
Arnesby Road
Fleckney Road
The Chestnuts
The Elms
1 grid square represents 500 metres

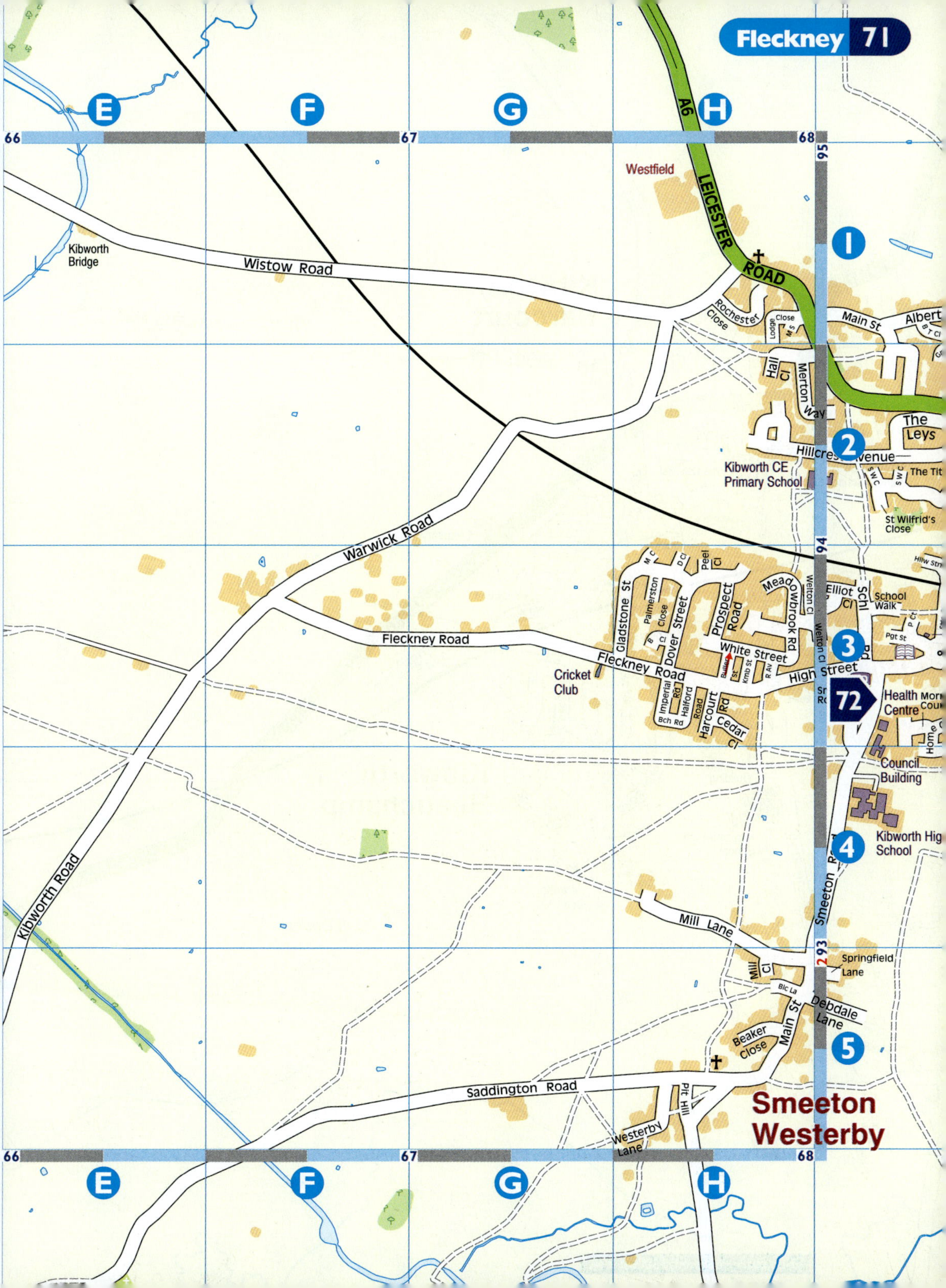
E
F
G
H
66
67
68
95
94
293
A6
LEICESTER ROAD
Westfield
Kibworth Bridge
Wistow Road
Rochester Close
Lodge Close
M S
Main St
Albert
B T Cl
Hall Cl
Merton Way
The Leys
Hillcrest Avenue
Kibworth CE Primary School
S W C
The Tit
St Wilfrid's Close
I
2
3
4
5
Warwick Road
Fleckney Road
M C
D Cl
Peel Cl
Gladstone St
Palmerston Close
Dover Street
Prospect Road
Meadowbrook Rd
Welton Cl
Elliot Cl
Schl
School Walk
P Ct
Pgt St
Hllw Strt
B Cl
White Street
R Av
Kmb St
Bullers St
High Street
Cricket Club
Imperial Rd
Halford Road
Harcourt Rd
Cedar Cl
Bch Rd
72
Health Centre
Home
Council Building
Kibworth High School
Smeeton Road
Kibworth Road
Mill Lane
Mill Cl
Springfield Lane
Blc La
Debdale Lane
Beaker Close
Main St
Saddington Road
Pit Hill
Westerby Lane
Smeeton Westerby

Kibworth Hall
Carlton
A
B
C
D
468
69
95
94
293
1
2
3
4
5
71
LEICESTER ROAD
Kibworth Harcourt
Rochester Close
Lodge Close
M S
Main St
Albert St
B T Cl
Gns Rd
Windmill Gdns
Marsh Dr
Marsh Avenue
Langton Road
Kibworth Road
Hall Cl
Merton Way
The Leys
Hillcrest Avenue
Kibworth CE Primary School
S W C
The Tithings
St Wilfrid's Close
Church Road
Church Cl
Okt Cl
Rectory Lane
S W S
The Lea
Cemetery
Hllw Stn
Peel Cl
Meadowbrook
Prospect Road
Welton Cl
Elliot Cl
Schl Rd
School Walk
Works
Rookery Cl
Brookfield Way
Larkswood
HARBOROUGH ROAD
Stn St
P Ct
Pgt St
Surgery
Stuart St
White St
Kmb St
High Street
PO
Smeeton Road
Harcourt Road
Cedar Cl
Health Centre
Morrison Court
Home Close
New Road
Gm Paddock
T Dr
The Links Road
Brd Cl
Fairway
Marriott Drive
Mls Cl
B C
Council Building
Weir Road
Springfield Crescent
Sprngf Cl
Wentworth Close
Kibworth Beauchamp
Kibworth High School
Granary Close
Kibworth Golf Club
Golf Course
Mill Lane
Mill Cl
Springfield Lane
Blc La
Main St
Debdale Lane
Beaker Close
Smeeton Westerby
1 grid square represents 500 metres

Sheepthorns Spinney
E
F
G
H
70
71
72
95
94
93
SHANGTON
B6047
I
Kibworth Road
PO
Main Street
Cranoe Road
The Manor
Tur Langton
2
B6047
MELTON ROAD
3
Church Langton
4
West Langton Road
Langton Hall
West Langton Road
HARBOROUGH ROAD
5
B6047
MELTON ROAD
Grange Farm

A6
A
B
C
D
472
73
90
89
88
1
2
3
4
5
B6047
HARBOROUGH
ROAD
Field
Road
Leicester Lane
Leicester Lane
Great
Bowden Hall
White
Lodge
Hill Crest
Farm
Upper
Green Pl
Top Yard
Farm
Bates
Cl
Kingston
Wy
Way
Smyth
Cl
Davies Cl
Coales Gardens
Monroe Cl
Kigston
Wy
Deacon Cl
Tymecrosse Gdns
Timson
Cl
Alvington
Turnpike Cl
The Robert
Smyth School
Burnmill Road
Scott Cl
Marlborough Wy
Overfield
Av
Ridgeway
Primary School
Pochin Dr
Cn Cl
The
Ridgeway
Ridgeway West
Blenheim
Wy
Wr
Dr
Rd
Sherrard
Russett Cl
Warwick Cl
Lincoln
Ct
Arden
Douglass Dr
Oak
Cl
St Lukes
Hosp
Kestian
Cl
B6047
The Woodlands
Victoria Av
Edward Rd
Hillcrest Av
Birtley
Coppice
Poplars
Ct
Park
Dr
The Oval
Hammond Way
The Crs
Ct Cl
St Marys
Business
Park
Birch Tree
Gdns
Perkins Cl
The
Headland
Southleigh
Gr
LEICESTER ROAD
Holly Cl
Holly Cl
Meadow Street
Meadow St
The
Broadway
Hillside
Rd
Fairway
Northleigh Gr
Logan Crs
Logan
Ct
Horsefair Cl
Fairfield
Brooke
House
College
Heygate
Orch St
Shrpshr Pl
Bn La
Saxon Cl
Roman Way
Connaught Rd
Close
Edmbrgh
Works
Albany Rd
Bowden La
Doddridge
Ad Rd
Rd
PO
Market
Harborough CE
Primary School
Norbury Cl
Austin
Cl
472
73
Road
Three
Swans
Htl
King's Rd
Ks Hd Pl
Works
Albert Rd
Fernie Road
York
St
Clarence
St
Andrew St
Macdonald
Dngly
Ter
A
77
B
C
D
Adam Wood
Cl
Knoll Str
Highcro
Logan
Stevens
St
Spencer
St
Works
Hearth Street
High Street
ABBEY ST
HIGH ST
THE SQ
Fieldhead
Cl
Spinney
Cl
Morley St
Clarke
Harcourt
St
East
St
Highfield St
Nelson St
Goward
St
F RD
School La
Talbot
Yd
Ch St
Symington Wy
Mill Hl
Rd
C Sq
F La
ST MARY'S RD
A5
Works
1 grid square represents 500 metres

Langton Road
Road
E
F
G
H
74
75
76
90
89
88
1
2
3
4
5
Welham Rd
Welham Road
A6
Langton Road
Welham
Sutton Road
Works
Chater Cl
Manor Rd
Main St
The Pines
PO
Gunnsbrook Cl
Great Bowden CE Primary School
Knight's End Road
Dingley Road
Cem
Horse Shoe La
Station Road
Great Bowden
Madeline Cl
Berry Cl
Bankfield Dr
Bowden Rdg
B664 SUTTON ROAD
B664
SUTTON ROAD
A427
HARBOROUGH ROAD
River Welland
ROCKINGHAM ROAD
A4304
Arden Cl
Great Bowden Road
Harborough Athletic Club
Euro Business Park
Rockingham Industrial Est
Valley Wy
Welland Ct
Welland Ind Est
Meadowdale Prim Sch
Lodge Farm
Market Harborough Stn
Works
Riverside
Valley Wy
Rylands Cl
Ashley Way
78
ROCKINGHAM RD
Works
Hartland Dr
The Furlongs
Thatch Meadow Dr
Woodbreach Dr
Simborough
Medway Cl
Lane

Laughton Road
Laughton Rd
The Green
MAIN STREET
Lubenham
HARBOROUGH ROAD
Paget Rd
PO
Westland Cl
Westgate
Connell Cl
Rushes Lane
Tower Ct
School Lane
La
Acorn Cl
Church Wk
Lubenham All Saints Prim Sch
Old Hall La
River Welland
THEDDINGWORTH RD
Theddingworth Rd
Farndon Road
Marston Road
Thorpe Lubenham Hall
Upper Highfield Plantation
PH
Lubenham Road
Marston Trussell
Road
Farndon Rd
Rectory Farm Cottages
Marston Trussell Road
Grange Farm
Marston Trussell Road
The Dales
Rectory Farm
A
B
C
D
1
2
3
4
5
470
71
87
86
285
1 grid square represents 500 metres

MARKET HARBOROUGH
East Farndon
LE16
LUBENHAM HILL
A4304
COVENTRY ROAD
ABBEY ST
HIGH ST
HIGH ST THE SQ
KETTERING RD
NORTHAMPTON
HARBOROUGH RD
A508
Welland Park Road
Western Avenue
Farndon Road
Harborough Road
Main Street
Lubenham Road
The Lealand
Leicestershire
Northamptonshire
County
Market Harborough CE Primary School
Mkt Harborough District Hospital
St Josephs RC Prim Sch
Medical Centre
The Welland Park College
Three Swans Htl
Theatre
Superstore
Works
Brooke House Coll
Sovereign Park Industri
Leisure Centre
Club House
Farndon Fields Primary School
Brierley Farm
New House Farm
Market Harborough Golf Club
Golf Course
Knoll Street
Highcross St
Logan St
Gardiner Street
Wartnaby Street
Clarke Street
Charles St
Morley St
Brookfield Road
Farndale View
Farndale
Elm Dr
Willow Crs
Rugby Close
Summers Wy
Pear Tree Gdns
Stuart Road
Ireton Road
Fairfax Road
Bath Street
Granville Street
Caxton St
Clipston Street
Lathkill St
Cross St
Essex Gdns
Cromwell Crescent
Balfour Gdns
Howard Wy
Rupert Road
Rainsborough Gardens
Watson Av
Gerrard Gdns
Hopton Flds
Argyle Pk
Ritchie Pk
Fleetwood Gdns
Butler Gdns
Fairway
Fairfield Road
Roman Way
Hearth Street
Walcot Rd
Northampton Rd
72
73
74
78
86
87
285
E
F
G
H
I
2
3
4
5

78
75
77
A
B
C
D
1
2
3
4
5
Lodge Farm
Meadowdale Prim Sch
Welland Ind Est
Rockingham Industrial Est
Market Harborough Stn
St Marys Business Park
Perkins Cl
Park
The Headlands
Great Bowden Rd
The Broadway
Heygate St
Orch St
Brooke House College
Hillside Rd
Saxon Cl
Roman Way
Works
Albany Rd
Albert Rd
York St
Clarence St
Fernie Road
Andrew St
Macdonald Cl
Symington Wy
Mill Hl Rd
High St
The Sq
Talbot Yd
School La
St Mary's Rd
Rockingham Rd
A508
A4304
Theatre
Josephs Prim Sch
Brooklands Gdns
Northampton Rd
Superstore
Kettering Road
Britannia Wk
Walcot Rd
Welland Park College
Springfield Ct
Nithsdale Crs
Nithsdale Av
Auriga St
Jerwood Wy
St Nicholas Wy
St Nicholas Cl
Rectory Lane
Jordan Cl
Riverside
Gores Lane
Claremont Dr
Medway Cl
Hartland Dr
Chatsworth Drive
Middledale Rd
The Furlongs
Thatch Meadow Dr
Ashley Way
Rylands Cl
Simborough
Picks Cl
Woodbreach Dr
Sandringham Way
Audley Cl
Fern Ley Cl
Shelland Cl
Roundhill Cl
Stinford Leys
Petworth Dr
Bellfields La
Bellfields St
Glebe Road
Dunslade Cl
Dunslade Grove
The Hghts
Shrewsbury Av
Launde Pk
Little Bowden Primary School
Scotland Rd
Queen St
Braybrooke Rd
LC
Little Bowden
Patrick St
Gladstone St
Cross St
Newcombe St
Naseby Cl
Granville Street
Bath Street
Caxton St
Clipston Street
Lathkill St
Crosby Rd
Rookwell Dr
Sovereign Park Industrial Est
Cem
Harborough Leisure Centre
Club House
Kibworth RUFC
Selby Cl
Dallison Cl
Vaughan Cl
River Jordan
Braybrooke Road
Harborough Road
Leicestershire County
Northamptonshire County
Market Harborough Golf Club
Harborough Rd
4 74
75
86
87
2 85
1 grid square represents 500 metres

Dingley
A427
MAIN
ROAD
A427
Dingley Lane
Church Lane
Dingley Lodge
Woodlands
Home Close
Dingley Warren
Braybrooke Road
Dingley Wood
HARBOROUGH ROAD
HARBOROUGH
ROAD
A6
Commons Farm
Road
Harborough
Road
Braybrooke Lower Lodge
Church Close
E
F
G
H
E
F
G
H
1
2
3
4
5
76
77
76
77
87
86
285

Springfields Farm
Bitteswell Lodge
A
B
C
D
451
52
86
85
284
1
2
3
4
5
Woodby Lane
Hawke Way
Hunter Boulevard
Harrier Parkway
Vulcan Way
Wellington Pkwy
Hunter Bvd
Field Farm
Blakenhall Farm
Magna Park Distribution Centre
Wellington Parkway
Hunter Boulevard
Shackelton Wy
Wood Bridge
COVENTRY ROAD A4303
Lane
Padge Hall Farm
Glebe Fm
Moorbarns Farm
1 grid square represents 500 metres

Bitteswell
LUTTERWORTH
LE17
Ullesthorpe Road
Ashby Lane
Deacon Close
St Marys CE Primary School
Valley La
Manor Rd
The Nook
Lutterworth Rd
PO
Manor House
Valley Farm
Dennis David Close
Bill Crane Way
Bmnt Cl
Noble Cl
Douglas Cl
Bader Cl
Page Cl
Maxwell Wy
Johnnie Johnson Drive
Dempsey Cl
Burrough Way
Mackenzie Close
Lacey Cl
Gale Close
Oakberry Road Industrial Estate
Bilton Wy
Works
Oakberry Rd
Tpk Cl
Gilmorton Road
Byron Cl
Shelley Dr
Macaulay Road
Dyson Cl
Tennyson Rd
Sherrier Wy
Dunley Wy
Denbigh Pl
Cncl Bldg
Swift Way
Central Av
Canada Flds
Feildingway
Wiclifway
Crescent Road
Elizabethan Wy
Industrial Park
Wycliffe Farm
Wycliffe Industrial Estate
LOWER LEICESTER ROAD
LEICESTER ROAD
A426
Way
Juniper Cl
Mulberry Cl
Magnolia Dr
Acacia Av
Sprc Wy
Aspen Wy
Brookfield
Pine Cl
Greenacres Drive
Sherrier CE Primary School
Bitteswell Road
Blackthorn Cl
Pear Tree
Woodlea Av
Hazel Dr
Conifer Cl
Holly
Larch Dr
The Hawthorns
Lutterworth Grammar School & Community College
New Street
Spencer Rd
Newall Cl
Cncl St
Hazeland Court
Goscote Dr
Guthlaxton Av
Gladstone St
Pol Stn
Health Cen
Hosp
Rmsy Cl
Amb Stn
Boundary Rd
Frngdn Av
Almond Wy
Honeysuckle Cl
Yew Tree Cl
Sycamore Dr
Ash
Jasmine Cl
Lilac Drive
Lavender Cl
Forsythia Cl
Allfrey Cl
Maple Dr
Laburnum Av
Cedar Av
Beech Av
Okfld Av
Linden Dr
Rowan Dr
Drive
Lutterworth Sports Centre
Coventry Road
MARKET STREET
George St
Fire Stn
Carlson Gdns
Walker Ct
Marylebone Dr
Wlw
Tr Crs
Chstnt Av
Poplar Av
Elm Av
Alder Crs
Himfld Cl
Firtree Av
Church Close
The Sherrier Centre
Church Gate
Cncl Bldg
Cpl St
Bl St
Station Rd
Leyton Cl
Rye Hl Av
Lilac Dr
Robinia Cl
Cherrytree Av
Azalea Cl
Hunters Drive
St Mary's Road
Church St
Bank St
HIGH ST
Misterton Wy
Coventry Road
Meriton Road
Avery Cl
Woodbine Crs
Baker St
Regent St
Orange Hl
Burton Close
De Verdon Rd
Elmhirst Rd
Whtl Rd
Palmer Drive
Wheeler Cl
Stoney Hollow
Mill Gv
Woodway Road
Ferrers Road
King's Wy
Orchard Rd
Woodmarket
Riverside Rd
Foxfield Close
Tedder Cl
Maino Crs
Ryderway
Spring Cl
RUGBY ROAD
Gibson Wy
Cunningham Drive
Chrchl Cl
Attlee Cl
Lutterworth High School
John Wycliffe Primary School
Mill Farm
Works
Mntgmry Cl
Cheshire Cl
Mntbttn Wy
Alexander Dr
A4303
LUTTERWORTH ROAD
Lutterworth Golf Club
Golf Course
Moorbarns Lane
Swinford Road
Junction 20
M1
River Swift
E
F
G
H
53
54
55
86
85
284
1
2
3
4
5

Anstey 17 G1
Aylestone 42 D2
Aylestone Park 43 E1
Barkby 13 H4
Barkby Thorpe 13 F5
Barwell 48 A3
Beaumont Leys 18 B3
Belgrave 26 B1
Birstall 19 G5
Bitteswell 81 E1
Blaby 54 B4
Bondman Hays 14 C4
Braunstone 33 G4
Broughton Astley 69 E3
Bushby 29 H5
Church Langton 73 H4
Clarendon Park 35 G4
Cosby 63 E3
Countesthorpe 65 F2
Croft 61 H3
Cropston 9 H2
Crown Hills 28 A5
Desford 30 C2
Earl Shilton 49 F4
East Farndon 77 E5
East Goscote 5 G1
Elmsthorpe 48 C5
Enderby 40 D5
Evington 37 E3
Eyres Monsell 42 D5
Field Head 6 D4
Fleckney 70 B3
Glenfield 24 A2
Glen Parva 42 B5
Great Bowden 75 F3
Great Glen 59 E3
Great Stretton 46 C2
Groby 16 B3
Highfields 3 J6
Houghton on the Hill 39 G1
Humberstone 27 H3
Huncote 51 H4
Kibworth Beauchamp 72 B4
Kibworth Harcourt 72 B1
Kilby Bridge 56 B5
Kirby Fields 32 B1
Kirby Muxloe 22 D4
Knighton 43 H1
Knighton Fields 35 F4
Leicester 3 F4
Leicester Forest East 32 C3
Little Bowden 78 B2
Little Stretton 47 G3
Littlethorpe 53 E5
Lubenham 76 C1
Lutterworth 81 E2
Market Harborough 77 E2
Markfield 6 A3
Mowmacre Hill 19 E2
Narborough 52 A3
Nether Hall 21 H5
New Parks 24 D3
Newton Harcourt 58 A5
Newtown Linford 7 H4
Normanton Turville 50 B2
North Evington 27 G4
Oadby 45 G1
Potters Marston 60 D1
Primethorpe 68 B2
Queniborough 5 G4
Ratby 22 C2
Red Hill 52 C3
Rushey Mead 20 C3
Sapcote 67 E1
Scotland 59 G1
Scraptoft 29 E2
Sharnford 66 C5
Smeeton Westerby 71 H5
South Knighton 44 B1
South Wigston 55 F2
Spinney Hills 27 E5
Stocking Farm 18 D4
Stoneygate 36 C5
Stoney Stanton 60 A3
Stoughton 38 A4
Sutton in the Elms 68 C1
Syston 13 G1
Thurcaston 10 A2
Thurmaston 13 E5
Thurnby 38 A1
Tur Langton 73 G2
Wanlip 12 A2
Westcotes 34 B1
Western Park 24 D4
Whetstone 53 G4
Wigston 44 A5
Wigston Magna 56 D1
The Woodlands 58 C5

USING THE STREET INDEX

Street names are listed alphabetically. Each street name is followed by its postal town or area locality, the Postcode District, the page number, and the reference to the square in which the name is found.

Standard index entries are shown as follows:
Abbey Ct *LEIN* LE4 ....**19** F5

Street names and selected addresses not shown on the map due to scale restrictions are shown in the index with an asterisk:
The Arcade *WGSTN* LE18 *......**44** B5

GENERAL ABBREVIATIONS

ACC	ACCESS
ALY	ALLEY
AP	APPROACH
AR	ARCADE
ASS	ASSOCIATION
AV	AVENUE
BCH	BEACH
BLDS	BUILDINGS
BND	BEND
BNK	BANK
BR	BRIDGE
BRK	BROOK
BTM	BOTTOM
BUS	BUSINESS
BVD	BOULEVARD
BY	BYPASS
CATH	CATHEDRAL
CEM	CEMETERY
CEN	CENTRE
CFT	CROFT
CH	CHURCH
CHA	CHASE
CHYD	CHURCHYARD
CIR	CIRCLE
CIRC	CIRCUS
CL	CLOSE
CLFS	CLIFFS
CMP	CAMP
CNR	CORNER
CO	COUNTY
COLL	COLLEGE
COM	COMMON
COMM	COMMISSION
CON	CONVENT
COT	COTTAGE
COTS	COTTAGES
CP	CAPE
CPS	COPSE
CR	CREEK
CREM	CREMATORIUM
CRS	CRESCENT
CSWY	CAUSEWAY
CT	COURT
CTRL	CENTRAL
CTS	COURTS
CTYD	COURTYARD
CUTT	CUTTINGS
CV	COVE
CYN	CANYON
DEPT	DEPARTMENT
DL	DALE
DM	DAM
DR	DRIVE
DRO	DROVE
DRY	DRIVEWAY
DWGS	DWELLINGS
E	EAST
EMB	EMBANKMENT
EMBY	EMBASSY
ESP	ESPLANADE
EST	ESTATE
EX	EXCHANGE
EXPY	EXPRESSWAY
EXT	EXTENSION
F/O	FLYOVER
FC	FOOTBALL CLUB
FK	FORK
FLD	FIELD
FLDS	FIELDS
FLS	FALLS
FLS	FLATS
FM	FARM
FT	FORT
FWY	FREEWAY
FY	FERRY
GA	GATE
GAL	GALLERY
GDN	GARDEN
GDNS	GARDENS
GLD	GLADE
GLN	GLEN
GN	GREEN
GND	GROUND
GRA	GRANGE
GRG	GARAGE
GT	GREAT
GTWY	GATEWAY
GV	GROVE
HGR	HIGHER
HL	HILL
HLS	HILLS
HO	HOUSE
HOL	HOLLOW
HOSP	HOSPITAL
HRB	HARBOUR
HTH	HEATH
HTS	HEIGHTS
HVN	HAVEN
HWY	HIGHWAY
IMP	IMPERIAL
IN	INLET
IND EST	INDUSTRIAL ESTATE
INF	INFIRMARY
INFO	INFORMATION
INT	INTERCHANGE
IS	ISLAND
JCT	JUNCTION
JTY	JETTY
KG	KING
KNL	KNOLL
L	LAKE
LA	LANE
LDG	LODGE
LGT	LIGHT
LK	LOCK
LKS	LAKES
LNDG	LANDING
LTL	LITTLE
LWR	LOWER
MAG	MAGISTRATE
MAN	MANSIONS
MD	MEAD
MDW	MEADOWS
MEM	MEMORIAL
MKT	MARKET
MKTS	MARKETS
ML	MALL
ML	MILL
MNR	MANOR
MS	MEWS
MSN	MISSION
MT	MOUNT
MTN	MOUNTAIN
MTS	MOUNTAINS
MUS	MUSEUM
MWY	MOTORWAY
N	NORTH
NE	NORTH EAST
NW	NORTH WEST
O/P	OVERPASS
OFF	OFFICE
ORCH	ORCHARD
OV	OVAL
PAL	PALACE
PAS	PASSAGE
PAV	PAVILION
PDE	PARADE
PH	PUBLIC HOUSE
PK	PARK
PKWY	PARKWAY
PL	PLACE
PLN	PLAIN
PLNS	PLAINS
PLZ	PLAZA
POL	POLICE STATION
PR	PRINCE
PREC	PRECINCT
PREP	PREPARATORY
PRIM	PRIMARY
PROM	PROMENADE
PRS	PRINCESS
PRT	PORT
PT	POINT
PTH	PATH
PZ	PIAZZA
QD	QUADRANT
QU	QUEEN
QY	QUAY
R	RIVER
RBT	ROUNDABOUT
RD	ROAD
RDG	RIDGE
REP	REPUBLIC
RES	RESERVOIR
RFC	RUGBY FOOTBALL CLUB
RI	RISE
RP	RAMP
RW	ROW
S	SOUTH
SCH	SCHOOL
SE	SOUTH EAST
SER	SERVICE AREA
SH	SHORE
SHOP	SHOPPING
SKWY	SKYWAY
SMT	SUMMIT
SOC	SOCIETY
SP	SPUR
SPR	SPRING
SQ	SQUARE
ST	STREET
STN	STATION
STR	STREAM
STRD	STRAND
SW	SOUTH WEST
TDG	TRADING
TER	TERRACE
THWY	THROUGHWAY
TNL	TUNNEL
TOLL	TOLLWAY
TPK	TURNPIKE
TR	TRACK
TRL	TRAIL
TWR	TOWER
U/P	UNDERPASS
UNI	UNIVERSITY
UPR	UPPER
V	VALE
VA	VALLEY
VIAD	VIADUCT
VIL	VILLA
VIS	VISTA
VLG	VILLAGE
VLS	VILLAS
VW	VIEW
W	WEST
WD	WOOD
WHF	WHARF
WK	WALK
WKS	WALKS
WLS	WELLS
WY	WAY
YD	YARD
YHA	YOUTH HOSTEL

POSTCODE TOWNS AND AREA ABBREVIATIONS

COAL	Coalville
END/NAR	Enderby/Narborough
GBY/RBY	Groby/Ratby
HINC	Hinckley
LEI	Leicester
LEIE	Leicester east
LEIN	Leicester north
LEIS	Leicester south
LEIW	Leicester west
LUTT	Lutterworth
MKTHBORO	Market Harborough
RLEINE/SYS	Rural Leicester north & east/Syston
RLEIS/BBY	Rural Leicester south/Blaby
RLEIW/BAR	Rural Leicester west/Barwell
WGSTN	Wigston

A

Abbey Ct LEIN LE4 19 F5
Abbey Court Rd LEIN LE4 19 F4
Abbey Dr LEIN LE4 19 F4
Abbey Ga LEIW LE3 26 A3
Abbey La LEIN LE4 19 E5
Abbey Mdw LEIN LE4 26 B1
Abbeymead Rd LEIN LE4 19 F4
Abbey Park Rd LEI LE1 26 B1
Abbey Park St LEIN LE4 26 C2
Abbey Ri LEIN LE4 19 F4
Abbey Rd END/NAR LE19 53 F2
Abbey St LEI LE1 3 F1
MKTHBORO LE16 77 H1
Abbots Cl LEIE LE5 28 B2
Abbotsford Rd LEIE LE5 27 H3
Abbots Rd North LEIE LE5 28 B2
Abbots Rd South LEIE LE5 28 B2
Abbotts Cl RLEINE/SYS LE7 12 D1
Aberdale Rd LEIS LE2 43 H2
Aber Rd LEIS LE2 36 B4
Abingdon Rd LEIS LE2 3 K7
Abney St LEIE LE5 36 A1
Acacia Av LEIN LE4 11 H4
LUTT LE17 81 F2
Acacia Cl LEIW LE3 32 B3
Acan Wy END/NAR LE19 52 C4
Acer Cl END/NAR LE19 52 C3
LEIN LE4 18 C3
Achurch Cl RLEIW/BAR LE9 60 B3
Acorn Cl LEIN LE4 19 G1
MKTHBORO LE16 76 B1
Acorn St LEIN LE4 19 H5
Acorn Wy WGSTN LE18 56 C1
Acres Rd LEIW LE3 32 C2
Adam & Eve St
MKTHBORO LE16 * 74 D5
Adamswood Cl
MKTHBORO LE16 77 F1
Adcock Rd LEIW LE3 25 F3
Adcote Cl RLEIW/BAR LE9 48 A5
Adderley Rd LEIS LE2 35 H4
Adelaide Cl LEIN LE4 10 C5
Adlington Rd LEIS LE2 45 G2
Adrian Dr RLEIW/BAR LE9 48 A4
Agar St LEIN LE4 26 D1
Aikman Av LEIW LE3 24 D2
Aikman Cl LEIW LE3 25 E3
Ainsdale RLEIS/BBY LE8 70 C4
Ainsdale Rd LEIW LE3 25 E5
Aintree Cl LEIE LE5 37 H1
Aintree Crs LEIS LE2 44 D2
Aisne Rd WGSTN LE18 43 E5
Alan Cl LEIN LE4 19 H3
Aland Gdns RLEIW/BAR LE9 69 E3
Albany Rd MKTHBORO LE16 74 D5
Alberta St LEIE LE5 3 J2
Albert Ct RLEIS/BBY LE8 53 H3
Albert Rd LEIS LE2 36 A3
MKTHBORO LE16 78 A1
Albert St RLEINE/SYS LE7 13 F1
RLEIS/BBY LE8 70 B3
RLEIS/BBY LE8 72 A1
Albion St LEI LE1 3 F5
LEIS LE2 45 E3
RLEINE/SYS LE7 13 F1
RLEINE/SYS LE7 17 G1
WGSTN LE18 55 F1
Alcester Dr LEIE LE5 37 H1
Alcott Cl LEIW LE3 25 E5
Aldeby Cl END/NAR LE19 41 G5
LEIS LE2 42 B4
Alder Cl LEIW LE3 32 B3
Alder Crs LUTT LE17 81 F3
Alderleigh Rd LEIS LE2 55 E2
Alderstone Cl WGSTN LE18 56 A3
Alderton Cl LEIN LE4 20 A2
Aldgate Av LEIE LE5 37 F2
Alexander Av
END/NAR LE19 40 C5
RLEIW/BAR LE9 49 G3
Alexander Dr LUTT LE17 81 F5
Alexander St LEIW LE3 2 C3
Alexandra Rd LEIS LE2 36 B4
Alexandra St END/NAR LE19 53 E3
LEIN LE4 12 C4
Alfreton Rd WGSTN LE18 44 A4
Alice Gdns RLEIS/BBY LE8 63 H1
Allandale Rd LEIE LE5 36 C3
Allenwood Rd LEIS LE2 43 E4
Allerton Dr LEIW LE3 25 E1
Allexton Gdns LEIW LE3 24 B4
Allfrey Cl LUTT LE17 81 E3
Alliance Rd LEIW LE3 24 A3
Allington Dr
RLEINE/SYS LE7 11 H4
Allington St LEIN LE4 26 D2
Allinson Cl LEIE LE5 28 A4
Alloway Cl LEIN LE4 20 B3
All Saints Cl RLEIW/BAR LE9 66 D2
All Saints Rd LEIW LE3 2 C3
RLEINE/SYS LE7 10 B2
Alma St LEIW LE3 25 G4
Almey's La RLEIW/BAR LE9 49 F3
Almond Cl RLEIS/BBY LE8 65 E2
Almond Rd LEIS LE2 35 F2
Almond Wy LUTT LE17 81 E3
RLEIW/BAR LE9 49 E5
Alport Wy WGSTN LE18 56 C1
Altar Stones La COAL LE67 6 A2
Althorp Cl LEIS LE2 42 B3
MKTHBORO LE16 78 C1
Alton Rd LEIS LE2 43 E3
Alvaston Rd LEIW LE3 34 B4
Alvecote Rd LEIS LE2 42 D3
Alvington Wy
MKTHBORO LE16 74 B4
Alyssum Wy END/NAR LE19 52 B2
Amadis Rd LEIN LE4 18 A4
Amanda Rd LEIS LE2 42 B4
Ambassador Rd LEIE LE5 28 A4
Amber Gate Cl
RLEIW/BAR LE9 69 E4
Ambergate Dr LEIN LE4 11 F4
Amberley Cl LEIN LE4 20 C1
Ambler Cl WGSTN LE18 56 B2
Ambleside RLEIW/BAR LE9 48 C4
Ambleside Cl LEIS LE2 42 C5
Ambleside Dr LEIS LE2 42 C5
Ambleside Wy LEIS LE2 42 C5
Ambrose Cl LEIW LE3 25 F4
Amersham Rd LEIN LE4 25 H1
Amesbury Rd WGSTN LE18 56 A3
Amhurst Cl LEIW LE3 24 D1
Amos Rd LEIW LE3 24 B4
Amsden Ri RLEIW/BAR LE9 68 B2
Amyson Rd LEIE LE5 28 C4
Amy St LEIW LE3 42 A1
Anchor St LEIN LE4 19 F5
Andover St LEIS LE2 3 H5
Andrew Av RLEIW/BAR LE9 63 F2
Andrewes Cl LEIW LE3 2 A4
Andrewes St LEIW LE3 2 A5
Andrewes Wk LEIW LE3 2 A5
Andrew Macdonald Cl
MKTHBORO LE16 78 A1
Andrew Rd RLEINE/SYS LE7 17 G1
Aneford Rd LEIN LE4 27 G1
Angela Dr LEIE LE5 37 F1
Anglesey Rd WGSTN LE18 43 F5
Angus Cl RLEINE/SYS LE7 29 F4
Angus Rd RLEIW/BAR LE9 48 A5
Ann St LEIE LE5 3 H3
Ann's Wy LEIS LE2 45 G3
Anstey La GBY/RBY LE6 16 D3
LEIN LE4 17 H3
RLEINE/SYS LE7 9 H4
Anthony Dr RLEINE/SYS LE7 29 F5
Anthony Rd LEIN LE4 25 H1
Apollo Cl LEIS LE2 3 K4
Apollo Ct LEIS LE2 3 K5
Appleby Cl LEIW LE3 24 A5
Appleby Rd LEIN LE4 13 E5
Appleton Av LEIN LE4 18 D3
Apple Tree Cl
RLEIW/BAR LE9 48 B2
The Approach LEIE LE5 36 D1
Aquitaine Cl END/NAR LE19 40 C5
Arbor Rd RLEIW/BAR LE9 61 G2
Arbour Rd LEIN LE4 19 H5
The Arcade WGSTN LE18 * 44 B5
Archdale St RLEINE/SYS LE7 12 D2
Archdeacon La LEI LE1 3 F1
Archer Cl LEIN LE4 20 C3
Archery Cl RLEIS/BBY LE8 65 F2
Archway Rd LEIE LE5 29 E1
Ardath Rd LEIN LE4 27 E1
Arden Av LEIW LE3 33 H3
Arden Cl MKTHBORO LE16 75 E5
Arden Wy MKTHBORO LE16 74 D4
Ardern Ter LEIW LE3 34 A3
Argyle Pk MKTHBORO LE16 77 H4
Armadale Dr LEIE LE5 28 C2
Armadale Gn LEIE LE5 28 C2
Armson Av RLEIW/BAR LE9 23 E5
Armston Rd RLEIW/BAR LE9 63 F3
Arncliffe Rd LEIE LE5 28 C2
Arndale WGSTN LE18 56 D2
Arnesby Crs LEIS LE2 43 F3
Arnesby Rd RLEIS/BBY LE8 70 A5
Arnhem St LEI LE1 3 G5
Arnold Av WGSTN LE18 55 G2
Arnold Cl RLEIW/BAR LE9 63 F4
Arnold St LEI LE1 3 J1
Arran Rd LEIN LE4 20 B3
Arran Wy RLEIS/BBY LE8 65 F3
Arreton Cl LEIS LE2 44 A1
Arum Wy LEIW LE3 24 B4
Ascot Rd LEIN LE4 19 H5
Asfordby St LEIE LE5 27 F4
Asha Margh LEIN LE4 19 G5
Ashbourne Rd WGSTN LE18 44 A4
Ashbourne St LEIS LE2 27 E5
Ashby Gld LEIE LE5 28 C5
Ashby Ri RLEIS/BBY LE8 58 D2
Ashby Rd COAL LE67 6 B2
Ash Cl GBY/RBY LE6 22 B1
Ashclose Av LEIS LE2 44 A1
Ash Ct GBY/RBY LE6 16 A5
Ashdown Av LEIW LE3 25 F4
Ashdown Rd WGSTN LE18 44 B4
Ash Dr RLEINE/SYS LE7 13 F2
Ashfield Dr RLEINE/SYS LE7 17 F2
Ashfield Rd LEIN LE4 12 D4
LEIS LE2 36 A2
MKTHBORO LE16 74 C5
Ashford Rd LEIS LE2 35 G4
Ash Gv RLEIS/BBY LE8 54 B3
Ashington Cl LEIW LE3 25 F2
Ashlands Wy END/NAR LE19 52 B2
Ashleigh Dr LUTT LE17 81 E3
Ashleigh Gdns LEIW LE3 * 34 C2
RLEIW/BAR LE9 48 C3
Ashleigh Rd LEIW LE3 23 H2
LEIW LE3 34 C1
Ashley Wy MKTHBORO LE16 78 C1
Ashlyns Ri LEIW LE3 24 C5
Ashmead Crs
RLEINE/SYS LE7 12 A3
Ashover Cl RLEIW/BAR LE9 63 F2
Ashover Rd LEIE LE5 36 A1
Ash Rd RLEIW/BAR LE9 48 D4
RLEIW/BAR LE9 61 H3
Ash St LEIE LE5 27 E3
Ashthorpe Rd LEIW LE3 34 A1
Ashton Cl LEIS LE2 45 E5
WGSTN LE18 * 56 A2
Ash Tree Cl LEIS LE2 45 F4
Ashtree Rd LEIE LE5 21 G5
Ash Tree Rd LEIS LE2 45 F4
Ash-Tree Rd RLEIW/BAR LE9 63 F3
Ashurst Cl WGSTN LE18 56 C3
Ashurst Rd LEIW LE3 33 H5
Ashville Wy RLEIS/BBY LE8 63 G2
Ashwell St LEI LE1 3 G6
Askrigg Wy WGSTN LE18 56 C1
Aspen Dr RLEIS/BBY LE8 65 E2
Aspen Wy LUTT LE17 81 F2
Asplin Rd LEIS LE2 43 E3
Asquith Bvd LEIS LE2 43 H2
Asquith Wy LEIS LE2 43 G3
Assured Dr LEIN LE4 12 B5
Astill Cl GBY/RBY LE6 23 E2
Astill Dr LEIN LE4 19 F3
Astill Lodge Rd LEIN LE4 11 A1
Astley Cl LEIW LE3 34 B2
MKTHBORO LE16 77 G3
Astley Rd RLEIW/BAR LE9 49 F4
Aston Hl LEIS LE2 35 G5
Aston La HINC LE10 66 B4
Atherstone Cl LEIS LE2 45 H4
Atkinson St LEIE LE5 27 F4
Atkins St LEIS LE2 2 E6
Atlas Cl LEIS LE2 3 K4
Attenborough Cl LEIW LE3 33 E4
Attfield Dr RLEIS/BBY LE8 53 H4
Attingham Cl LEIE LE5 27 F2
Attlee Cl LUTT LE17 81 F4
Attlee Wy LEIS LE2 43 F3
Auburn Rd RLEIS/BBY LE8 54 A3
Auden Cl LEIN LE4 18 B5
Audley Cl MKTHBORO LE16 78 C2
Audley End LEIW LE3 34 A4
Augusta Cl LEIW LE3 24 A4
Augustus Cl RLEINE/SYS LE7 12 C2
Auriga St MKTHBORO LE16 78 A2
Austin Ri LEIE LE5 28 C1
Austins Cl MKTHBORO LE16 77 G1
Austwick Cl LEIN LE4 18 C4
Autumn Rd LEIS LE2 42 C5
Avebury Av LEIN LE4 25 G1
Avenue Cl RLEINE/SYS LE7 5 F4
Avenue Gdns LEIS LE2 36 A4
Avenue North
RLEIW/BAR LE9 49 G2
Avenue Rd LEIS LE2 36 A4
RLEINE/SYS LE7 5 G4
Avenue Rd Extension
LEIS LE2 35 G4
Avenue South
RLEIW/BAR LE9 49 G3
The Avenue LEIS LE2 36 A3
LEIS LE2 46 C4
LEIW LE3 23 H1
RLEIS/BBY LE8 54 A3
RLEIW/BAR LE9 68 C2
Averil Rd LEIE LE5 28 B4
Avery Cl LUTT LE17 81 F4
Avery Dr COAL LE67 6 B3
RLEINE/SYS LE7 4 D5
Avery Hl LEIW LE3 33 F1
Avington Cl LEIW LE3 18 A5
Avoca Cl LEIE LE5 28 B4
Avon Cl LEIS LE2 45 G3
Avondale Rd WGSTN LE18 44 B5
Avon Dr RLEIS/BBY LE8 53 H4
Avon Rd LEIW LE3 33 G3
Avonside Dr LEIE LE5 27 H5
Avon St LEIS LE2 3 K6
Axbridge Cl LEIN LE4 25 H1
Aylestone Dr LEIS LE2 42 D3
Aylestone La WGSTN LE18 43 H4
Aylestone Rd LEIS LE2 35 F2
LEIS LE2 42 D1
Aylestone Wk LEIS LE2 35 F2
Aylmer Rd LEIW LE3 33 H1
Ayrshire Cl RLEIW/BAR LE9 48 A5
Aysgarth Rd LEIN LE4 18 C4
Ayston Rd LEIW LE3 34 A4
Azalea Cl LUTT LE17 81 E4

B

Babingdon Rw LEIS LE2 43 G3
Babingley Dr LEIN LE4 18 D5
Back La RLEIS/BBY LE8 59 H3
Badcock Wy RLEIS/BBY LE8 70 C5
Baddely Dr WGSTN LE18 43 H4
Baden Rd LEIE LE5 36 C2
Badger Cl END/NAR LE19 52 C4
Badger Dr RLEIS/BBY LE8 63 H1
Badger's Cnr RLEINE/SYS LE7 5 F1
Badgers Holt LEIS LE2 45 E4
Badminton Rd LEIN LE4 20 B2
RLEINE/SYS LE7 4 D4
Baggrave St LEIE LE5 27 F4
Baileys La RLEIS/BBY LE8 59 H2
Bainbridge Rd LEIW LE3 34 B4
WGSTN LE18 56 C2
Baines La LEIW LE3 32 D3
Baker St LUTT LE17 81 G4
Bakery Cl RLEIW/BAR LE9 63 F4
Bakewell Rd WGSTN LE18 44 A4
Bakewell St LEIE LE5 27 E5
Bala Rd RLEIW/BAR LE9 61 H2
Balcombe Av LEIW LE3 25 F4
Balderstone Cl LEIE LE5 28 A5
Baldwin Av WGSTN LE18 55 G2
Baldwin Ri RLEIW/BAR LE9 68 B2
Baldwin Rd WGSTN LE18 43 H3
Bale Rd LEIN LE4 27 G1
Balfour Gdns
MKTHBORO LE16 77 G3
Balfour St LEIW LE3 25 H3
Balisfire Gv LEIN LE4 18 B4
The Balk LEIW LE3 23 H1
Balladine Rd RLEINE/SYS LE7 9 G5
Ballards Cl LEIN LE4 18 B4
Ballater Cl LEIE LE5 37 H2
Balliol Av RLEINE/SYS LE7 13 G2
Balmoral Cl LEIS LE2 44 A1
MKTHBORO LE16 78 C2
Balmoral Dr LEIW LE3 33 G3
Balmoral Rd
RLEIW/BAR LE9 48 D4
Bambrook Cl
RLEIW/BAR LE9 30 B2
Bamburgh Cl
MKTHBORO LE16 78 C1
Bambury La RLEIS/BBY LE8 64 D5
Bampton Cl WGSTN LE18 56 B3
Bankart Av LEIS LE2 36 C4
Bankfield Dr
MKTHBORO LE16 75 E4
Bankside LEIE LE5 29 E2
Banks Rd LEIS LE2 42 D1
The Banks RLEINE/SYS LE7 5 H4
RLEIW/BAR LE9 63 F4
Bank St LUTT LE17 81 G4
Bank Ter RLEIW/BAR LE9 48 A5
Bannerman Rd LEIE LE5 36 B2
Bantlam La END/NAR LE19 40 D5
Barbara Av LEIE LE5 28 B3
RLEIW/BAR LE9 32 A2
Barbara Cl END/NAR LE19 40 C5
Barbara Rd LEIW LE3 34 B4
Barclay St LEIW LE3 34 C1
Bardolph St LEIN LE4 26 D2
Bardolph St East LEIN LE4 27 E2
Bardon Cl LEIW LE3 17 H4
Bardon Rd RLEIW/BAR LE9 48 B3
Barfoot Cl RLEIS/BBY LE8 70 A2
Barfoot Rd LEIS LE2 43 F3
Barford Cl WGSTN LE18 56 A3
Barge Cl WGSTN LE18 55 G3
Barkby La RLEINE/SYS LE7 13 F3
Barkby Rd LEIN LE4 20 C5
RLEINE/SYS LE7 5 G5
RLEINE/SYS LE7 13 F1
Barkby Thorpe La
RLEINE/SYS LE7 12 C3
Barkbythorpe Rd LEIN LE4 20 D3
Barker St LEIE LE5 27 F3
Barkford Cl LEIE LE5 29 E1
Barley Cl LEIW LE3 24 A2
Barling Rd LEIE LE5 27 H2
Barmouth Av LEIS LE2 43 G2
Barnard Cl LEIS LE2 3 J5
Barnard Gdns
MKTHBORO LE16 77 G4
Barnby Av WGSTN LE18 44 A4
Barn Cl WGSTN LE18 56 C3
Barnes Cl LEIN LE4 20 C2
RLEIS/BBY LE8 71 H3
Barnes Heath Rd LEIE LE5 28 A5
Barnet Cl LEIS LE2 45 E5
Barnfield Cl RLEIS/BBY LE8 58 D2
Barngate Cl LEIN LE4 11 F4
Barnley Cl RLEIS/BBY LE8 65 E2
Barns Cl RLEIW/BAR LE9 22 C5
Barnsdale Rd LEIN LE4 17 H2
Barnstaple Cl WGSTN LE18 56 B3
Barnstaple Rd LEIE LE5 37 H2
Barns Wy RLEIW/BAR LE9 30 C1
Barn Wy COAL LE67 6 C4
Barnwell Av LEIN LE4 19 F3
Baronet Wy LEIE LE5 29 E1
Barons Cl RLEIW/BAR LE9 22 C5
Baron St LEI LE1 3 H4
The Barracks
RLEIW/BAR LE9 48 A5
Barratt Cl LEIS LE2 36 B3
Barrington Rd LEIS LE2 36 C4
Barrow Cl WGSTN LE18 56 D2
Barry Cl RLEIW/BAR LE9 32 A2
Barry Dr RLEINE/SYS LE7 4 D5
RLEIW/BAR LE9 32 A2
Barry Rd LEIE LE5 28 D1
Barston St LEI LE1 2 E1
Bartholomew St LEIS LE2 36 A1
Barton Cl GBY/RBY LE6 22 D3
WGSTN LE18 * 56 A2
Barton Rd LEIW LE3 25 G2
Barwell Rd RLEIW/BAR LE9 22 D5
Baslow Rd LEIE LE5 36 A1
Bassett Av RLEIS/BBY LE8 65 E3
Bassett La RLEIW/BAR LE9 66 D2
Bassett St LEIW LE3 2 A1
WGSTN LE18 55 F2
Batchelor Rd RLEIS/BBY LE8 70 B3
Bateman Rd LEIW LE3 25 E3
Bates Cl MKTHBORO LE16 74 C3
Bath Cl RLEIW/BAR LE9 66 D1
Bath La LEIW LE3 2 C3

Bath St LEIN LE4 19 G4
MKTHBORO LE16 77 H3
RLEINE/SYS LE7 4 C5
Bathurst Rd LEIE LE5 37 H1
Battenberg Rd LEIW LE3 25 G4
Batten St LEIS LE2 35 E4
Battersbee Rd LEIW LE3 24 C2
Battersbee Wy LEIW LE3 24 C2
Baxters Cl LEIN LE4 18 B5
Bayberry Gdns LEIS LE2 43 E4
Baycliff Cl LEIW LE3 25 F2
Bayham Cl LEIE LE5 28 B5
Baysdale WGSTN LE18 56 D1
Baysdale Rd LEIS LE2 2 D7
Bay St LEI LE1 2 D1
Bayswater Dr LEIS LE2 54 D2
Beacon Av LEIN LE4 12 D5
Beacon Cl COAL LE67 6 C3
GBY/RBY LE6 16 B5
LEIN LE4 18 A1
Beaconsfield Rd LEIW LE3 34 C1
Beaker Cl RLEIS/BBY LE8 71 H5
Beal St LEIS LE2 3 K3
Beamont Cl LUTT LE17 81 G1
Beatrice Rd LEIW LE3 25 F3
Beatty Av LEIE LE5 27 G3
Beatty Rd LEIE LE5 27 G3
RLEINE/SYS LE7 4 D5
Beauchamp Rd
RLEIS/BBY LE8 71 H3
Beaufort Cl LEIS LE2 45 H4
RLEIW/BAR LE9 30 B3
Beaufort Rd LEIW LE3 34 A4
Beaufort Wy LEIS LE2 45 H4
Beaumanor Rd LEIN LE4 19 F5
Beaumont Gn GBY/RBY LE6 16 B5
Beaumont Leys Cl LEIN LE4 18 D4
Beaumont Leys La LEIN LE4 18 D3
Beaumont Lodge Rd
LEIN LE4 18 B1
Beaumont Rd LEIE LE5 27 E4
Beaumont St LEIS LE2 45 E2
Beaumont Wy LEIN LE4 18 B3
Beauville Dr LEIN LE4 18 A4
Beaver Cl RLEIS/BBY LE8 63 H1
Beck Cl LEIS LE2 42 A5
Beckett Rd LEIE LE5 27 G2
Beckingham Rd LEIS LE2 36 A2
Bedale Dr LEIN LE4 18 D2
Bede St LEIW LE3 2 B6
Bedford Cl RLEIW/BAR LE9 30 B2
Bedford Dr GBY/RBY LE6 16 B5
Bedford Rd WGSTN LE18 43 G5
Bedford St North LEI LE1 3 G1
Bedford St South LEI LE1 3 F2
Beeby Cl RLEINE/SYS LE7 13 G1
Beeby Rd LEIE LE5 27 F4
RLEINE/SYS LE7 13 H4
RLEINE/SYS LE7 29 G2
Beech Av GBY/RBY LE6 23 E1
LUTT LE17 81 E3
Beech Cl COAL LE67 6 C4
Beechcroft Av LEIW LE3 34 A5
Beechcroft Rd LEIS LE2 36 A4
Beech Dr LEIW LE3 33 F2
RLEINE/SYS LE7 13 F2
The Beeches
RLEIW/BAR LE9 49 F2
Beechfield Av LEIN LE4 11 G5
Beechfield Cl
RLEIS/BBY LE8 58 D2
Beechings Cl RLEIS/BBY LE8 64 C3
Beech Rd LEIS LE2 45 E3
RLEIS/BBY LE8 54 B4
Beech St LEIE LE5 27 E3
Beech Tree Cl
RLEIS/BBY LE8 72 A1
Beech Wy RLEIW/BAR LE9 30 A2
Beechwood Av LEIN LE4 20 C1
RLEINE/SYS LE7 5 F4
RLEIW/BAR LE9 32 B1
Beechwood Cl LEIE LE5 28 C5
Beechwood Rd
END/NAR LE19 52 D5
Beggar's La LEIW LE3 32 A3
Begonia Cl LEIW LE3 32 B3
Belfry Dr LEIW LE3 24 A5
Belgrave Av LEIN LE4 19 G4
Belgrave Bvd LEIN LE4 18 C2
Belgrave F/O LEI LE1 26 C3
Belgrave Ga LEI LE1 3 F2
Belgrave Rd LEIN LE4 26 C2
Bellamy Cl LEIS LE2 42 A5
Bell Cl GBY/RBY LE6 22 D2
RLEIW/BAR LE9 69 E5
Belleville Dr LEIS LE2 45 G2
Belle Vue Av LEIN LE4 19 E5
Belle Vue Rd
RLEIW/BAR LE9 48 C3
Bellfields La
MKTHBORO LE16 78 B2
Bellfields St
MKTHBORO LE16 78 B2
Bellflower Rd LEIE LE5 21 F5
Bellholme Cl LEIN LE4 19 H4
Bell La END/NAR LE19 53 E4
LEIE LE5 3 J2
RLEIS/BBY LE8 59 H3
Bell St LUTT LE17 81 G4
WGSTN LE18 44 B5
Bell Vw END/NAR LE19 * 53 E3
Belmont St LEIS LE2 42 D1
Belper Cl LEIS LE2 45 E4
WGSTN LE18 55 G3
Belper St LEIN LE4 26 D1
Belton Cl LEIS LE2 43 F3
Belton Rd LEIW LE3 34 A5
Belvoir Cl LEIS LE2 45 G4
RLEIW/BAR LE9 30 B2
Belvoir Dr LEIS LE2 42 C2
RLEINE/SYS LE7 5 E5
Belvoir Dr East LEIS LE2 42 D2
Belvoir St LEI LE1 3 F5
Beman Cl LEIN LE4 20 C2
Bembridge Cl LEIN LE4 25 H2
Bembridge Rd LEIN LE4 25 G2
Bencroft Cl RLEINE/SYS LE7 17 F1
Bendbow Ri LEIW LE3 33 G2
Benford Cl RLEIW/BAR LE9 68 D5
Bennett Ri RLEIW/BAR LE9 52 A3
Bennett Wy WGSTN LE18 55 G1
Bennion Rd LEIN LE4 18 A3
RLEINE/SYS LE7 38 C1
Benskins Ov LEIN LE4 10 C5
Benskyn Cl RLEIS/BBY LE8 64 D2
Benson St LEIE LE5 27 G5
Bentinghouse Rd LEIS LE2 42 D4
Bentley Rd LEIN LE4 11 G4
Beresford Dr LEIS LE2 36 B5
Berford Cl RLEIW/BAR LE9 68 D4
Berkeley Cl LEIS LE2 45 H3
Berkley St LEI LE1 2 D1
Berkshire Rd LEIS LE2 42 D1
Berners St LEIS LE2 3 K3
Berridge Dr LEIS LE2 45 F4
Berridge La LEIN LE4 19 H4
Berridge St LEI LE1 2 E4
Berrington Cl LEIE LE5 27 G2
Berry Cl MKTHBORO LE16 75 E4
Berry's La GBY/RBY LE6 22 C2
Bessingham Cl LEIE LE5 21 G5
Best Cl WGSTN LE18 55 F2
Beth-El WGSTN LE18 * 56 A3
Bevan Rd LEIN LE4 10 C5
Beverley Av LEIN LE4 26 D1
Beverley Cl LEIN LE4 12 C5
Beverley Dr
RLEIW/BAR LE9 68 C1
Bevington Cl GBY/RBY LE6 22 B1
Bewcastle Gv LEIN LE4 18 D2
Bewicke Rd LEIW LE3 34 B3
Bexhill Ri LEIE LE5 29 E3
Biam Wy LEIW LE3 34 A5
Biddle Rd END/NAR LE19 53 E5
LEIW LE3 25 F3
Biddulph Av LEIE LE5 36 A1
Biddulph St LEIS LE2 36 A1
Bideford Cl WGSTN LE18 56 B4
Bideford Rd LEIE LE5 37 H2
Bidford Cl LEIW LE3 33 G3
Bidford Rd LEIW LE3 33 G3
Biggin Hill Rd LEIE LE5 37 F2
Bigg's Cl RLEIS/BBY LE8 64 A1
Bignal Dr LEIW LE3 32 D1
Bilberry Cl LEIW LE3 42 A2
Bill Crane Wy LUTT LE17 81 G1
Billington Cl LEIN LE4 19 E4
Bilsdale Rd WGSTN LE18 56 D2
Bilton Wy LUTT LE17 81 H1
Bindley La RLEIS/BBY LE8 58 C2
Bingley Rd END/NAR LE19 52 D5
Birch Cl COAL LE67 14 C1
LEIN LE4 27 F1
RLEIW/BAR LE9 48 D5
Birchfield Av COAL LE67 6 B4
Birch Tree Av
RLEINE/SYS LE7 11 G3
Birch Tree Gdns
MKTHBORO LE16 74 D5
Birchtree Rd WGSTN LE18 44 B4
Birchwood Cl LEIW LE3 32 B3
RLEINE/SYS LE7 13 G1
Birdie Cl RLEIS/BBY LE8 72 B3
Birds Nest Av LEIW LE3 24 D2
Birkdale Av LEIS LE2 36 B4
Birkdale Rd RLEINE/SYS LE7 17 E1
Birkenshaw Rd LEIW LE3 25 E1
Birsmore Av LEIN LE4 20 B3
Birstall Rd LEIN LE4 19 G2
Birstall St LEI LE1 26 D3
Birstow Crs LEIN LE4 18 D2
Birtley Coppice
MKTHBORO LE16 74 B5
Bishop Cl MKTHBORO LE16 77 H4
Bishopdale Rd LEIN LE4 18 C4
Bishop St LEI LE1 3 F4
Bisley St LEIW LE3 34 D2
Bitteswell Rd LUTT LE17 81 G2
Blaby By-Pass
RLEIS/BBY LE8 54 A4
Blaby Rd END/NAR LE19 40 D5
WGSTN LE18 55 G2
Blackberry La
RLEINE/SYS LE7 4 A1
Blackbird Av LEIN LE4 25 H2
Blackbird Rd LEIN LE4 25 H2
Blackburn Rd
RLEIW/BAR LE9 48 A5
Blackett Av LEIW LE3 25 E2
Blackfriars St LEI LE1 2 C3
Blackmore Dr LEIW LE3 25 E5
Blacksmiths La
RLEIS/BBY LE8 71 H5
Blackthorn Cl LUTT LE17 81 E3
Blackthorn Dr LEIN LE4 17 H1
RLEINE/SYS LE7 12 C1
Blackthorn La LEIS LE2 37 F5
Blackthorn Rd LEIW LE3 23 H3
Blackwell Cl WGSTN LE18 56 C2
Bladen Cl RLEIS/BBY LE8 64 D2
Blairmore Rd LEIW LE3 24 A4
Blaise Gv LEIN LE4 27 F1
Blake Ct END/NAR LE19 40 C5
Blakenhall Cl END/NAR LE19 52 B3
Blakenhall Rd LEIE LE5 28 A5
Blakeshay Cl LEIW LE3 17 H5
Blakesley Rd WGSTN LE18 44 D5
Blake St LEI LE1 2 E2
Bland Rd LEIW LE3 24 D2
Blankley Dr LEIS LE2 36 B4
Blanklyn Av LEIE LE5 27 F5
Blaydon Cl LEIW LE3 25 F2
Bleasby Cl LEIN LE4 21 E3
Blenheim Cl WGSTN LE18 55 F3
Blenheim Crs
RLEIW/BAR LE9 68 B2
Blenheim Rd LEIN LE4 11 H4
Blenheim Wy LEIN LE4 19 E3
MKTHBORO LE16 74 C4
Blissett Rd LEIW LE3 25 F3
Bloomfield Rd LEIS LE2 43 F1
Blossom Rd LEIW LE3 34 A1
The Blossoms COAL LE67 14 C1
Blount Rd LEIN LE4 20 D1
Bloxams Cl LEIW LE3 41 H2
Bloxham Rd LEIW LE3 25 F3
Blue Banks Av LEIS LE2 42 A5
Bluebell Cl RLEINE/SYS LE7 5 G3
RLEIW/BAR LE9 23 F4
Bluebell Dr GBY/RBY LE6 16 C4
LEIS LE2 43 F4
Blue Gates Rd LEIN LE4 17 H2
Blue Pots Cl LEIW LE3 32 A3
Blundell Rd LEIE LE5 37 E2
Blunt's La WGSTN LE18 56 B1
Bodenham Cl WGSTN LE18 56 A3
Bodicoat Cl RLEIS/BBY LE8 63 H1
Bodmin Av WGSTN LE18 56 A3
Bodnant Av LEIE LE5 36 C2
Bodycote Cl RLEIW/BAR LE9 68 D4
Bollington Rd LEIS LE2 45 G2
Bolsover St LEIE LE5 27 G4
Bolton Rd LEIW LE3 25 G5
Bolus Rd LEIW LE3 33 E3
Bondman Cl LEIN LE4 19 E3
Bonner Cl LEIS LE2 45 H4
Bonners La LEIS LE2 2 D6
Bonney Rd LEIW LE3 25 E1
Bonnington Rd LEIS LE2 35 H4
Bonsall St LEIE LE5 36 A1
Bonville Pl LEIW LE3 34 B4
Booth Cl LEIE LE5 28 B5
Bordeaux Cl
END/NAR LE19 40 C5
Border Dr LEIN LE4 18 D2
Borlace St LEIW LE3 2 A2
Borrowcup Cl
RLEIS/BBY LE8 64 C2
Borrowdale Cl
RLEIW/BAR LE9 49 F4
Boston Rd LEIN LE4 17 H3
Boswell St END/NAR LE19 52 C2
Bosworth Gn
RLEIW/BAR LE9 49 H2
Bosworth St LEIW LE3 2 A3
Boulder La LEIS LE2 43 F2
Boulter Crs WGSTN LE18 44 B5
Boulton Ct LEIS LE2 46 A4
Boundary Rd LEIS LE2 34 D4
LUTT LE17 81 H3
Bourton Crs LEIS LE2 45 G3
Bow Br LEIW LE3 2 B4
Bowden La
MKTHBORO LE16 74 C5
Bowden Rdg
MKTHBORO LE16 75 E4
Bowhill Gv LEIE LE5 29 E4
Bowling Green St LEI LE1 3 F4
Bowmans Wy LEIW LE3 23 H2
Bowmars La LEIW LE3 2 C1
Boyers Wk LEIW LE3 32 B2
Boynton Rd LEIW LE3 34 A1
Brabazon Cl LEIS LE2 44 D3
Brabazon Rd LEIS LE2 44 D2
Bracken Cl LEIE LE5 37 F1
LEIW LE3 32 B3
Bracken Dl RLEINE/SYS LE7 5 G2
Brackenfield Wy LEIN LE4 12 D4
Bracken Hl GBY/RBY LE6 8 A4
Brackenthwaite LEIN LE4 20 B4
Bracken Wy COAL LE67 6 C3
Bradbourne Rd LEIE LE5 27 F5
Bradbury Cl RLEIW/BAR LE9 63 F3
Bradfield Cl LEIE LE5 36 C1
Bradgate Av LEIN LE4 12 D5
Bradgate Cl RLEINE/SYS LE7 29 E5
Bradgate Dr GBY/RBY LE6 22 C1
WGSTN LE18 43 H3
Bradgate Hl GBY/RBY LE6 7 E5
Bradgate Rd COAL LE67 6 C3
GBY/RBY LE6 8 B4
RLEINE/SYS LE7 9 G1
RLEIW/BAR LE9 48 B3
Bradgate St LEIN LE4 25 H2
Brading Rd LEIW LE3 25 G2
Bradshaw Av LEIS LE2 42 C5
Bradstone Cl
RLEIW/BAR LE9 69 F4
Bradston Rd LEIS LE2 43 E3
Braemar Dr LEIN LE4 20 A3
Brailsford Rd WGSTN LE18 43 H4
Bramall Ct LEIE LE5 27 G2
Bramall Rd LEIE LE5 27 F3
Bramber Cl LEIN LE4 20 C1
Bramble Cl LEIE LE5 21 H5
LEIW LE3 24 B3
Bramble Wy LEIW LE3 34 A4
Brambling Rd LEIE LE5 27 F4
Brambling Wy LEIS LE2 45 E4
Bramcote Rd LEIW LE3 34 B5
WGSTN LE18 44 A5
Bramham Cl LEIW LE3 25 E1
Bramley Cl RLEIW/BAR LE9 68 C3
Bramley Ct LEIW LE3 23 H2
Bramley Orch
RLEINE/SYS LE7 29 G5
Bramley Rd LEIN LE4 11 H5
LEIW LE3 25 G5
Brampton Av LEIW LE3 25 E4
Brampton Wy LEIS LE2 44 D2
Brancaster Cl LEIN LE4 18 D5
Brandon St LEIN LE4 26 C2
Bransdale Rd WGSTN LE18 56 D1
Branting Hl GBY/RBY LE6 16 D4
Branting Hill Av LEIW LE3 16 D5
Branting Hill Gv LEIW LE3 16 D5
Bratmyr RLEIS/BBY LE8 70 B2
Braunstone Av LEIW LE3 33 H3
Braunstone Cl LEIW LE3 33 H4
Braunstone Ga LEIW LE3 2 B5
Braunstone La LEIW LE3 33 F2
LEIW LE3 34 A4
Braunstone La East
LEIW LE3 34 B5
Braunstone Wy LEIW LE3 33 G2
Braybrooke Rd LEIN LE4 27 G1
MKTHBORO LE16 78 C3
MKTHBORO LE16 79 H1
Braymish Cl RLEIS/BBY LE8 72 B3
Brazil St LEIS LE2 35 E2
Breach La RLEIW/BAR LE9 49 F5
Brecon Cl WGSTN LE18 55 F1
Breedon Av WGSTN LE18 44 A5
Breedon St LEIS LE2 27 E5
Brent Knowle Gdns
LEIE LE5 28 D5
Brentwood Rd LEIS LE2 35 G4
Bretby Rd LEIS LE2 43 E2
Brettell Rd LEIS LE2 42 D4
Bretton Cl LEIN LE4 19 E4
Brewer Cl LEIN LE4 20 C2
Brex Ri LEIW LE3 24 B4
Brian Rd LEIN LE4 25 H1
The Brianway LEIE LE5 27 H3
Briar Cl LEIS LE2 45 F4
Briarfield Dr LEIE LE5 29 E1
Briargate Dr LEIN LE4 11 E4
Briar Meads LEIS LE2 45 F5
Briar Rd LEIE LE5 28 D3
Briar Wk LEIS LE2 45 F4
Brickman Cl LEIW LE3 32 A3
Bridevale Rd LEIS LE2 43 E3
Bridge Cl LEIN LE4 12 D4
Bridgemere Cl LEIS LE2 42 B4
Bridge Park Rd LEIN LE4 12 B5
Bridge Rd LEIE LE5 27 F4
Bridgewater Dr
RLEIS/BBY LE8 58 D2
Bridge Wy RLEIS/BBY LE8 53 H5
Bridle Cl RLEIW/BAR LE9 61 G3
Bridlespur Wy LEIN LE4 19 E2
The Bridle LEIS LE2 42 B4
Bridport Cl WGSTN LE18 56 A2
Brierfield Rd
RLEIW/BAR LE9 63 F4
Briers Cl END/NAR LE19 52 D4
Brighton Av RLEINE/SYS LE7 5 E5
WGSTN LE18 44 A3
Brighton Cl WGSTN LE18 44 A3
Brighton Rd LEIE LE5 27 F2
Brightside Rd LEIE LE5 36 C2
Brightwell Dr LEIW LE3 32 D1
Brindley Ri LEIE LE5 29 E1
Bringhurst Rd LEIW LE3 24 B3
Brington Cl WGSTN LE18 56 C1
Brinsmead Rd LEIS LE2 43 H1
Bristol Av LEIN LE4 25 H1
Britannia St LEI LE1 26 B2
Britannia Wk
MKTHBORO LE16 78 A2
Britannia Wy
RLEINE/SYS LE7 12 C3
Britford Av WGSTN LE18 55 H3
Briton St LEIW LE3 2 A7
Brixham Dr WGSTN LE18 43 G3
Brixworth Ri LEIE LE5 29 E4
Broad Av LEIE LE5 27 H5
Broadbent Cl
RLEIS/BBY LE8 53 H4
Broadfield Wy
RLEIS/BBY LE8 64 C2
Broadford Cl LEIN LE4 20 B3
Broadgate Cl LEIN LE4 11 G4
Broadhurst St LEIN LE4 19 H5
Broad Meadow
WGSTN LE18 56 C2
Broadmead Rd
RLEIS/BBY LE8 54 A5
Broad St END/NAR LE19 40 D5
RLEINE/SYS LE7 13 E1
Broadway RLEINE/SYS LE7 13 E1
Broadway Furlong
RLEINE/SYS LE7 9 G5
Broadway Rd LEIE LE5 36 B3
The Broadway LEIS LE2 37 E5
MKTHBORO LE16 74 D5
Brockenhurst Dr LEIW LE3 33 G5
Brockey Cl RLEIW/BAR LE9 48 B4
Brocklesby Wy LEIE LE5 29 E2
Brocks Hill Cl LEIS LE2 45 F4

Brocks Hill Dr LEIS LE2 45 E3
Broctone Cl RLEIW/BAR LE9 69 F4
Broctone Dr RLEIW/BAR LE9 68 C2
Bromwich Cl LEIW LE3 33 E3
Bronte Cl LEIW LE3 34 A1
Bronze WGSTN LE18 56 D2
Brook Ct RLEIS/BBY LE8 65 F2
Brookdale Rd LEIW LE3 24 B5
Brook Dr GBY/RBY LE6 22 C3
Brookes Av
RLEIW/BAR LE9 61 G3
Brookfield HINC LE10 66 C4
Brookfield Av
RLEINE/SYS LE7 4 D5
Brookfield Ri LEIS LE2 43 F2
Brookfield Rd
MKTHBORO LE16 77 F1
Brookfield St
RLEINE/SYS LE7 13 F1
Brookfield Wy LUTT LE17 81 E2
RLEIS/BBY LE8 72 B3
Brook Gdns LEIS LE2 42 B5
Brookhouse Av LEIS LE2 3 J6
Brookhouse St LEIS LE2 3 J6
Brookland Rd LEIS LE2 35 G4
Brooklands Cl
RLEIS/BBY LE8 53 H5
RLEIW/BAR LE9 68 D3
Brooklands Gdns
MKTHBORO LE16 77 H1
Brooklands Rd
RLEIW/BAR LE9 63 F2
Brook Rd LEIE LE5 28 D3
Brooksby Dr LEIS LE2 45 E3
Brooksby St LEIS LE2 35 E4
Brookside LEIS LE2 36 B2
RLEINE/SYS LE7 4 D5
RLEIS/BBY LE8 53 H5
Brookside Dr LEIS LE2 45 G3
Brookside Gdns
RLEIS/BBY LE8 * 70 B4
Brook St END/NAR LE19 40 D5
LEIN LE4 12 B5
RLEINE/SYS LE7 4 C5
RLEIS/BBY LE8 53 H4
RLEIW/BAR LE9 51 H4
Broombriggs Rd LEIW LE3 17 H4
Broome Av RLEINE/SYS LE7 5 G1
Broomfield RLEINE/SYS LE7 5 G2
Broomhills Rd
END/NAR LE19 52 B3
Broomleys RLEIS/BBY LE8 64 D2
Broom Wy END/NAR LE19 52 B2
Brougham St LEI LE1 3 H2
Broughton Cl
RLEINE/SYS LE7 9 G5
Broughton Fld WGSTN LE18 56 C3
Broughton La
RLEIW/BAR LE9 68 C5
Broughton Rd LEIS LE2 43 E2
RLEIW/BAR LE9 60 C4
RLEIW/BAR LE9 61 E5
RLEIW/BAR LE9 61 G3
RLEIW/BAR LE9 69 F1
Broughton Wy
RLEIW/BAR LE9 68 D2
Browning St END/NAR LE19 52 C2
LEIW LE3 34 C1
Brown's Cl RLEIW/BAR LE9 67 E1
Brown's Wy RLEIS/BBY LE8 63 H1
Broxburn Cl LEIN LE4 20 B3
Broxfield Cl LEIS LE2 45 E5
Bruce St LEIW LE3 34 D2
Bruce Wy RLEIS/BBY LE8 63 G1
Bruin St LEIN LE4 26 C1
Bruins Wk LEIS LE2 44 D3
Brunel Av LEIW LE3 25 E1
Brunswick St LEI LE1 3 J2
Bruxby St RLEINE/SYS LE7 12 D1
Bryngarth Crs LEIE LE5 28 B3
Bryony Rd LEIE LE5 21 H5
Buckfast Cl LEIE LE5 36 D2
WGSTN LE18 56 A2
Buckhaven Cl LEIN LE4 20 B3
Buckingham Cl
GBY/RBY LE6 16 A5
Buckingham Dr LEIS LE2 42 B3
Buckingham Rd
RLEIS/BBY LE8 65 F2
Buckingham's Wy
HINC LE10 66 B5
Buckland Rd LEIE LE5 27 F2
Buckminster Rd LEIN LE4 25 G2
Buckwell Rd
RLEIW/BAR LE9 66 D1
Bude Dr LEIW LE3 24 A1
Bude Rd WGSTN LE18 56 B2
Buller Rd LEIN LE4 26 C1
Buller St RLEIS/BBY LE8 71 H3
Bull Head St WGSTN LE18 56 B1
Bulwer Rd LEIS LE2 35 H4
Burchnall Rd LEIW LE3 33 E4
Burdet Cl LEIW LE3 33 G4
Burdett Wy LEIN LE4 18 D3
Burdock Cl LEIE LE5 21 H5
Burfield St LEIN LE4 26 D2
Burgess Rd LEIS LE2 43 E2
Burgess St LEI LE1 2 D1
WGSTN LE18 44 B5
Burghley Cl
MKTHBORO LE16 78 B1
Burgin Rd RLEINE/SYS LE7 17 F2
Burleigh Av WGSTN LE18 44 A4
Burley Cl RLEIW/BAR LE9 30 B2
RLEIW/BAR LE9 63 F3
Burleys F/O LEI LE1 3 F1
Burleys Wy LEI LE1 2 E1
Burlington Rd LEIS LE2 36 A4
Burnaby Av LEIE LE5 27 F4
Burnaston Rd LEIS LE2 43 E2
Burnell Rd LEIW LE3 34 B3
Burneston Wy WGSTN LE18 56 C1
Burnet Cl LEIE LE5 21 G5
Burnham Cl WGSTN LE18 56 B4
Burnham Dr LEIN LE4 18 D5
RLEIS/BBY LE8 53 H5
Burnmill Rd
MKTHBORO LE16 74 C4
Burnmoor St LEIS LE2 35 E3
Burnside Rd LEIS LE2 43 G2
RLEIW/BAR LE9 68 D4
Burns St END/NAR LE19 52 C2
LEIS LE2 35 G5
Burroughs Rd GBY/RBY LE6 22 A1
Burrough Wy LUTT LE17 81 G1
Burrows Cl END/NAR LE19 52 D4
The Burrows END/NAR LE19 52 B3
Bursdon Cl LEIW LE3 24 B4
Bursom Rd LEIN LE4 18 B1
Burton Cl LEIS LE2 45 H4
LUTT LE17 81 H4
Burton St LEI LE1 3 H3
Buscot Cl LEIN LE4 27 F2
Bushby Rd LEIE LE5 27 F3
Bushey Cl END/NAR LE19 52 D3
Bush Lock Cl WGSTN LE18 55 G3
Bushloe End WGSTN LE18 56 A1
Bushnell Cl RLEIW/BAR LE9 69 E5
Butcombe Rd LEIN LE4 25 H1
Bute Wy RLEIS/BBY LE8 65 F3
Butler Cl LEIN LE4 20 C3
Butler Gdns
MKTHBORO LE16 77 F3
Butt Cl WGSTN LE18 56 C2
Butt Close La LEI LE1 2 E2
Buttercup Cl END/NAR LE19 52 C2
GBY/RBY LE6 16 C4
Buttermere St LEIS LE2 35 E2
Butterwick Dr LEIN LE4 18 C3
Buxton Cl RLEIS/BBY LE8 53 H4
Buxton St LEIS LE2 27 E4
Buzzard Cl RLEIW/BAR LE9 68 D2
Byfield Dr WGSTN LE18 44 C5
Byford Rd LEIN LE4 19 E5
Byre Crs RLEIW/BAR LE9 68 D4
Byron Cl END/NAR LE19 52 C1
LUTT LE17 81 G1
RLEIS/BBY LE8 70 B4
Byron St LEI LE1 3 G2
RLEIW/BAR LE9 48 B3
RLEIW/BAR LE9 49 E4
Byway Rd LEIE LE5 36 C3

C

Cademan Cl LEIS LE2 43 H1
Cadles Cl RLEIW/BAR LE9 60 B3
Cairngorm Cl LEIS LE2 43 F1
Cairnsford Rd LEIS LE2 43 H2
Calais Hl LEI LE1 3 G5
Calais St LEI LE1 3 G5
Caldecote Rd LEIW LE3 34 A4
Caldecott Cl WGSTN LE18 56 C1
Calder Rd LEIN LE4 18 C4
Caledine Rd LEIW LE3 24 D2
Calgary Rd LEI LE1 26 C3
Callan Cl END/NAR LE19 52 C3
Calver Hey Rd LEIN LE4 18 A4
Calvert Crs RLEIW/BAR LE9 67 E2
Calverton Av WGSTN LE18 44 A4
Calverton Cl GBY/RBY LE6 22 D2
Camborne Cl WGSTN LE18 56 A2
Cambrian Cl
RLEIW/BAR LE9 63 F4
Cambridge Cl
RLEINE/SYS LE7 13 F1
Cambridge Dr
RLEIW/BAR LE9 30 A2
Cambridge Rd
RLEIW/BAR LE9 63 F3
Cambridge St LEIW LE3 34 C1
Camden Rd LEIW LE3 34 A4
Camden St LEI LE1 3 G2
Camellia Cl END/NAR LE19 52 B2
Camelot Wy END/NAR LE19 52 C2
Cameron Av LEIN LE4 19 H4
Camfield Ri LEIS LE2 42 D4
Campbell Av LEIN LE4 20 C1
Campbell St LEI LE1 3 G5
Campion Cl END/NAR LE19 52 C3
Camville Rd LEIW LE3 33 H1
Canada Flds LUTT LE17 81 G2
Canal St LEIN LE4 12 B4
LEIS LE2 42 C1
WGSTN LE18 55 F3
Candle La RLEIW/BAR LE9 49 F3
Cank St LEI LE1 2 E3
Cannam Cl RLEIS/BBY LE8 64 A1
Canning Pl LEI LE1 2 E1
Canning St LEI LE1 2 E1
Cannock St LEIN LE4 21 E4
Canon Cl LEIS LE2 45 F4
Canons Cl END/NAR LE19 52 D3
Canonsleigh Rd LEIN LE4 19 E4
Canon St LEIN LE4 19 H5
Canterbury Ter LEIW LE3 34 B2
Cantrell Rd LEIW LE3 33 F2
Canvey Cl WGSTN LE18 44 D5
Capers Cl END/NAR LE19 40 C5
Capesthorne Cl LEIE LE5 27 F2
Cara Cl LEIS LE2 36 A5
Carbery Cl LEIS LE2 45 H4
Cardigan Dr WGSTN LE18 55 F1
Cardinal Cl GBY/RBY LE6 22 D2
Cardinals Wk LEIE LE5 28 C2
Carey Cl WGSTN LE18 56 B3
Carey Hill Rd
RLEIW/BAR LE9 60 B4
Carey Rd RLEIW/BAR LE9 51 H4
Careys Cl LEI LE1 2 D4
Carfax Av LEIS LE2 44 D1
Carisbrooke Av LEIS LE2 44 A1
Carisbrooke Gdns LEIS LE2 36 A5
Carisbrooke Pk LEIS LE2 44 A1
Carisbrooke Rd LEIS LE2 36 A5
Carlisle St LEIW LE3 25 F5
Carlson Gdns LUTT LE17 81 H3
Carl St LEIS LE2 42 C2
Carlton Av END/NAR LE19 53 E3
Carlton Dr WGSTN LE18 44 A5
Carlton Gdns
RLEIS/BBY LE8 * 58 D4
Carlton La RLEIS/BBY LE8 59 H3
Carlton St LEI LE1 2 E6
Carmen Gv GBY/RBY LE6 15 H4
Carnation Cl LEIW LE3 32 B3
Carnation St LEIN LE4 19 F5
Carnoustie Rd LEIW LE3 24 B4
Caroline Ct LEIS LE2 43 E2
Carpenter's Cl LEIW LE3 23 H3
Carpe Rd LEIN LE4 27 F1
Carrow Rd LEIW LE3 23 H5
Carr's Dr RLEIW/BAR LE9 49 F3
Carrs Hl RLEIW/BAR LE9 48 C5
Carr's Rd RLEIW/BAR LE9 49 F3
Carter Cl END/NAR LE19 40 C5
Carter St LEIN LE4 27 E2
Carts La LEI LE1 2 E3
Cartwright Dr LEIS LE2 45 E3
Carvers Cnr LEIS LE2 * 42 B5
Cashmore Vw LEIN LE4 18 D3
Castell Dr GBY/RBY LE6 16 B4
Castle Cl RLEIW/BAR LE9 66 D2
Castle Flds LEIN LE4 17 H2
Castleford Rd LEIW LE3 33 G5
Castlegate Av LEIN LE4 11 F4
Castle Ri GBY/RBY LE6 16 B5
Castle Rd RLEIW/BAR LE9 22 D5
Castle St LEI LE1 2 D5
Castleton Rd WGSTN LE18 44 A4
Castle Vw LEI LE1 2 D5
Castle Yd LEI LE1 2 D5
Caswell Cl LEIN LE4 18 D3
Caters Cl RLEINE/SYS LE7 17 F1
Catesby St LEIW LE3 2 A5
Catherine St LEI LE1 26 D2
LEIN LE4 27 E1
Cathkin Cl LEIW LE3 24 B5
Caudle Cl RLEINE/SYS LE7 9 H1
Causeway La GBY/RBY LE6 9 F2
LEI LE1 2 D2
Cavendish Rd LEIS LE2 35 E5
Caversham Rd LEIS LE2 42 C5
Cawsand Rd WGSTN LE18 56 A2
Caxton St MKTHBORO LE16 78 A3
Cecilia Rd LEIS LE2 35 H3
Cecil Rd LEIE LE5 27 E4
LEIS LE2 3 K3
Cedar Av LEIN LE4 11 G5
LUTT LE17 81 F3
WGSTN LE18 56 B2
Cedar Cl LEIW LE3 24 C1
RLEIS/BBY LE8 71 H3
Cedar Ct GBY/RBY LE6 16 B5
Cedar Crs END/NAR LE19 52 D4
Cedar Dr RLEINE/SYS LE7 13 F2
Cedar Rd LEIS LE2 36 A1
RLEIS/BBY LE8 54 B5
RLEIW/BAR LE9 48 D4
Cedars Ct LEIS LE2 36 A3
The Cedars LEIS LE2 43 H1
Cedarwood Cl LEIN LE4 27 F1
Celandine Cl LEIS LE2 46 A4
Celandine Rd LEIE LE5 21 G5
Celt St LEIW LE3 2 B6
Cemetery Rd
RLEIS/BBY LE8 53 H4
Central Av LEIS LE2 36 A3
LUTT LE17 81 G2
RLEINE/SYS LE7 4 D5
WGSTN LE18 56 A1
Central Cl RLEIS/BBY LE8 53 H3
Central Rd LEIW LE3 25 H3
Central St RLEIS/BBY LE8 65 F3
Centre Ct END/NAR LE19 41 F1
Centurion Wy
END/NAR LE19 33 F5
Century Ct LEIE LE5 28 C4
Chadderton Cl LEIS LE2 43 G1
Chadwell Rd LEIW LE3 24 C3
Chaffinch Cl LEIN LE4 18 A1
Chainama Cl LEIW LE3 24 A4
Chale Rd LEIN LE4 19 F5
Chalvington Cl LEIE LE5 37 G2
Chambers Cl COAL LE67 6 D4
Champion Cl LEIE LE5 28 B5
Chancel Rd LEIN LE4 10 D4
Chancery Pl LEI LE1 * 2 E4
Chancery St LEI LE1 2 E5
Chandler Wy
RLEIW/BAR LE9 69 F4
Chantry Cl RLEIW/BAR LE9 51 G3
Chapel Cl RLEINE/SYS LE7 4 C5
RLEINE/SYS LE7 10 B1
RLEINE/SYS LE7 39 H1
Chapel Gn LEIW LE3 32 D3
Chapel Hl GBY/RBY LE6 16 A4
Chapel La GBY/RBY LE6 22 C2
HINC LE10 66 C5
LEIS LE2 43 H1
RLEIW/BAR LE9 30 B1
RLEIW/BAR LE9 63 F4
WGSTN LE18 56 B1
Chapel St END/NAR LE19 40 C5
HINC LE10 66 C5
LEIS LE2 45 E3
LUTT LE17 81 G3
RLEINE/SYS LE7 4 D5
RLEIS/BBY LE8 54 B2
RLEIW/BAR LE9 48 A5
RLEIW/BAR LE9 49 G2
Chaplin Ct LEIW LE3 33 F2
Chappell Cl LEIN LE4 12 C5
Charlecote Av LEIW LE3 33 G4
Charles Dr RLEINE/SYS LE7 17 G1
Charles St LEI LE1 3 F2
MKTHBORO LE16 77 G1
Charleston Crs
RLEIW/BAR LE9 48 A5
Charles Wy RLEIS/BBY LE8 64 A1
Charlock Rd LEIE LE5 21 H5
Charlton Cl RLEIS/BBY LE8 54 A5
Charnor Rd LEIW LE3 24 C2
Charnwood GBY/RBY LE6 22 B1
Charnwood Av LEIN LE4 12 D4
RLEIS/BBY LE8 53 H3
Charnwood Cl LEIN LE4 12 D4
LEIW LE3 32 C1
Charnwood Dr COAL LE67 6 D4
LEIW LE3 32 C2
RLEINE/SYS LE7 29 F5
Charnwood Rd
RLEINE/SYS LE7 9 F5
RLEIW/BAR LE9 48 B3
Charnwood St LEIS LE2 26 E4
Charter St LEI LE1 26 B3
Chartley Rd LEIW LE3 34 C2
Chartwell Dr WGSTN LE18 43 G5
The Chase COAL LE67 6 C4
LEIW LE3 41 H1
RLEINE/SYS LE7 5 F1
RLEIS/BBY LE8 59 E2
Chater Cl LEIE LE5 28 D3
MKTHBORO LE16 75 E3
Chatham St LEI LE1 3 F5
Chatsworth Av WGSTN LE18 55 G2
Chatsworth Dr
MKTHBORO LE16 78 B1
RLEINE/SYS LE7 12 D1
Chatsworth St LEIS LE2 27 E5
Chatteris Av LEIE LE5 37 H2
Chaucer St END/NAR LE19 52 C2
LEIS LE2 36 A2
Checketts Cl LEIN LE4 19 H5
Checketts Rd LEIN LE4 19 H4
Checkland Rd LEIN LE4 12 C4
Cheddar Rd WGSTN LE18 44 C5
Cheer Cl RLEIS/BBY LE8 63 H2
Chellaston Rd WGSTN LE18 44 A4
Chelsea Cl LEIS LE2 54 D2
Cheltenham Rd LEIN LE4 18 C5
Cheney End RLEIW/BAR LE9 51 H3
Cheney Rd LEIN LE4 21 E2
Chepstow Rd LEIS LE2 36 A2
Cheriton Rd LEIS LE2 42 D3
Cherrybrook Cl LEIN LE4 10 B5
Cherry Dr RLEINE/SYS LE7 13 F2
Cherry Gv RLEIS/BBY LE8 59 E3
Cherry Hills Rd LEIW LE3 24 A4
Cherryleas Dr LEIW LE3 34 C1
Cherry Rd RLEIS/BBY LE8 54 B4
Cherry St WGSTN LE18 55 H1
Cherrytree Av LUTT LE17 81 E4
Cherry Tree Av
RLEIW/BAR LE9 32 A2
Cherrytree Cl
RLEINE/SYS LE7 17 F2
RLEIS/BBY LE8 64 D2
Cherry Tree Dr
RLEIW/BAR LE9 48 B3
Cherry Tree Gv
END/NAR LE19 40 C5
Cheshire Cl LUTT LE17 81 E5
Cheshire Dr WGSTN LE18 43 F5
Cheshire Gdns LEIS LE2 42 D1
Cheshire Rd LEIS LE2 42 D1
Chester Cl LEI LE1 3 J1
RLEIS/BBY LE8 54 C4
Chesterfield Rd LEIE LE5 36 B1
Chesterfield Wy
RLEIW/BAR LE9 48 C4
Chester Rd RLEIS/BBY LE8 54 C4
Chestnut Av LEIE LE5 28 C1
LEIS LE2 44 D3
LUTT LE17 81 E3
Chestnut Cl END/NAR LE19 52 D5
RLEINE/SYS LE7 5 F4
RLEINE/SYS LE7 13 F2
RLEIW/BAR LE9 69 E4
Chestnut Dr LEIS LE2 46 C4
RLEINE/SYS LE7 38 C1
Chestnut Rd LEIW LE3 24 A2
The Chestnuts
RLEIS/BBY LE8 65 E2
Chestnut Wk COAL LE67 14 C1
GBY/RBY LE6 16 B5
Chestnut Wy RLEINE/SYS LE7 5 G2

Chettle Rd LEIW LE3 25 E3
Chevin Av LEIW LE3 24 B5
Cheviot Rd LEIS LE2 43 F2
Chilcombe Cl LEIN LE4 19 E4
Chiltern Av RLEIW/BAR LE9 63 F4
Chiltern Cl MKTHBORO LE16 74 D4
Chiltern Gn LEIS LE2 43 G2
Chislehurst Av LEIW LE3 33 G5
Chiswick Rd LEIS LE2 35 F4
Chitterman Wy COAL LE67 6 C4
Chorley Wood Rd LEIE LE5 37 H1
Chrisett Cl LEIE LE5 28 B4
Christopher Cl
RLEIS/BBY LE8 65 E3
Christopher Dr LEIN LE4 20 D3
Christow St LEI LE1 3 H1
Church Av LEIW LE3 25 G5
Church Cl LUTT LE17 81 G3
RLEINE/SYS LE7 4 D5
RLEIS/BBY LE8 72 A2
RLEIW/BAR LE9 48 A5
RLEIW/BAR LE9 68 D3
Church Dr COAL LE67 6 B4
Church Ga LEI LE1 2 E3
LUTT LE17 81 G3
Church Hl LEIN LE4 19 H1
RLEINE/SYS LE7 29 F2
Church Hill Rd LEIN LE4 12 C5
Churchill Cl LEIS LE2 45 E3
LUTT LE17 81 E4
Churchill Dr LEIW LE3 32 D1
Churchill St LEIS LE2 3 K7
Churchill Wy RLEIS/BBY LE8 70 C5
Church La END/NAR LE19 53 E3
GBY/RBY LE6 22 C2
LEIN LE4 12 B5
LEIS LE2 38 A4
LEIS LE2 43 H1
MKTHBORO LE16 79 H1
RLEINE/SYS LE7 17 F1
RLEINE/SYS LE7 38 B1
RLEIS/BBY LE8 53 H3
RLEIS/BBY LE8 70 B4
RLEIW/BAR LE9 30 B2
RLEIW/BAR LE9 48 A5
Church Nook WGSTN LE18 44 B5
Church Rd LEIE LE5 37 F3
LEIS LE2 42 C2
LEIW LE3 23 H1
RLEINE/SYS LE7 12 A2
RLEIS/BBY LE8 58 C3
RLEIS/BBY LE8 72 A3
RLEIW/BAR LE9 22 D5
Church Sq MKTHBORO LE16 77 H1
Church St LEI LE1 3 G4
LEIN LE4 20 B1
LEIS LE2 45 E3
LUTT LE17 81 G4
MKTHBORO LE16 77 H1
RLEIS/BBY LE8 54 C3
RLEIS/BBY LE8 65 F3
RLEIW/BAR LE9 49 F2
RLEIW/BAR LE9 60 B4
RLEIW/BAR LE9 66 D2
Church Vw END/NAR LE19 53 E3
Church Wk
MKTHBORO LE16 76 C1
Churchward Av LEIN LE4 18 C3
The Circle LEIE LE5 27 H5
Clarefield Rd LEIW LE3 25 F5
Clare Gv LEIW LE3 33 F3
Claremont Dr
MKTHBORO LE16 78 B1
Claremont St LEIN LE4 19 G4
Clarence Rd END/NAR LE19 53 F1
Clarence St LEI LE1 3 F3
MKTHBORO LE16 78 A1
Clarendon Park Rd
LEIS LE2 35 G4
Clarendon St LEIS LE2 2 D7
Clarke Gv LEIN LE4 19 G1
Clarkes Rd WGSTN LE18 55 H1
Clarke St LEIN LE4 19 H4
MKTHBORO LE16 77 G1
Clark Gdns RLEIS/BBY LE8 54 A3
Claybrook Av LEIW LE3 34 A5
Claydon Rd LEIE LE5 27 G2
Claymill Rd LEIN LE4 20 D3
Clayton Dr LEIN LE4 20 D1
Clear View Crs
RLEIW/BAR LE9 49 F2
Clematis Cl LEIN LE4 18 A2
Clement Av LEIN LE4 19 G4
Clevedon Crs LEIN LE4 27 G2
Cleveland Rd WGSTN LE18 44 B5
Cleveleys Av LEIW LE3 34 A5
Cliffe House Ms
RLEIS/BBY LE8 53 H4
Cliffe Rd LEIN LE4 19 F1
Clifford St LEIW LE3 2 A3
WGSTN LE18 55 F1
Cliffwood Av LEIN LE4 11 F5
Clifton Dr WGSTN LE18 55 G3
Clifton Rd LEIS LE2 35 E5
Clint Hill Dr RLEIW/BAR LE9 60 C4
Clipper Rd LEIN LE4 20 D4
Clipstone Cl WGSTN LE18 56 C1
Clipstone Gdns WGSTN LE18 56 C1
Clipston St MKTHBORO LE16 78 A3
The Cloisters
RLEIW/BAR LE9 49 E3
The Close END/NAR LE19 * 52 C1
RLEINE/SYS LE7 9 F5
RLEIW/BAR LE9 48 B4
Clovelly Rd LEIE LE5 36 D1
LEIW LE3 24 B2
Clover Cl END/NAR LE19 52 C3
Cloverdale Rd LEIE LE5 21 G5
Clumber Cl RLEINE/SYS LE7 4 D4
Clumber Rd LEIE LE5 27 G5
Clyde St LEI LE1 3 H2
Coalbourn Cl LEIN LE4 19 E3
Coales Av RLEIS/BBY LE8 64 A1
Coales Gdns
MKTHBORO LE16 74 B4
Coatbridge Av LEIN LE4 20 B4
Coates Av LEIW LE3 25 E3
Cobden St LEI LE1 3 K1
Cobwells Cl RLEIS/BBY LE8 70 C4
Cokayne Rd LEIW LE3 24 B4
Colbert Dr LEIW LE3 42 A1
Colby Dr LEIN LE4 21 E1
Colby Rd LEIN LE4 20 D2
Colchester Rd LEIE LE5 28 B4
Colebrook Cl LEIE LE5 36 C2
Coleford Rd LEIN LE4 21 E2
Coleman Cl LEIE LE5 27 H3
Coleman Rd LEIE LE5 27 H3
RLEIS/BBY LE8 70 A3
Coleridge Dr
END/NAR LE19 52 C1
Coles Cl LEIN LE4 20 B2
Colindale Av LEIN LE4 11 G4
Colin Grundy Dr LEIE LE5 28 B1
Collaton Rd WGSTN LE18 56 A2
College Av LEIS LE2 3 J6
College Rd RLEINE/SYS LE7 13 F1
RLEIS/BBY LE8 53 H3
College St LEIS LE2 3 J6
College Wk LEIS LE2 3 J6
Collett Rd LEIN LE4 18 C3
Collingham Rd LEIW LE3 34 C3
Collin Pl LEIN LE4 20 A5
Collins Cl LEIW LE3 33 F3
Colne Cl LEIS LE2 45 H3
Colsterdale Cl LEIN LE4 18 D2
Coltbeck Av END/NAR LE19 52 C4
Colthurst Wy LEIE LE5 29 E4
Colton St LEI LE1 3 G4
Coltsfoot Rd LEIE LE5 21 G5
Columbia Cl END/NAR LE19 40 C5
Columbine Cl LEIW LE3 33 G3
Columbine Rd LEIE LE5 21 G4
Colwell Rd LEIN LE4 25 H2
Combe Cl LEIW LE3 25 G2
Comet Cl LEIW LE3 25 F3
Commercial Sq LEIS LE2 35 F4
The Common LEIE LE5 37 E2
RLEIW/BAR LE9 48 B5
Compass Rd LEIE LE5 28 C3
Compton Dr
RLEIW/BAR LE9 51 H3
Compton Rd LEIW LE3 34 C3
Conaglen Rd LEIS LE2 42 B2
Condor Cl RLEIW/BAR LE9 68 D2
Conduit St LEIS LE2 3 H5
Cone La LEIS LE2 36 A3
Conery La END/NAR LE19 40 C5
Coneygrey RLEIS/BBY LE8 70 B2
Conifer Cl LUTT LE17 81 F3
Coninsby Cl LEIW LE3 34 B4
Coniston Av LEIS LE2 35 E2
Coniston Cl
RLEIW/BAR LE9 49 F3
Coniston Wy
RLEIW/BAR LE9 61 H2
Connaught Rd
MKTHBORO LE16 74 D5
Connaught St LEIS LE2 3 K7
Connell Cl MKTHBORO LE16 76 C1
Constable Av LEIN LE4 26 D2
Constance Rd LEIE LE5 27 F5
Constitution Hl LEI LE1 3 H4
Conway Rd LEIS LE2 36 B2
Cooden Av LEIW LE3 34 B1
Cooke Cl LEIW LE3 33 F3
Cooke's Dr RLEIW/BAR LE9 68 C3
Cook's La RLEIW/BAR LE9 66 D2
WGSTN LE18 56 D4
Cookson Rd LEIN LE4 21 E2
Coombe Pl LEIS LE2 45 F4
Coombe Ri LEIS LE2 45 G5
Co-operation St
END/NAR LE19 40 D5
Cooper Cl LEIS LE2 42 C2
RLEIW/BAR LE9 51 H3
Cooper Gdns LEIS LE2 45 H4
Cooper La GBY/RBY LE6 22 D2
Cooper's Nook
RLEINE/SYS LE7 5 F2
Cooper St LEIN LE4 26 C1
Copdale Rd LEIE LE5 27 G5
Copeland Av LEIW LE3 25 E1
Copeland Rd LEIN LE4 19 F1
Copinger Rd LEIS LE2 43 F1
Coplow Av LEIE LE5 36 C3
Coplow Crs RLEINE/SYS LE7 13 E2
Coppice La RLEINE/SYS LE7 5 H4
The Coppice COAL LE67 6 C4
END/NAR LE19 52 C3
LEIN LE4 13 E5
Copse Cl LEIS LE2 42 C5
LEIS LE2 45 G1
LEIW LE3 32 A4
Copthorne Cl LEIW LE3 24 B5
Copt Oak Rd END/NAR LE19 52 C3
Corah St LEIW LE3 2 C5
Coral St LEIN LE4 26 C1
Corbet Cl LEIN LE4 18 B4
Cordelia Cl LEIE LE5 27 G2
Cordery Rd LEIE LE5 37 F2
Cordonnier Cl
RLEIW/BAR LE9 69 E5
Corfield Ri LEIW LE3 33 G2
Coriander Rd LEIS LE2 2 B7
Cork La LEIS LE2 54 A1
Cork St LEIE LE5 27 E5
Cornfield Cl END/NAR LE19 53 E4
Cornfields LEIS LE2 * 47 F3
Cornwallis Av LEIN LE4 18 B5
Cornwall Rd LEIN LE4 25 H1
WGSTN LE18 55 F1
Cornwall St END/NAR LE19 40 D5
Coronation Av
RLEIW/BAR LE9 68 C3
WGSTN LE18 55 H1
Coronation Rd
RLEIW/BAR LE9 48 D5
Coronet Cl RLEINE/SYS LE7 17 G1
Corporation Rd LEIN LE4 19 F5
Corshaw Wk LEIE LE5 27 F2
Cort Crs LEIW LE3 33 G1
Cosby Rd END/NAR LE19 53 E5
RLEIS/BBY LE8 64 C3
RLEIW/BAR LE9 69 E2
Cossington La
RLEINE/SYS LE7 4 C2
Cossington St LEIN LE4 26 D1
Cotley Rd LEIN LE4 18 C2
Cotswold Av
RLEIW/BAR LE9 63 F4
Cottage Cl GBY/RBY LE6 22 C1
Cottage Farm Cl LEIW LE3 41 H2
Cottage Gdns
RLEIW/BAR LE9 49 F3
Cottage La COAL LE67 6 A1
RLEIW/BAR LE9 30 B1
RLEIW/BAR LE9 69 E3
Cottage Rd WGSTN LE18 56 C2
Cottage Rw LEIW LE3 34 B5
Cottagers Cl LEIS LE2 43 E3
Cottesbrooke Cl
WGSTN LE18 56 B1
Cottesmore Av LEIS LE2 45 G4
Cottesmore Rd LEIE LE5 27 F3
Cotton Cl LEIN LE4 20 B2
RLEIW/BAR LE9 69 E4
Coulson Cl RLEIS/BBY LE8 54 A5
Council St LUTT LE17 81 G3
Countesthorpe Rd
RLEIS/BBY LE8 55 F5
RLEIW/BAR LE9 63 F4
Counting House Rd
LEIS LE2 35 F3
Countryman's Wy
RLEINE/SYS LE7 5 F1
Countryman Wy COAL LE67 6 C4
Court Cl RLEIW/BAR LE9 23 E5
Courtenay Rd LEIN LE4 25 G1
Court Rd LEIS LE2 54 B1
RLEINE/SYS LE7 38 B1
Coventry Rd END/NAR LE19 62 B1
LUTT LE17 67 E4
LUTT LE17 80 B4
MKTHBORO LE16 77 G2
RLEIW/BAR LE9 61 G5
Coventry St LEIW LE3 2 A5
Coverdale Rd WGSTN LE18 56 D2
Coverside Rd
RLEIS/BBY LE8 59 E2
Covert Cl LEIS LE2 45 G2
RLEINE/SYS LE7 12 C1
Covert La RLEINE/SYS LE7 29 G2
Covett Wy LEIW LE3 24 C5
Cowdall Rd LEIW LE3 33 F2
Cow La GBY/RBY LE6 14 D5
Cowley Wy LEIE LE5 29 E4
Cowslip Cl END/NAR LE19 52 B3
Crabtree Cnr LEIS LE2 43 G3
Cradock Rd LEIS LE2 35 H3
Cradock St LEI LE1 3 J2
Crafton St East LEI LE1 3 H2
Crafton St West LEI LE1 3 G2
Craftsmans Wy
RLEINE/SYS LE7 5 F2
Craig Gdns LEIW LE3 24 B4
Craighill Rd LEIS LE2 35 H5
Cranberry Cl LEIW LE3 33 F3
Cranbourne Gdns LEIS LE2 37 F5
Cranbrook Rd
RLEINE/SYS LE7 29 F4
Crane-Ley Rd GBY/RBY LE6 16 A4
Cranesbill Rd LEIE LE5 28 C1
Crane St LEI LE1 2 E1
Cranfield Rd LEIS LE2 42 D2
Cranmer Cl RLEIS/BBY LE8 54 A5
Cranmer Dr RLEINE/SYS LE7 12 D1
Cranmer St LEIW LE3 2 A6
Cranoe Rd RLEIS/BBY LE8 73 H2
Cransley Cl LEIE LE5 21 G4
Cranstone Crs LEIW LE3 24 A3
Crantock Cl LEIE LE5 37 G2
Cranwell Cl LEIE LE5 37 F3
Craven St LEI LE1 2 D1
Crawford Rd LEIW LE3 25 F4
Crayford Wy LEIE LE5 28 D1
Craythorne Wy
WGSTN LE18 56 C1
Creaton Ct WGSTN LE18 56 C1
Creaton Rd WGSTN LE18 56 C1
Crediton Cl WGSTN LE18 56 B3
Crescent Cl
MKTHBORO LE16 74 D5
Crescent Rd LUTT LE17 81 G2
Crescent St LEI LE1 3 F6
The Crescent LEI LE1 * 3 F6
MKTHBORO LE16 74 D5
RLEIS/BBY LE8 54 B4
RLEIS/BBY LE8 * 58 D3
WGSTN LE18 44 A4
Cressida Pl LEIW LE3 * 33 G3
Cresswell Cl LEIN LE4 21 E1
The Crestway
RLEIS/BBY LE8 53 H3
Crete Av WGSTN LE18 55 E1
Critchlow Rd
RLEIW/BAR LE9 51 H3
Croft Av LEIS LE2 42 C2
Croft Cl RLEIW/BAR LE9 48 B5
Croft Dr WGSTN LE18 43 H4
Crofters Cl LEIW LE3 23 G2
Crofters Dr LEIE LE5 28 A3
Croft Hill Rd
RLEIW/BAR LE9 51 G5
Croft La RLEIW/BAR LE9 51 E3
Croft Rd LEIN LE4 10 C5
RLEIW/BAR LE9 51 E1
RLEIW/BAR LE9 62 B2
The Croft RLEIW/BAR LE9 22 D5
Croftway COAL LE67 6 B4
Croft Wy RLEIW/BAR LE9 69 E3
Cromarty Cl LEIN LE4 20 B4
Cromer St LEIS LE2 36 A2
Cromford Av WGSTN LE18 55 G2
Cromford Rd
RLEIW/BAR LE9 63 F2
Cromford St LEIS LE2 27 E4
Cromford Wy
RLEIW/BAR LE9 69 F3
Cromwell Crs
MKTHBORO LE16 77 G3
Cromwell Rd RLEIS/BBY LE8 58 D3
Cropston Cl LEIW LE3 24 B4
Cropston Rd GBY/RBY LE6 9 G2
RLEINE/SYS LE7 17 G1
Cropthorne Av LEIE LE5 27 H5
Crosby Rd
MKTHBORO LE16 78 A3
Cross Hedge Cl LEIN LE4 18 C3
Cross Keys Gn LEIE LE5 29 E3
Crossleys RLEIS/BBY LE8 70 B4
Crossley St LEIW LE3 24 A2
Cross Rd LEIS LE2 36 A3
Cross St END/NAR LE19 40 D5
LEIN LE4 26 C1
LEIS LE2 45 E1
MKTHBORO LE16 77 H2
RLEINE/SYS LE7 13 F1
RLEIS/BBY LE8 54 B3
WGSTN LE18 56 B1
The Cross END/NAR LE19 40 D5
The Crossways LEIN LE4 11 G5
The Crossway LEIS LE2 43 F2
LEIW LE3 34 A5
Crowan Dr WGSTN LE18 56 A3
Crowfoot Wy
RLEIW/BAR LE9 68 D5
Crowhurst Dr LEIW LE3 33 G5
Crow La LEIW LE3 34 D2
Crown Hills Av LEIE LE5 27 G5
Crown Hills Ri LEIE LE5 27 G5
Croyland Gn LEIE LE5 29 E4
Cufflin Cl GBY/RBY LE6 22 D2
Cuffling Cl LEIW LE3 24 B4
Cuffling Dr LEIW LE3 24 B4
Culham Av LEIE LE5 27 F2
Culver Rd LEIW LE3 25 G2
Culworth Dr WGSTN LE18 56 C1
Cumberland Rd
WGSTN LE18 43 E5
Cumberland St LEI LE1 2 C2
Cumberland Wy
RLEIW/BAR LE9 48 A4
Cumberwell Dr
END/NAR LE19 53 E2
Cunningham Dr LUTT LE17 81 E4
Curlew Cl RLEINE/SYS LE7 4 B5
Curlew Wk LEIE LE5 * 27 E3
Curteys Cl LEIW LE3 34 B4
Curtis Cl RLEIS/BBY LE8 53 H4
Curzon Av LEIN LE4 19 G1
WGSTN LE18 55 G2
Curzon Cl RLEINE/SYS LE7 5 F4
Curzon Rd LEIS LE2 43 E1
Curzon St LEI LE1 26 D3
Cutters Cl END/NAR LE19 52 C4
The Cuttings
RLEINE/SYS LE7 29 F4
Cygnet Cl RLEINE/SYS LE7 4 B5
Cyprus Rd LEIS LE2 43 E2
Cyril St LEIW LE3 34 A5

D

Dabey Cl COAL LE67 6 B4
Daisy Cl GBY/RBY LE6 16 C4
Dakyn Rd LEIE LE5 28 D4
Dalby Av RLEINE/SYS LE7 11 H4
RLEINE/SYS LE7 29 G5
Dalby Dr GBY/RBY LE6 16 B4
Dalby Rd RLEINE/SYS LE7 9 F5
Dale Acre RLEIS/BBY LE8 65 F2
Dale Av WGSTN LE18 43 G4
The Dales RLEIS/BBY LE8 64 C2
Dale St LEIS LE2 27 E5
Dalkeith Rd LEIN LE4 20 B3
Dalley Cl RLEINE/SYS LE7 13 F2

Dallison Cl
MKTHBORO LE16 77 H4
Danbury Dr LEIN LE4 18 D5
Dandees Cl COAL LE67 6 C3
Dane Hl GBY/RBY LE6 22 D2
Danehurst Av LEIW LE3 25 F4
Daneshill Rd LEIW LE3 25 G5
Dane St LEIW LE3 2 A4
Dannett St LEIW LE3 2 A3
Dannett Wk LEIW LE3 2 A3
Danvers Rd LEIW LE3 34 C2
Darenth Dr LEIN LE4 18 A4
Darien Wy LEIW LE3 33 E3
Darker St LEI LE1 2 E2
Darley Av WGSTN LE18 55 G2
Darley Rd RLEIS/BBY LE8 54 A4
Darley St LEIS LE2 27 E5
Darlington Rd LEIW LE3 25 E2
Dart Cl LEIS LE2 45 G3
Dartford Rd LEIS LE2 34 D4
Darwen Cl LEIW LE3 25 F2
Darwin Cl LEIW LE3 33 E4
RLEIW/BAR LE9 68 D4
Dashwood Rd LEIS LE2 36 A2
Davenport Av LEIS LE2 44 D2
Davenport Rd LEIE LE5 28 B5
WGSTN LE18 56 B2
Davett Cl LEIE LE5 28 B4
David Av LEIN LE4 19 E2
Davies Cl MKTHBORO LE16 74 B4
Davison Cl LEIE LE5 28 A4
Dawlish Cl LEIE LE5 28 D5
Dawson's La
RLEIW/BAR LE9 48 B5
Daybell Cl RLEIS/BBY LE8 53 H2
Day St LEIN LE4 19 G4
Deacon Cl LUTT LE17 81 E1
MKTHBORO LE16 74 B4
Deacon Rd LEIN LE4 10 D4
Deacon St LEIS LE2 2 D7
Deancourt Rd LEIS LE2 43 H2
Deane Gate Dr
RLEINE/SYS LE7 39 H1
Deanery Crs LEIN LE4 10 D4
Dean Rd LEIN LE4 27 E1
Debdale La RLEIS/BBY LE8 71 H5
Deene Cl MKTHBORO LE16 * 78 D1
Deepdale LEIE LE5 27 H4
Delaware Rd LEIE LE5 38 A2
De Lisle Cl MKTHBORO LE16 77 G2
De Montfort Ms LEIS LE2 3 H6
De Montfort Sq LEI LE1 3 G7
De Montfort St LEI LE1 3 G7
Dempsey Cl LUTT LE17 81 G1
Denacre Av WGSTN LE18 55 G2
Denbigh Pl LUTT LE17 81 G2
Denbydale WGSTN LE18 56 D2
Denegate Av LEIN LE4 11 F4
Denham Cl LEIW LE3 24 A4
Denis Cl LEIW LE3 25 F5
Deniston Cl RLEIW/BAR LE9 68 B2
Denman La RLEIW/BAR LE9 51 H3
Denmark Rd LEIS LE2 35 E5
Denmead Av WGSTN LE18 44 A5
Denton St LEIW LE3 25 F5
Derby Cl RLEIW/BAR LE9 69 E4
Dersingham Rd LEIN LE4 18 D5
Derwent Cl RLEIW/BAR LE9 49 F4
Derwent St LEIS LE2 27 E5
Derwent Wk LEIS LE2 45 G3
Desford La RLEIW/BAR LE9 30 A5
Desford Rd END/NAR LE19 40 B3
END/NAR LE19 52 D3
GBY/RBY LE6 22 D4
Devana Rd LEIS LE2 36 A2
Devenports Hl
RLEINE/SYS LE7 29 H5
Devenports Wy
RLEINE/SYS LE7 29 H5
De Verdon Rd LUTT LE17 81 E4
Devitt Wy RLEIW/BAR LE9 68 D5
Devonia Rd LEIS LE2 45 H4
Devonshire Av
WGSTN LE18 55 G2
Devonshire Rd LEIN LE4 26 A1
Devonshire St LEI LE1 2 E1
Devon Wy LEIE LE5 27 H5
Dickens Ct LEIW LE3 25 E5
The Dicken RLEIS/BBY LE8 53 H4
Dickinson Wy LEIN LE4 12 D5
Didsbury St LEIW LE3 33 G2
Digby Cl LEIW LE3 34 B1
Dillon Ri LEIW LE3 24 D2
Dillon Rd LEIW LE3 24 D2
Dillon Wy LEIW LE3 24 D1
Dimmingsdale Cl
RLEINE/SYS LE7 9 G5
Dingley Av LEIN LE4 27 E1
Dingley Link WGSTN LE18 44 C5
Dingley Rd
MKTHBORO LE16 75 F3
Dingley Ter
MKTHBORO LE16 78 A1
Diseworth St LEIS LE2 27 E5
Disney Cl RLEIW/BAR LE9 60 B4
Disraeli Cl RLEIS/BBY LE8 71 H3
Disraeli St LEIS LE2 42 C1
Ditchling Av LEIW LE3 25 E4
Dixon Dr LEIS LE2 36 A2
Dobney Av RLEINE/SYS LE7 5 E4
Doctor Cookes Cl
RLEIW/BAR LE9 48 A5
Doctors Flds
RLEIW/BAR LE9 48 D4
Doddridge Rd
MKTHBORO LE16 74 C5
Dog & Gun La
RLEIS/BBY LE8 63 H1
Dogwood Ct LEIS LE2 45 E1
Dominion Rd LEIW LE3 24 B2
Dominus Wy END/NAR LE19 33 F5
Donald Cl LEIN LE4 20 D3
Donaldson Rd LEIN LE4 26 C2
Doncaster Rd LEIN LE4 26 D1
Donnett Cl LEIE LE5 28 B4
Donnington St LEIS LE2 27 E5
Dorchester Cl
RLEIS/BBY LE8 54 C5
WGSTN LE18 56 A3
Dorchester Rd LEIW LE3 34 B1
Dore Rd LEIE LE5 36 A1
Dorothy Av LEIN LE4 20 B1
LEIS LE2 42 B5
Dorothy Rd LEIE LE5 27 F5
Dorset Av LEIW LE3 24 A1
WGSTN LE18 43 F5
Dorset St LEIN LE4 26 C2
Double Rail Cl WGSTN LE18 55 G2
Doudney Cl RLEIW/BAR LE9 60 B5
Douglas Bader Cl LUTT LE17 81 G1
Douglass Dr
MKTHBORO LE16 74 D4
Dovecote Cl RLEIW/BAR LE9 66 D2
Dovecote La
RLEIW/BAR LE9 61 G1
Dovecote Rd
RLEIW/BAR LE9 61 G1
Dovecote Wy
RLEIW/BAR LE9 48 B5
Dovedale Av RLEIS/BBY LE8 54 B4
Dovedale Rd LEIN LE4 12 C5
LEIS LE2 36 C4
Dove Ri LEIS LE2 45 G2
Dover St LEI LE1 3 G5
RLEIS/BBY LE8 71 H3
Downham Av LEIN LE4 19 E5
Downing Dr LEIE LE5 37 G2
Down St LEIN LE4 26 D1
Draper St LEIS LE2 36 A2
Drayton Rd LEIW LE3 24 C3
Dribdale RLEIS/BBY LE8 70 C4
Drinkstone Rd LEIE LE5 36 C1
The Drive LEIN LE4 19 G1
RLEINE/SYS LE7 29 F2
RLEIS/BBY LE8 64 B2
RLEIS/BBY LE8 72 B3
RLEIW/BAR LE9 48 B3
Dronfield St LEIE LE5 27 E5
Drovers Wy END/NAR LE19 52 D4
RLEIW/BAR LE9 30 B2
Drumcliff Rd LEIE LE5 29 E4
Drummond Rd
END/NAR LE19 40 C5
LEIN LE4 19 F4
Drury La LEIS LE2 44 D2
Dryden St LEI LE1 3 G2
Dudleston Cl LEIE LE5 28 A5
Dudley Av LEIE LE5 28 C4
Dudley Cl LEIE LE5 28 C4
Duffield Av WGSTN LE18 43 H4
Duffield St LEIS LE2 27 E5
Dukes Cl LEIN LE4 12 D5
WGSTN LE18 43 H5
Dukes Dr LEIS LE2 36 A3
Duke St LEI LE1 3 F6
Dulverton Cl WGSTN LE18 56 B3
Dulverton Rd LEIW LE3 25 G5
Dumbleton Av LEIW LE3 34 C4
Dunbar Rd LEIN LE4 20 C5
Dunblane Av LEIN LE4 20 B3
Duncan Av RLEIW/BAR LE9 51 H4
Duncan Rd LEIS LE2 42 D1
Duncombe Rd LEIW LE3 25 F1
Dundee Rd RLEIS/BBY LE8 54 B5
Dundonald Rd LEIN LE4 26 C1
Dunholme Rd LEIN LE4 27 G1
Dunire Cl LEIN LE4 18 C4
Dunkirk St LEI LE1 3 G6
Dunley Wy LUTT LE17 81 G2
Dunlin Rd LEIE LE5 27 E3
Dunslade Cl
MKTHBORO LE16 78 C2
Dunslade Gv
MKTHBORO LE16 78 B2
Dunslade Rd
MKTHBORO LE16 78 B2
Duns La LEIW LE3 2 C5
Dunstall Av LEIW LE3 33 F3
Dunster St LEIW LE3 25 F5
Dunton Rd RLEIW/BAR LE9 69 F5
Dunton St LEIW LE3 2 B1
WGSTN LE18 55 F2
Dupont Gdns LEIW LE3 24 B3
Durban Rd LEIN LE4 10 C5
Durham Dr WGSTN LE18 43 G4
Durnford Rd WGSTN LE18 56 A3
Durston Cl LEIE LE5 37 H1
Duxbury Rd LEIE LE5 27 G3
Dwyer Cl RLEINE/SYS LE7 12 D2
Dysart Wy LEI LE1 3 K1
Dyson Cl LUTT LE17 81 G2

E

Eagle Cl RLEIW/BAR LE9 68 C2
Ealing Rd LEIS LE2 35 F4
Eamont Cl LEIS LE2 42 D5
Earle Smith Cl
RLEIS/BBY LE8 53 H4
Earl Howe St LEIS LE2 3 K6
Earl Howe Ter LEIW LE3 2 B5
Earl Russell St LEIS LE2 42 C2
Earls Cl LEIN LE4 12 D5
Earl Shilton Rd
RLEIW/BAR LE9 50 A2
Earl St LEI LE1 3 G2
RLEIW/BAR LE9 49 G2
Earls Wy LEIN LE4 12 D5
Earlswood Rd LEIE LE5 37 H2
East Av LEIS LE2 36 A3
RLEINE/SYS LE7 5 E5
RLEIS/BBY LE8 53 H3
East Bond St LEI LE1 2 E2
Eastcourt Rd LEIS LE2 44 A2
East Equity Rd
RLEIW/BAR LE9 49 F4
Eastern Bvd LEIS LE2 35 E2
Eastfield Rd LEIN LE4 12 D4
LEIW LE3 25 F5
East Gn RLEIW/BAR LE9 48 A5
Eastleigh Rd LEIW LE3 34 C2
East Link END/NAR LE19 41 F1
Eastmere Rd WGSTN LE18 44 D5
East Park Rd LEIE LE5 36 A1
East Rd LEIN LE4 19 G3
East St LEI LE1 3 G5
LEIS LE2 45 E2
MKTHBORO LE16 77 G1
Eastway Rd WGSTN LE18 44 B4
Eastwood Rd LEIS LE2 42 D3
Ebchester Cl LEIS LE2 42 C5
Ebchester Rd LEIS LE2 42 C5
Edale Cl LEIW LE3 33 G2
Eddystone Rd LEIE LE5 29 E3
Eden Cl LEIS LE2 45 G2
Edenhall Cl LEIN LE4 20 B4
LEIS LE2 45 H4
Edenhurst Av LEIW LE3 41 H1
Eden Rd LEIS LE2 45 G2
Edensor St LEIN LE4 20 A4
Eden Wy LEIS LE2 54 D1
Edgbaston Cl LEIN LE4 10 D5
Edgcote Ct LEIE LE5 27 G2
Edgefield Cl LEIE LE5 21 F4
Edgehill Cl RLEIS/BBY LE8 58 D3
Edgehill Rd LEIN LE4 27 G1
Edgeley Cl LEIW LE3 25 E1
Edgeley Rd RLEIS/BBY LE8 65 F2
Edinburgh Cl
MKTHBORO LE16 74 D5
Edinburgh Rd
RLEIW/BAR LE9 48 D4
Edith Av LEIW LE3 42 A1
Edmonton Rd LEI LE1 3 H1
Edward Av LEIW LE3 33 H5
Edward Cl LEIS LE2 45 G3
Edward Dr LEIS LE2 55 E2
Edward Rd LEIS LE2 35 H3
MKTHBORO LE16 74 B4
RLEIS/BBY LE8 70 B4
Edward St LEIS LE5 27 E3
RLEINE/SYS LE7 17 G1
Egerton Av LEIN LE4 19 E5
Egginton St LEIE LE5 36 A1
Eglantine Cl LEIS LE2 45 E1
Eider Cl RLEIS/BBY LE8 63 G2
Eileen Av LEIN LE4 19 E5
Elbow La LEI LE1 2 D2
Eldon St LEI LE1 3 G2
Elgin Av LEIW LE3 24 D2
Elizabethan Wy LUTT LE17 81 H2
Elizabeth Cl RLEINE/SYS LE7 39 H1
RLEIS/BBY LE8 70 B5
Elizabeth Ct WGSTN LE18 56 A1
Elizabeth Crs WGSTN LE18 43 H4
Elizabeth Dr LEIN LE4 12 C4
LEIS LE2 45 G4
Elizabeth Gdns
RLEIS/BBY LE8 53 H4
Elizabeth Rd RLEIS/BBY LE8 70 B4
Elizabeth St LEIE LE5 27 G5
Elland Rd LEIW LE3 23 H5
Ellesmere Pl LEIW LE3 34 B3
Ellesmere Rd LEIW LE3 34 B3
Elliot Cl LEIS LE2 46 A4
RLEIS/BBY LE8 64 A2
RLEIS/BBY LE8 72 A3
Elliott Dr LEIN LE4 21 E1
LEIW LE3 32 D2
Elliott Rd LEIN LE4 18 D3
Ellis Av LEIN LE4 26 C1
Ellis Cl LEIW LE3 23 H2
Ellis Dr RLEIW/BAR LE9 32 B2
Ellis Flds LEIS LE2 46 A5
Ellison Cl RLEIW/BAR LE9 60 B3
WGSTN LE18 55 F3
Ellis St RLEINE/SYS LE7 17 F1
Ellwood Cl LEIE LE5 37 F1
Elm Av LUTT LE17 81 F3
Elm Cl GBY/RBY LE6 16 B5
Elmcroft Av LEIE LE5 28 B3
Elmdale Rd RLEIW/BAR LE9 48 D5
Elmdale St LEIN LE4 19 G5
Elm Dr MKTHBORO LE16 77 F2
Elmesthorpe La
RLEIW/BAR LE9 48 D5
Elmfield Av LEIN LE4 11 F5
LEIS LE2 36 A2
Elmhirst Rd LUTT LE17 81 F4
Elmhurst Cl END/NAR LE19 52 C4
Elms Cl LEIS LE2 45 E4
Elms La RLEIS/BBY LE8 59 H2
Elmsleigh Av LEIS LE2 36 B4
Elms Rd LEIS LE2 36 A5
The Elms RLEIS/BBY LE8 54 B3
RLEIS/BBY LE8 65 E2
Elmsthorpe Ri LEIW LE3 34 A2
Elm Tree Av LEIW LE3 23 G2
Elmtree Cl LEIE LE5 21 G5
Elm Tree Rd RLEIW/BAR LE9 63 E4
Elmwood Rw LEIS LE2 43 G4
Elsadene Av LEIN LE4 19 H4
Elsalene Dr GBY/RBY LE6 15 G2
Elsham Cl LEIW LE3 24 B5
Elston Flds LEIS LE2 43 F2
Elstree Av LEIE LE5 29 E2
Elsworthy Wk LEIW LE3 24 B4
Elwell Av RLEIW/BAR LE9 48 B2
Elwin Av WGSTN LE18 44 B4
Emberton Cl WGSTN LE18 44 D5
Emerson Cl LEIN LE4 18 A4
Emperor Wy RLEIS/BBY LE8 63 H2
Empire Rd LEIW LE3 2 A1
End Cl LEIW LE3 17 H4
Enderby Rd RLEIS/BBY LE8 53 G2
End Forsells
RLEINE/SYS LE7 39 H2
Englefield Rd LEIE LE5 28 D5
Ennerdale Cl LEIS LE2 45 H4
Ensbury Gdns LEIE LE5 37 F2
Epping Wy LEIS LE2 42 C5
Epsom Rd LEIN LE4 19 H5
Equity Rd END/NAR LE19 40 C5
LEIW LE3 2 A7
RLEIW/BAR LE9 49 E4
Erdyngton Rd LEIW LE3 33 H1
Erith Rd LEIS LE2 34 D4
Ernee Cl LEIW LE3 24 B3
Erskine St LEI LE1 3 H2
Ervin's Lock WGSTN LE18 55 G3
Ervin Wy RLEINE/SYS LE7 5 G3
Eskdale Cl LEIS LE2 45 H4
Essex Cl RLEIW/BAR LE9 30 B2
Essex Gdns
MKTHBORO LE16 77 G3
Essex Rd LEIN LE4 20 C5
WGSTN LE18 43 F5
Estima Cl LEIS LE2 36 A5
Estley Rd RLEIW/BAR LE9 68 C2
Estoril Av WGSTN LE18 44 D5
Ethel Rd LEIE LE5 36 C1
Eton Cl LEIS LE2 35 H5
Eunice Av RLEIW/BAR LE9 51 H4
Euston St LEIS LE2 35 F4
Evelyn Dr LEIW LE3 34 C3
Evelyn Rd LEIW LE3 33 G3
Everard Wy END/NAR LE19 41 G3
Everest Ct LEI LE1 3 J1
Everett Cl LEIN LE4 21 E1
Every St LEI LE1 3 F4
Evesham Rd LEIW LE3 34 C3
Evington Cl LEIE LE5 36 C1
Evington Dr LEIE LE5 36 C2
Evington La LEIE LE5 36 D2
Evington Ms LEIE LE5 37 F2
Evington Parks Rd LEIS LE2 36 B2
Evington Rd LEIE LE5 36 A2
LEIS LE2 3 K7
Evington St LEIS LE2 3 K6
Evington Valley Rd LEIE LE5 36 B2
Excalibur Cl LEIW LE3 32 C3
Exeter Rd WGSTN LE18 43 H5
Exmoor Av LEIN LE4 25 H2
Exmoor Cl WGSTN LE18 56 B2
Exploration Dr LEIN LE4 19 F5
Exton Rd LEIE LE5 27 G3
Eyebrook Cl LEIE LE5 21 G4
Eynsford Cl LEIS LE2 36 D5

F

Factory La MKTHBORO LE16 77 H1
Fair Acre Rd
RLEIW/BAR LE9 * 48 A5
Fairacre Rd RLEIW/BAR LE9 48 A5
Fairbourne Rd LEIW LE3 34 A4
Fairefield Crs LEIW LE3 17 F5
Faire Rd LEIW LE3 24 B1
Fairestone Av LEIW LE3 24 A2
Fairfax Cl LEIN LE4 20 C5
Fairfax Rd LEIN LE4 20 C5
MKTHBORO LE16 77 H2
Fairfield Rd LEIS LE2 45 F2
MKTHBORO LE16 74 B5
Fairfield St LEIE LE5 27 E5
WGSTN LE18 55 F1
Fairford Av LEIE LE5 37 F2
Fairhaven Rd
RLEINE/SYS LE7 9 G4
Fairholme Rd LEIS LE2 43 G2
Fairisle Wy RLEIS/BBY LE8 65 F3
Fairstone Hl LEIS LE2 45 F4
Fairview Av RLEIS/BBY LE8 53 H4
Fairway MKTHBORO LE16 74 B5
RLEIS/BBY LE8 72 B4
The Fairway LEIS LE2 36 D5
LEIS LE2 43 F2
RLEIS/BBY LE8 54 A4
RLEIW/BAR LE9 32 B1
Falcon Cl LEIW LE3 32 A3
RLEIW/BAR LE9 68 C2
Falconer Crs LEIW LE3 24 C2
Falcon Rd RLEINE/SYS LE7 17 F1
Faldo Cl LEIN LE4 20 C2

Fallow Cl RLEIW/BAR LE9 ......68 D5
Fallowfield Rd LEIE LE5 ....37 H1
Falmouth Dr WGSTN LE18......56 A2
Falmouth Rd LEIE LE5 ....36 D1
Faringdon Av LUTT LE17 ....81 H3
Farleigh Av WGSTN LE18 ....44 A5
Farleigh Cl RLEIW/BAR LE9 ....68 C2
Farley Rd LEIS LE2 ....36 B5
Farley Wy RLEIW/BAR LE9......23 F4
Farm Cl END/NAR LE19 ....53 E5
LEIN LE4 ....11 H5
LEIS LE2 ....43 F3
Farmers Cl LEIW LE3...............23 G2
Farm Rd RLEIW/BAR LE9 ....48 C3
Farmway LEIW LE3..................41 G1
Farndale WGSTN LE18 ....56 D1
Farndale Vw
MKTHBORO LE16..................77 E2
Farndon Dr RLEIW/BAR LE9 ..60 A4
Farndon Rd
MKTHBORO LE16..................76 B5
MKTHBORO LE16..................77 G3
Farnham St LEIE LE5 ....27 E4
Farnworth Cl LEIN LE4...........20 B4
Farrier La LEIN LE4 ....18 B4
Farriers' Wy RLEINE/SYS LE7 ..5 F2
Farringdon St LEIE LE5 ....27 E3
Farr Wood Cl GBY/RBY LE6....16 A4
Farthingdale Cl
RLEIW/BAR LE9 ....63 G3
Fastnet Rd LEIE LE5 ....29 E3
Faversham Cl LEIW LE3 ....24 A4
Fayrhurst Rd LEIS LE2 ....43 E2
Featherby Dr LEIS LE2 ....42 A5
Featherstone Dr LEIS LE2 ......54 C1
Feature Rd LEIN LE4...............12 C4
Federation St
END/NAR LE19......................52 C1
Feildingway LUTT LE17 ....81 G2
Feldspar Cl END/NAR LE19 ....40 C3
Felley Wy LEIW LE3 ....25 G2
Felstead Rd LEIN LE4 ....18 D3
Fenners Cl LEIN LE4 ....10 C5
Fenton Cl LEIS LE2 ....45 E5
Fenwick Rd LEIS LE2 ....46 A4
Fermain Cl LEIE LE5 ....28 D5
Fern Bank LEIE LE5 * 27 E4
Fern Cl LEIE LE5.......................29 E5
Fern Crs GBY/RBY LE6 ....15 H3
Ferndale Dr GBY/RBY LE6 ......22 D2
Ferndale Rd LEIN LE4.............20 C1
LEIS LE2 ....43 H2
Ferndown Cl LEIW LE3............24 A4
Fernhurst Rd LEIW LE3 ....33 H5
Fernie Cl LEIS LE2 ....45 G4
Fernie Dene RLEIS/BBY LE8 ..59 E2
Fernie Rd LEIE LE5 ....27 F3
MKTHBORO LE16..................78 A1
Fernlea END/NAR LE19 ....52 B2
Fern Ley Cl
MKTHBORO LE16..................78 C2
Fernleys Cl LEIN LE4...............18 B4
Fern Ri LEIE LE5 ....28 C1
Ferrars Ct LEIW LE3 ....33 F4
Ferrers Ri GBY/RBY LE6..........16 A4
Ferrers Rd LUTT LE17.............81 F4
Ferrers St LEIS LE2 ....43 F3
Ferrous Cl LEIN LE4 ....27 E2
Festival Av LEIN LE4...............20 B1
Field Cl END/NAR LE19...........53 E4
Field Court Rd GBY/RBY LE6..16 B4
Fieldfare Wk LEIE LE5 * 27 E3
Fieldgate Crs LEIN LE4...........11 E4
Fieldhead Cl
MKTHBORO LE16..................77 F1
Fieldhouse Rd LEIN LE4..........19 G4
Fieldhurst Av LEIW LE3 ....33 G5
Fielding Rd LEIN LE4 ....11 F5
Field Vw LEIN LE4...................13 E5
Field Wy RLEIW/BAR LE9........48 D3
Fieldway Crs RLEIS/BBY LE8..58 D2
The Fieldway
RLEIW/BAR LE9 ....68 D4
Filbert St LEIS LE2..................35 E2
Filbert St East LEIS LE2 ....35 F2
Fillingate RLEINE/SYS LE7 ......11 H1
Finch Cl LEIW LE3 ....24 C5
Finch Wy END/NAR LE19 ....52 B4
Fineshade Av LEIW LE3 ....25 G2
Finsbury Rd LEIN LE4..............27 E1
Finson Cl WGSTN LE18 ....44 B5
Fiona Dr LEIE LE5 ....29 E5
Firestone Cl LEIW LE3 ....24 A4
Firfield Av LEIN LE4 ....11 G5
The Firs RLEINE/SYS LE7 ....13 E2
Firtree Av LUTT LE17 ....81 F3
Fir Tree Av RLEIS/BBY LE8......65 E2
Firtree Cl RLEIW/BAR LE9 ......48 B3
Fir Tree Cl WGSTN LE18 ....44 A3
Fir Tree La GBY/RBY LE6 ....16 A3
Fisher Cl RLEIW/BAR LE9 ....60 A4
Fishley Cl LEIW LE3..................23 H3
Fishponds Cl LEIW LE3...........23 H2
Fishpools LEIW LE3..................41 G1
Fitzroy St LEIW LE3 ....2 A4
Fitzwilliam Cl LEIS LE2 ....45 H4
Flamborough Rd LEIE LE5 ....28 D3
Flamingo Dr RLEIS/BBY LE8 ..63 H2
Flatholme Rd LEIE LE5............29 E2
Flaxfield Cl GBY/RBY LE6........16 B4
Flaxland Cl
MKTHBORO LE16..................78 C2
Flax Rd LEIN LE4 ....19 H5
Fleckney Rd RLEIS/BBY LE8 ..70 C5
RLEIS/BBY LE8......................71 F3
The Fleet RLEIW/BAR LE9 ......60 C3
Fleetwood Cl
MKTHBORO LE16..................77 G3
Fleetwood Gdns
MKTHBORO LE16..................77 G3
Fleetwood Rd LEIS LE2 ....35 G4
Fletcher Rd RLEIW/BAR LE9 ..60 C3
Fletchers Cl END/NAR LE19....52 D4
Fletchers' Wy
RLEINE/SYS LE7......................5 F2
Flora St LEIW LE3 ....2 A4
Florence Av WGSTN LE18........55 G2
Florence Rd LEIE LE5 ....27 E4
Florence St LEIS LE2...............43 E1
Florence Wragg Wy
LEIS LE2 ....46 A4
Floyd Cl LEIN LE4 ....20 C2
Folville Ri LEIW LE3.................34 A3
Fontwell Dr LEIS LE2 ....42 B3
Forbes Cl LEIW LE3 ....24 A3
Ford Cl LEIS LE2......................42 C5
Ford Ri LEIS LE2 ....42 C5
The Ford RLEIS/BBY LE8 ....54 C3
Fordview Cl RLEIS/BBY LE8....58 C2
Forest Av LEIN LE4 ....12 B4
Forest Cl GBY/RBY LE6............15 H4
Forest Dr RLEIW/BAR LE9 ......32 A1
Foresters Cl LEIW LE3 ....23 H2
Forest Ga RLEINE/SYS LE7......17 F1
Forest House La LEIW LE3.....32 B4
Forest Ri GBY/RBY LE6 ....15 H4
LEIS LE2 ....45 G2
RLEINE/SYS LE7....................29 F5
RLEIW/BAR LE9 ....30 C2
RLEIW/BAR LE9 ....32 B2
Forest Rd COAL LE67 ....6 A4
END/NAR LE19......................40 B3
LEIE LE5 ....27 E3
RLEIW/BAR LE9 ....51 H1
Forest Vw GBY/RBY LE6 ....15 H3
Forest View Rd
RLEIW/BAR LE9 ....48 C4
Forge Cl LEIW LE3 ....23 G2
RLEIS/BBY LE8......................70 B3
Forrester Cl RLEIW/BAR LE9 ..63 F3
Forryan Cl RLEIW/BAR LE9 ....63 F4
Forryans Cl WGSTN LE18 ......56 C3
Forsythia Cl LUTT LE17 ....81 E3
Fosse Cl END/NAR LE19 ....53 F1
HINC LE10.............................66 B5
Fosse La LEIW LE3..................25 G3
Fosse Park Av
END/NAR LE19......................41 H2
Fosse Pk South
END/NAR LE19......................41 H4
Fosse Rd Central LEIW LE3 ....25 G5
Fosse Rd North LEIW LE3 ......25 G4
Fosse Rd South LEIW LE3 ......34 B3
Fosse Wy RLEINE/SYS LE7 ......12 D2
Foston Ga WGSTN LE18 ....56 C3
Foston La RLEIS/BBY LE8 ......65 F2
Fothergill Cl
MKTHBORO LE16..................78 C1
Foulds La RLEIS/BBY LE8........54 A2
Foundry La LEI LE1.................26 B3
RLEINE/SYS LE7....................12 D1
Foundry Sq LEI LE1 * 26 C3
Fountains Av LEIS LE2 ....42 D5
Fowler Cl LEIN LE4 ....18 C3
Fox Covert RLEIS/BBY LE8 ....63 H1
Foxcroft Cl LEIW LE3 ....34 C5
Foxfield Cl LUTT LE17.............81 H4
Foxglove Cl END/NAR LE19....52 C3
RLEINE/SYS LE7......................5 G2
RLEIW/BAR LE9 ....69 E5
Foxglove Dr GBY/RBY LE6 ....16 C4
Foxglove Rd LEIE LE5 ....21 G5
Foxhill Dr LEIS LE2 ....42 A5
Foxholes Rd LEIW LE3 ....33 E1
Fox Hollies HINC LE10 ....66 B5
Fox Hollow LEIS LE2...............45 H4
RLEINE/SYS LE7......................5 F1
Foxhunter Dr LEIS LE2...........44 D2
Fox La LEI LE1 ....3 F3
RLEIW/BAR LE9 ....22 D4
Foxon St LEIW LE3 ....2 B5
Foxon Wy LEIW LE3 ....33 F4
Foxpond La RLEIS/BBY LE8....58 A2
Fox St LEI LE1 ....3 H4
Foxton Lock Cl WGSTN LE18..55 G3
Fox Yd MKTHBORO LE16 *......78 A1
Frampton Av LEIW LE3 ....25 F5
Franche Rd LEIW LE3 ....25 G4
Francis Av LEIW LE3 ....41 H1
Francis St LEIS LE2 ....36 B4
Frank Booton Cl
RLEIW/BAR LE9 ....49 H3
Franklin Wy RLEIS/BBY LE8 ..63 H1
Franklyn Rd LEIS LE2 ....42 B3
Frankson Av LEIW LE3 ....34 A4
Fraser Cl LEI LE1 ....3 H1
Frederick Cl RLEINE/SYS LE7....5 G3
Frederick Rd LEIE LE5 ....27 E4
Frederick St WGSTN LE18 ......44 B5
Fredscott Cl LEIE LE5 ....29 E3
Freeboard Rd LEIW LE3.........41 H1
Freehold Rd LEIN LE4.............19 G2
Freehold St LEI LE1 ....3 K1
Freeman Rd North
LEIE LE5 ....27 H3
Freeman's Wy
RLEINE/SYS LE7......................5 G1
Freemantle Rd LEIS LE2 ....36 C4
Freemens Common Rd
LEIS LE2 ....35 F3
Freer Cl RLEINE/SYS LE7 ....39 G2
RLEIS/BBY LE8......................54 B3
WGSTN LE18.........................56 C3
Freeschool La LEI LE1 ....2 D3
French Rd LEIE LE5..................27 G3
Frensham Cl LEIS LE2.............45 E4
Freshwater Cl WGSTN LE18....56 A3
Frewen Dr RLEIW/BAR LE9 ....66 D1
Frewin St LEIE LE5 ....27 G3
Friar La LEI LE1 ....2 D5
Friars Cswy LEI LE1 ....2 C3
Friday St LEI LE1 ....2 D1
Frinton Av LEIE LE5 ....37 H1
Frisby Rd LEIE LE5 ....27 E2
RLEIW/BAR LE9 ....48 B4
Friswell La RLEIW/BAR LE9 ....48 A4
Fritchley Cl RLEIW/BAR LE9 ..52 A4
Frith Cl LEIW LE3....................24 A2
Froanes Cl END/NAR LE19......40 C4
Frog Island LEIW LE3 ....25 H3
Frolesworth Rd LEIW LE3 ......24 C4
RLEIW/BAR LE9 ....68 C4
Frolesworth Wy LEIW LE3......24 C4
Frome Av LEIS LE2 ....45 H2
Front St LEIN LE4 ....19 H1
Fulbeck Av LEIE LE5...............37 H1
Fulford Rd LEIW LE3...............24 A5
Fuller Cl RLEIW/BAR LE9 ....30 C1
Fullhurst Av LEIW LE3 ....34 B2
Fulmar Rd RLEINE/SYS LE7 ....17 F2
Furlong Cl RLEINE/SYS LE7 * ..13 G1
Furlongs Cl RLEINE/SYS LE7 ..13 G1
The Furlongs
MKTHBORO LE16..................78 C1
Furnival Cl RLEIS/BBY LE8......70 A3
Furrows Cl END/NAR LE19 ....53 E5

G

Gaddesby Av LEIW LE3...........34 C2
Gainsborough Rd LEIS LE2 ....35 H5
RLEIS/BBY LE8......................72 A2
Galahad Cl LEIW LE3...............32 C3
Galby St LEIE LE5 ....27 F3
Gale Cl LUTT LE17 ....81 G1
Gallards Hl LEIW LE3..............33 G1
Galleywood Dr LEIN LE4 ....18 D5
Gallimore Cl LEIW LE3 ....24 C1
Gallowtree Ga LEI LE1 ....3 F3
Galsworthy Ct LEIW LE3 ....25 E5
Galway Rd LEIN LE4 ....19 E2
Gamekeepers Ct LEIE LE5 ......21 G4
Gamel Rd LEIE LE5 ....28 B5
Ganton Rd LEIW LE3...............24 A4
Garden Cl LEIS LE2 ....45 E3
Gardenfield Rd LEIN LE4 ....20 D3
Garden St LEI LE1 ....3 F1
LEIN LE4 ....12 C5
WGSTN LE18.........................55 F2
Gardiner St
MKTHBORO LE16..................77 F1
Garendon St LEIS LE2...............3 K3
Garendon Wy GBY/RBY LE6 ..16 A5
Garfield Pk RLEIS/BBY LE8 ....58 D2
Garfield St LEIN LE4 ....26 C2
Garfit Rd RLEIW/BAR LE9........23 E5
Garland Crs LEIW LE3 ....25 F2
Garnett Crs LEIS LE2...............42 C4
Garsdale WGSTN LE18 ....56 D1
Garth Av LEIN LE4..................19 E3
Gartree Crs RLEIW/BAR LE9 ..48 D3
Gartree Rd LEIS LE2 ....36 D4
LEIS LE2 ....47 E3
Gascoigne Av
RLEINE/SYS LE7......................5 G4
Gas La WGSTN LE18.................56 A2
Gas St LEI LE1 ....26 B3
Gateway St LEIS LE2.................2 D6
Gaulby La LEIS LE2 ....37 H5
Gaul St LEIW LE3 ....2 A7
Gavin Cl LEIW LE3 ....33 E3
Gayhurst Cl LEIW LE3 ....41 H1
WGSTN LE18.........................56 C1
Gayton Av LEIN LE4 ....27 E1
Gayton Hts END/NAR LE19 ....40 C4
Geary Cl END/NAR LE19..........52 D4
GBY/RBY LE6 ....23 E2
Gedding Rd LEIE LE5 ....27 G5
Geddington Cl WGSTN LE18 ..56 C1
Gedge Wy LEIS LE2.................43 E2
Gees Lock Cl LEIS LE2 ....42 B4
Gelert Av LEIE LE5..................28 D4
George Foster Cl
RLEIW/BAR LE9 ....49 F2
George Geary Cl
RLEIW/BAR LE9 ....48 C4
Georgeham Cl WGSTN LE18 ..56 B2
George Hill Cl
RLEIW/BAR LE9 ....60 B3
George Marriott Cl
RLEIW/BAR LE9 ....60 A5
George St END/NAR LE19 ......40 C5
LEI LE1 ....3 G1
LUTT LE17.............................81 G3
RLEINE/SYS LE7....................17 F1
RLEIW/BAR LE9 ....48 B4
George Toon Ct
RLEINE/SYS LE7 * 4 C5
George Ward Ct
RLEIW/BAR LE9 ....48 B4
Gerrard Gdns
MKTHBORO LE16..................77 G4
Gervas Rd LEIE LE5.................28 C3
Geveze Wy RLEIW/BAR LE9....69 E5
Gibbons Cl LEIN LE4 ....26 C2
Gibson Cl WGSTN LE18 ....44 B5
Gibson Wy LUTT LE17.............81 E4
Gifford Cl LEIE LE5 ....37 F2
Gilbert Cl LEIN LE4 ....20 C3
MKTHBORO LE16..................78 C2
Gillam Butts RLEIS/BBY LE8 ..65 E3
Gillbank Dr GBY/RBY LE6........22 C2
Gilliver St LEIS LE2 ....35 H5
Gillman Rd LEIW LE3..............25 E2
Gilmorton Av LEIS LE2 ....42 B4
Gilmorton Cl LEIS LE2............42 B4
Gilmour Cl LEIN LE4 ....18 B2
Gilstead Cl RLEINE/SYS LE7 ....38 B1
Gimson Av RLEIW/BAR LE9 ....63 F3
Gimson Cl LEIE LE5 ....28 A1
Gimson Rd LEIW LE3...............25 F5
Gipsy La LEIE LE5 ....27 H1
LEIN LE4 ....20 A5
Gipsy Rd LEIN LE4...................19 H5
The Glade LEIW LE3 ....41 H1
Gladstone Ms
RLEIW/BAR LE9 *..................68 C2
Gladstone St LEI LE1 ....3 G2
LUTT LE17.............................81 H3
MKTHBORO LE16..................78 A2
RLEINE/SYS LE7....................17 G1
RLEIS/BBY LE8......................70 B4
RLEIS/BBY LE8......................71 H3
WGSTN LE18.........................44 B5
Glaisdale Cl LEIN LE4 ....18 C4
Glaisdale Rd WGSTN LE18 ......56 C2
Glamorgan Av WGSTN LE18 ..55 F1
Glazebrook Rd LEIW LE3 ....24 D1
Glazebrook Sq LEIW LE3 ....25 E2
Glean Cl RLEIW/BAR LE9 ....68 D5
Glebe Cl LEIS LE2....................44 C1
LEIW LE3...............................23 H2
WGSTN LE18.........................44 B5
Glebe Dr RLEIS/BBY LE8..........64 D3
Glebelands Rd LEIN LE4.........10 D4
The Glebelands
RLEIS/BBY LE8......................58 C3
Glebe Rd GBY/RBY LE6...........16 A4
LEIS LE2 ....44 D1
MKTHBORO LE16..................78 B2
RLEINE/SYS LE7......................5 G4
RLEIW/BAR LE9 ....68 C3
Glebe St LEIS LE2.....................3 H6
Glebe Wy RLEINE/SYS LE7 ....4 B5
RLEINE/SYS LE7....................12 C1
Glenbarr Av LEIN LE4 ....25 H2
Glenborne Rd LEIS LE2...........43 G4
Glencoe Av LEIN LE4...............20 A3
Glendale Av LEIW LE3.............16 D4
Glendon St LEIN LE4...............26 D1
Glendower Cl LEIE LE5 ....28 B4
Gleneagles Av LEIN LE4 ....20 B3
Glenfield Crs LEIW LE3 ....24 A2
Glenfield Frith Dr LEIW LE3....24 B1
Glenfield La RLEIW/BAR LE9 ..23 E4
Glenfield Rd LEIW LE3 ....24 D3
Glenfield Rd East LEIW LE3 ....25 G5
Glenfrith Cl LEIW LE3 ....17 H4
Glenfrith Wy LEIW LE3 ....17 H5
Glengarry Cl LEIW LE3 ....25 E3
Glengarry Ct LEIW LE3 ....24 D3
Glengarry Wy LEIW LE3 ....24 D2
Glen Ga WGSTN LE18 ....55 F1
Glenhills Bvd LEIS LE2 ....42 D3
Glenhills Wy LEIS LE2 ....42 D3
Glenmore Rd LEIN LE4 ....20 B4
Glen Park Av LEIW LE3 ....16 D5
Glen Ri LEIS LE2 ....42 B5
RLEIS/BBY LE8......................58 B2
Glen Rd LEIS LE2 ....45 G4
RLEIS/BBY LE8......................57 H4
Glenrothes Cl LEIW LE3 ....24 A5
Glen St LEIN LE4 ....26 D1
Glenville Av LEIS LE2..............54 B1
LEIW LE3...............................17 E5
Glen Wy LEIS LE2....................45 G4
Glossop St LEIE LE5 ....36 A2
Gloucester Av
RLEINE/SYS LE7......................5 E5
Gloucester Cl
RLEIW/BAR LE9 ....30 B3
Gloucester Crs WGSTN LE18 ..43 F5
Glyn Cl RLEIW/BAR LE9..........48 A4
Goddard Cl RLEINE/SYS LE7 ..29 G5
Goddards Cl LEIN LE4 ....18 B5
Goddards Slang LEIS LE2........45 E3
Godfrey Cl LEIN LE4 ....18 A1
Godwin Av WGSTN LE18..........56 C1
Godwin Ct WGSTN LE18 * 56 B1
Goldhill LEIS LE2 ....43 G4
Goldhill Gdns LEIS LE2 ....44 B1
Goldsmith Rd LEIW LE3 ....34 A1
Golf Course La LEIW LE3 ....24 A5
Goode's Av RLEINE/SYS LE7 ..13 F2
Goode's La RLEINE/SYS LE7....13 E1
Goodheart Wy LEIW LE3 ....33 E3
Gooding Av LEIW LE3..............33 H2
Gooding Cl LEIW LE3 ....34 B2
Goodwood Cl
MKTHBORO LE16..................78 C1
Goodwood Crs LEIE LE5 ....37 F1
Goodwood Rd LEIE LE5..........28 B5
Gopsall St LEIS LE2 ....3 K6
Gordon Av LEIS LE2 ....3 K7
Gores La MKTHBORO LE16......78 B1
Gorham Ri RLEIW/BAR LE9 ....68 B2
Gorse Hl LEIN LE4 ....17 H2

Gorse La LEIS LE2 45 H5
RLEINE/SYS LE7 12 D1
Gorsty Cl LEIN LE4 18 B4
Goscote Dr LUTT LE17 81 G3
Goscote Hall Rd LEIN LE4 19 F1
Goshawk Cl RLEIW/BAR LE9 68 C2
Gosling St LEIS LE2 2 D6
Gotham St LEIS LE2 3 J6
Gough Rd LEIE LE5 27 G4
Goward St MKTHBORO LE16 77 H1
Gower St LEI LE1 3 G1
Grace Gdns LEIS LE2 * 43 E1
Grace Rd LEIS LE2 35 E5
RLEIW/BAR LE9 30 B2
RLEIW/BAR LE9 67 E1
Grafton Dr WGSTN LE18 56 D1
Grafton Pl LEI LE1 2 E1
Graham St LEIE LE5 3 J2
Grampian Cl LEIS LE2 43 F1
Granary Cl LEIW LE3 23 H3
RLEIS/BBY LE8 72 A4
Granby Av LEIE LE5 * 27 F4
Granby Rd LEIS LE2 42 D1
Granby St LEI LE1 3 G4
Grange Av LEIW LE3 32 C2
RLEINE/SYS LE7 5 H1
Grange Cl GBY/RBY LE6 22 D2
LEIS LE2 42 C5
LEIW LE3 23 H2
RLEIS/BBY LE8 58 D2
Grange Ct RLEIW/BAR LE9 30 B1
Grange Dr LEIS LE2 42 B5
RLEIS/BBY LE8 53 H3
Grange La LEIS LE2 2 E6
RLEINE/SYS LE7 38 A1
Grange Rd RLEIW/BAR LE9 68 C3
WGSTN LE18 44 B4
The Grange RLEIW/BAR LE9 49 E4
Grangeway Rd WGSTN LE18 44 A4
Granite Cl END/NAR LE19 40 C4
Grantham Av
RLEIW/BAR LE9 68 B1
Grantham Rd LEIE LE5 28 C2
Granville Av LEIS LE2 44 D2
Granville Crs WGSTN LE18 43 H3
Granville Rd LEI LE1 35 H2
WGSTN LE18 44 A3
Granville St
MKTHBORO LE16 77 H3
Grape St LEI LE1 2 D2
Grasmere Rd WGSTN LE18 44 D5
Grasmere St LEIS LE2 2 C7
Grass Acres LEIW LE3 41 G1
Grassington Cl LEIN LE4 18 C3
Grassington Dr WGSTN LE18 56 C2
Gravel St LEI LE1 2 E2
The Gravel RLEIS/BBY LE8 59 H3
Grays Ct END/NAR LE19 40 C5
Gray St LEIS LE2 2 C6
Grayswood Dr LEIN LE4 10 A5
Great Arler Rd LEIS LE2 35 G5
Great Bowden Rd
MKTHBORO LE16 75 E5
Great Central St LEIW LE3 2 C2
Great Central Wy LEIW LE3 34 D3
Great Meadow Rd LEIN LE4 18 B5
Grebe Wy RLEIS/BBY LE8 63 H2
Greenacre Dr LEIE LE5 37 F1
Greenacres Dr LUTT LE17 81 F3
Greenbank Dr LEIS LE2 45 F3
Greenbank Rd LEIE LE5 28 D1
Greencoat Rd LEIW LE3 24 C3
Greendale Rd LEIS LE2 42 B5
Greenfields RLEIS/BBY LE8 53 H4
Greengate La LEIN LE4 11 E5
Greenhill Cl END/NAR LE19 52 B4
Greenhill Dr RLEIW/BAR LE9 48 B4
Greenhill Rd LEIS LE2 35 H4
Greenhithe Rd LEIS LE2 34 D4
Greenland Av LEIE LE5 28 A2
Greenland Dr LEIE LE5 28 A2
Green La MKTHBORO LE16 77 H3
RLEIS/BBY LE8 65 F2
RLEIW/BAR LE9 49 E2
Green Lane Cl LEIE LE5 27 H4
Green Lane Rd LEIE LE5 27 F3
Green Rd RLEIW/BAR LE9 68 C2
Greenside Pl LEIS LE2 43 F3
Greensward
RLEINE/SYS LE7 5 G1
The Green COAL LE67 6 B4
MKTHBORO LE16 76 B1
RLEIW/BAR LE9 51 H4
RLEIW/BAR LE9 61 G1
Green Wk LEIW LE3 24 C5
Greenway RLEIS/BBY LE8 72 A3
The Greenway LEIN LE4 19 G5
Greenwich Cl
END/NAR LE19 52 D3
Greenwood Rd LEIE LE5 27 H4
Gregory Cl LEIN LE4 13 E5
Gregorys Cl LEIW LE3 33 F4
Gregson Cl LEIN LE4 20 B2
Grendon Cl WGSTN LE18 44 C5
Grenfell Rd LEIS LE2 44 C1
Grenville Gdns
MKTHBORO LE16 77 G3
Gresley Cl LEIN LE4 18 C3
RLEINE/SYS LE7 29 F4
Gretna Wy LEIE LE5 29 E3
Grey Cl GBY/RBY LE6 16 B4
Grey Crs GBY/RBY LE6 7 H3
Grey Friars LEI LE1 2 E4
Greylag Wy RLEIS/BBY LE8 63 H2
Greyland Paddock
GBY/RBY LE6 16 B4
Greys Dr GBY/RBY LE6 16 A5
Greystoke Cl LEIN LE4 19 E4
Greystone Av LEIE LE5 28 B4
Griffin Cl LEIN LE4 20 D2
Grimston Cl LEIN LE4 21 E3
Grisedale Cl LEIS LE2 35 E2
Grizedale Gv END/NAR LE19 52 B2
Groby La GBY/RBY LE6 7 H5
Groby Rd GBY/RBY LE6 22 D1
LEIW LE3 16 D4
LEIW LE3 24 D1
LEIW LE3 25 G2
RLEINE/SYS LE7 17 E2
Grocot Rd LEIE LE5 37 E2
Grosvenor Cl LEIS LE2 54 D2
Grosvenor Crs LEIS LE2 44 D1
Grosvenor St LEI LE1 3 G1
Grovebury Rd LEIN LE4 19 E4
Grove Rd LEIE LE5 27 E4
RLEIS/BBY LE8 53 H5
The Grove RLEIW/BAR LE9 30 A2
Grove Wy END/NAR LE19 41 H3
Guild Cl RLEINE/SYS LE7 9 H1
Guildford Dr WGSTN LE18 43 H3
Guildford Rd LEIS LE2 36 C4
Guildhall La LEI LE1 2 D4
Guinevere Wy LEIW LE3 32 C3
Gullet La RLEIW/BAR LE9 22 C5
Gumley Sq END/NAR LE19 40 D5
Gunnsbrook Cl
MKTHBORO LE16 75 E3
Gunthorpe Rd LEIW LE3 33 F1
Gurnall Rd LEIN LE4 18 A3
Gurney Crs END/NAR LE19 53 E5
Guthlaxton Av LEIS LE2 3 J5
LUTT LE17 81 G3
Guthlaxton Gap
RLEIW/BAR LE9 62 A2
Guthlaxton St LEIS LE2 3 K5
Guthlaxton Wy WGSTN LE18 56 C3
Guthridge Crs LEIW LE3 34 B2
Gwencole Av LEIW LE3 34 A5
Gwencole Crs LEIW LE3 42 A1
Gwendolen Rd LEIE LE5 27 F5
Gwendolin Av LEIN LE4 11 H5
Gwendoline Dr
RLEIS/BBY LE8 64 D2
Gynsill Cl RLEINE/SYS LE7 17 G2
Gynsill La RLEINE/SYS LE7 17 F4

H

Hackett Rd LEIW LE3 24 D2
Haddenham Rd LEIW LE3 34 C3
Haddon Cl RLEINE/SYS LE7 12 D1
Haddon St LEIS LE2 27 E5
Hadrian Cl RLEINE/SYS LE7 12 C2
Hadrian Rd LEIN LE4 12 C5
LEIN LE4 19 E2
Hagley Cl MKTHBORO LE16 78 C1
Haig Pl LEIW LE3 * 34 A3
Halcroft Ri WGSTN LE18 56 B2
The Half Cft RLEINE/SYS LE7 4 C5
Half Moon Crs LEIS LE2 45 G2
Halford Cl RLEIS/BBY LE8 53 H5
RLEIS/BBY LE8 58 D3
Halford Rd RLEIS/BBY LE8 71 H3
Halford St LEI LE1 3 F4
RLEINE/SYS LE7 13 E1
Halifax Dr LEIN LE4 19 E4
Halkin St LEIN LE4 26 D1
Hallam Av LEIN LE4 11 F5
Hallam Crs East LEIW LE3 33 H3
Hallaton Rd LEIE LE5 27 H2
Hallaton St LEIS LE2 43 E1
Hallbrook Rd
RLEIW/BAR LE9 68 D5
Hall Cl LEIS LE2 42 B5
RLEIS/BBY LE8 71 H2
Hallcroft Av RLEIS/BBY LE8 65 E3
Hall Dr LEIS LE2 45 F2
Halley Cl LEIN LE4 18 A1
Hall Farm Cl RLEINE/SYS LE7 5 H4
Hall Farm Crs
RLEIW/BAR LE9 69 E4
Hall Farm Rd
RLEINE/SYS LE7 10 B2
Hall Gdns RLEIS/BBY LE8 58 D3
Hall La LEIS LE2 42 C1
Hall Rd RLEINE/SYS LE7 29 F2
Halls Crs HINC LE10 66 C5
Hall Wk END/NAR LE19 40 D4
Halsbury St LEIS LE2 36 B2
Halstead St LEIE LE5 27 F4
Halter Slade WGSTN LE18 56 C2
Hamble Cl RLEIW/BAR LE9 30 B2
Hamble Rd LEIS LE2 45 G2
Hambleton Cl LEIW LE3 32 B3
Hamelin Rd LEIW LE3 33 H1
Hamilford Cl LEIE LE5 29 E1
Hamilton St LEIS LE2 3 K7
Hamilton Wy LEIE LE5 21 F5
Hammond Wy
MKTHBORO LE16 74 C5
Hampden Rd LEIN LE4 20 C5
Hampshire Rd LEIS LE2 42 D1
Hampstead Cl
END/NAR LE19 52 D3
Hampton Cl LEIS LE2 54 D2
WGSTN LE18 56 C1
Hanbury Rd LEIE LE5 37 H1
Hand Av LEIW LE3 33 G2
Handley St LEIS LE2 43 E1
Hanover Cl LEIE LE5 28 B1
Hansen Ct WGSTN LE18 55 G1
Haramead Rd LEI LE1 3 K1
Harborough Rd
MKTHBORO LE16 74 A1
MKTHBORO LE16 75 H4
MKTHBORO LE16 76 C1
MKTHBORO LE16 78 D4
MKTHBORO LE16 79 E2
RLEIS/BBY LE8 72 B3
Harcourt Cl RLEINE/SYS LE7 4 C5
Harcourt Rd
RLEIS/BBY LE8 71 H3
WGSTN LE18 56 C2
Harcourt St
MKTHBORO LE16 77 G1
Harcourt Wy END/NAR LE19 41 F2
Hardie Crs LEIW LE3 33 F3
Harding St LEI LE1 2 C1
Hardwick Ct LEIW LE3 34 C2
Hardwick Crs
RLEINE/SYS LE7 12 D1
Hardwicke Rd
END/NAR LE19 52 B3
Hardwick Rd LEIE LE5 37 H1
Hardy's Av LEIN LE4 20 A3
Harebell Cl LEIE LE5 21 F5
Harecroft Crs
RLEIW/BAR LE9 67 E1
Harefield Av LEIW LE3 34 B5
Harene Crs RLEIW/BAR LE9 32 A3
Harewood St LEIE LE5 27 F3
Harland Cl RLEIW/BAR LE9 63 F3
Harlaxton St LEIW LE3 34 B3
Harlequin Wy
RLEIS/BBY LE8 63 H2
Harolds La END/NAR LE19 40 D3
Harold St LEIS LE2 35 E5
Harrier Cl RLEIW/BAR LE9 68 C2
Harrier Pkwy LUTT LE17 80 B2
Harrington Rd WGSTN LE18 44 C5
Harrington St LEIN LE4 27 E2
Harringworth Rd LEIE LE5 37 F1
Harris Cl RLEIW/BAR LE9 69 E4
Harrison Cl LEIW LE3 24 A2
MKTHBORO LE16 77 G4
RLEIS/BBY LE8 64 A1
RLEIW/BAR LE9 49 F3
WGSTN LE18 55 H2
Harrison Rd LEIN LE4 20 A5
Harrison St LEIN LE4 12 C4
Harris Rd LEIN LE4 18 B4
Harrod Dr MKTHBORO LE16 74 D5
Harrogate Rd LEIN LE4 27 E1
Harrogate Wy
WGSTN LE18 56 C2
Harrop Cl RLEIS/BBY LE8 54 A3
Harrow Cl LEIW LE3 32 B4
Harrowden Ri LEIE LE5 28 A4
Harrowgate Dr LEIN LE4 11 F4
Harrow Rd LEIW LE3 34 C1
Hart Cl RLEIS/BBY LE8 63 H1
Hartfield Rd LEIE LE5 28 D2
Hartington Rd LEIE LE5 27 E4
Hartland Dr
MKTHBORO LE16 78 B1
Hartopp Cl RLEINE/SYS LE7 29 G5
Hartopp Rd LEIS LE2 35 H3
Hart Rd LEIE LE5 27 E4
Hartshorn Cl LEIN LE4 20 D1
Harvard Cl LEIS LE2 45 F2
Harvest Cl END/NAR LE19 53 F5
LEIN LE4 18 B4
Harvester Cl LEIW LE3 32 B4
Harvest Wy RLEIW/BAR LE9 68 D5
Harwin Rd LEIE LE5 37 F1
Haskell Cl LEIW LE3 33 F3
Hassal Rd LEIW LE3 24 C2
Hastings Cl RLEIS/BBY LE8 70 C5
Hastings Dr RLEIW/BAR LE9 48 B4
Hastings Rd LEIE LE5 27 F2
RLEIW/BAR LE9 32 A1
The Hastings LEIW LE3 33 F4
Hathaway Av LEIW LE3 33 H4
Hatherleigh Rd LEIE LE5 36 D2
Hat Rd LEIW LE3 41 G1
Hattern Av LEIN LE4 18 D3
Havelock St LEIS LE2 2 D7
Haven Cl LEIW LE3 32 B3
Havencrest Dr LEIE LE5 28 B3
Hawarden Av LEIE LE5 27 H3
Hawk Cl RLEIW/BAR LE9 68 C2
Hawker Rd LEIS LE2 45 H4
Hawkesbury Rd LEIS LE2 43 E1
Hawkes Hl LEIS LE2 43 F3
Hawke Wy LUTT LE17 80 A1
Hawthorn Av
RLEINE/SYS LE7 11 H4
Hawthorn Cl
RLEIW/BAR LE9 32 A3
Hawthorn Dr
RLEIS/BBY LE8 54 B5
Hawthorne Dr LEIE LE5 37 E2
Hawthorne St LEIW LE3 25 F4
Hawthorne Wy
RLEIW/BAR LE9 48 B5
Hawthorn Gv LEIS LE2 45 F1
Hawthorn Ri GBY/RBY LE6 16 B4
The Hawthorns COAL LE67 6 C4
LUTT LE17 81 F3
RLEIS/BBY LE8 65 E2
Haybarn Cl END/NAR LE19 53 F5
Hayden Av LEIS LE2 45 H4
Hayden Cl LEIN LE4 19 E4
Hayes End RLEIW/BAR LE9 30 B2
Hayes Rd WGSTN LE18 44 C5
Hayfield Cl LEIW LE3 23 H2
Hayling Crs LEIE LE5 28 A2
Haymarket LEI LE1 3 F3
Haynes Rd LEIE LE5 27 G3
Haywood Cl LEIE LE5 37 F1
Hazeland Ct LUTT LE17 81 G3
Hazelbank Rd
RLEIS/BBY LE8 65 F2
Hazel Cl END/NAR LE19 53 E5
LEIN LE4 11 H4
Hazeldene Rd LEIE LE5 21 H5
Hazel Dr LEIW LE3 41 H2
LUTT LE17 81 F3
Hazelhead Rd
RLEINE/SYS LE7 17 F1
Hazelnut Cl LEIE LE5 37 F1
Hazel St LEIS LE2 35 F2
RLEIW/BAR LE9 30 A2
Hazel Wy RLEIW/BAR LE9 48 A4
Hazelwood Rd LEIE LE5 36 B2
WGSTN LE18 55 G3
Heacham Dr LEIN LE4 18 B4
Headingly Cl LEIN LE4 10 C5
Headland Rd LEIE LE5 37 E2
The Headlands
MKTHBORO LE16 74 D5
RLEINE/SYS LE7 5 G1
Headley Rd LEIW LE3 41 H1
Healey St WGSTN LE18 55 F2
Healy Cl LEIN LE4 18 D3
Heanor St LEI LE1 2 D1
Heards Cl WGSTN LE18 56 C3
Hearth St MKTHBORO LE16 77 G1
Heath Av END/NAR LE19 53 G1
RLEINE/SYS LE7 12 D1
Heathbrook Dr
GBY/RBY LE6 22 D2
Heathcott Rd LEIS LE2 43 F1
Heatherbrook Rd LEIN LE4 17 H2
Heather Rd LEIS LE2 35 G5
Heather Wy RLEIS/BBY LE8 65 F3
Heathfield Rd WGSTN LE18 44 B3
Heathgate Cl LEIN LE4 11 F4
Heath La RLEIW/BAR LE9 48 C3
Heath La South
RLEIW/BAR LE9 48 D3
Heathley Cl LEIW LE3 32 B3
Heathley Park Dr LEIW LE3 25 E1
Heawood Wy LEIW LE3 33 F4
Heays Cl LEIW LE3 24 C2
Hebden Cl LEIS LE2 54 C1
Heddington Cl WGSTN LE18 43 G3
Heddington Wy
WGSTN LE18 43 G3
Hedgerow La
RLEIW/BAR LE9 22 C5
Hedgerow Rd LEIW LE3 34 A1
Hefford Gdns LEIN LE4 18 D3
Heighton Crs
END/NAR LE19 53 E5
The Heights
MKTHBORO LE16 78 C2
Helena Crs LEIN LE4 19 E3
Helmsley Rd LEIS LE2 43 F3
Helston Cl WGSTN LE18 56 A2
Hemington Rd LEIE LE5 37 H2
Hemlock Cl END/NAR LE19 52 B2
Henley Crs LEIW LE3 33 H4
Henley Rd LEIW LE3 25 G4
Henray Av LEIS LE2 54 C1
Henry Cl LEIW LE3 32 B3
Henshaw St LEIS LE2 2 E6
Hensman Cl RLEIS/BBY LE8 70 C5
Henson Cl LEIN LE4 19 F1
Henson Wy HINC LE10 66 B4
Henton Rd LEIW LE3 25 G5
Herbert Av LEIN LE4 19 H5
Herbert Cl RLEIS/BBY LE8 53 H4
Herdsmans Cl
END/NAR LE19 53 E4
Hereford Rd LEIS LE2 42 D1
Hereward Dr
RLEINE/SYS LE7 29 F5
Herle Av LEIW LE3 33 H3
Hermitage Cl LEIS LE2 45 E3
Hermitage Rd LEIN LE4 19 G2
Heron Cl RLEIS/BBY LE8 58 D2
Herongate Rd LEIE LE5 27 H2
Heron Rd LEIE LE5 27 E3
Heron Wy END/NAR LE19 53 F1
RLEINE/SYS LE7 4 B5
Herrick Cl END/NAR LE19 40 C5
Herrick Dr RLEINE/SYS LE7 29 F5
Herrick Rd LEIS LE2 35 G5
Herricks Av LEIN LE4 20 D2
Herrick Wy WGSTN LE18 56 C2
Herschell St LEIS LE2 36 A2
Hesketh Av LEIS LE2 42 C5
Hesketh Cl LEIS LE2 42 C5
Hewes Cl LEIS LE2 42 B5
Hewett Cl RLEIS/BBY LE8 58 C3
Hewitt Dr RLEIW/BAR LE9 32 B1
Hextall Rd LEIE LE5 37 E2
Hexter Cl RLEIS/BBY LE8 63 H2
Heybridge Rd LEIE LE5 27 H2
Heybrook Av RLEIS/BBY LE8 54 A4
Heycock Cl RLEIS/BBY LE8 70 C5
Heyford Rd LEIW LE3 33 F1
Heygate St
MKTHBORO LE16 74 C5
Heythrop Cl LEIS LE2 45 H4
Heyworth Rd LEIW LE3 34 C4

Hidcote Rd LEIS LE2 45 E4
Higgs Cl LEIE LE5 28 A5
Highbury Rd LEIN LE4 27 E2
Highcliffe Rd LEIN LE4 21 E4
Highcroft Av LEIS LE2 45 G4
Highcroft Rd LEIS LE2 45 H5
Highcross St LEI LE1 2 D3
MKTHBORO LE16 77 F1
Higher Gn RLEIS/BBY LE8 58 D3
Highfield Crs WGSTN LE18 44 B4
Highfield Dr WGSTN LE18 44 B4
Highfield Rd GBY/RBY LE6 16 A5
Highfield St LEIS LE2 3 J7
MKTHBORO LE16 77 G1
RLEINE/SYS LE7 17 G1
RLEIS/BBY LE8 70 A3
RLEIW/BAR LE9 48 D4
RLEIW/BAR LE9 60 B3
Highgate LEIS LE2 43 G4
Highgate Av LEIN LE4 11 E4
Highgate Dr WGSTN LE18 43 H3
Highgrove Crs LEIS LE2 42 B3
Highland Av RLEIW/BAR LE9 32 A3
Highmeres Rd LEIN LE4 20 D4
High St END/NAR LE19 40 D5
LEI LE1 2 E3
LEIE LE5 37 F3
LEIS LE2 45 E2
LUTT LE17 81 G4
MKTHBORO LE16 77 H1
RLEINE/SYS LE7 4 C5
RLEIS/BBY LE8 53 H4
RLEIS/BBY LE8 58 C3
RLEIS/BBY LE8 70 B3
RLEIS/BBY LE8 71 H3
RLEIW/BAR LE9 30 B2
RLEIW/BAR LE9 49 F3
High Tor East
RLEIW/BAR LE9 49 E2
High Tor West
RLEIW/BAR LE9 49 E2
Highway Rd LEIE LE5 36 C3
LEIN LE4 12 D4
Hilary Crs GBY/RBY LE6 15 H4
Hilcot Gn LEIW LE3 33 E4
Hilders Rd LEIW LE3 25 E4
Hildyard Rd LEIN LE4 26 C1
Hillary Pl LEIW LE3 34 A3
Hillberry Cl END/NAR LE19 52 C3
Hillcrest Av
MKTHBORO LE16 74 B5
RLEIS/BBY LE8 71 H2
Hillcrest Rd WGSTN LE18 43 H3
Hillcroft Cl LEIN LE4 12 C4
Hillcroft Rd LEIE LE5 27 G5
Hill Fld LEIS LE2 46 A4
Hill Gdns MKTHBORO LE16 77 F1
Hill La COAL LE67 6 A3
RLEIS/BBY LE8 64 A3
Hill Lane Cl COAL LE67 6 B2
Hill Ri LEIN LE4 11 G4
LEIN LE4 20 D2
Hillrise Av LEIW LE3 34 A5
Hillsborough Cl LEIS LE2 54 C1
Hillsborough Crs LEIS LE2 54 C1
Hillsborough Rd LEIS LE2 54 C1
Hillside COAL LE67 6 B3
Hillside Av WGSTN LE18 56 B2
Hillside Rd MKTHBORO LE16 74 D5
Hill St LEI LE1 3 G2
RLEIW/BAR LE9 48 B5
RLEIW/BAR LE9 61 G2
Hill Top RLEIW/BAR LE9 49 F2
Hilltop Av RLEIS/BBY LE8 59 E3
Hilltop Rd LEIN LE4 21 F4
Hill Vw END/NAR LE19 41 G5
Hill View Dr RLEIW/BAR LE9 63 F3
Hill Wy LEIS LE2 45 G4
Hinckley Rd LEIW LE3 24 C5
LEIW LE3 32 C2
RLEIW/BAR LE9 31 H5
RLEIW/BAR LE9 48 D4
RLEIW/BAR LE9 66 A1
Hind Cl RLEIS/BBY LE8 54 A5
Hindoostan Av WGSTN LE18 43 E5
Hinks Av RLEINE/SYS LE7 29 F2
Hipwell Crs LEIN LE4 19 E4
Hoball Cl LEIW LE3 24 C2
Hobart St LEIS LE2 3 J5
Hobby Cl RLEIW/BAR LE9 68 C2
Hobill Cl LEIW LE3 32 D3
RLEIW/BAR LE9 52 A3
Hobrook Rd RLEIS/BBY LE8 70 C5
Hobson Rd LEIN LE4 19 E4
Hoby St LEIW LE3 2 A2
Hockley Farm Rd LEIW LE3 33 F1
Hodgson Cl LEIW LE3 25 E1
Hodson Cl RLEIS/BBY LE8 53 H5
Hogarth Rd LEIN LE4 10 C3
Holbeck Dr RLEIW/BAR LE9 69 E3
Holbrook LEIS LE2 46 A4
Holbrook Rd LEIS LE2 44 C1
Holdenby Cl
MKTHBORO LE16 78 C1
Holden Cl RLEIS/BBY LE8 64 A1
Holden St LEIN LE4 19 G5
Holderness Rd LEIN LE4 18 D2
Holgate Cl RLEINE/SYS LE7 9 G5
Holkham Av LEIN LE4 27 F1
Holland Rd LEIS LE2 3 K2
Holland Wy END/NAR LE19 52 D3
Holliers Wy RLEIW/BAR LE9 61 G2
Hollies Wy RLEINE/SYS LE7 38 B1
Hollington Rd LEIE LE5 36 B1
Hollins Rd LEIW LE3 33 G1
Hollinwell Cl LEIW LE3 24 A5
Hollow Rd RLEINE/SYS LE7 17 F1
Hollow Station
RLEIS/BBY LE8 72 A3
The Hollow LEIE LE5 37 F3
RLEIW/BAR LE9 49 F3
Hollowtree Rd LEIE LE5 21 G5
Holly Bank Cl LEIE LE5 21 G5
Hollybrook Cl LEIN LE4 21 E1
Hollybush Cl LEIE LE5 28 D3
RLEINE/SYS LE7 12 D1
Holly Cl MKTHBORO LE16 74 C5
Holly Ct LEIS LE2 45 E1
Hollydene Crs
RLEIW/BAR LE9 48 D4
Holly Dr LUTT LE17 81 F3
Holly Gv RLEIS/BBY LE8 54 B3
Holly La RLEIW/BAR LE9 48 B4
Holly Tree Av LEIN LE4 11 G4
Holman Rw LEIE LE5 28 A4
Holmdale Rd
RLEINE/SYS LE7 13 E1
Holmden Av WGSTN LE18 55 H1
Holme Dr LEIS LE2 45 F1
Holmes Cl GBY/RBY LE6 16 A4
Holmewood Dr
RLEIW/BAR LE9 32 B1
Holmfield Av LEIS LE2 36 B3
Holmfield Av East LEIW LE3 33 E2
Holmfield Av West
LEIW LE3 33 E2
Holmfield Cl LUTT LE17 81 E3
Holmfield Rd LEIS LE2 36 A3
RLEIW/BAR LE9 30 B2
Holmleigh Gdns
RLEINE/SYS LE7 38 B1
Holmwood Dr LEIW LE3 24 C1
Holt Dr RLEIW/BAR LE9 32 B1
Holt Rd LEIN LE4 19 G2
Holts Cl LEIS LE2 42 B4
Holyoak Dr HINC LE10 66 B4
Holyoake St END/NAR LE19 52 C1
Holyrood Dr RLEIS/BBY LE8 64 D2
Holywell Rd LEIS LE2 42 C2
Home Cl MKTHBORO LE16 79 H1
RLEIS/BBY LE8 54 B3
RLEIS/BBY LE8 72 A4
Home Farm Cl LEIN LE4 18 C4
Homemead Av LEIN LE4 18 D5
Homer Dr END/NAR LE19 52 C3
Homestead Dr WGSTN LE18 56 B2
Homestone Gdns LEIE LE5 29 E4
Homestone Ri LEIE LE5 29 E4
Homeway Rd LEIE LE5 36 C2
Honeybourne Cl LEIS LE2 45 E3
Honeycomb Cl
END/NAR LE19 52 C3
Honeysuckle Cl LUTT LE17 81 E3
RLEINE/SYS LE7 5 H2
Honeysuckle Rd LEIE LE5 21 G5
Honiton Cl WGSTN LE18 56 A2
Hoods Cl LEIN LE4 18 D1
Hopefield Rd LEIW LE3 34 C3
Hopton Flds
MKTHBORO LE16 77 G4
Hopwood Cl LEIN LE4 18 B4
Hopyard Cl LEIS LE2 42 B4
Hornbeam Cl
END/NAR LE19 52 C3
LEIS LE2 45 E1
Horndean Av WGSTN LE18 44 A5
Horsefair Cl
MKTHBORO LE16 74 B5
Horsefair St LEI LE1 2 E4
Horseshoe Cl
RLEIW/BAR LE9 63 F2
Horse Shoe La
MKTHBORO LE16 75 E3
Horsewell La WGSTN LE18 56 B3
Horston Rd LEIE LE5 36 C2
Horton Ct RLEIS/BBY LE8 * 54 A3
Horwood Cl WGSTN LE18 44 C4
Hoskins Cl WGSTN LE18 56 C3
Hospital Cl LEIE LE5 36 D1
Hospital La RLEIS/BBY LE8 54 D5
Hotel St LEI LE1 2 E4
Hotoft Rd LEIE LE5 28 B2
Houghton La LEIS LE2 38 C4
Houghton St LEIE LE5 27 F3
Houlditch Rd LEIS LE2 35 H5
Housman Wk LEIN LE4 26 D2
Howard Cl RLEIW/BAR LE9 48 A4
Howard Rd LEIS LE2 35 H3
LEIS LE2 54 B1
Howard Wy
MKTHBORO LE16 77 G3
Howden Rd LEIS LE2 42 C4
Howdon Rd LEIS LE2 45 F5
Howe Cl RLEIW/BAR LE9 60 A5
Hoylake Cl LEIE LE5 36 C3
Hubbard Cl RLEIS/BBY LE8 64 A1
Hudson Cl LEIW LE3 25 E2
Huggett Cl LEIN LE4 20 C3
Hughenden Dr LEIS LE2 35 E4
Humber Cl LEIE LE5 28 B1
Humberstone Dr LEIE LE5 27 H2
Humberstone Ga LEI LE1 2 E3
Humberstone La LEIN LE4 20 D2
Humberstone Rd LEIE LE5 3 G3
Humes Cl RLEIS/BBY LE8 63 H2
Humphries Cl LEIE LE5 28 A5
Huncote Rd RLEIW/BAR LE9 60 B2
Hungarton Bvd LEIE LE5 28 B2
Hungarton Dr
RLEINE/SYS LE7 13 G1
Hunter Bvd LUTT LE17 80 A2
Hunter Rd LEIN LE4 26 C1
Hunters Dr LUTT LE17 81 F4
Hunters Rw
RLEIW/BAR LE9 * 63 F3
Hunters Wy LEIS LE2 45 H3
LEIW LE3 32 B3
Huntingdon Gdns
MKTHBORO LE16 77 G3
Huntingdon Rd LEIN LE4 20 B5
The Huntings
RLEIW/BAR LE9 22 C5
Huntsmans Cl COAL LE67 6 C4
Huntsman's Dl
RLEINE/SYS LE7 5 F1
Huntsmans Wy LEIN LE4 20 B4
Hursley Cl LEIS LE2 45 G3
Hurst Ri LEIE LE5 28 A5
Hurst Rd RLEIW/BAR LE9 49 E4
Hutchinson St LEIS LE2 3 J4
Hyde Cl END/NAR LE19 52 D3
LEIS LE2 45 G5
Hydra Wk LEIS LE2 3 K4
Hylion Rd LEIS LE2 43 G2

I

Ibbetson Av LEIW LE3 24 A3
Ibsley Wy LEIS LE2 42 D5
Ickworth Cl LEIE LE5 27 G2
Iffley Cl LEIE LE5 27 H5
Iliffe Av LEIS LE2 44 D3
Iliffe Rd LEIN LE4 27 G1
Illingworth Rd LEIE LE5 28 A4
Ilmington Cl LEIW LE3 24 A1
Imperial Av LEIW LE3 34 B2
Imperial Rd RLEIS/BBY LE8 71 H3
Impey Cl LEIW LE3 33 F4
Infirmary Cl LEIS LE2 2 E7
Infirmary Rd LEI LE1 2 E6
Infirmary Sq LEIS LE2 2 E6
Ingarsby Cl RLEINE/SYS LE7 39 H1
Ingarsby Dr LEIE LE5 37 G2
Ingleby Rd WGSTN LE18 44 A5
Ingle Dr GBY/RBY LE6 22 C2
Ingle St LEIW LE3 25 F3
Ingold Av LEIN LE4 18 D4
Ingrams Wy WGSTN LE18 56 C3
Invergary Cl LEIN LE4 20 B3
Iona Cl LEIN LE4 18 B4
Iona Rd RLEINE/SYS LE7 4 B5
Iona Wy RLEIS/BBY LE8 65 F3
Ipswich Cl LEIN LE4 18 A1
Ireton Av LEIN LE4 20 D5
Ireton Rd LEIN LE4 27 G1
MKTHBORO LE16 77 G3
Iris Av LEIN LE4 11 H4
LEIS LE2 42 B5
Irlam St WGSTN LE18 55 F3
Ironworks Rd LEIN LE4 27 E2
Isis Cl LEIS LE2 45 H2
Islington St LEIS LE2 35 F3
Isobella Rd LEIW LE3 33 E4
Ivanhoe Cl LEIW LE3 24 A3
Ivanhoe Rd WGSTN LE18 55 F1
Ivanhoe St LEIW LE3 25 G4
Ivatt Cl RLEINE/SYS LE7 29 G5
Ivychurch Crs LEIE LE5 29 E1
Ivydale Rd LEIN LE4 20 D1
Ivydene Cl RLEIW/BAR LE9 49 F3
Ivy Rd LEIW LE3 34 C2

J

Jacklin Dr LEIN LE4 20 B2
Jackson Cl LEIS LE2 45 H3
MKTHBORO LE16 77 H4
Jackson St LEIN LE4 19 H4
Jacob Cl END/NAR LE19 40 C5
Jacqueline Rd COAL LE67 6 D4
Jacques Cl END/NAR LE19 40 C5
James Gavin Wy LEIS LE2 46 A4
James St RLEINE/SYS LE7 9 F5
RLEIS/BBY LE8 54 A3
RLEIW/BAR LE9 49 E4
RLEIW/BAR LE9 60 B3
Jamesway RLEIW/BAR LE9 63 F2
Janes Wy COAL LE67 6 C4
Jarrett Cl END/NAR LE19 40 C5
Jarrom St LEIS LE2 35 E2
Jarvis St LEIW LE3 2 C3
Jasmine Cl LEIE LE5 21 F4
LUTT LE17 81 E3
Jasmine Ct END/NAR LE19 52 B2
WGSTN LE18 55 F1
Jean Dr LEIN LE4 25 H1
Jellicoe Rd LEIE LE5 27 G4
Jennett Cl LEIE LE5 28 C4
Jeremy Cl LEIN LE4 19 H5
Jermyn St LEIN LE4 19 H5
Jersey Rd LEIN LE4 18 D3
Jersey Wy RLEIW/BAR LE9 48 A5
Jerwood Wy
MKTHBORO LE16 78 A2
Jessons Cl LEIN LE4 20 B4
Jessop Cl LEIW LE3 25 E2
Jewsbury Wy LEIW LE3 33 E3
John Bold Av
RLEIW/BAR LE9 60 C3
Johnnie Johnson Dr
LUTT LE17 81 G1
Johnscliffe Cl GBY/RBY LE6 7 H3
Johnson Cl RLEIS/BBY LE8 53 H4
RLEIW/BAR LE9 69 E4
Johnson Ri RLEIW/BAR LE9 60 C4
Johnson Rd LEIN LE4 11 F5
Johnson St LEI LE1 2 C1
John St END/NAR LE19 52 D1
Jonathan Cl GBY/RBY LE6 16 C4
Jordan Av WGSTN LE18 55 G2
Jordan Cl LEIW LE3 24 A2
MKTHBORO LE16 78 B1
Journeyman's Gn
GBY/RBY LE6 22 D2
Jowett Cl LEIW LE3 25 E1
Joyce Rd LEIW LE3 25 F2
Jubilee Crs END/NAR LE19 53 E4
Jubilee Dr LEIW LE3 24 A3
RLEIW/BAR LE9 49 E4
Jubilee Gdns LEIE LE5 27 F2
Jubilee Rd LEI LE1 3 F1
RLEIW/BAR LE9 68 C3
Judith Dr LEIE LE5 37 F1
RLEIS/BBY LE8 65 F2
Julian Rd LEIS LE2 54 C1
Junction Rd LEI LE1 26 C3
WGSTN LE18 44 B5
June Av LEIN LE4 21 E2
Junior St LEI LE1 2 D2
Juniper Cl LEIW LE3 32 B3
LUTT LE17 81 F2
Juno Cl LEIW LE3 24 A3
Jupiter Cl LEIS LE2 3 K3

K

Kamloops Crs LEI LE1 3 G1
Kashmir Rd LEI LE1 26 D3
Kate St LEIW LE3 2 A4
Kay Rd LEIW LE3 24 D2
Keats Cl END/NAR LE19 40 C5
RLEIW/BAR LE9 49 F2
Keats La RLEIW/BAR LE9 49 E2
Keats Wk LEIN LE4 26 D2
Keays Wy RLEINE/SYS LE7 29 F2
Keble Dr RLEINE/SYS LE7 13 F1
Keble Rd LEIS LE2 35 G4
Kedleston Av LEIN LE4 19 G2
Kedleston Rd LEIE LE5 36 B1
Keenan Cl LEIS LE2 42 B3
Keepers' Cft RLEINE/SYS LE7 5 G2
The Keep RLEIW/BAR LE9 22 D5
Kegworth Av LEIE LE5 27 H5
Keightley Rd LEIW LE3 24 D2
Kelbrook Cl LEIN LE4 18 C3
Kelmarsh Av WGSTN LE18 56 B1
Kelso Gn LEIS LE2 42 D5
Kelvon Cl LEIW LE3 24 B1
Kemble Sq LEI LE1 3 F3
Kemp Rd LEIW LE3 24 C1
Kempson Rd LEIS LE2 35 E5
Kendall's Av RLEIW/BAR LE9 61 G2
Kendal Rd LEIN LE4 20 B4
Kendrick Dr LEIS LE2 45 F3
Kenilworth Cl
RLEIW/BAR LE9 68 C1
Kenilworth Dr LEIS LE2 44 D3
Kenilworth Rd WGSTN LE18 43 F5
Kennedy Wy LEIW LE3 32 C3
Kenneth Gamble Ct
WGSTN LE18 43 H4
Kenny Cl RLEIS/BBY LE8 54 A5
Kensington Cl LEIS LE2 45 G5
LEIS LE2 54 D2
Kensington Dr WGSTN LE18 44 B3
Kensington St LEIN LE4 26 C1
Kent Crs WGSTN LE18 43 F5
Kent Dr LEIS LE2 45 G3
Kenton Av WGSTN LE18 56 A2
Kent St LEIE LE5 3 J2
Kenwood Rd LEIS LE2 44 A1
Kepston Cl LEIS LE2 42 D4
Kerrial Rd LEIW LE3 24 C3
Kerry Cl RLEIW/BAR LE9 48 A4
Kerrysdale Av LEIN LE4 20 B5
Kertley RLEIS/BBY LE8 70 B3
Kestian Cl MKTHBORO LE16 74 B4
Kestral La LEIE LE5 21 G5
Kestrel Cl LEIE LE5 27 E3
LEIW LE3 32 A3
RLEINE/SYS LE7 4 B5
RLEIS/BBY LE8 70 C5
RLEIW/BAR LE9 68 C2
Keswick Cl LEIN LE4 11 H4
Keswick Rd RLEIS/BBY LE8 54 A4
Kettering Rd
MKTHBORO LE16 78 A2
Kevern Cl WGSTN LE18 56 A2
Kew Dr LEIS LE2 45 G5
WGSTN LE18 43 H3
Keyham Cl LEIE LE5 28 B1
Keyham La LEIE LE5 28 C1
Keyham La West LEIE LE5 28 D1
Keythorpe St LEIS LE2 3 K3
Kibworth Br RLEIS/BBY LE8 71 E1
Kibworth Rd
RLEIS/BBY LE8 70 B4
RLEIS/BBY LE8 72 C1
Kielder Cl END/NAR LE19 52 B1
Kigston Wy
MKTHBORO LE16 74 C4

Kilburn Av LEIS LE2 44 D2
Kilby Av LEIN LE4 19 G2
Kilby Dr WGSTN LE18 56 C2
Kilby Rd RLEIS/BBY LE8 70 B3
Kildare St LEI LE1 3 F3
Kilmelford Cl LEIN LE4 20 B3
Kiln Av LEIN LE4 20 D1
Kiln Cl RLEIW/BAR LE9 69 E4
Kilverstone Av LEIE LE5 37 H2
Kilworth Dr LEIE LE5 36 C2
Kimberley Rd LEIS LE2 36 A2
Kimberley St
RLEIS/BBY LE8 71 H3
Kincaple Rd LEIN LE4 20 B3
Kincraig Rd LEIN LE4 20 B3
Kinder Cl RLEIS/BBY LE8 64 A1
Kingcup Cl LEIW LE3 32 B3
King Edward Av
END/NAR LE19 53 E3
King Edward Rd LEIE LE5 27 H3
Kingfisher Av LEIE LE5 27 E3
Kingfisher Cl LEIW LE3 32 A3
RLEINE/SYS LE7 4 B5
RLEIS/BBY LE8 58 D2
Kingfisher Wk LEIE LE5 * 27 E3
King Richard's Hl
RLEIW/BAR LE9 49 H2
King Richards Rd LEIW LE3 25 E5
Kingsbridge Cl
END/NAR LE19 52 C3
Kingsbridge Crs LEIN LE4 10 B5
Kingsbury Av LEIE LE5 37 G1
Kingscliffe Crs LEIE LE5 37 H1
Kings Ct RLEIW/BAR LE9 * 48 B4
Kings Dr LEIW LE3 32 C2
WGSTN LE18 44 A5
Kingsfield Rd
RLEIW/BAR LE9 48 B4
RLEIW/BAR LE9 63 E4
Kingsgate Av LEIN LE4 11 F4
King's Head Pl
MKTHBORO LE16 77 H1
Kingsley Cl END/NAR LE19 52 C2
Kingsley St LEIS LE2 35 G5
Kingsmead Rd LEIS LE2 44 A2
Kings Newton St LEIS LE2 36 A1
King's Rd MKTHBORO LE16 77 H1
Kingsthorpe Cl LEIN LE4 19 F4
Kingston Av WGSTN LE18 43 H4
Kingston Rd LEIS LE2 36 A2
Kingston Wy
MKTHBORO LE16 74 B3
King St END/NAR LE19 40 D5
LEI LE1 3 F6
LEIS LE2 45 F3
RLEINE/SYS LE7 21 H1
RLEIS/BBY LE8 53 H4
RLEIW/BAR LE9 48 B5
Kings Wk LEIW LE3 32 C3
RLEIW/BAR LE9 49 E3
Kings Wy GBY/RBY LE6 16 B5
Kingsway LEIW LE3 33 H5
King's Wy LUTT LE17 81 F4
Kingsway North LEIW LE3 33 G3
Kingsway Rd LEIE LE5 36 C3
Kingswood Av LEIW LE3 34 B1
King Williams Wy
RLEINE/SYS LE7 9 G5
Kinley Rd LEIN LE4 19 E3
Kinross Av LEIE LE5 29 E4
Kinsdale Dr LEIE LE5 29 F4
Kintyre Dr LEIN LE4 20 A3
Kiplin Dr END/NAR LE19 52 C1
Kipling Gv LEIN LE4 18 A5
Kirby Cl RLEIW/BAR LE9 66 D1
Kirby La RLEIW/BAR LE9 32 B2
Kirby Rd GBY/RBY LE6 23 F3
LEIW LE3 25 G5
Kirkby Rd RLEIW/BAR LE9 48 B4
Kirkdale Rd WGSTN LE18 55 F1
Kirkfield Rd RLEIS/BBY LE8 65 F2
Kirkland Rd LEIW LE3 33 H5
Kirk La END/NAR LE19 41 E5
Kirkstone Cl LEIW LE3 24 B1
Kirkwall Crs LEIE LE5 29 E3
Kirloe Av LEIW LE3 32 B2
Kirminton Gdns LEIE LE5 28 C4
Kirtley Wy RLEIW/BAR LE9 69 E3
Kitchener Rd LEIE LE5 27 G5
RLEINE/SYS LE7 9 G5
Kite Cl RLEIW/BAR LE9 68 C1
Knight Cl LEIN LE4 12 D5
Knighton Church Rd
LEIS LE2 44 A1
Knighton Cl
RLEIW/BAR LE9 69 E5
Knighton Dr LEIS LE2 36 A5
Knighton Fields Rd East
LEIS LE2 35 F5
Knighton Fields Rd West
LEIS LE2 * 35 F5
Knighton Grange Rd
LEIS LE2 36 C5
Knighton Junction La
LEIS LE2 35 G4
Knighton La LEIS LE2 35 E5
Knighton La East LEIS LE2 35 F5
Knighton Park Rd LEIS LE2 36 A3
Knighton Ri LEIS LE2 36 C4
Knighton Rd LEIS LE2 35 H5
Knighton St LEIS LE2 2 E7
Knightsbridge Rd LEIS LE2 54 D2
Knights Cl RLEIW/BAR LE9 60 B3
Knight's End Rd
MKTHBORO LE16 75 F3
Knights Link
RLEIW/BAR LE9 49 H2
Knights Rd LEIN LE4 18 C1
Knollgate Cl LEIN LE4 11 E4
Knoll St MKTHBORO LE16 77 F1
Knowles Rd LEIW LE3 24 C3
Krefeld Wy LEIN LE4 18 B3

L

Labrador Cl LEI LE1 3 H1
Laburnum Av LUTT LE17 81 F3
Laburnum Dr
RLEIW/BAR LE9 48 D4
Laburnum Rd LEIE LE5 28 C1
Lacey Cl LUTT LE17 81 G1
Ladbroke Gv RLEIS/BBY LE8 65 F2
Lady Hay Rd LEIW LE3 17 H4
Lady Leys RLEIW/BAR LE9 63 F3
Ladysmith Rd
RLEIW/BAR LE9 22 D4
WGSTN LE18 43 E5
Laithwaite Cl LEIN LE4 18 B1
Lakeside Ct RLEINE/SYS LE7 38 A1
Lakeview Cha LEIE LE5 21 G4
Lakin Dr LEIW LE3 33 E3
Lambert Rd LEIW LE3 34 C3
Lamborne Rd LEIS LE2 43 G2
Lambourne Rd LEIN LE4 11 H4
Lamen Rd LEIW LE3 24 C1
Lamplighters
RLEIS/BBY LE8 70 B4
Lamport Cl WGSTN LE18 56 D1
Lancashire St LEIN LE4 19 H4
Lancaster Cl RLEIW/BAR LE9 30 B3
Lancaster Ct GBY/RBY LE6 16 A5
Lancaster Rd LEI LE1 3 F7
Lancaster St LEIE LE5 27 F4
Lancaster Wy LEIS LE2 55 E2
Lancelot Cl LEIW LE3 32 C3
Lancing Av LEIW LE3 25 E4
Landscape Dr LEIE LE5 37 G1
Landsdowne Rd LEIS LE2 35 E5
Landseer Rd LEIS LE2 35 H4
Land Society La
RLEIW/BAR LE9 49 E3
Lane Cl LEIW LE3 24 A2
Lanesborough Cl
RLEINE/SYS LE7 10 B1
Lanesborough Dr
RLEINE/SYS LE7 10 B1
Lanesborough Rd LEIN LE4 19 H3
Lanes Hill Gv
RLEIW/BAR LE9 60 C5
Langdale RLEIS/BBY LE8 70 B3
Langdale Rd LEIN LE4 12 D5
Langham Dr END/NAR LE19 52 D3
Langham Rd LEIN LE4 20 D4
The Langhill LEIE LE5 27 H4
Langholm Rd LEIE LE5 29 E4
Langley Av LEIN LE4 19 F4
Langley Cl RLEIW/BAR LE9 51 H3
Langton Rd
MKTHBORO LE16 75 E1
RLEIS/BBY LE8 72 B2
WGSTN LE18 56 B2
Langton St LEI LE1 3 F2
Lansdowne Gv WGSTN LE18 55 G3
Lapwing Cl LEIN LE4 18 B1
Lapwing Ct END/NAR LE19 52 C4
Larch Dr LUTT LE17 81 F3
Larch Gv LEIW LE3 33 E2
Larchmont Rd LEIN LE4 25 H2
Larch St LEIE LE5 27 E3
Larchwood RLEIS/BBY LE8 65 E2
Larchwood Av GBY/RBY LE6 16 B4
Larchwood Cl LEIS LE2 43 G1
Lark Cl LEIW LE3 32 B3
Larkspur Cl LEIE LE5 21 F4
Larkswood RLEIS/BBY LE8 72 B3
Lastingham Cl LEIS LE2 43 G2
Lathkill St MKTHBORO LE16 78 A3
Latimer Cl RLEIS/BBY LE8 54 A5
Latimer Ct RLEINE/SYS LE7 17 F2
Latimer Crs
MKTHBORO LE16 78 B1
Latimer Pl LEIN LE4 * 26 C2
Latimer Rd RLEINE/SYS LE7 9 H1
Latimer St LEIW LE3 2 A6
RLEINE/SYS LE7 17 G2
Laughton Rd
MKTHBORO LE16 76 B1
Launceston Rd WGSTN LE18 56 A3
Launde Pk MKTHBORO LE16 78 B2
Launde Rd COAL LE67 6 C4
LEIS LE2 45 G1
Laundon Cl GBY/RBY LE6 16 B5
Laundon Wy GBY/RBY LE6 23 E1
RLEIS/BBY LE8 64 A1
Laundry La LEIN LE4 19 H5
Laurel Cl LEIW LE3 24 C2
Laurel Dr LEIS LE2 45 H5
RLEIS/BBY LE8 65 E2
Laurel Rd LEIE LE5 36 A1
RLEIS/BBY LE8 54 B4
The Laurels COAL LE67 14 C1
Laureston Dr LEIS LE2 36 B3
Lavender Cl LUTT LE17 81 E3
RLEIS/BBY LE8 54 A3
Lavender Rd LEIW LE3 34 C2
Laverstock Rd WGSTN LE18 56 A3
Lawford Rd LEIS LE2 42 D4
Lawn Av LEIN LE4 11 H5
The Lawns LEIS LE2 * 36 A3
Lawnwood Rd
GBY/RBY LE6 15 H4
Lawrence Cl LEIN LE4 10 C3
Law St LEIN LE4 26 C1
Lawyers La LEIS LE2 45 E3
Laxford Cl LEIN LE4 18 C5
Laxton Cl LEIN LE4 11 H4
WGSTN LE18 56 D1
Layton Rd LEIE LE5 27 G3
Lea Cl LEIN LE4 12 B5
RLEIW/BAR LE9 69 E4
The Lealand
MKTHBORO LE16 77 E4
Leamington Dr
RLEIS/BBY LE8 54 B5
Leas Cl RLEINE/SYS LE7 29 F4
The Lea RLEIS/BBY LE8 72 B3
Ledbury Cl LEIS LE2 45 H4
Ledbury Gn LEIN LE4 18 D2
Ledwell Dr LEIW LE3 24 A1
Lee Cir LEI LE1 3 G2
Lee Cl RLEIW/BAR LE9 60 C3
The Leecrofts
RLEIW/BAR LE9 49 F3
Lee Ri GBY/RBY LE6 22 D2
Lees High HINC LE10 66 B5
Leeson St LEIS LE2 43 E1
Lee St LEI LE1 3 G2
Legion Wy END/NAR LE19 33 F5
Leicester La END/NAR LE19 40 D5
MKTHBORO LE16 74 A2
RLEIW/BAR LE9 30 D2
Leicester Rd COAL LE67 6 D4
END/NAR LE19 53 F2
GBY/RBY LE6 16 B4
HINC LE10 66 B5
LEIN LE4 10 D4
LEIS LE2 45 E2
LEIS LE2 54 B1
LEIW LE3 17 F5
MKTHBORO LE16 74 B5
RLEINE/SYS LE7 10 A1
RLEINE/SYS LE7 17 G1
RLEIS/BBY LE8 54 B3
RLEIS/BBY LE8 65 F2
RLEIS/BBY LE8 70 B2
RLEIS/BBY LE8 71 H1
RLEIW/BAR LE9 48 C5
RLEIW/BAR LE9 49 F1
RLEIW/BAR LE9 61 H5
RLEIW/BAR LE9 67 E2
WGSTN LE18 44 A3
Leicestershire Round
COAL LE67 7 E3
GBY/RBY LE6 8 A4
Leicester St LEIE LE5 27 F4
Leire La RLEIW/BAR LE9 68 B5
Leire St LEIN LE4 19 H5
Lema Cl LEIN LE4 20 C2
Lena Dr GBY/RBY LE6 15 G2
Lenthall Sq
MKTHBORO LE16 77 H3
Leopold Cl RLEIS/BBY LE8 64 D2
Leopold Rd LEIS LE2 35 G4
Leopold St WGSTN LE18 55 F1
Letchworth Rd LEIW LE3 25 E4
Lethbridge Cl LEI LE1 3 G1
Leveret Dr RLEIS/BBY LE8 63 H1
Leveric Rd LEIE LE5 27 G2
Lewett Cl LEIN LE4 18 D3
Lewin Br RLEINE/SYS LE7 4 C3
Lewis Cl LEIN LE4 18 B5
Lewisher Rd LEIN LE4 20 C4
Lewis Wy RLEIS/BBY LE8 65 F3
Lexham St LEIN LE4 19 H5
Leybury Wy RLEINE/SYS LE7 29 F3
Leycroft Rd LEIN LE4 18 B1
Leyland Rd LEIW LE3 41 H1
Leys Cl LEIS LE2 45 G2
Leysdale Cl LEIN LE4 18 B4
Leys Dr LEIS LE2 45 E4
Leysland Av RLEIS/BBY LE8 64 C2
The Leys RLEIS/BBY LE8 64 C3
RLEIS/BBY LE8 72 A2
Leyton Cl LUTT LE17 81 H4
Liberty Rd LEIW LE3 24 B4
Lichfield Av RLEIW/BAR LE9 68 B1
Lichfield Dr RLEIS/BBY LE8 54 B5
Lichfield St LEI LE1 2 E1
Lidster Cl LEIE LE5 28 B2
Lilac Av LEIE LE5 28 C1
Lilac Dr LUTT LE17 81 E3
Lilac Wy RLEINE/SYS LE7 5 G2
Lillingstone Cl COAL LE67 6 C3
Limber Crs LEIW LE3 33 G2
Lime Av GBY/RBY LE6 23 E1
Lime Cl RLEINE/SYS LE7 13 F1
Lime Dr RLEINE/SYS LE7 13 F2
Lime Gv RLEIS/BBY LE8 54 B3
RLEIW/BAR LE9 22 D5
RLEIW/BAR LE9 49 E4
Lime Grove Cl LEIN LE4 18 C3
Limehurst Rd LEIE LE5 28 D1
Lime Kilns WGSTN LE18 56 C3
Lime Tree Av
RLEINE/SYS LE7 11 G4
Lime Tree Rd END/NAR LE19 53 F1
Linacres Rd LEIW LE3 33 G2
Lincoln Ct MKTHBORO LE16 74 D4
Lincoln Dr RLEINE/SYS LE7 13 G2
RLEIS/BBY LE8 54 B5
WGSTN LE18 55 F1
Lincoln Rd RLEIW/BAR LE9 48 A5
Lincoln St LEIS LE2 3 J5
Linden Av RLEIS/BBY LE8 64 C2
Linden Dr LEIE LE5 36 D2
LUTT LE17 81 F3
Linden Farm Dr
RLEIS/BBY LE8 64 D2
Linden La RLEIW/BAR LE9 32 B1
Linden St LEIE LE5 27 G5
Lindfield Rd LEIW LE3 25 E4
Lindisfarne Rd
RLEINE/SYS LE7 12 D1
Lindrick Dr LEIE LE5 36 C3
Lindridge La RLEIW/BAR LE9 30 B1
Lindsay Rd LEIW LE3 34 B4
Lindsey Gdns
MKTHBORO LE16 77 G4
Lindum Cl RLEINE/SYS LE7 12 D2
Linford Cl WGSTN LE18 56 C1
Linford Crs COAL LE67 6 C4
Linford St LEIN LE4 19 G4
Ling Dl RLEINE/SYS LE7 5 G2
Link Ri COAL LE67 6 D4
Link Rd LEIS LE2 44 C1
RLEINE/SYS LE7 5 F4
RLEINE/SYS LE7 9 F5
Links Rd RLEIS/BBY LE8 72 B3
Linkway Gdns LEIW LE3 25 G5
Linley Gn RLEIW/BAR LE9 63 F3
Linnett Cl END/NAR LE19 52 C4
Linney Rd LEIN LE4 18 C4
Lintlaw Cl LEIN LE4 20 B3
Linton St LEIE LE5 36 A2
Linwal Av RLEINE/SYS LE7 39 H1
Linwood La LEIS LE2 43 F2
Lipton Rd LEIN LE4 18 A1
Litelmede LEIE LE5 27 G3
Little Av LEIN LE4 19 H4
Little Dl WGSTN LE18 56 C2
Little Dunmow Rd LEIE LE5 27 H2
The Littlefare LEIW LE3 33 F3
Littlegarth LEIS LE2 43 F4
Little Glen Rd LEIS LE2 54 C2
Little Hl WGSTN LE18 56 B1
Little Holme St LEIW LE3 2 B5
Littlejohn Rd LEIS LE2 42 D4
Little La RLEIW/BAR LE9 30 B1
Little Masons Cl LEIW LE3 33 F4
Littlemeer Cl LEIW LE3 33 F4
Littlemore Cl LEIE LE5 27 H4
Littleton St LEIW LE3 25 H3
The Littleway LEIE LE5 27 H4
Little Wood Cl LEIN LE4 18 C3
Livesey Dr RLEIW/BAR LE9 66 C2
Livingstone St LEIW LE3 34 C1
Lobbs Wood Ct LEIE LE5 28 B2
Lobelia Cl END/NAR LE19 52 B3
Locke Av LEIN LE4 20 B2
Lockerbie Av LEIN LE4 20 A3
Lock Gate Cl WGSTN LE18 55 G3
Lockhouse Cl LEIS LE2 42 B4
Lockley Cl GBY/RBY LE6 22 D2
Lodge Cl LEIN LE4 20 D1
RLEINE/SYS LE7 5 E5
RLEIS/BBY LE8 71 H1
RLEIW/BAR LE9 51 H3
Lodge Farm Rd LEIE LE5 28 C5
Lodge La RLEINE/SYS LE7 9 F1
Lodge Rd RLEIS/BBY LE8 70 B5
Lodgewood Av LEIN LE4 11 F5
Logan Av LEIS LE2 42 C2
Logan Ct MKTHBORO LE16 74 B5
Logan Crs MKTHBORO LE16 74 A5
Logan St MKTHBORO LE16 77 G1
Lombardy Ri LEIE LE5 27 E3
Lomond Crs LEIN LE4 18 C5
London Rd COAL LE67 6 B4
LEIS LE2 3 J6
LEIS LE2 45 F3
RLEIS/BBY LE8 58 B2
London St LEIE LE5 27 F4
Long Brimley Cl
MKTHBORO LE16 78 C1
Longcliffe Rd LEIE LE5 27 E3
Longfellow Rd LEIS LE2 35 G5
Longford Cl WGSTN LE18 56 A3
Long Furrow RLEINE/SYS LE7 5 G2
Longgrey RLEIS/BBY LE8 70 A2
Longhade Furlong
RLEINE/SYS LE7 9 H4
Longhurst Cl LEIN LE4 20 C2
The Longlands
MKTHBORO LE16 78 C1
Long La LEI LE1 2 D2
WGSTN LE18 56 B1
Longleat Cl LEIE LE5 27 F2
MKTHBORO LE16 78 C1
Long Meadow WGSTN LE18 56 C3
Longstone Gn LEIE LE5 29 E3
Long St RLEIW/BAR LE9 60 C3
WGSTN LE18 56 B1
Lonsdale Rd LEIN LE4 20 C1
Lonsdale St LEIS LE2 36 A1
Lord Byron St LEIS LE2 35 G5
Lord Cl END/NAR LE19 52 D4
Lords Av LEIN LE4 10 C5
Lorne Rd LEIS LE2 35 G4
Lorraine Rd LEIS LE2 42 D1
Lorrimer Rd LEIS LE2 35 E5
Loseby La LEI LE1 2 E4
Lothair Rd LEIS LE2 35 E4
Loughborough Rd LEIN LE4 11 G4
Loughland Cl RLEIS/BBY LE8 54 A3
Louise Av GBY/RBY LE6 16 B5
Lovelace Wy RLEIS/BBY LE8 70 B4
Lowcroft Dr LEIS LE2 45 G4

Lower Brown St LEI LE1 ....2 E6
Lower Church St
RLEINE/SYS LE7 ....4 D5
Lower Hastings St LEI LE1 ......3 G7
Lower Hill St LEI LE1........3 F2
Lower Keyham La LEIE LE5....28 B1
Lower Lee St LEI LE1 ....3 F2
Lower Leicester Rd
LUTT LE17........81 H2
Lower Willow St LEI LE1 ....26 C3
Lowick Dr WGSTN LE18 ....56 C1
Lowland Av LEIW LE3........32 C3
Loxley Rd LEIW LE3 ....24 A1
Lubbesthorpe Bridle Rd
END/NAR LE19........32 C5
LEIW LE3........33 G4
Lubbesthorpe Rd LEIW LE3....41 G1
Lubbesthorpe Wy
END/NAR LE19........33 F5
Lubenham Hl
MKTHBORO LE16........77 E1
Lubenham Rd
MKTHBORO LE16........77 E3
Lucas Wy RLEIW/BAR LE9 ......49 E4
Ludgate Cl LEIN LE4 ....11 E4
Ludlam Cl RLEIS/BBY LE8........64 C2
Ludlow Cl LEIS LE2 ....45 G3
Lulworth Cl LEIE LE5 ....37 E1
WGSTN LE18........56 B4
Lunsford Rd LEIE LE5........27 F2
Luther St LEIW LE3 ....34 C1
Lutterworth Rd LEIS LE2........42 C3
LUTT LE17........81 F1
RLEIS/BBY LE8........54 A5
Lychgate Cl GBY/RBY LE6 ....9 G2
Lydall Rd LEIS LE2 ....42 D4
Lydford Rd LEIN LE4........20 C5
Lyle Cl LEIN LE4 ....20 C2
Lymington Rd LEIE LE5 ....28 D2
Lyn Cl LEIW LE3 ....17 H4
Lyncote Rd LEIW LE3 ....34 B5
Lyncroft Leys LEIE LE5........29 F3
Lyndale Cl LEIN LE4........20 C1
Lyndale Rd LEIW LE3 ....33 H5
Lyndene Cl RLEIW/BAR LE9 ....49 E4
Lyndhurst Rd LEIS LE2 *........45 E2
Lyndon Dr LEIS LE2........44 D2
Lyngate Av LEIN LE4........11 G4
Lynholme Rd LEIS LE2 ....43 H2
Lynmouth Cl LEIW LE3........24 A3
Lynmouth Dr WGSTN LE18 ....43 G3
Lynmouth Rd LEIE LE5........28 D2
Lynwood Cl RLEIW/BAR LE9 ..30 B2
Lyon Cl WGSTN LE18........43 G4
Lytham Rd LEIS LE2 ....35 G4
Lytton Rd LEIS LE2 ....35 H4

M

Mablowe Fld WGSTN LE18.....56 C3
Macaulay Rd LUTT LE17........81 G2
Macaulay St LEIS LE2 ....35 F4
Macdonald Rd LEIN LE4........26 C1
Machin Dr RLEIW/BAR LE9 ....69 E5
Mackenzie Cl LUTT LE17 ....81 G1
Mackenzie Wy LEI LE1 ....3 H1
Madeline Cl
MKTHBORO LE16........75 E4
Madeline Rd LEIN LE4 ....18 C1
Madras Rd LEI LE1 ....3 J2
Magna Rd WGSTN LE18 ....55 G2
Magnolia Cl LEIS LE2 ....42 C3
LEIW LE3........32 A3
Magnolia Dr LUTT LE17 ....81 F2
Magnus Rd LEIN LE4........20 A5
Maiden St RLEINE/SYS LE7 ....12 D1
Maidenwell Av LEIE LE5........21 H5
Maidstone Rd LEIS LE2 ....3 J5
Maidwell Cl WGSTN LE18 ....56 D1
Maino Crs LUTT LE17 ....81 E4
Main Rd MKTHBORO LE16 ......79 G1
Main St COAL LE67 ....6 B3
GBY/RBY LE6 ....7 H3
GBY/RBY LE6 ....22 C2
LEIE LE5 ....28 A2
LEIE LE5 ....37 F2
LEIW LE3........23 H1
LEIW LE3........33 H3
MKTHBORO LE16........75 E3
MKTHBORO LE16........76 B1
MKTHBORO LE16........77 E5
RLEINE/SYS LE7........5 H4
RLEINE/SYS LE7........13 G4
RLEINE/SYS LE7........29 F2
RLEINE/SYS LE7........38 B1
RLEINE/SYS LE7........39 H2
RLEIS/BBY LE8........58 D3
RLEIS/BBY LE8........59 H3
RLEIS/BBY LE8........65 F3
RLEIS/BBY LE8........70 B4
RLEIS/BBY LE8........71 H1
RLEIS/BBY LE8........71 H5
RLEIS/BBY LE8........72 A1
RLEIW/BAR LE9........22 D5
RLEIW/BAR LE9........30 B1
RLEIW/BAR LE9........51 H4
RLEIW/BAR LE9........63 F4
RLEIW/BAR LE9........68 C2
Malabar Rd LEI LE1........3 J2
Malcolm Ar LEI LE1 * 2 E3
Malham Cl LEIN LE4 ....18 B4
Malham Wy LEIS LE2 ....45 H3
Mallard Av GBY/RBY LE6 ......16 A4
Mallard Dr RLEINE/SYS LE7 ......4 B5
Mallard Wy LEIW LE3 ....32 A3
Malling Av RLEIW/BAR LE9 ....68 B2
Malling Cl RLEINE/SYS LE7......11 H3
Mallory Pl LEIE LE5........27 G2
Mallory St RLEIW/BAR LE9......48 C3
Mallow Cl LEIE LE5 ....21 G4
The Maltings LEIW LE3........23 H1
Malton Dr LEIS LE2 ....45 G2
Malvern Crs RLEIW/BAR LE9 ..63 F3
Malvern Rd LEIS LE2........36 B3
Mandarin Wy
RLEIS/BBY LE8........63 H2
Mandervell Rd LEIS LE2........44 D3
Mandora La LEIS LE2 ....3 J7
Manitoba Rd LEI LE1 ....3 G1
Mann Cl LEIW LE3 ....33 F3
Manners Rd LEIS LE2 ....43 E1
Manor Brook Cl
RLEIW/BAR LE9 ....60 C3
Manor Cl LEIS LE2 ....37 F5
Manor Ct RLEIS/BBY LE8 ....54 C3
Manor Dr LEIN LE4 ....18 A2
Manor Farm Cl
RLEIW/BAR LE9 ....68 D3
Manor Farm Wy LEIW LE3......23 H3
Manor Gdns LEIW LE3 ....24 A2
RLEIW/BAR LE9 ....30 A2
Manor House Gdns
LEIE LE5 ....28 B2
Manor Rd LEIN LE4........20 B1
LEIS LE2 ....36 D5
LUTT LE17........81 F1
MKTHBORO LE16........75 E3
RLEIS/BBY LE8........70 C4
RLEIW/BAR LE9........30 A2
RLEIW/BAR LE9........63 F2
RLEIW/BAR LE9........66 D1
Manor Rd Extension
LEIS LE2 ....45 F1
Manor St WGSTN LE18 ....55 H1
Mansfield St LEI LE1........2 E2
Manston Cl LEIN LE4........21 E2
Mantle Rd LEIW LE3 ....2 A2
Manton Cl RLEIW/BAR LE9 ....69 F3
Maple Av LEIW LE3 ....33 E2
RLEIS/BBY LE8........54 B5
RLEIS/BBY LE8........65 E2
Maple Dr LUTT LE17 ....81 F3
Maple Rd LEIN LE4 ....20 B1
Mapleton Rd WGSTN LE18......44 A5
Maple Tree Wk
END/NAR LE19........53 E4
Maple Wy RLEIW/BAR LE9......30 A2
RLEIW/BAR LE9 ....48 D5
Maplewell Dr LEIN LE4........18 A1
Maplin Rd LEIE LE5........29 E1
Marble St LEI LE1 ....2 E5
Marcus Cl RLEINE/SYS LE7......12 C2
Marefield Cl RLEINE/SYS LE7..29 G5
Marfitt St LEIN LE4 ....19 H5
Margam Cl LEIW LE3........18 B5
Margaret Anne Rd
LEIS LE2 ....45 F4
Margaret Cl LEIN LE4 ....12 C4
Margaret Crs WGSTN LE18 ....43 H5
Margaret Rd LEIE LE5 ....27 G5
Marigold Wy END/NAR LE19..52 B3
Marina Dr GBY/RBY LE6........16 C4
Marina Rd LEIE LE5........36 B1
Marion Cl LEIW LE3 ....17 H5
Marion's Wy
RLEIW/BAR LE9 ....61 H2
Marjorie St LEIN LE4........26 C1
Market Pl LEI LE1 ....2 E4
Market Pl South LEI LE1 ....2 E4
Market St LEI LE1 ....2 E4
LUTT LE17........81 H3
Markfield La COAL LE67 ....7 E4
Markfield Rd COAL LE67 ....14 C3
GBY/RBY LE6 ....15 F5
Markland LEIS LE2 ....42 C4
Marlborough Dr
RLEIS/BBY LE8........70 C5
Marlborough St LEI LE1........3 F5
Marlborough Wy
MKTHBORO LE16........74 C4
Marlow Rd LEIW LE3 ....34 D3
Marmion Cl RLEIS/BBY LE8 ....70 C5
Maromme Sq WGSTN LE18 ....44 B5
Marquis St LEI LE1 ....3 F6
Marriott Dr RLEIS/BBY LE8 ....72 B3
Marriott Rd LEIS LE2 ....43 E3
Marsden Av RLEINE/SYS LE7....5 F4
Marsden La LEIS LE2........42 B2
Marshall Cl LEIW LE3 ....33 E3
Marsh Av RLEIS/BBY LE8 ....72 B2
Marsh Cl LEIN LE4 ....20 D2
Marsh Dr RLEIS/BBY LE8 ....72 A2
Marston Cl LEIS LE2 ....45 E5
Marston Crs RLEIS/BBY LE8 ..65 E3
Marston Dr GBY/RBY LE6 ......16 B4
Marston Rd LEIN LE4 ....20 C5
MKTHBORO LE16........76 A3
RLEIW/BAR LE9 ....61 F1
Marston Trussell Rd
MKTHBORO LE16........76 B5
Marstown Av WGSTN LE18 ....55 F1
Martin Av LEIS LE2 ....45 F3
RLEIW/BAR LE9 ....32 B2
Martin Cl LEIN LE4........26 D2
RLEIW/BAR LE9 ....60 B5
Martindale Cl LEIS LE2 ....35 F2
Martin Dr RLEINE/SYS LE7........4 A5
Martinshaw La
GBY/RBY LE6 ....16 A4
Martin St LEIN LE4 ....27 E2
Martival LEIE LE5 ....27 G3
Marvin Cl LEIW LE3........25 F3
Marwell Cl LEIN LE4 ....19 F3
Marwood Rd LEIN LE4........18 D3
Marydene Ct LEIE LE5 ....37 G2
Marydene Dr LEIE LE5 ....37 G2
Marylebone Dr LUTT LE17........81 H3
Mary Rd LEIW LE3........25 F2
Mary St RLEIW/BAR LE9........49 F3
Masefield Av
END/NAR LE19........52 C1
Masefield Cl RLEIW/BAR LE9..48 B3
Masons Cl END/NAR LE19 ......52 D4
Matlock Av WGSTN LE18 ....55 G2
Matlock St LEIE LE5 ....27 E4
Matts Cl LEIS LE2........42 D3
Maughan St RLEIW/BAR LE9..49 F2
Maura Cl RLEIS/BBY LE8 ....63 H1
Maurice Dr RLEIS/BBY LE8 ....64 D3
Maurice Rd
MKTHBORO LE16........77 G4
Mavis Av LEIW LE3 ....34 C3
Mawby Cl RLEIS/BBY LE8........64 A1
Maxwell Wy LUTT LE17 ....81 G1
May Cl LEIW LE3 ....34 A1
Mayfield Dr WGSTN LE18........44 B4
Mayfield Rd LEIS LE2 ....36 A2
Mayfield Wy
RLEIW/BAR LE9 ....48 C4
Mayflower Cl COAL LE67 ....6 C4
Mayflower Rd LEIE LE5 ....36 C2
Maynard Rd LEIE LE5........3 K3
LEIE LE5 ....27 E4
Mayns La RLEIS/BBY LE8 ....59 F5
Mayor's Wk LEI LE1 ....35 G2
Mays Farm Dr
RLEIW/BAR LE9 ....60 B3
Maytree Cl RLEIW/BAR LE9 ....32 A2
Maytree Dr RLEIW/BAR LE9 ..32 A2
McDowell Wy
END/NAR LE19........52 D4
McVicker Cl LEIE LE5 ....28 A4
Meadhurst Rd LEIW LE3 ....25 E5
Meadowbrook Rd
RLEIS/BBY LE8........71 H3
Meadow Cl GBY/RBY LE6........22 D2
RLEIW/BAR LE9 ....60 B3
Meadow Ct END/NAR LE19 ....52 C2
WGSTN LE18 * 56 B1
Meadow Court Rd
GBY/RBY LE6 ....16 B4
RLEIW/BAR LE9 ....49 F4
Meadowcourt Rd LEIS LE2 ....44 D1
Meadowcroft Cl LEIW LE3......23 H3
Meadow Edge
END/NAR LE19........52 C1
Meadow Gdns LEIS LE2 ....43 F3
Meadow Hl RLEIS/BBY LE8 ....58 C3
Meadow La COAL LE67........6 C3
LEIN LE4 ....11 H4
RLEINE/SYS LE7........4 A5
Meadow Rd RLEIW/BAR LE9 ..48 C4
The Meadows
END/NAR LE19........53 F4
RLEINE/SYS LE7........5 G1
Meadow St
MKTHBORO LE16........74 C5
Meadowsweet Rd LEIE LE5 ..28 C1
The Meadow
RLEIW/BAR LE9 ....69 E4
Meadow Vw LEIS LE2........45 F3
RLEINE/SYS LE7........5 H2
Meadow Wy GBY/RBY LE6 ....16 B4
RLEIW/BAR LE9 ....30 B3
WGSTN LE18........44 D5
The Meads LEIW LE3........24 C5
Meadvale Rd LEIS LE2 ....44 A1
Meadway LEIW LE3 ....25 E4
The Meadway LEIN LE4........11 G4
RLEINE/SYS LE7........12 D2
Meadwell Rd LEIW LE3........33 F1
Medhurst Cl RLEIS/BBY LE8 ..64 A1
Medina Rd LEIW LE3........25 H2
Medway Cl
MKTHBORO LE16........78 B1
Medway St LEIS LE2 ....36 A1
The Meer RLEIS/BBY LE8 ....70 C5
Melba Wy RLEINE/SYS LE7 ....11 H3
Melbourne Cl
RLEIS/BBY LE8........71 H3
Melbourne Rd LEIS LE2 ....27 E5
Melbourne St LEIS LE2........3 K3
Melcroft Av LEIW LE3........25 F5
Melford St LEIE LE5 ....27 H3
Melland Pl LEIS LE2........43 E3
Mellier Cl END/NAR LE19 ....52 C1
Mellor Rd LEIW LE3........25 E5
Melody Av RLEINE/SYS LE7 ....17 G1
Melrose St LEIN LE4 ....26 D1
Melton Av LEIN LE4........20 A2
Melton Dr RLEIW/BAR LE9......68 C1
Melton Rd LEIN LE4 ....12 B5
RLEINE/SYS LE7........5 H1
RLEINE/SYS LE7........12 C3
Melton St LEI LE1 ....26 C3
RLEIW/BAR LE9 ....49 E3
Memory La LEI LE1 ....26 C3
Mendip Av LEIN LE4 ....25 G1
Mennecy Cl RLEIS/BBY LE8 ....64 D3
Mensa Cl LEIS LE2 ....27 E5
Menzies Rd LEIN LE4 ....19 E5
Mercia Dr LEIS LE2 ....44 D2
Mercury Cl LEIS LE2 ....3 K5
Mere Cl LEIE LE5 ....27 E4
Meredith Rd LEIW LE3 ....34 B4
Mere La RLEINE/SYS LE7 ....5 H4
RLEIS/BBY LE8........57 H1
Mere Rd LEIE LE5 ....27 E5
LEIS LE2 ....47 E2
WGSTN LE18........44 C5
The Mere RLEIS/BBY LE8 ....58 C3
Mereworth Cl LEIE LE5 ....27 F2
Meridian East
END/NAR LE19........33 F5
Meridian North
END/NAR LE19........41 F1
Meridian South
END/NAR LE19........41 F2
Meridian Wy END/NAR LE19 ..33 F4
Meridian West
END/NAR LE19........41 F1
Meriton Rd LUTT LE17 ....81 F4
Merlin Cl LEIW LE3 ....32 C3
RLEIW/BAR LE9 ....68 C2
Merthull Rd LEIE LE5 ....28 C4
Merton Av LEIW LE3........25 G5
RLEINE/SYS LE7........13 F1
Merton Cl RLEIW/BAR LE9 ......68 B2
Merton Wy RLEIS/BBY LE8 ....71 H2
Mervyn Rd LEIE LE5 ....36 B1
Metcalf Cl RLEIW/BAR LE9......60 B4
Metcalfe St RLEIW/BAR LE9 ..49 E4
Methuen Av LEIN LE4........12 C4
Meynell Cl LEIS LE2........45 G4
Meynell Rd LEIE LE5 ....27 F3
Michael Cl RLEINE/SYS LE7 ......5 G3
Michael Ramsey Ct LEIS LE2 ..42 C5
Mickleton Dr LEIE LE5 ....37 F2
Middlebrook Cl
GBY/RBY LE6 ....22 D2
Middledale Rd
MKTHBORO LE16........78 B1
Middlesex Rd LEIS LE2........42 D1
Middleton Cl
RLEIW/BAR LE9 ....60 C4
WGSTN LE18........44 D5
Middletons Cl
RLEIS/BBY LE8........70 B3
Middleton St LEIS LE2 ....42 C1
Midhurst Av LEIW LE3 ....33 H5
Midland St LEI LE1 ....3 H3
Midway Rd LEIE LE5........36 B3
Milestone Cl RLEIS/BBY LE8 ..72 C3
Milford Cl END/NAR LE19........52 C3
Milford Rd LEIS LE2 ....35 H5
Millbrook Cl LEIN LE4 ....19 F4
Millbrook Dr
RLEIW/BAR LE9 ....68 D4
Mill Cl LEIN LE4 ....19 H1
RLEIS/BBY LE8........71 H5
RLEIW/BAR LE9 ....67 E1
WGSTN LE18........55 F3
Mill Dr GBY/RBY LE6........22 D3
Miller Cl LEIN LE4........20 C2
Millers Cl LEIW LE3 ....23 G2
RLEINE/SYS LE7........13 E2
Millersdale Av LEIE LE5 ....28 D5
Millers Gdns
MKTHBORO LE16........77 E2
Millers Gra RLEIW/BAR LE9 ....68 D4
Millfield Cl RLEINE/SYS LE7 ....17 F2
Millfield Crs LEIW LE3........41 H2
Mill Gv LUTT LE17 ....81 H4
Mill Hl END/NAR LE19 ....40 B3
Mill Hill Cl RLEIS/BBY LE8........53 H4
Mill Hill La COAL LE67 ....6 B3
LEIS LE2 ....3 J7
Mill Hill Rd MKTHBORO LE16 ..78 A1
Milligan Rd LEIS LE2 ....43 E2
Mill La END/NAR LE19........40 D5
HINC LE10........66 C4
LEIN LE4 ....12 B4
LEIS LE2 ....2 C6
RLEIS/BBY LE8........54 D3
RLEIS/BBY LE8........71 H4
RLEIW/BAR LE9 ....49 G2
RLEIW/BAR LE9 ....50 B4
The Mill La GBY/RBY LE6 ....23 G2
Mill Rd RLEINE/SYS LE7 ....10 B1
Millstone La LEI LE1 ....2 E5
RLEINE/SYS LE7........5 E4
Mill St LEI LE1........3 F6
Mill Vw RLEIW/BAR LE9 ....51 H4
Millwood Cl LEIN LE4 ....19 E2
Milnroy Rd LEIE LE5 ....29 E4
Milton Cl WGSTN LE18 ....56 C1
Milton Crs LEIN LE4........18 B5
Milton Gdns LEIS LE2 ....45 E3
Milton St END/NAR LE19 ....52 C2
Milverton Av LEIN LE4 ....25 H1
Milverton Cl WGSTN LE18 ....44 A4
Milverton Dr WGSTN LE18......44 A4
Minehead St LEIW LE3 ....25 F5
Minster Crs LEIN LE4 ....25 H1
Mint Rd LEIS LE2 ....2 B7
Misterton Wy LUTT LE17 ....81 H4
Mitchell Rd END/NAR LE19 ....40 C5
Moat Ct LEIE LE5........28 C2
Moat Rd LEIE LE5 ....27 F5
Moat St WGSTN LE18 ....56 A1
Modbury Av LEIN LE4........19 E3
Moira St LEIN LE4 ....26 D1
Monal Cl RLEIS/BBY LE8........63 H2
Monar Cl LEIN LE4........20 B3
Mona St RLEIW/BAR LE9 ....49 E4
Monica Rd LEIW LE3........41 H1
Monks Crs LEIN LE4 ....10 C4

Monmouth Dr LEIS LE2 54 C1
Monroe Cl MKTHBORO LE16 74 B4
Monsell Dr LEIS LE2 42 C3
Montague Av
RLEINE/SYS LE7 13 F2
Montague Rd LEIS LE2 35 H4
RLEIW/BAR LE9 68 D2
Montgomery Cl LUTT LE17 81 E5
Montgomery Rd
RLEIW/BAR LE9 49 G3
Montreal Cl LEI LE1 26 C3
Montreal Rd LEI LE1 26 C3
Montrose Cl
MKTHBORO LE16 77 G3
Montrose Rd LEIS LE2 42 C3
Montrose Rd South
LEIS LE2 42 C3
Montvale Gdns LEIN LE4 25 H2
Moon Cl LEIS LE2 3 J5
Moore Rd RLEIW/BAR LE9 48 B4
Moores Cl WGSTN LE18 55 E1
Moores La END/NAR LE19 40 D5
Moores Rd LEIN LE4 19 H5
Moorfields LEIE LE5 28 D2
Moorgate Av LEIN LE4 11 F4
Moorgate St LEIN LE4 26 C2
Moorland Rd
RLEINE/SYS LE7 12 C1
Morban Rd LEIS LE2 42 B2
Morcote Rd LEIW LE3 33 G1
Morland Av LEIS LE2 36 C5
Morledge St LEIE LE5 3 H3
Morley Rd LEIE LE5 27 E4
RLEIW/BAR LE9 67 E2
Morley St MKTHBORO LE16 77 G1
Mornington St LEIE LE5 27 F3
Morpeth Av LEIN LE4 18 D2
Morpeth Dr LEIS LE2 45 H4
Morris Cl LEIW LE3 33 F3
Morrison Ct RLEIS/BBY LE8 72 A3
Morris Rd LEIS LE2 35 G4
Mortiboys Wy
RLEIW/BAR LE9 60 B4
Mortimer Pl LEIW LE3 34 B4
Mortimer Rd END/NAR LE19 52 C4
Mortimer Wy LEIW LE3 34 A4
Mortoft Rd LEIN LE4 19 G4
Morton Wk LEIE LE5 27 F2
The Morwoods LEIS LE2 45 E3
Mossdale Rd LEIW LE3 33 G5
Mosse Wy LEIS LE2 45 G2
Mossgate LEIW LE3 25 E3
Mosswithy RLEIS/BBY LE8 70 B5
Mostyn Av RLEINE/SYS LE7 5 E5
Mostyn St LEIW LE3 25 F5
Mottisford Rd LEIN LE4 19 F3
Mountain Rd LEIN LE4 21 E3
Mount Av LEIE LE5 27 F4
RLEIW/BAR LE9 48 C4
Mountbatten Wy LUTT LE17 81 F4
Mountcastle Rd LEIW LE3 34 C3
Mountfield Rd
RLEIW/BAR LE9 49 E3
Mount Pleasant LEIS LE2 45 H4
Mount Rd LEIE LE5 27 E4
LEIS LE2 45 F3
RLEIW/BAR LE9 63 F3
The Mount RLEINE/SYS LE7 29 F2
Mount Vw RLEIS/BBY LE8 58 D2
Mowbray Dr RLEINE/SYS LE7 5 E5
Mowmacre Hl LEIN LE4 19 E2
Mowsley End WGSTN LE18 56 B1
Muirfield Cl LEIW LE3 24 A4
Mulberry Av LEIW LE3 24 A4
Mulberry Cl LUTT LE17 81 F2
Mull Wy RLEIS/BBY LE8 65 F3
Muncaster Cl
RLEIW/BAR LE9 69 E5
Mundella St LEIS LE2 36 A2
Munnings Cl LEIN LE4 26 D2
Muntjack Rd
RLEIS/BBY LE8 63 H1
Murby Wy LEIW LE3 33 E4
Muriel Rd LEIW LE3 25 G5
Murray Cl RLEIW/BAR LE9 68 D5
Murrayfield Rd LEIW LE3 24 A5
Murray St LEIS LE2 3 K3
Museum Sq LEI LE1 3 G6
Musgrove Cl LEIW LE3 2 A5
Musson Rd LEIW LE3 24 C3
Muston Gdns LEIS LE2 43 H1
Myrtle Av RLEINE/SYS LE7 11 H3
Myrtle Cl RLEIW/BAR LE9 48 A4
Myrtle Rd LEIS LE2 36 A1

N

Nagle Gv LEIN LE4 20 B2
Namur Rd WGSTN LE18 43 E5
Nansen Rd LEIE LE5 36 C1
Narborough Rd LEIW LE3 34 B4
RLEIW/BAR LE9 51 H4
RLEIW/BAR LE9 63 E1
Narborough Rd North
LEIW LE3 2 B5
Narborough Rd South
END/NAR LE19 41 G3
Narborough Wood Pk
END/NAR LE19 * 40 A1
Narrow Boat Cl
WGSTN LE18 55 G3
Narrow La LEIS LE2 42 C2
Naseby Cl MKTHBORO LE16 77 H2
WGSTN LE18 56 C1
Naseby Rd LEIN LE4 20 C5
Naseby Sq
MKTHBORO LE16 77 H2
Naseby Wy RLEIS/BBY LE8 58 D3
Navigation St LEI LE1 26 B3
Naylor Rd RLEINE/SYS LE7 5 E4
Neal Av LEIW LE3 33 G3
Necton St RLEINE/SYS LE7 13 E1
Nedham St LEIE LE5 3 K2
Needham Av LEIS LE2 42 A5
Needham Cl LEIS LE2 46 A4
Needwood Wy
END/NAR LE19 52 B1
Nelot Wy LEIE LE5 28 B5
Nelson St LEIS LE2 3 H6
MKTHBORO LE16 77 G1
RLEINE/SYS LE7 13 F1
Nene Dr LEIS LE2 45 G3
Neptune Cl LEIS LE2 27 E5
Neston Gdns LEIS LE2 43 F2
Neston Rd LEIS LE2 43 F2
Netherfield Cl
RLEIW/BAR LE9 69 F3
Netherfield Rd
RLEINE/SYS LE7 9 F5
Nether Field Wy LEIW LE3 33 F4
Netherhall La LEIN LE4 19 H1
Netherhall Rd LEIE LE5 28 C2
Netton Cl WGSTN LE18 56 A3
Nevanthon Rd LEIW LE3 25 F5
Neville Dr COAL LE67 6 B4
Neville Rd LEIW LE3 25 F5
Neville Smith Cl
RLEIW/BAR LE9 66 D2
Newall Cl LUTT LE17 81 G3
Newarke Cl LEIS LE2 2 C6
Newarke St LEI LE1 2 D5
The Newarke LEIS LE2 2 C5
Newark Rd LEIN LE4 12 C5
New Bond St LEI LE1 2 E3
New Bridge Rd LEIS LE2 54 B1
New Bridge St LEIS LE2 35 E2
Newbury Cl WGSTN LE18 56 A2
Newby Cl RLEIS/BBY LE8 53 H3
Newby Gdns LEIS LE2 45 H4
Newcombe Rd LEIW LE3 34 B3
Newcombe St
MKTHBORO LE16 77 H2
New Fields Av LEIW LE3 34 B3
New Fields Sq LEIW LE3 34 B4
New Forest Cl WGSTN LE18 56 B3
Newgate End WGSTN LE18 56 A1
Newham Cl LEIN LE4 21 E2
Newhaven Rd LEIE LE5 37 H2
New Henry St LEIW LE3 2 C1
Newington St LEIN LE4 19 H5
New Inn Cl RLEIW/BAR LE9 69 E4
Newlands Rd
RLEIW/BAR LE9 48 B4
Newlyn Pde LEIE LE5 28 D1
Newmarket St LEIS LE2 35 H5
New Park Rd LEIS LE2 35 E5
New Parks Bvd LEIW LE3 24 B5
New Parks Crs LEIW LE3 25 E2
New Park St LEIW LE3 2 B5
New Parks Wy LEIW LE3 24 C4
New Pingle St LEIW LE3 2 C1
Newpool Bank LEIS LE2 46 A4
Newport Pl LEI LE1 3 G5
Newport St LEIW LE3 25 G4
Newquay Dr LEIW LE3 24 A1
New Rd LEI LE1 2 E2
RLEIS/BBY LE8 72 B3
RLEIW/BAR LE9 60 B4
New Romney Cl LEIE LE5 29 E2
The Newry LEIS LE2 43 F3
New Star Rd LEIN LE4 20 D4
Newstead Av LEIW LE3 25 G1
RLEINE/SYS LE7 38 C1
WGSTN LE18 44 A4
Newstead Rd LEIS LE2 36 A5
New St LEI LE1 2 E4
LEIS LE2 45 F3
LUTT LE17 81 G3
RLEINE/SYS LE7 5 G4
RLEIS/BBY LE8 54 B2
RLEIS/BBY LE8 65 F2
RLEIW/BAR LE9 49 E3
Newton La RLEIS/BBY LE8 58 B4
WGSTN LE18 56 D2
Newton Wy
RLEIW/BAR LE9 68 D5
Newtown Linford La
GBY/RBY LE6 16 A2
Newtown St LEI LE1 3 F7
New Wk LEI LE1 3 H6
RLEIW/BAR LE9 66 D2
New Way Rd LEIE LE5 36 B3
New Zealand La
RLEINE/SYS LE7 5 E3
Nicholas Dr GBY/RBY LE6 22 D2
Nichols St LEIE LE5 3 H3
Nicklaus Rd LEIN LE4 20 B2
Nidderdale Rd
WGSTN LE18 56 D1
Nithsdale Av
MKTHBORO LE16 77 H2
Nithsdale Crs
MKTHBORO LE16 78 A2
Noble Cl LUTT LE17 81 G1
Noble St LEIW LE3 25 G5
Nock Verges
RLEIW/BAR LE9 49 G2
RLEIW/BAR LE9 60 B4
Noel St LEIW LE3 34 D2
Nook Cl GBY/RBY LE6 22 C1
Nook St LEIW LE3 25 F3
The Nook END/NAR LE19 40 C5
LUTT LE17 81 F1
RLEINE/SYS LE7 17 G1
RLEIS/BBY LE8 53 H4
RLEIS/BBY LE8 58 C4
RLEIW/BAR LE9 63 F4
Norbury Av LEIN LE4 27 E1
Norbury Cl
MKTHBORO LE16 74 B5
Norfolk Rd RLEIW/BAR LE9 30 B3
WGSTN LE18 43 F5
Norfolk St LEIW LE3 2 A5
Norfolk Wk LEIW LE3 2 A4
Norman Ct LEIS LE2 45 H5
Norman Dagley Cl
RLEIW/BAR LE9 49 E4
Normandy Cl LEIW LE3 24 A3
Norman Rd LEIN LE4 12 B4
Norman St LEIW LE3 2 A7
Normanton Rd LEIE LE5 36 A1
Norris Cl LEIN LE4 18 A4
Northampton Rd
MKTHBORO LE16 77 H1
Northampton St LEI LE1 3 G5
North Av LEIS LE2 36 A3
Northcote Rd LEIS LE2 35 H5
Northdene Rd LEIS LE2 43 H3
Northdown Dr LEIN LE4 20 C1
North Dr LEIE LE5 28 A2
North End Cl LEIS LE2 43 F2
Northfield Av LEIN LE4 11 G4
WGSTN LE18 43 H4
Northfield Rd LEIN LE4 27 G1
RLEIS/BBY LE8 54 B2
Northfields RLEINE/SYS LE7 4 D5
Northfold Rd LEIS LE2 44 A2
Northgate St LEIW LE3 2 C1
Northleigh Gv
MKTHBORO LE16 74 B5
Northleigh Wy
RLEIW/BAR LE9 49 F4
North Mills LEIW LE3 * 2 B1
North St RLEINE/SYS LE7 4 C5
WGSTN LE18 44 B5
Northumberland Av
LEIN LE4 20 A5
Northumberland Rd
WGSTN LE18 43 F5
Northumberland St LEI LE1 2 D1
North Wy RLEINE/SYS LE7 39 H1
Norton Rd RLEIW/BAR LE9 48 C4
Norton St LEI LE1 2 E6
Norwich Rd LEIN LE4 18 D4
Norwood Rd LEIE LE5 36 C2
Nottingham Rd LEIE LE5 27 F4
Nowell Cl LEIS LE2 54 D2
Nugent St LEIW LE3 2 A2
Nunneley Wy
MKTHBORO LE16 74 D5
Nursery Cl LEIN LE4 20 B1
RLEINE/SYS LE7 5 G4
RLEIW/BAR LE9 51 E1
Nursery Gdns
RLEIW/BAR LE9 48 D4
Nursery Hollow LEIS LE2 42 A5
Nursery Rd LEIE LE5 28 D3
Nutfield Rd LEIW LE3 34 C2
Nuthall Gv LEIS LE2 42 B4

O

Oadby Hill Dr LEIS LE2 44 D2
Oadby Rd WGSTN LE18 44 C5
Oakberry Rd LUTT LE17 81 H1
Oak Cl MKTHBORO LE16 74 D5
Oakcroft Av
RLEIW/BAR LE9 23 E5
Oakdale Cl LEIW LE3 24 A4
Oakdale Rd
RLEIW/BAR LE9 48 D4
Oakdene Rd LEIS LE2 43 G2
Oak Dr RLEINE/SYS LE7 13 F2
Oakenshaw Cl LEIN LE4 19 E2
Oakfield Av COAL LE67 6 B4
LEIN LE4 11 F5
LEIW LE3 17 F5
LUTT LE17 81 F3
Oakfield Cl RLEIS/BBY LE8 58 D2
Oakfield Crs RLEIS/BBY LE8 54 C4
Oakfield Rd LEIS LE2 36 A2
Oakland Av LEIN LE4 20 A2
Oakland Rd LEIS LE2 35 G4
Oakleigh Av WGSTN LE18 55 E2
Oakley Rd LEIE LE5 27 F3
Oakmeadow LEIW LE3 23 H3
Oakmeadow Wy
GBY/RBY LE6 16 A5
Oak Pool Gdns LEIS LE2 42 D5
Oakridge Cl LEIE LE5 21 G4
Oak Rd END/NAR LE19 52 D5
RLEIW/BAR LE9 30 A2
Oaks Dr RLEIS/BBY LE8 54 C4
Oakside Crs LEIE LE5 28 C5
Oak Spinney Pk
RLEIW/BAR LE9 32 D1
Oaks Rd RLEIS/BBY LE8 58 D3
Oak St LEIE LE5 27 E3
Oaks Wy LEIS LE2 36 D5
RLEIW/BAR LE9 49 E3
Oakthorpe Av LEIW LE3 34 B1
Oaktree Cl GBY/RBY LE6 16 A4
LEIE LE5 21 G5
RLEIS/BBY LE8 72 B2
Oakwood Av WGSTN LE18 44 B4
Oakwood Cl LEIW LE3 32 B3
Oakwood Rd LEIN LE4 25 H1
The Oasis LEIW LE3 23 H2
Oban St LEIW LE3 25 G4
Ocean Cl LEIE LE5 28 C3
Ocean Rd LEIE LE5 28 C4
Odam Cl LEIW LE3 33 H3
Odeon Ar LEI LE1 2 E4
Offranville Cl LEIN LE4 20 D1
Ogwen Cl LEIE LE5 28 D4
Okehampton Av LEIE LE5 36 D2
Old Church St LEIS LE2 42 C2
Old Field Cl RLEIS/BBY LE8 64 C2
Old Hall Cl GBY/RBY LE6 16 B5
LEIN LE4 12 C4
Old Hall La
MKTHBORO LE16 76 C1
Old Mill Cl RLEIW/BAR LE9 68 D4
Old Mill La LEI LE1 2 C2
Old Mill Rd RLEIW/BAR LE9 68 D4
Old Milton St LEI LE1 3 G1
Old Rectory Cl
RLEIW/BAR LE9 68 C3
Oliver Rd LEIN LE4 20 B5
Oliver St LEIS LE2 35 E5
Olphin St LEIN LE4 26 C2
Olympic Cl LEIW LE3 24 B2
Onslow St LEIS LE2 36 A1
Ontario Cl LEI LE1 3 G1
Orange Hl LUTT LE17 81 H4
Orange St WGSTN LE18 55 F3
Orchard Av LEIS LE2 54 B1
Orchard Cl LEIS LE2 45 E4
Orchard Gdns LEIN LE4 20 D1
Orchard La RLEIS/BBY LE8 58 D4
RLEIS/BBY LE8 65 F3
Orchard Rd LEIN LE4 11 H5
LUTT LE17 81 F4
RLEIW/BAR LE9 68 C2
Orchards Dr WGSTN LE18 55 H1
Orchardson Av LEI LE1 26 D2
The Orchards LEIE LE5 29 E3
Orchard St LEI LE1 3 F1
MKTHBORO LE16 74 C5
RLEIS/BBY LE8 70 B4
The Orchard GBY/RBY LE6 16 A4
RLEIW/BAR LE9 60 C4
Orchard Wy
RLEINE/SYS LE7 13 G1
Orchid Cl END/NAR LE19 52 C2
LEIE LE5 21 G5
Orchid Pl RLEIW/BAR LE9 69 F5
Oriel Dr RLEINE/SYS LE7 13 F1
Orkney Wy RLEIS/BBY LE8 65 F3
Orlando Rd LEIS LE2 35 H3
Orme Cl LEIN LE4 18 A4
Ormen Gn LEIW LE3 24 B4
Ormond Cl RLEIW/BAR LE9 48 A4
Oronsay Rd LEIN LE4 18 B4
Orpine Rd LEIE LE5 21 F4
Orsett Cl LEIE LE5 27 H2
Orson Dr WGSTN LE18 43 H5
Orson St LEIE LE5 27 F5
Orton Rd LEIN LE4 19 E4
RLEIW/BAR LE9 49 F3
Orwell Dr LEIN LE4 18 A3
Osborne Rd LEIE LE5 27 F5
The Osiers LEIW LE3 41 H1
Osmaston Rd LEIE LE5 36 A1
Osprey Cl RLEIW/BAR LE9 68 C2
Osprey Rd LEIN LE4 18 A1
Oswin Rd LEIW LE3 24 D5
Ottawa Rd LEI LE1 3 H2
Otter Wy RLEIS/BBY LE8 63 H1
Outfields Dr
RLEINE/SYS LE7 9 H2
Outwood Cl LEIW LE3 24 B5
The Oval LEIS LE2 3 H7
MKTHBORO LE16 74 C5
RLEIW/BAR LE9 60 C4
WGSTN LE18 44 D4
Overdale Av LEIW LE3 16 D4
Overdale Cl LEIW LE3 16 D5
MKTHBORO LE16 78 B2
Overdale Rd LEIN LE4 20 D1
LEIS LE2 44 A1
Overfield Av
MKTHBORO LE16 74 D4
Overfield Cl END/NAR LE19 52 C4
GBY/RBY LE6 22 D2
Overing Cl LEIN LE4 19 G4
Overpark Av LEIW LE3 33 H1
Overseal Rd LEIW LE3 24 C2
Overton Rd LEIE LE5 27 F3
Owen Cl LEIN LE4 20 C2
LEIW LE3 33 F4
Owston Dr WGSTN LE18 43 H5
Oxendon St LEIS LE2 3 K5
Oxendon Wk LEIS LE2 3 K5
Oxen Wy LEIE LE5 28 A5
Oxford Av LEIS LE2 35 H2
Oxford Ct RLEINE/SYS LE7 5 E5
Oxford Dr WGSTN LE18 43 F5
Oxford Rd LEIS LE2 35 H3
RLEIW/BAR LE9 30 A2
Oxford St LEI LE1 2 E5
RLEINE/SYS LE7 5 E5
RLEIW/BAR LE9 48 B4
RLEIW/BAR LE9 49 F3
Oxted Ri LEIS LE2 45 E5

P

Packer Av LEIW LE3 .... 32 D1
Packhorse Dr
END/NAR LE19 .... 53 F1
Packhorse Rd LEIS LE2 .... 42 D5
Packwood Rd LEIN LE4 .... 19 E3
Paddock Cl LEIS LE2 .... 44 D3
RLEIS/BBY LE8 .... 65 E2
The Paddocks
END/NAR LE19 .... 53 E4
Paddock St WGSTN LE18 .... 56 B1
The Paddock COAL LE67 .... 6 C3
RLEIS/BBY LE8 .... 72 B3
Paddock Vw
RLEINE/SYS LE7 .... 12 D1
Padgate Cl RLEINE/SYS LE7 .... 29 F4
Padstow Rd LEIN LE4 .... 20 C5
Padwell La RLEINE/SYS LE7 .... 38 C1
Page Cl LUTT LE17 .... 81 G1
Paget Av LEIN LE4 .... 11 H4
Paget Ct RLEIS/BBY LE8 .... 72 A3
Paget Rd LEIW LE3 .... 25 G4
MKTHBORO LE16 .... 76 B1
Paget St LEIS LE2 .... 42 C2
RLEIS/BBY LE8 .... 72 A3
Paigle Rd LEIS LE2 .... 42 C2
Painter St LEI LE1 .... 26 C2
Palfreyman La LEIS LE2 .... 46 A4
Palmer Dr LUTT LE17 .... 81 G4
Palmerston Bvd
WGSTN LE18 .... 44 A2
Palmerston Cl
RLEIS/BBY LE8 .... 71 H3
Palmerston Wy LEIS LE2 .... 44 B2
Palmer St LEIN LE4 .... 19 G4
Pamela Pl LEIN LE4 .... 19 E3
Pankhurst Rd LEIN LE4 .... 18 A1
Paper Mill Cl
RLEINE/SYS LE7 .... 17 F1
The Parade LEIS LE2 .... 45 E2
LEIS LE2 * 54 A1
Paramore Cl RLEIS/BBY LE8 .. 64 A1
Pares St LEI LE1 .... 26 B3
Parham Cl LEIW LE3 .... 25 F1
Park Av COAL LE67 .... 6 C3
LEIS LE2 .... 35 E5
Park Cl RLEIW/BAR LE9 .... 49 E2
RLEIW/BAR LE9 .... 63 F4
Park Crs LEIS LE2 .... 45 G4
Parkdale Rd LEIN LE4 .... 20 D1
Park Dr LEIW LE3 .... 23 H2
LEIW LE3 .... 33 E2
MKTHBORO LE16 .... 74 C5
Parker Dr LEIN LE4 .... 18 D5
Parkfield Cl GBY/RBY LE6 .... 22 D2
Parkhill LEIS LE2 .... 34 D5
Park Hill Av LEIS LE2 .... 42 D1
Park Hill Dr LEIS LE2 .... 42 D1
Parkhouse Cl LEIN LE4 .... 19 G2
Parkland Dr LEIS LE2 .... 45 E2
Parklands Av GBY/RBY LE6 .... 15 H4
Park La LEIS LE2 .... 36 B3
Park Ri LEIW LE3 .... 24 C5
Park Rd END/NAR LE19 .... 52 D4
GBY/RBY LE6 .... 22 C3
LEIN LE4 .... 19 F1
RLEINE/SYS LE7 .... 17 F1
RLEIS/BBY LE8 .... 54 A3
RLEIW/BAR LE9 .... 49 F3
RLEIW/BAR LE9 .... 63 F4
RLEIW/BAR LE9 .... 66 D2
WGSTN LE18 .... 55 F3
Parkside GBY/RBY LE6 .... 16 B3
Parkside Cl LEIN LE4 .... 18 A1
Parkstone Rd LEIE LE5 .... 28 D2
RLEINE/SYS LE7 .... 4 D4
RLEIW/BAR LE9 .... 30 B3
Park St LEI LE1 .... 3 F5
RLEIS/BBY LE8 .... 70 B3
Park Vale Rd LEIE LE5 .... 27 E5
Park Vw HINC LE10 .... 66 B5
LEIW LE3 .... 24 C4
Park View Cl
RLEIW/BAR LE9 .... 68 D3
The Parkway LEIE LE5 .... 28 B3
Parliament St LEIS LE2 .... 2 E7
Parlour Cl WGSTN LE18 .... 56 A1
Parry St LEIE LE5 .... 27 E3
Parsons Dr LEIS LE2 .... 42 A5
Partridge Cl RLEINE/SYS LE7 .... 4 B5
Partridge Rd LEIN LE4 .... 20 D2
Parvian Rd LEIS LE2 .... 43 G4
Pasley Cl LEIS LE2 .... 42 D4
Pasley Rd LEIS LE2 .... 42 D4
Pasture La LEI LE1 .... 2 D1
The Pastures
END/NAR LE19 .... 52 C2
LEIS LE2 .... 46 A4
MKTHBORO LE16 .... 77 F1
RLEINE/SYS LE7 .... 12 C1
RLEIW/BAR LE9 .... 68 D4
Paterson Cl LEIN LE4 .... 18 A1
Paton St LEIW LE3 .... 2 A7
Patrick St MKTHBORO LE16 .... 78 A2
Patterdale Rd LEIN LE4 .... 12 C5
Paul Dr LEIN LE4 .... 20 D3
Pauline Av LEIN LE4 .... 19 H3
Pawley Cl RLEIS/BBY LE8 .... 64 A1
Pawley Gdns LEIS LE2 .... 42 D4
Payne St LEIN LE4 .... 19 H4
Peacock Dr RLEIS/BBY LE8 .... 63 H1
Peacock La LEI LE1 .... 2 D4
Peakdale WGSTN LE18 .... 56 D2
Peake Rd LEIN LE4 .... 27 F1
Pear Tree Cl LUTT LE17 .... 81 E3
RLEIW/BAR LE9 .... 48 B3
Peartree Cl LEIW LE3 .... 23 H3
RLEINE/SYS LE7 .... 17 F2
Pear Tree Gdns
MKTHBORO LE16 .... 77 G2
Peatling Rd RLEIS/BBY LE8 .... 65 G4
Peckleton Gn
RLEIW/BAR LE9 .... 48 B3
Peckleton La
RLEIW/BAR LE9 .... 30 B2
RLEIW/BAR LE9 .... 31 E5
Peckleton Vw
RLEIW/BAR LE9 .... 30 B3
Pedlars Cl LEIN LE4 .... 18 B4
Peebles Wy LEIN LE4 .... 20 B4
Peel Cl RLEIS/BBY LE8 .... 71 H3
Peewit Cl LEIS LE2 .... 42 A5
Pegasus Cl LEIS LE2 .... 3 K4
Peggs Cl RLEIW/BAR LE9 .... 49 F3
Peggs La RLEINE/SYS LE7 .... 5 H4
Peldon Cl LEIN LE4 .... 18 D5
Pelham St LEI LE1 .... 2 E6
LEIS LE2 .... 45 E2
Pelham Wy LEI LE1 .... 2 E6
Pells Cl RLEIS/BBY LE8 .... 70 B3
Pembroke Av
RLEINE/SYS LE7 .... 13 F2
WGSTN LE18 .... 55 F1
Pembroke St LEIN LE4 .... 27 E3
Pembury Cl RLEIS/BBY LE8 .... 58 D2
Pen Cl LEIS LE2 .... 43 E4
Penclose Rd RLEIS/BBY LE8 .. 70 A3
Pendene Rd LEIS LE2 .... 36 A4
Pendlebury Dr LEIS LE2 .... 43 G1
Pendragon Wy LEIW LE3 .... 32 B3
Penfold Cl RLEIW/BAR LE9 .... 66 D1
Penfold Dr RLEIS/BBY LE8 .... 64 D3
Penhale Rd LEIW LE3 .... 33 G5
Penman Wy END/NAR LE19 .. 41 G3
Pennant Cl LEIW LE3 .... 24 B3
Penney Cl WGSTN LE18 .... 44 A5
Pennine Cl LEIS LE2 .... 45 H3
Penny La RLEIW/BAR LE9 .... 48 A5
Penny Long La LEIW LE3 .... 32 B2
Penrith Rd LEIN LE4 .... 20 A5
Penryn Dr WGSTN LE18 .... 56 A2
Pensilva Cl WGSTN LE18 .... 56 A2
Pentridge Cl WGSTN LE18 .... 56 A3
Penzance Av WGSTN LE18 .... 56 A2
Peppercorn Cl LEIN LE4 .... 18 C4
Percival St LEIE LE5 .... 27 F3
Percy Rd LEIS LE2 .... 43 E1
Percy St LEIW LE3 .... 34 A5
Peregrine Ri LEIN LE4 .... 18 A1
Peregrine Rd
RLEIW/BAR LE9 .... 68 C2
Perkins Cl MKTHBORO LE16 .. 74 D5
Perkyn Rd LEIE LE5 .... 28 C4
Perseverance Rd LEIN LE4 .... 19 G2
Perth Av LEIW LE3 .... 25 E3
Peter's Cl RLEIW/BAR LE9 .... 60 A4
Peters Dr LEIE LE5 .... 28 B3
Petersfield RLEIW/BAR LE9 .... 61 G2
Petunia Cl LEIW LE3 .... 32 B3
Petworth Dr LEIW LE3 .... 25 F4
MKTHBORO LE16 .... 78 C1
Pevensey Av LEIE LE5 .... 37 H2
Peverel Rd LEIW LE3 .... 34 A3
Phillip Dr LEIS LE2 .... 55 E2
Phillips Crs LEIN LE4 .... 18 A1
Phipps Cl RLEIS/BBY LE8 .... 54 A5
Phoenix Cl LEIW LE3 .... 25 F3
Piccaver Ri LEIW LE3 .... 24 B4
Pickering Cl LEIN LE4 .... 27 F1
Pickering Rd
RLEIW/BAR LE9 .... 68 D5
Picks Cl MKTHBORO LE16 .... 78 C1
Pickwell Cl LEIW LE3 .... 24 C2
Piers Rd LEIW LE3 .... 24 A1
Pilkington Rd LEIW LE3 .... 33 G2
Pimpernel Cl END/NAR LE19 .. 52 B2
Pindar Rd LEIW LE3 .... 25 E2
Pine Cl LUTT LE17 .... 81 E3
Pine Dr RLEINE/SYS LE7 .... 13 F2
Pinehurst Cl LEIW LE3 .... 24 A4
Pinel Cl RLEIW/BAR LE9 .... 69 E5
Pine Rd LEIW LE3 .... 24 A2
The Pines MKTHBORO LE16 .... 75 E3
Pine Tree Av GBY/RBY LE6 .... 16 B5
LEIE LE5 .... 28 A3
Pine Tree Cl LEIS LE2 .... 45 F4
Pine Tree Gv
RLEIW/BAR LE9 .... 32 A3
Pinewood Av LEIN LE4 .... 20 C2
Pinewood Cl LEIN LE4 .... 18 A2
RLEIS/BBY LE8 .... 65 E2
Pinewood Dr COAL LE67 .... 14 C1
Pinfold LEIW LE3 .... 41 G1
Pinfold Rd LEIN LE4 .... 20 A1
The Pinfold COAL LE67 .... 6 C4
GBY/RBY LE6 .... 22 C2
Pingle La RLEIW/BAR LE9 .... 50 C4
Pingle St LEIW LE3 .... 2 C1
Pintail Cl RLEIS/BBY LE8 .... 63 G2
Piper Cl LEIW LE3 .... 25 E3
Piper Wy LEIW LE3 .... 25 E3
Pipistrelle Wy LEIS LE2 .... 46 A4
Pitchens Cl LEIN LE4 .... 17 H2
Pit Hl RLEIS/BBY LE8 .... 71 H5
Pits Av LEIW LE3 .... 41 G1
Pitton Cl WGSTN LE18 .... 56 A3
Plantation Av LEIS LE2 .... 42 C2
The Plantation
RLEIS/BBY LE8 .... 65 E2
Player Cl LEIN LE4 .... 20 B2
Pleasant Cl LEIW LE3 .... 32 B3
Plough Cl LEIW LE3 .... 32 B4
RLEIW/BAR LE9 .... 69 E5
Ploughman's Lea
RLEINE/SYS LE7 .... 5 F2
Plover Crs LEIN LE4 .... 18 B1
Plowman Cl LEIW LE3 .... 24 A1
Plumtree Wy
RLEINE/SYS LE7 .... 13 F2
Pluto Cl LEIS LE2 .... 3 K4
Plymouth Dr LEIE LE5 .... 36 D2
Plymstock Cl LEIW LE3 .... 25 F4
Poachers Cl LEIW LE3 .... 23 H2
Poachers Pl LEIS LE2 .... 45 H4
Pochin Dr MKTHBORO LE16 .. 74 D4
Pochin's Bridge Rd
WGSTN LE18 .... 55 G3
Pochins Cl WGSTN LE18 .... 56 A2
Pochin St RLEIW/BAR LE9 .... 61 G2
Pocklingtons Wk LEI LE1 .... 2 E4
Polaris Cl LEIS LE2 .... 3 K4
Pollard Rd LEIW LE3 .... 33 G2
Pomeroy Dr LEIS LE2 .... 44 D3
Pool Rd LEIW LE3 .... 25 F4
Pope Crs END/NAR LE19 .... 40 C5
Pope St LEIS LE2 .... 35 G5
Poplar Av COAL LE67 .... 6 B4
LEIN LE4 .... 11 G4
LUTT LE17 .... 81 F3
RLEIS/BBY LE8 .... 65 E3
Poplar Rd END/NAR LE19 .... 52 D5
Poplars Cl GBY/RBY LE6 .... 16 A4
Poplars Ct MKTHBORO LE16 .. 74 B5
The Poplars LEIW LE3 .... 42 A1
RLEIW/BAR LE9 .... 49 G2
The Poppins LEIN LE4 .... 18 B1
Popple Cl RLEIW/BAR LE9 * 69 E4
Poppy Cl GBY/RBY LE6 .... 16 C4
LEIS LE2 .... 43 F4
Porlock St LEIW LE3 .... 25 F5
Portcullis Rd LEIE LE5 .... 29 E1
Portgate WGSTN LE18 .... 56 C2
Portishead Rd LEIE LE5 .... 27 G2
Portland Rd LEIS LE2 .... 35 H3
RLEIW/BAR LE9 .... 23 E5
Portland St RLEIW/BAR LE9 .. 63 F3
Portland Wk LEIS LE2 .... 45 G5
Portloc Dr WGSTN LE18 .... 56 A3
Portman St LEIN LE4 .... 19 H5
Portmore Cl LEIN LE4 .... 18 C5
Portsdown Rd LEIS LE2 .... 44 B2
Portsmouth Rd LEIN LE4 .... 26 C1
The Portwey LEIE LE5 .... 27 G2
Post Office La
RLEIS/BBY LE8 .... 57 H4
Post Rd RLEINE/SYS LE7 .... 12 C3
Potter St LEI LE1 .... 3 G2
Potterton Rd LEIN LE4 .... 18 D3
Pougher Cl RLEIW/BAR LE9 .... 67 E2
Powys Av LEIS LE2 .... 36 C4
Poynings Av LEIW LE3 .... 25 E4
Prebend St LEIS LE2 .... 3 H6
Preston Cl GBY/RBY LE6 .... 23 E2
Preston Ri LEIE LE5 .... 28 C1
Prestwold Rd LEIE LE5 .... 27 F2
Pretoria Cl LEIN LE4 .... 10 C5
Pretoria Rd RLEIW/BAR LE9 .. 22 D4
Price Wy LEIN LE4 .... 12 D5
Pride Pl MKTHBORO LE16 .... 77 G2
Priestley Rd LEIW LE3 .... 34 A1
Priestman Rd LEIW LE3 .... 33 E4
Priest Meadow
RLEIS/BBY LE8 .... 70 B3
Primerose Wy
RLEINE/SYS LE7 .... 5 G3
Primrose Cl END/NAR LE19 .... 52 C3
GBY/RBY LE6 .... 16 C4
Primrose Hl LEIS LE2 .... 44 D2
Primrose Wy
RLEIW/BAR LE9 .... 23 F4
Prince Albert Dr LEIW LE3 .... 24 A3
Prince Dr LEIS LE2 .... 45 G3
Princes Cl RLEINE/SYS LE7 .... 17 G1
Princess Av LEIS LE2 .... 45 G4
Princess Rd Backways
LEI LE1 .... 3 F6
Princess Rd East LEI LE1 .... 3 G7
Princess Rd West LEI LE1 .... 3 F6
Princess St END/NAR LE19 .... 53 E3
Priory Cl RLEINE/SYS LE7 .... 12 D1
Priory Crs LEIW LE3 .... 24 C5
Priory La COAL LE67 .... 6 B1
Priory Wk LEIW LE3 .... 32 C2
Progress Wy LEIN LE4 .... 21 E4
Prospect Hl LEIE LE5 .... 27 E4
Prospect Rd LEIE LE5 .... 27 F4
RLEIS/BBY LE8 .... 71 H3
Prospect Wy
RLEIW/BAR LE9 .... 49 E3
Pulford Dr RLEINE/SYS LE7 .... 29 F4
Pullman Rd WGSTN LE18 .... 55 H1
Purbeck Cl WGSTN LE18 .... 56 B3
Purcell Rd LEIN LE4 .... 26 C2
Purley Rd LEIN LE4 .... 27 E1
Putney Rd LEIS LE2 .... 35 G3
Putney Rd West LEIS LE2 .... 35 E3
Pymm Ley Cl GBY/RBY LE6 .... 16 B4
Pymm Ley La GBY/RBY LE6 .. 16 B5
Pytchley Cl LEIN LE4 .... 19 E3

Q

The Quadrant LEIN LE4 * 19 F5
Quarry La END/NAR LE19 .... 40 C4
Quebec Rd LEI LE1 .... 3 H2
Queen Mary St LEI LE1 .... 26 B3
Queens Dr END/NAR LE19 .... 53 F1
LEIW LE3 .... 32 C2
WGSTN LE18 .... 55 H1
Queensferry Pde LEIS LE2 .... 42 C5
Queensgate Dr LEIN LE4 .... 11 E4
Queensmead Cl
GBY/RBY LE6 .... 16 A5
Queens Park Wy LEIS LE2 .... 54 D1
Queens Rd LEIS LE2 .... 35 H4
RLEIS/BBY LE8 .... 54 A4
Queen St COAL LE67 .... 6 B4
LEI LE1 .... 3 G3
LEIS LE2 .... 45 F3
MKTHBORO LE16 .... 78 B2
RLEINE/SYS LE7 .... 13 G5
RLEIW/BAR LE9 .... 48 B5
Queensway RLEIW/BAR LE9 .. 48 C4
Quemby Cl LEIN LE4 .... 19 G5
Quenby Crs RLEINE/SYS LE7 .. 13 G1
Quenby St LEIE LE5 .... 27 F3
Queniborough Rd LEIN LE4 .. 27 E1
RLEINE/SYS LE7 .... 5 G4
RLEINE/SYS LE7 .... 13 H4
Quickthorns LEIS LE2 .... 45 F1
Quiney Wy LEIS LE2 .... 45 G2
Quinton Ri LEIS LE2 .... 45 E3
Quorn Av LEIS LE2 .... 45 G4
Quorndon Ri GBY/RBY LE6 .... 16 A5
Quorn Rd LEIE LE5 .... 27 F3

R

Radar Rd LEIW LE3 .... 24 B5
Radcot Lawns LEIS LE2 .... 42 D5
Radford Dr LEIW LE3 .... 33 E2
Radiant Rd LEIE LE5 .... 28 C3
Radnor Ct END/NAR LE19 .... 52 B1
Radnor Rd WGSTN LE18 .... 55 G1
Raeburn Rd LEIS LE2 .... 35 H4
Ragdale Rd LEIN LE4 .... 27 F1
Railway St WGSTN LE18 .... 55 F3
Raine Wy LEIS LE2 .... 45 H5
Rainsborough Gdns
MKTHBORO LE16 .... 77 G3
Rainsford Crs LEIN LE4 .... 19 E4
Ramsbury Rd WGSTN LE18 .... 43 G3
Ramsdean Av WGSTN LE18 .... 44 A5
Ramsey Cl LUTT LE17 .... 81 H3
Ramsey Gdns LEIE LE5 .... 29 E1
Ramsey Wy LEIE LE5 .... 29 E1
Ramson Cl LEIE LE5 .... 21 G5
Rancliffe Crs LEIW LE3 .... 34 A1
Randles Cl RLEINE/SYS LE7 .... 38 C1
Rannoch Cl LEIN LE4 .... 18 C4
Ranton Wy LEIW LE3 .... 25 G2
Ratby La COAL LE67 .... 6 C5
GBY/RBY LE6 .... 23 E3
Ratby Meadow La
END/NAR LE19 .... 41 G5
Ratby Rd GBY/RBY LE6 .... 16 A4
Ratcliffe Ct LEIS LE2 .... 36 B5
Ratcliffe Dr RLEIW/BAR LE9 .. 51 H4
Ratcliffe Rd LEIS LE2 .... 36 A5
Ratcliffe St LEIN LE4 .... 19 H5
Ravenhurst Rd LEIW LE3 .... 33 H5
Raven Rd LEIW LE3 .... 33 G2
Ravensbridge Dr LEIN LE4 .... 25 H2
Ravensthorpe Rd
WGSTN LE18 .... 56 B1
Raw Dykes Rd LEIS LE2 .... 35 E3
Rawlings Ct LEIS LE2 .... 46 A4
Rawson St END/NAR LE19 .... 40 D5
LEI LE1 .... 3 F6
Rawsthorne Wk LEIN LE4 .... 26 C2
Rayleigh Gn LEIE LE5 .... 29 E1
Rayleigh Wy LEIE LE5 .... 29 E1
Raymond Rd LEIW LE3 .... 34 C2
Rayner Rd LEIN LE4 .... 20 C4
Rearsby Rd LEIN LE4 .... 27 E1
RLEINE/SYS LE7 .... 5 G3
Rectory Gdns LEIS LE2 .... 37 F3
Rectory La MKTHBORO LE16 .. 78 B2
RLEINE/SYS LE7 .... 10 B2
RLEIS/BBY LE8 .... 72 A2
Rectory Rd COAL LE67 .... 6 C3
RLEINE/SYS LE7 .... 11 H2
Redcar Rd LEIN LE4 .... 19 H5
Red Hall Dr RLEIW/BAR LE9 .... 48 B4
Red Hall Rd RLEIW/BAR LE9 .. 48 C4
Red Hl LEIN LE4 .... 19 F2
Red Hill Av END/NAR LE19 .... 52 C3
Red Hill Cl LEIN LE4 .... 12 C4
Red Hill La LEIN LE4 .... 12 D4
Red Hill Wy LEIN LE4 .... 18 D2
Red House Cl LEIS LE2 .... 42 C4
Red House Gdns LEIS LE2 .... 42 C4
Red House Ri LEIS LE2 .... 42 C4
Red House Rd LEIS LE2 .... 42 C4
Redliech Cl
MKTHBORO LE16 .... 78 C2
Redmarle Rd LEIW LE3 .... 34 A2
Redpath Cl LEI LE1 .... 26 D3
Redruth Av WGSTN LE18 .... 56 A3
Redwing Wk LEIE LE5 * 27 E3
Redwood Wk LEIE LE5 * 27 E3

Reedpool Cl *RLEIS/BBY* LE8 65 F2
Rees Gv *LEIN* LE4 20 B2
Reeth Cl *LEIN* LE4 18 C4
Reeves Cl *RLEIS/BBY* LE8 63 H1
Regal Ct *END/NAR* LE19 53 F1
Regency Cl *LEIS* LE2 54 D2
Regent Cl *WGSTN* LE18 43 H5
Regent Rd *LEI* LE1 3 F6
RLEIS/BBY LE8 65 F2
Regent St *END/NAR* LE19 53 E3
LEI LE1 3 H6
LEIS LE2 45 E2
LUTT LE17 81 G4
RLEIW/BAR LE9 48 B4
Regents Wk *LEIW* LE3 32 C2
Rendell Rd *LEIN* LE4 26 D1
Renfrew Rd *LEIE* LE5 29 E2
Renishaw Dr *LEIE* LE5 36 C3
Repington Rw *LEIS* LE2 43 F3
Repton Rd *WGSTN* LE18 43 H4
Repton St *LEIW* LE3 2 B1
Reservoir Rd *RLEINE/SYS* LE7 9 F1
The Retreat *LEIE* LE5 27 H5
Reynolds Pl *LEIW* LE3 34 A3
Rhodes Cl *MKTHBORO* LE16 77 F2
Ribble Av *LEIS* LE2 45 H2
Richard Cl *LEIW* LE3 33 E2
Richard Iii Rd *LEIW* LE3 2 B3
Richardson Cl
RLEIW/BAR LE9 60 B5
Richardsons Cl
RLEIW/BAR LE9 69 E4
Richmond Cl *LEIS* LE2 35 E5
RLEIW/BAR LE9 30 B3
RLEIW/BAR LE9 63 E4
Richmond Dr *LEIS* LE2 55 E2
Richmond Rd *LEIS* LE2 35 E4
Richmond St *LEIS* LE2 2 D6
Richmond Wy *LEIS* LE2 45 G5
Riddington Rd
END/NAR LE19 53 E5
LEIW LE3 41 H1
Ridgemere Cl
RLEINE/SYS LE7 5 F5
Ridgeway *END/NAR* LE19 53 E5
Ridge Wy *LEIS* LE2 45 F5
Ridgeway Dr *LEIN* LE4 20 D1
The Ridgeway
MKTHBORO LE16 74 D4
Ridgeway West
MKTHBORO LE16 74 C4
Ridgway Rd *LEIS* LE2 36 B5
The Ridings *RLEINE/SYS* LE7 5 G4
The Riding *LEIN* LE4 18 B1
Ridley Cl *RLEINE/SYS* LE7 9 G2
RLEIS/BBY LE8 54 A5
Ridley St *LEIW* LE3 2 A6
Riley Cl *MKTHBORO* LE16 77 E2
RLEIW/BAR LE9 60 B5
Ringers Cl *LEIS* LE2 37 E5
Ringer's Spinney *LEIS* LE2 37 F5
Ring Rd *LEIS* LE2 44 B2
The Ringway *RLEINE/SYS* LE7 5 G3
Ringwood Cl
RLEIW/BAR LE9 30 B2
WGSTN LE18 56 A2
Ringwood Rd *LEIE* LE5 29 E1
Ripley Cl *MKTHBORO* LE16 78 C1
Ripon Dr *RLEIS/BBY* LE8 54 B5
Ripon St *LEIS* LE2 36 A2
The Rise *END/NAR* LE19 52 C1
RLEINE/SYS LE7 39 H1
Riston Cl *LEIS* LE2 45 E5
Ritchie Pk *MKTHBORO* LE16 77 H4
Riversdale Cl *LEIN* LE4 11 H5
Riverside *MKTHBORO* LE16 78 B1
Riverside Cl *RLEIS/BBY* LE8 58 D2
Riverside Ct
END/NAR LE19 * 53 E4
Riverside Dr *LEIS* LE2 42 B2
Riverside Rd *LUTT* LE17 81 H4
Riverside Wy
END/NAR LE19 53 E4
Rivers St *LEIW* LE3 2 B3
Rivets Meadow Cl
LEIW LE3 33 F4
Robert Hall St *LEIN* LE4 19 F4
Robertsbridge Av *LEIN* LE4 19 E4
Robertson Cl
RLEIW/BAR LE9 60 B4
Roberts Rd *LEIN* LE4 26 C1
Robin Cl *LEIS* LE2 43 E1
Robinia Cl *LUTT* LE17 81 E3
Robinson Rd *LEIE* LE5 27 G4
Robinson Wy *COAL* LE67 6 D4
Roborough Gn *LEIE* LE5 29 E4
Robotham Cl
END/NAR LE19 52 D4
RLEIW/BAR LE9 51 H4
Roche Cl *LEIS* LE2 42 C4
Rochester Cl *RLEIS/BBY* LE8 71 H1
Rochester Gdns
MKTHBORO LE16 77 G3
Rockbridge Rd *LEIS* LE2 45 H4
Rockery Cl *LEIE* LE5 28 A3
Rockingham Cl *LEIE* LE5 28 B4
RLEIS/BBY LE8 54 B5
Rockingham Rd
MKTHBORO LE16 75 F5
Rockley Rd *LEIN* LE4 25 G1
Roebuck Cl *RLEIS/BBY* LE8 63 H1
Roecliff Cl *COAL* LE67 6 C4
Roehampton Dr
WGSTN LE18 43 H3
Rogerstone Rd *LEIE* LE5 37 H1
Rolleston Cl
MKTHBORO LE16 78 B1
Rolleston Rd *WGSTN* LE18 43 H5
Rolleston St *LEIE* LE5 27 F4
Roman Cl *RLEIW/BAR* LE9 30 C2
RLEIW/BAR LE9 * 49 G2
Roman Hl *WGSTN* LE18 56 C3
Roman Rd *LEIN* LE4 19 G2
Roman St *LEIW* LE3 2 A6
Roman Wy
MKTHBORO LE16 77 H1
RLEINE/SYS LE7 12 C2
Romway Av *LEIE* LE5 36 C3
Romway Rd *LEIE* LE5 36 C3
Rona Gdns *LEIE* LE5 29 E3
Ronald Toon Rd
RLEIW/BAR LE9 49 G3
Rookery *GBY/RBY* LE6 16 B4
Rookery Cl *RLEIS/BBY* LE8 72 B3
Rookery La *GBY/RBY* LE6 16 A4
LEIN LE4 20 B1
Rookwell Dr
MKTHBORO LE16 78 A3
Rosamund Av *LEIW* LE3 33 H5
Rose Acre Cl *LEIE* LE5 29 F3
Rosebank Rd
RLEIS/BBY LE8 65 F2
Rosebarn Wy *LEIE* LE5 28 D1
Rosebery Av *RLEIS/BBY* LE8 71 H3
Rosebery Rd *RLEINE/SYS* LE7 9 G5
Rosebery St *LEIE* LE5 27 F4
Rose Crs *LEIW* LE3 32 B3
Rosedale Av *LEIN* LE4 20 B5
Rosedale Rd *WGSTN* LE18 56 D1
Rosedene Av *LEIN* LE4 20 C1
Rosedene Cl *RLEIW/BAR* LE9 32 B1
Rose Farm Cl *LEIW* LE3 33 H1
Rosemead Dr *LEIS* LE2 45 F3
Rosemoor Cl
MKTHBORO LE16 78 C1
Roseneath Av *LEIN* LE4 20 C5
Rose St *LEIN* LE4 19 F5
Rose Tree Av *LEIN* LE4 11 G4
Roseway *LEIN* LE4 20 B4
Rossendale Rd
RLEIW/BAR LE9 48 D3
Rossett Dr *LEIN* LE4 18 D5
Rossetti Rd *END/NAR* LE19 40 C5
Rosshill Crs *LEIE* LE5 29 E3
Ross's La *WGSTN* LE18 56 B1
Ross' Wk *LEIN* LE4 26 C2
Rotherby Av *LEIN* LE4 27 F1
Rothley St *LEIN* LE4 26 C1
Roughton St *LEIN* LE4 19 G5
Roundhay Rd *LEIW* LE3 34 C3
Roundhill *RLEIW/BAR* LE9 23 E5
Roundhill Cl
MKTHBORO LE16 78 C2
RLEINE/SYS LE7 12 D2
Roundhill Rd *LEIE* LE5 36 B2
The Roundway *LEIN* LE4 20 D2
Rowan Av *MKTHBORO* LE16 77 H3
Rowanberry Av *LEIW* LE3 24 A4
Rowan Dr *LUTT* LE17 81 F3
The Rowans *RLEIS/BBY* LE8 65 E2
Rowan St *LEIW* LE3 25 G4
Rowlanson Cl *LEIN* LE4 10 D3
Rowlatts Hill Rd *LEIE* LE5 27 H4
Rowley Cl *RLEIS/BBY* LE8 70 B5
Rowley Fields Av *LEIW* LE3 34 B4
Rowsley Av *LEIE* LE5 36 B1
Rowsley St *LEIE* LE5 36 B1
Royal Ct *END/NAR* LE19 * 53 E3
Royal East St *LEI* LE1 3 F1
Royal Rd *LEIN* LE4 19 H5
Royce Cl *LEIW* LE3 33 E3
Roy Cl *END/NAR* LE19 53 E3
Roydene Crs *LEIN* LE4 25 G1
Royston Cl *LEIS* LE2 54 C1
Ruby St *LEIW* LE3 25 G4
Ruding Rd *LEIW* LE3 2 B6
Ruding St *LEI* LE1 2 C3
Rufford St *LEIE* LE5 27 G4
Rugby Cl *MKTHBORO* LE16 77 G2
Rugby St *LEIW* LE3 25 H3
Rumsey Dr *RLEIS/BBY* LE8 53 H3
Runcorn Cl *LEIS* LE2 42 C5
Runcorn Rd *LEIS* LE2 42 D5
Rupert Crs *RLEINE/SYS* LE7 5 G3
Rupert Rd *MKTHBORO* LE16 77 H3
Rupert St *LEI* LE1 2 E4
Rupert Wy *RLEIS/BBY* LE8 58 D3
Rushes La *MKTHBORO* LE16 76 C1
The Rushes *COAL* LE67 6 C3
Rushey Cl *LEIN* LE4 20 A3
Rushford Cl *LEIN* LE4 27 F1
Rushford Dr *LEIN* LE4 27 F1
Rushmere Wk *LEIW* LE3 32 C3
Rushton Dr *LEIS* LE2 42 B4
Ruskin Av *RLEINE/SYS* LE7 13 G2
Ruskington Dr *WGSTN* LE18 44 B3
Russett Cl *MKTHBORO* LE16 74 D4
RLEIW/BAR LE9 48 A4
Russet Wy *RLEINE/SYS* LE7 12 A3
Rutherford Rd *LEIN* LE4 18 A3
Rutland Av *LEIS* LE2 35 E4
WGSTN LE18 43 H5
Rutland Cl *LEIW* LE3 32 C2
Rutland Dr *LEIN* LE4 12 C5
Rutland St *LEI* LE1 3 G4
Rydal St *LEIS* LE2 2 C7
Ryde Av *LEIS* LE2 44 B1
Ryder Rd *LEIW* LE3 24 A4
Ryderway *LUTT* LE17 81 F4
Rye Cl *LEIS* LE2 43 E4
Ryegate Crs *LEIN* LE4 11 F4
Rye Hill Av *LUTT* LE17 81 H3
Rylands Cl *MKTHBORO* LE16 75 F5

S

Sacheverell Wy
GBY/RBY LE6 23 E1
Sacheverel Rd *LEIW* LE3 24 B4
Sackville Gdns *LEIS* LE2 36 A5
Saddington Rd
RLEIS/BBY LE8 70 C4
Saddlers Cl *LEIW* LE3 23 H2
RLEINE/SYS LE7 5 F2
Saffron Cl *RLEIW/BAR* LE9 48 C3
Saffron Hill Rd *LEIS* LE2 35 E5
Saffron La *LEIS* LE2 35 E4
Saffron Rd *WGSTN* LE18 43 E5
Saffron Wy *LEIS* LE2 43 E2
Sage Rd *LEIS* LE2 2 B7
St Aidan's Av
RLEINE/SYS LE7 12 D2
St Albans Rd *LEIS* LE2 3 K7
St Andrew's Dr *LEIS* LE2 36 C4
St Andrews Rd *LEIS* LE2 43 E1
St Annes Cl *RLEINE/SYS* LE7 13 G2
St Anne's Dr *LEIS* LE2 42 D2
St Augustine Rd *LEIW* LE3 2 B4
St Austell Rd *LEIE* LE5 29 E3
St Barnabas Rd *LEIE* LE5 27 F4
St Bernards Av *LEIN* LE4 19 H4
St Bernard St *LEIN* LE4 19 H5
Saintbury Rd *LEIW* LE3 24 B1
St Catharines Wy
RLEINE/SYS LE7 39 H2
St Columba Wy
RLEINE/SYS LE7 4 B5
St Crispin's Wy
RLEINE/SYS LE7 12 C3
St Cuthbert's Av
RLEIS/BBY LE8 58 D3
St David's Cl *LEIS* LE2 36 C4
LEIW LE3 32 B3
St Davids Rd *LEIW* LE3 24 A4
St Denys Rd *LEIE* LE5 37 F1
St Dunstan Rd *LEIW* LE3 25 G4
St George St *LEI* LE1 3 H4
St Georges Wy *LEI* LE1 3 G5
St Helen's Cl *HINC* LE10 66 C5
LEIN LE4 25 G1
St Helens Dr *LEIN* LE4 25 H2
St Hildas Cl *RLEINE/SYS* LE7 13 G2
St Ives Rd *LEIN* LE4 20 C5
WGSTN LE18 56 A2
St James Cl *LEIS* LE2 45 G5
RLEIW/BAR LE9 51 H4
St James Rd *LEIS* LE2 36 A2
St James St *LEI* LE1 3 G2
St Johns *END/NAR* LE19 41 G5
St John's Av
RLEINE/SYS LE7 13 G2
St Johns Rd *LEIS* LE2 36 A3
St John St *LEI* LE1 2 E1
St Leonards Rd *LEIS* LE2 35 H4
St Luke's Cl *RLEINE/SYS* LE7 38 B1
St Margaret's St *LEI* LE1 2 E1
St Margaret's Wy *LEI* LE1 2 E1
LEIN LE4 26 A2
St Marks St *LEI* LE1 26 C3
St Martins *LEI* LE1 2 E4
St Martin's Dr
RLEIW/BAR LE9 30 A2
St Martins Sq *LEI* LE1 2 E4
St Marys Av *LEIE* LE5 28 C2
LEIW LE3 33 E2
St Marys Cl *RLEIW/BAR* LE9 68 C3
St Mary's Ct *LEIW* LE3 33 E2
RLEIW/BAR LE9 48 A5
St Marys Rd *LEIS* LE2 35 H3
LUTT LE17 81 F3
MKTHBORO LE16 78 A1
St Matthews Wy *LEI* LE1 3 G1
St Mellion Cl *LEIN* LE4 10 B5
St Michaels Av *LEIN* LE4 19 H4
St Michael's Cl *COAL* LE67 6 B3
St Nicholas Cir *LEI* LE1 2 C4
St Nicholas Cl
MKTHBORO LE16 78 A2
St Nicholas Pl *LEI* LE1 2 D4
St Nicholas Wy
MKTHBORO LE16 78 A2
St Oswalds Rd *LEIW* LE3 24 D3
St Pauls Cl *LEIS* LE2 45 H2
St Paul's Dr *RLEINE/SYS* LE7 13 E2
St Pauls Rd *LEIW* LE3 25 G5
St Peter's Cl *LEIW* LE3 23 H2
St Peters Dr *RLEIS/BBY* LE8 53 H3
St Peters La *LEI* LE1 2 D3
St Peters Rd *LEIS* LE2 3 K6
St Peter's St
RLEINE/SYS LE7 13 E1
St Philips Rd *LEIE* LE5 36 B2
St Saviour's Hl *LEIE* LE5 27 E4
St Saviour's Rd *LEIE* LE5 27 F5
St Stephens Rd *LEIS* LE2 36 A1
St Swithin's Rd *LEIE* LE5 28 D5
St Thomas Rd *LEIS* LE2 55 E2
St Thomas's Rd
RLEIS/BBY LE8 59 E3
St Wilfrid's Cl
RLEIS/BBY LE8 72 A2
St Wolstan's Cl *WGSTN* LE18 44 B5
Salcombe Cl *WGSTN* LE18 56 A2
Salcombe Dr *LEIW* LE3 24 A2
Salisbury Av *LEI* LE1 3 J7
RLEIW/BAR LE9 61 G2
Salisbury Cl *RLEIS/BBY* LE8 54 B5
RLEIW/BAR LE9 30 B2
Salisbury Rd *LEI* LE1 35 H2
Salkeld Rd *LEIS* LE2 54 C1
Saltash Cl *WGSTN* LE18 56 A2
Saltcoates Av *LEIN* LE4 20 A3
Saltersford Rd *LEIE* LE5 27 H3
Saltersgate Dr *LEIN* LE4 11 G4
Salt's Cl *END/NAR* LE19 52 D1
Samphire Cl *LEIE* LE5 21 H5
Samson Rd *LEIW* LE3 25 F3
Samuel St *LEI* LE1 3 J3
Sandacre St *LEI* LE1 2 E2
Sanderson Cl *RLEIS/BBY* LE8 54 A5
Sandfield Cl *LEIN* LE4 20 C2
Sandford Cl *LEIE* LE5 28 A4
Sandford Rd
RLEINE/SYS LE7 13 E1
Sandgate Av *LEIN* LE4 11 F4
Sandham Bridge Rd
RLEINE/SYS LE7 9 H1
Sandhill Dr *END/NAR* LE19 53 F2
Sandhills Av *LEIE* LE5 21 G4
Sandhurst Cl *LEIW* LE3 25 F4
Sandhurst Gdns *LEIW* LE3 25 F4
Sandhurst Rd *LEIW* LE3 25 F3
Sandhurst St *LEIS* LE2 45 E2
Sandiacre Dr *LEIN* LE4 12 D4
Sandown Rd *LEIS* LE2 36 B4
LEIW LE3 24 A1
WGSTN LE18 44 B4
Sandpiper Cl *LEIE* LE5 27 E3
Sandringham Av *LEIN* LE4 19 H4
RLEIW/BAR LE9 48 D4
Sandringham Rd *LEIS* LE2 55 E2
Sandringham Wy
MKTHBORO LE16 78 C2
Sandy Ri *WGSTN* LE18 44 C4
Sanvey Ga *LEI* LE1 2 D2
Sanvey La *LEIS* LE2 42 B2
Sapcote Rd *RLEIW/BAR* LE9 60 C4
Saunderson Rd *LEIN* LE4 18 D3
Savernake Rd *LEIN* LE4 25 G1
Saville Rd *RLEIS/BBY* LE8 54 C5
Saville St *LEIE* LE5 27 G4
Sawbrook *RLEIS/BBY* LE8 70 C4
Sawday St *LEIS* LE2 35 E2
Sawley St *LEIE* LE5 36 B2
Saxby St *LEIS* LE2 3 J6
Saxon Cl *MKTHBORO* LE16 74 D5
Saxon Dl *LEIS* LE2 54 C1
Saxondale Rd *WGSTN* LE18 56 C3
Saxons Ri *GBY/RBY* LE6 22 C1
Saxon St *LEIW* LE3 2 A6
Scalborough Cl
RLEIS/BBY LE8 64 C2
Scalpay Cl *LEIN* LE4 18 B4
Scarborough Rd *LEIN* LE4 19 H5
School Cl *RLEIW/BAR* LE9 61 G3
School Crs *RLEIW/BAR* LE9 68 C2
Schoolgate *LEIS* LE2 43 F4
School House Cl
RLEINE/SYS LE7 17 F2
School La *END/NAR* LE19 52 D4
HINC LE10 66 C5
LEIE LE5 37 F3
LEIN LE4 19 G1
MKTHBORO LE16 76 C1
MKTHBORO LE16 77 H1
RLEINE/SYS LE7 5 H4
RLEINE/SYS LE7 13 H4
RLEINE/SYS LE7 39 H2
RLEIW/BAR LE9 51 H4
School Rd *RLEIS/BBY* LE8 72 A3
School St *RLEINE/SYS* LE7 4 D5
RLEIS/BBY LE8 70 B4
School Wk *RLEIS/BBY* LE8 72 A3
Scotland La *RLEINE/SYS* LE7 39 H1
Scotland Rd
MKTHBORO LE16 78 B2
Scotland Wy *RLEIS/BBY* LE8 65 F3
Scotswood Crs *LEIS* LE2 42 C5
Scott Cl *MKTHBORO* LE16 74 C4
Scott Ct *LEIS* LE2 35 G5
Scott St *LEIS* LE2 35 G5
Scraptoft La *LEIE* LE5 28 A3
Scraptoft Ms *LEIE* LE5 28 A3
Scraptoft Ri *LEIE* LE5 29 F2
Scrivener Cl *RLEINE/SYS* LE7 29 G5
Scudamore Rd *LEIW* LE3 23 H5
Seacole Cl *LEIW* LE3 33 F3
Seaford Rd *LEIS* LE2 42 D3
Seagrave Dr *LEIS* LE2 44 D2
Seaton Ri *LEIE* LE5 29 E1
Seaton Rd *LEIW* LE3 33 E4
WGSTN LE18 56 A2
Seddons Cl *LEIN* LE4 18 D3
Sedgebrook Rd *LEIE* LE5 37 H1
Sedgefield Dr
RLEINE/SYS LE7 12 C1
RLEINE/SYS LE7 29 F4
Segrave Rd *LEIW* LE3 34 B3
Seine La *END/NAR* LE19 40 B4
Selbury Dr *LEIS* LE2 44 D3
Selby Av *LEIE* LE5 28 D1
Selby Cl *MKTHBORO* LE16 77 H3
Selkirk Rd *LEIN* LE4 20 B4
Senator Cl *RLEINE/SYS* LE7 12 D2
Sence Crs *RLEIS/BBY* LE8 58 C3
Severn Cl *RLEIW/BAR* LE9 63 F3
Severn Rd *LEIS* LE2 45 H3

Severn St LEIS LE2 3 K6
Sextant Rd LEIE LE5 28 C3
Seymour Rd LEIS LE2 35 H3
Seymour St LEIS LE2 3 J6
Seymour Wy LEIW LE3 32 B3
Shackelton Wy LUTT LE17 80 A4
Shackerdale Rd WGSTN LE18 43 H3
Shackleton St LEI LE1 26 C3
Shades Cl RLEIW/BAR LE9 61 G2
Shadrack Cl RLEIW/BAR LE9 60 B5
Shady La LEIS LE2 37 F4
Shaeffer Ct LEIN LE4 18 B5
Shaftesbury Av LEIN LE4 19 G5
Shaftesbury Rd LEIW LE3 34 C1
Shakespeare Cl LEIW LE3 33 G4
Shakespeare Dr LEIW LE3 33 H4
Shakespeare St LEIS LE2 35 F5
Shanklin Av LEIS LE2 44 B1
Shanklin Dr LEIS LE2 44 B1
Shanklin Gdns LEIS LE2 44 B1
Shanti Margh LEIN LE4 20 A5
Shardlow Rd WGSTN LE18 44 A5
Sharmon Crs LEIW LE3 24 B4
Sharnbrook Gdns HINC LE10 66 C5
Sharnford Rd RLEIW/BAR LE9 67 E3
Sharpe Wy END/NAR LE19 52 D4
Sharpland LEIS LE2 42 C3
Sharpley Dr LEIN LE4 18 A1
Sharply Hl GBY/RBY LE6 8 A1
Shaw Cl RLEIS/BBY LE8 53 H5
Shaw Wood Cl GBY/RBY LE6 16 A4
Shearer Cl LEIN LE4 20 C3
Shearsby Cl WGSTN LE18 56 B1
Sheene Rd LEIN LE4 18 A3
Sheffield St LEIW LE3 34 D2
Shelbourne St LEIE LE5 * 27 E4
Sheldon St LEIE LE5 3 J2
Shelland Cl MKTHBORO LE16 78 C2
Shellduck Cl RLEIS/BBY LE8 63 H2
Shelley Dr LUTT LE17 81 G2
Shelley Rd END/NAR LE19 52 C1
Shelley St LEIS LE2 35 G5
Shenley Rd WGSTN LE18 44 C4
Shenton Cl LEIN LE4 21 E1
RLEIS/BBY LE8 53 H4
WGSTN LE18 44 A5
Shenton Rd RLEIW/BAR LE9 48 B4
Sherborne Av WGSTN LE18 56 A3
Sherford Cl WGSTN LE18 56 A1
Sheridan Cl END/NAR LE19 52 C1
Sheridan St LEIS LE2 35 F5
Sheringham Rd LEIN LE4 18 D5
Sherloyd Cl LEIN LE4 20 D3
Sherrard Rd LEIE LE5 27 E4
MKTHBORO LE16 74 C4
Sherrard Wy LEIW LE3 33 F4
Sherrier Wy LUTT LE17 81 G1
Sherwood St LEIE LE5 27 G4
Shetland Rd LEIN LE4 20 A5
Shetland Wy RLEIS/BBY LE8 65 F3
Shield Crs LEIS LE2 54 C1
Shilton Rd RLEIW/BAR LE9 48 B5
Shipley Rd LEIE LE5 36 B1
Shipston Hl LEIS LE2 45 E4
Shipton Cl WGSTN LE18 56 D1
Shire Cl LEIW LE3 24 C5
Shires La LEI LE1 2 D3
Shires Wk LEI LE1 * 2 E3
Shirley Av LEIS LE2 36 B5
Shirley Dr RLEINE/SYS LE7 4 D4
Shirley Rd LEIS LE2 36 B5
Shirley St LEIN LE4 19 G5
Shoesmith Cl RLEIW/BAR LE9 48 A5
Short Cl RLEIS/BBY LE8 70 B4
Shortridge La END/NAR LE19 40 D5
Short St LEI LE1 2 E2
Shottens Cl LEIN LE4 18 B5
Shottery Av LEIW LE3 33 H4
Shoulbard RLEIS/BBY LE8 70 A3
Shrewsbury Av LEIS LE2 43 G2
MKTHBORO LE16 78 C2
Shrewsbury Cl RLEIW/BAR LE9 48 A4
Shropshire Pl MKTHBORO LE16 74 C5
Shropshire Rd LEIS LE2 42 D1
Shuttleworth La RLEIW/BAR LE9 63 F5
Sibson Rd LEIN LE4 11 G5
Sibton La LEIS LE2 45 E4
Sickleholm Dr LEIE LE5 36 C3
Sidmouth Av LEIE LE5 37 E1
Sidwell St LEIE LE5 27 G5
Silbury Rd LEIN LE4 25 G1
Silsden Ri LEIS LE2 42 D5
Silver Ar LEI LE1 2 E3
Silverdale Dr LEIN LE4 20 D1
Silverstone Dr LEIN LE4 20 B2
Silver St LEI LE1 2 E3
Silverton Rd LEIS LE2 45 G2
Silver Wk LEI LE1 * 2 E3
Silverwood Cl LEIE LE5 28 C5
Simborough Wy MKTHBORO LE16 78 C1
Simmins Crs LEIS LE2 42 D4
Simons Cl WGSTN LE18 56 C3
Simpson Cl RLEINE/SYS LE7 12 C2
RLEIS/BBY LE8 54 A5
Siskin Hl LEIS LE2 45 E4
Sitch Cl RLEIW/BAR LE9 69 E4
Sitwell Wk LEIE LE5 36 C3
Six Acre Cl GBY/RBY LE6 22 D2
Six Acres RLEIW/BAR LE9 68 C3
Skampton Rd LEIE LE5 37 F1
Skelton Dr LEIS LE2 43 G2
Sketchley Cl LEIE LE5 28 D4
Skippon Cl MKTHBORO LE16 77 G2
Skipworth St LEIS LE2 36 A1
Skye Wy RLEIS/BBY LE8 65 F3
The Slade Greens LEIS LE2 42 C4
Slate Brook Cl GBY/RBY LE6 16 B4
Slate Cl LEIW LE3 23 H2
Slater St LEIW LE3 26 A3
Slate St LEIS LE2 3 H5
Sloane Cl END/NAR LE19 40 C5
Smart Cl LEIW LE3 33 F3
Smedmore Rd LEIE LE5 27 F2
Smeeton Ct RLEIS/BBY LE8 * 72 A3
Smeeton Rd RLEIS/BBY LE8 72 A4
Smith Av LEIN LE4 20 D1
Smith Dorrien Rd LEIE LE5 27 G3
Smith Wy END/NAR LE19 41 G4
Smithy Farm Dr RLEIW/BAR LE9 60 A4
Smore Slade Hills LEIS LE2 46 A4
Smyth Cl MKTHBORO LE16 74 C4
Snowdens End WGSTN LE18 56 C2
Snowdrop Cl END/NAR LE19 52 B3
Snow Hl LEIN LE4 25 G1
Soar La LEIW LE3 2 B2
Soar Rd RLEINE/SYS LE7 12 C3
Soar Valley Wy END/NAR LE19 41 H4
Somerby Dr LEIS LE2 45 G3
Somerby Rd RLEINE/SYS LE7 29 F4
Somerfield Wy LEIW LE3 32 B3
Somerscales Wk LEIN LE4 26 D2
Somerset Av LEIN LE4 18 D5
Somerset Dr LEIW LE3 23 H3
Somers Rd LEIE LE5 28 C4
Somerville Rd LEIW LE3 34 B4
Sonning Wy LEIS LE2 54 B1
Sopers Rd RLEIW/BAR LE9 61 G3
Sorrel Rd LEIE LE5 21 G5
Sorrel Wy END/NAR LE19 52 B2
South Albion St LEI LE1 3 G5
Southampton St LEI LE1 3 G3
South Av LEIW LE3 32 D2
WGSTN LE18 56 A1
South Church Ga LEI LE1 2 D1
Southdown Dr LEIN LE4 20 C2
Southdown Rd LEIE LE5 27 F4
South Dr LEIE LE5 28 A2
RLEIW/BAR LE9 60 C5
Southernhay Av LEIS LE2 36 A5
Southernhay Cl LEIS LE2 36 A4
Southernhay Rd LEIS LE2 36 A4
Southey Cl END/NAR LE19 52 C1
LEIN LE4 26 D2
Southfield Av RLEINE/SYS LE7 13 F1
Southfield Cl LEIE LE5 29 F3
LEIS LE2 42 A5
Southfields Av LEIS LE2 44 D2
Southfields Dr LEIS LE2 43 F3
Southgates LEI LE1 2 D4
Southgates U/P LEI LE1 2 D4
South Kingsmead Rd WGSTN LE18 44 A2
South Knighton Rd LEIS LE2 44 B1
Southland Rd LEIS LE2 44 B2
Southleigh Gv MKTHBORO LE16 74 B5
Southmeads Cl LEIS LE2 44 D1
Southmeads Rd LEIS LE2 37 E5
South St LEIS LE2 45 E2
Southview Dr LEIE LE5 36 D3
Southway RLEIS/BBY LE8 54 B5
South Wy RLEIS/BBY LE8 72 B2
Spa Dr RLEIW/BAR LE9 66 D1
Spa La WGSTN LE18 56 B1
Spalding St LEIE LE5 27 G4
Sparkenhoe RLEIW/BAR LE9 61 G3
Sparkenhoe St LEIS LE2 3 J5
Sparsis Gdns END/NAR LE19 53 F2
Speedwell Cl END/NAR LE19 52 B2
Speedwell Dr LEIE LE5 21 F4
RLEIW/BAR LE9 69 E5
Speers Rd LEIW LE3 24 C2
Spencefield Dr LEIE LE5 37 F2
Spencefield La LEIE LE5 37 G2
Spencer Av LEIN LE4 12 C5
Spencer Rd LUTT LE17 81 G3
Spencer St LEIS LE2 45 E2
MKTHBORO LE16 77 G1
Spence St LEIE LE5 27 F3
Spendlow Gdns LEIS LE2 43 E4
Spiers Cl END/NAR LE19 52 D4
Spinney Av RLEIS/BBY LE8 65 E2
Spinney Cl GBY/RBY LE6 16 A5
LEIS LE2 42 A5
MKTHBORO LE16 77 F1
RLEINE/SYS LE7 12 C1
Spinney Halt RLEIS/BBY LE8 53 G4
Spinney Hill Rd LEIE LE5 27 E3
Spinney Ri LEIN LE4 11 F5
Spinneyside GBY/RBY LE6 16 A5
The Spinney LEIS LE2 46 C4
RLEINE/SYS LE7 38 A1
Spinney Vw RLEIS/BBY LE8 59 E2
Sponne Ri LEIS LE2 43 E4
Sports Field La RLEIW/BAR LE9 51 H3
Sports Rd LEIW LE3 24 A2
Springbrook Dr RLEINE/SYS LE7 29 F4
Spring Cl GBY/RBY LE6 22 D2
Springclose LEIS LE2 42 D3
Spring Cl LUTT LE17 81 G4
Springdale Rd LEIN LE4 20 C1
Spring Field Cl LEIW LE3 23 H3
Springfield Cl RLEIS/BBY LE8 72 B4
Springfield Ct MKTHBORO LE16 78 A2
Springfield Crs RLEIS/BBY LE8 72 A4
Springfield La RLEIS/BBY LE8 72 A5
Springfield Rd LEIS LE2 36 A4
Spring Gdns END/NAR LE19 * 53 E5
Springhill Gdns MKTHBORO LE16 77 F2
Spring La WGSTN LE18 44 B5
The Springs RLEIW/BAR LE9 * 68 D3
Springway Cl LEIE LE5 29 E5
Springwell Cl RLEIS/BBY LE8 65 E2
Springwell Dr RLEIS/BBY LE8 64 D2
Springwell La RLEIS/BBY LE8 63 H3
Spruce Wy LUTT LE17 81 F2
The Square END/NAR LE19 53 E5
LEIW LE3 23 H1
MKTHBORO LE16 77 H1
RLEIS/BBY LE8 57 H5
RLEIS/BBY LE8 65 F3
Squire's Ride RLEINE/SYS LE7 5 F1
Squirrel Cl END/NAR LE19 52 C4
Squirrel's Cnr RLEINE/SYS LE7 5 G1
Stable Cl END/NAR LE19 53 E4
Stablegate Wy MKTHBORO LE16 78 B1
Stackley Rd RLEIS/BBY LE8 58 D2
Stadium Pl LEIN LE4 19 E5
Stadium Ri LEIN LE4 * 25 H1
Stadon Rd RLEINE/SYS LE7 17 F1
Stafford Dr WGSTN LE18 55 F1
Stafford Leys LEIW LE3 32 B2
Stafford St LEIN LE4 20 A4
RLEIW/BAR LE9 48 A5
Staindale WGSTN LE18 56 D1
Stainmore Av END/NAR LE19 52 B1
Stamford Cl LEIW LE3 23 H2
MKTHBORO LE16 77 H2
Stamford Dr GBY/RBY LE6 16 B5
RLEINE/SYS LE7 9 H1
Stamford Rd RLEIW/BAR LE9 32 A1
Stamford St GBY/RBY LE6 22 B1
LEI LE1 3 F5
LEIW LE3 23 H2
Stanbrig WGSTN LE18 * 56 C3
Stancliff Rd LEIN LE4 20 D2
Stanfell Rd LEIS LE2 35 H5
Stanhope Rd WGSTN LE18 56 C2
Stanhope St LEIE LE5 27 F5
Stanier Dr LEIN LE4 21 E3
Stanier Rd RLEIW/BAR LE9 69 E3
Stanley Dr LEIE LE5 28 A2
Stanley Rd LEIS LE2 36 A2
Stanley St RLEIW/BAR LE9 48 A5
Stanton La RLEIW/BAR LE9 60 D2
RLEIW/BAR LE9 66 B1
Stanton Rd RLEIW/BAR LE9 66 D1
Stanton Rw LEIS LE2 43 F2
Stanway Cl MKTHBORO LE16 78 B1
Stanyon Cl RLEIS/BBY LE8 65 E2
Stapleford Rd LEIN LE4 18 D3
Staplehurst Av END/NAR LE19 33 G5
Starmer Cl RLEIW/BAR LE9 63 G3
Station Cl RLEIW/BAR LE9 32 A1
Station Dr RLEIW/BAR LE9 32 A1
Station La RLEINE/SYS LE7 29 F3
Station Rd END/NAR LE19 53 E4
GBY/RBY LE6 22 C2
LEIN LE4 19 F2
LEIW LE3 24 A1
LUTT LE17 81 H4
MKTHBORO LE16 75 E4
RLEINE/SYS LE7 10 A1
RLEINE/SYS LE7 13 E1
RLEINE/SYS LE7 29 F5
RLEIS/BBY LE8 58 C5
RLEIS/BBY LE8 64 D3
RLEIW/BAR LE9 22 D5
RLEIW/BAR LE9 30 C2
RLEIW/BAR LE9 49 E5
RLEIW/BAR LE9 60 A3
RLEIW/BAR LE9 61 G2
RLEIW/BAR LE9 68 D3
WGSTN LE18 55 H1
Station St LEIS LE2 3 H5
RLEIS/BBY LE8 53 G3
RLEIS/BBY LE8 72 A3
WGSTN LE18 55 F1
Staveley Cl WGSTN LE18 56 C1
Staveley Rd LEIE LE5 36 B2
Staythorpe Rd LEIN LE4 21 E2
Steadman Av RLEIW/BAR LE9 63 G3
Stebbings Rd LEIS LE2 42 D3
Steele Cl LEIE LE5 28 A5
Steeple Cl WGSTN LE18 44 C4
Steins La LEIE LE5 28 B2
Stelle Wy RLEINE/SYS LE7 17 F4
Stenor Cl RLEIS/BBY LE8 70 A3
Stenson Rd LEIW LE3 25 E1
Stephenson Ct LEIW LE3 17 E5
Stephenson Dr LEIW LE3 25 G3
Stephenson Wy GBY/RBY LE6 16 A4
Stevens Cl RLEIW/BAR LE9 60 C4
Stevenson Gdns RLEIW/BAR LE9 63 F2
Stevens St MKTHBORO LE16 77 G1
Stevenstone Cl LEIS LE2 45 H3
Stewards Ct RLEIW/BAR LE9 30 B2
Stewart Av END/NAR LE19 52 C2
Steyning Crs LEIW LE3 24 B1
Stiles Cl RLEIW/BAR LE9 68 D4
The Stiles RLEINE/SYS LE7 4 D5
Stinford Leys MKTHBORO LE16 78 C1
Stirling Dr RLEINE/SYS LE7 29 F4
Stockland Rd LEIS LE2 43 E4
Stocks Rd RLEINE/SYS LE7 29 F2
Stockton Rd LEIN LE4 27 F1
Stockwell Cl MKTHBORO LE16 78 C1
Stockwell Rd LEIS LE2 44 A2
Stokes Dr LEIW LE3 25 F2
Stonebridge St LEIE LE5 27 F4
Stonechat Wk LEIE LE5 * 27 E4
Stone Cl LEIN LE4 18 A1
Stonecroft RLEIS/BBY LE8 64 C3
Stonecrop Rd LEIE LE5 21 G5
Stonehaven Rd LEIN LE4 20 B3
Stonehill Av LEIN LE4 11 G4
Stonehill Dr RLEIS/BBY LE8 59 E2
Stonehurst Rd LEIW LE3 33 H5
Stoneleigh Wy LEIW LE3 25 F2
Stonesby Av LEIS LE2 43 E3
Stoneycroft Rd RLEIW/BAR LE9 48 D4
Stoneygate Av LEIS LE2 36 A4
Stoneygate Ct LEIS LE2 36 A3
Stoneygate Rd LEIS LE2 36 B3
Stoney Hollow LUTT LE17 81 G4
Stoneywell Rd LEIN LE4 17 H2
Stores La RLEIS/BBY LE8 70 B4
Storey Ct LEI LE1 3 F7
Storey St LEIW LE3 25 H3
Stornaway Rd LEIE LE5 28 D3
Stoughton Av LEIS LE2 36 B4
Stoughton Cl LEIS LE2 45 F2
Stoughton Dr LEIE LE5 36 D3
Stoughton Dr North LEIE LE5 36 B2
Stoughton Dr South LEIS LE2 36 D4
Stoughton La LEIS LE2 37 H4
Stoughton Rd LEIS LE2 36 B4
LEIS LE2 37 F5
RLEINE/SYS LE7 38 A2
Stoughton St LEIS LE2 3 K5
Stoughton St South LEIS LE2 3 K5
Stour Cl LEIS LE2 45 H2
Stowe Cl LEIW LE3 25 E1
Strasbourg Dr LEIN LE4 18 B4
Stratford Rd LEIW LE3 33 H4
Strathaven Rd LEIN LE4 20 B3
Strathern Rd LEIW LE3 17 H5
Strathmore Av LEIN LE4 20 B5
Stratton Cl MKTHBORO LE16 77 G3
Streamside Cl RLEIW/BAR LE9 68 D4
Strensall Rd LEIS LE2 42 D5
Stretton Hall Dr LEIS LE2 46 B5
Stretton La RLEINE/SYS LE7 39 G4
Stretton Rd LEIS LE2 47 E3
LEIW LE3 25 G5
RLEIS/BBY LE8 58 D1
Stroma Wy RLEIS/BBY LE8 65 F3
Stroud Rd LEIE LE5 27 F3
Strudwick Wy RLEIS/BBY LE8 54 A3
Stuart Rd LEIS LE2 42 C5
MKTHBORO LE16 77 G2
Stuart St LEIW LE3 34 D2
RLEIS/BBY LE8 72 A3
Stubbs Rd LEIN LE4 26 D2
Sturdee Cl LEIS LE2 42 D5
Sturdee Gn LEIS LE2 42 C4
Sturdee Rd LEIS LE2 42 D4
Sturrock Cl RLEINE/SYS LE7 29 F4
Styon Rd LEIW LE3 24 C1
Sudeley Av LEIN LE4 19 E5
Suffolk Cl WGSTN LE18 43 G5
Suffolk St LEIE LE5 27 G5
Suffolk Wy RLEIW/BAR LE9 30 B3
Sulgrave Rd LEIE LE5 27 F3
Summerlea Rd LEIE LE5 28 C4
Summers Wy MKTHBORO LE16 77 G2
Sunbury Gn LEIE LE5 29 E3
Sunbury Ri RLEIS/BBY LE8 64 C2
Sundew Rd LEIE LE5 21 G5
Sunningdale Rd LEIW LE3 32 D1
Sunnycroft Rd LEIW LE3 25 E5
Sunnyfield Cl LEIE LE5 28 C5
Sunny Side LEIS LE2 45 G4
Sunnyside Cl RLEIS/BBY LE8 53 H3
Sun Wy LEIW LE3 33 F2

Surrey St *LEIN* LE4 26 D1
Susan Av *LEIE* LE5 37 F1
Sussex Rd *WGSTN* LE18 43 F5
Sussex St *LEIE* LE5 3 J2
Sutherington Wy
RLEINE/SYS LE7 9 G5
Sutherland St *LEIS* LE2 36 A1
Sutton Av *LEIN* LE4 27 E1
Sutton Cl *LEIS* LE2 45 F5
Sutton Ct *RLEIW/BAR* LE9 68 C1
Sutton Pl *LEIN* LE4 20 A5
Sutton Rd *LEIS* LE2 43 G1
MKTHBORO LE16 75 F3
Swainson Rd *LEIN* LE4 27 G2
Swain St *LEI* LE1 3 H4
Swale Cl *LEIS* LE2 45 H2
Swallowdale Dr *LEIN* LE4 18 B1
Swallow Dr *RLEINE/SYS* LE7 4 B5
Swallows Cl *LEIW* LE3 32 A4
Swannington Rd *LEIW* LE3 25 G3
RLEIW/BAR LE9 69 E3
Swanscombe Rd *LEIS* LE2 34 D4
Swan St *LEIW* LE3 2 C2
Swan Wy *RLEINE/SYS* LE7 4 A5
Sweetbriar Rd *LEIW* LE3 34 C2
Swift Cl *RLEINE/SYS* LE7 4 B5
Swift Wy *LUTT* LE17 81 G2
Swindale Cl *LEIS* LE2 2 D7
Swinford Av *LEIS* LE2 54 D1
Swinford Rd *LUTT* LE17 81 H5
Swinstead Rd *LEIE* LE5 37 H1
Swithland Av *LEIN* LE4 26 A1
Swithland Cl *COAL* LE67 6 C4
Sword Cl *LEIW* LE3 24 A3
Sybil Rd *LEIW* LE3 34 B4
Sycamore Cl *LEIS* LE2 36 D4
LEIS LE2 46 C5
RLEINE/SYS LE7 13 F2
Sycamore Dr *GBY/RBY* LE6 16 B5
LUTT LE17 81 E3
Sycamore Gv *GBY/RBY* LE6 16 B4
Sycamore Rd
RLEINE/SYS LE7 11 G4
Sycamore St *RLEIS/BBY* LE8 54 B3
Sycamore Wy
END/NAR LE19 52 D5
Sykefield Av *LEIW* LE3 34 C1
Sylvan Av *LEIE* LE5 27 F4
Sylvan St *LEIW* LE3 25 G4
Sylvan Wy *LEIW* LE3 32 D1
Symington Wy
MKTHBORO LE16 77 H1
Syston Rd *RLEINE/SYS* LE7 4 B2
RLEINE/SYS LE7 5 F3
Syston St East *LEI* LE1 3 K1
Syston St West *LEI* LE1 26 C2
Sywell Dr *WGSTN* LE18 56 C1

T

Tadcaster Av *LEIS* LE2 42 D5
Tailby Av *LEIE* LE5 27 G2
Talbot La *LEI* LE1 2 C4
Talbot St *LEIN* LE4 19 G4
Talbott Cl *RLEIW/BAR* LE9 69 E5
Talbot Yd *MKTHBORO* LE16 77 H1
Tamar Rd *LEIN* LE4 20 C5
LEIS LE2 45 H3
Tamerton Rd *LEIS* LE2 32 E4
Tansey Crs *RLEIW/BAR* LE9 60 A4
Tansley Av *WGSTN* LE18 55 G2
Tarbat Rd *LEIE* LE5 28 D3
Tarragon Rd *LEIS* LE2 2 B7
Tatlow Rd *LEIW* LE3 24 A4
Tatton Cl *LEIW* LE3 25 E1
Taunton Cl *WGSTN* LE18 56 A2
Taunton Rd *LEIW* LE3 34 B1
Taurus Cl *LEIS* LE2 3 K4
Taverner Dr *GBY/RBY* LE6 22 D3
Taverners Rd *LEIN* LE4 10 C5
Tavistock Dr *LEIE* LE5 36 D2
Taylor Cl *RLEINE/SYS* LE7 13 E1
Taylor Rd *LEI* LE1 26 C3
Taylor's Bridge Rd
WGSTN LE18 55 G2
Taylors Cl *RLEIW/BAR* LE9 60 B4
Teal Cl *LEIW* LE3 32 A3
Teal Wy *RLEINE/SYS* LE7 4 A5
Teasel Cl *END/NAR* LE19 52 C3
Tebbs Cl *RLEIS/BBY* LE8 64 C2
Tedder Cl *LUTT* LE17 81 E4
Tedworth Gn *LEIN* LE4 18 D2
Teignmouth Cl *LEIE* LE5 36 D2
Telford Wy *LEIE* LE5 29 E5
Tempest Rd *LEIN* LE4 19 F1
Temple Rd *LEIE* LE5 27 G5
Tendring Dr *WGSTN* LE18 44 D5
Tennis Court Dr *LEIE* LE5 28 A3
Tennyson Rd *LUTT* LE17 81 G2
Tennyson St *END/NAR* LE19 52 C2
LEIS LE2 36 A1
Tentercroft Av
RLEINE/SYS LE7 5 E5
Tetuan Rd *LEIW* LE3 25 G4
Tewkesbury St *LEIW* LE3 2 A3
Thackeray St *LEIS* LE2 35 F4
Thames St *LEI* LE1 3 F1
Thatcher Cl *LEIN* LE4 18 B3
Thatchers' Cnr
RLEINE/SYS LE7 5 F2
Thatch Meadow Dr
MKTHBORO LE16 78 C1
Theddingworth Rd
MKTHBORO LE16 76 B2
Thirlmere Rd *WGSTN* LE18 44 C5
Thirlmere St *LEIS* LE2 35 E2
Thistle Cl *END/NAR* LE19 52 C3
RLEINE/SYS LE7 9 H2
Thomas Cl *RLEINE/SYS* LE7 39 H1
Thomasson Rd *LEIE* LE5 28 B4
Thomson Cl *LEIN* LE4 20 B1
Thoresby St *LEIE* LE5 27 G4
Thornborough Cl
END/NAR LE19 52 B4
MKTHBORO LE16 78 B2
Thornby Gdns *WGSTN* LE18 56 C1
Thorndale Rd *LEIN* LE4 20 D1
Thorneycroft Cl
RLEIW/BAR LE9 69 F5
Thornhills *END/NAR* LE19 52 B1
Thornhills Gv
END/NAR LE19 52 C1
Thornholme Cl *LEIN* LE4 18 C3
Thornton Cl *LEIW* LE3 33 F2
RLEIW/BAR LE9 69 E5
Thornton Dr *END/NAR* LE19 53 E3
Thornton La *COAL* LE67 14 A4
Thorntree Cl *LEIW* LE3 17 G5
Thornville Cl *LEIN* LE4 27 G1
Thorpe Dr *WGSTN* LE18 44 B4
Thorpe Field Dr *LEIN* LE4 12 D4
Thorpe La *RLEINE/SYS* LE7 13 H5
Thorpe St *LEIW* LE3 2 B5
Thorpe Wy *END/NAR* LE19 41 F4
Thorpewell *LEIE* LE5 27 H4
Threadgold Cl *LEIN* LE4 18 B1
Thurcaston Rd *LEIN* LE4 10 D5
Thurcroft Cl *LEIS* LE2 42 D5
Thurlaston La
RLEIW/BAR LE9 49 H2
RLEIW/BAR LE9 51 E4
Thurlby Rd *LEIE* LE5 27 F3
Thurlington Rd *LEIW* LE3 34 A2
Thurlow Cl *LEIS* LE2 45 H4
Thurlow Rd *LEIS* LE2 35 G4
Thurmaston Bvd *LEIN* LE4 20 D3
Thurmaston La *LEIE* LE5 21 E5
LEIN LE4 20 D4
Thurnby Hl *RLEINE/SYS* LE7 29 E5
Thurnby La *LEIS* LE2 38 A4
Thurncourt Cl *LEIE* LE5 28 C3
Thurncourt Gdns *LEIE* LE5 29 F3
Thurncourt Rd *LEIE* LE5 28 C3
Thurnview Rd *LEIE* LE5 37 G2
Thyme Cl *LEIS* LE2 2 B7
Tiber Wy *END/NAR* LE19 33 F5
Tichborne St *LEIS* LE2 3 J6
Tigers Cl *WGSTN* LE18 55 E1
Tigers Rd *WGSTN* LE18 55 E1
Tigers Wy *LEI* LE1 35 G2
Tilbury Crs *LEIN* LE4 21 E2
Tilford Crs *LEIS* LE2 54 D1
Tillett Rd *LEIW* LE3 33 F3
Tilley Cl *LEIW* LE3 33 F4
Tillingham Rd *LEIE* LE5 27 H2
Tilling Rd *LEIN* LE4 18 C3
Tilton Dr *LEIS* LE2 45 E5
Timber St *WGSTN* LE18 55 F2
Timberwood Dr
GBY/RBY LE6 16 A5
Timson Cl *MKTHBORO* LE16 74 B4
Tinker's Dell *RLEINE/SYS* LE7 5 F1
Tiptree Cl *LEIN* LE4 18 D5
Tithe St *LEIE* LE5 27 G3
The Tithings *RLEIS/BBY* LE8 72 A2
Tiverton Av *LEIN* LE4 20 A5
Tiverton Cl *END/NAR* LE19 52 B3
LEIS LE2 45 G3
The Tofts *WGSTN* LE18 56 B2
Tolcarne Rd *LEIE* LE5 28 C2
Tolchard Cl *LEIE* LE5 28 A5
Tollemache Av *LEIN* LE4 19 E5
Toller Rd *LEIS* LE2 36 A4
Tolton Rd *LEIN* LE4 18 D3
Tolwell Rd *LEIN* LE4 18 C1
Tomlin Rd *LEIN* LE4 27 G1
Tom Paine Cl *LEIW* LE3 33 F3
Top Cl *LEIW* LE3 33 F4
Tophall Dr *RLEIS/BBY* LE8 65 E3
Torcross Cl *LEIW* LE3 24 C2
Toronto Cl *LEI* LE1 3 H1
Torridon Cl *LEIN* LE4 18 D4
Torrington Cl *WGSTN* LE18 56 B3
Totland Rd *LEIW* LE3 25 G2
Tournament Rd *LEIW* LE3 24 B3
Tovey Crs *LEIS* LE2 42 D4
Tower Ct *MKTHBORO* LE16 76 C1
Tower Rd *RLEIW/BAR* LE9 49 F2
Towers Cl *RLEIW/BAR* LE9 32 A1
Towers Dr *RLEIW/BAR* LE9 32 A1
Tower St *LEI* LE1 3 F7
Towle Rd *LEIW* LE3 24 C2
Townend Rd
RLEIW/BAR LE9 48 A4
Townsend Cl *LEIN* LE4 20 B2
RLEIW/BAR LE9 69 F4
Townsend Rd
END/NAR LE19 40 C5
RLEIW/BAR LE9 60 B5
Towpath Link *WGSTN* LE18 55 G3
Trafalgar Wy *LEIS* LE2 54 D2
Trafford Rd *LEIE* LE5 27 H3
Tranter Pl *LEIN* LE4 20 B5
Treasure Cl *LEIW* LE3 24 A3
Treaty Rd *LEIW* LE3 24 B3
Tredington Rd *LEIW* LE3 24 B1
Treetops Cl *LEIE* LE5 28 A3
Trefoil Cl *LEIE* LE5 21 G5
RLEIW/BAR LE9 69 F5
Tremaine Dr *WGSTN* LE18 56 A2
Trenant Rd *LEIS* LE2 43 E4
Trent Av *LEIN* LE4 10 C5
Trent Cl *LEIS* LE2 45 H3
RLEIW/BAR LE9 69 E3
Trescoe Ri *LEIW* LE3 24 C5
Tressell Wy *LEIW* LE3 33 F3
Trevanth Rd *LEIN* LE4 20 D5
Trevino Dr *LEIN* LE4 20 B2
Trevose Gdns *LEIE* LE5 28 D3
Trigo Cl *LEIN* LE4 18 A3
Trillium Cl *LEIE* LE5 21 G4
Trinity Cl *RLEINE/SYS* LE7 13 F1
Trinity La *LEI* LE1 3 F7
Trinity Rd *END/NAR* LE19 53 G1
RLEIS/BBY LE8 53 H3
Tristram Cl *LEIW* LE3 32 C3
Triumph Rd *LEIW* LE3 24 A3
Trojan Wy *RLEINE/SYS* LE7 12 C2
Troon Wy *LEIN* LE4 20 B3
Trueway Rd *LEIE* LE5 36 C3
Truro Dr *WGSTN* LE18 56 B2
Tuckey Cl *RLEIW/BAR* LE9 66 D1
Tudor Cl *LEIW* LE3 2 B4
Tudor Dr *LEIS* LE2 45 F2
RLEIW/BAR LE9 63 F5
Tudor Gv *GBY/RBY* LE6 23 E1
Tudor Rd *LEIW* LE3 2 A2
Tunstall Crs *LEIN* LE4 27 G2
Turnbull Dr *LEIW* LE3 33 H5
Turnbury Wy *LEIE* LE5 36 C3
Turner Ri *LEIS* LE2 45 F4
Turner Rd *LEIE* LE5 27 H3
Turner St *LEI* LE1 3 F7
Turnpike Cl *LUTT* LE17 81 H1
MKTHBORO LE16 74 B4
Turnpike Wy *COAL* LE67 6 C4
Turnstone Wk *LEIE* LE5 * 27 E3
Turn St *RLEINE/SYS* LE7 4 C5
Turville Cl *WGSTN* LE18 56 C3
Turville Rd *LEIW* LE3 34 B2
Tuskar Rd *LEIE* LE5 28 D3
Tuxford Rd *LEIN* LE4 21 E4
Twickenham Rd *LEIS* LE2 54 C1
Twycross St *LEIE* LE5 27 E5
LEIS LE2 3 K5
Tyburn Cl *LEIW* LE3 17 H4
Tyes End *LEIN* LE4 18 A4
Tyler Rd *GBY/RBY* LE6 22 D2
Tymecrosse Gdns
MKTHBORO LE16 74 B4
Tyndale St *LEIW* LE3 2 A6
Tynedale Cl *LEIS* LE2 45 H3
Tyringham Rd *WGSTN* LE18 56 C1
Tyrrell St *LEIW* LE3 2 A2
Tysoe Hl *LEIW* LE3 24 B1
Tythorn Dr *WGSTN* LE18 43 G3

U

Ullswater Cl *RLEIW/BAR* LE9 49 F4
Ullswater Dr *LEIS* LE2 45 G4
Ullswater St *LEIS* LE2 2 C7
Ulvers Cft *COAL* LE67 6 C3
Ulverscroft Dr
GBY/RBY LE6 16 B5
Ulverscroft Rd *LEIN* LE4 27 E2
Una Av *LEIW* LE3 34 A5
Underwood Crs
RLEIW/BAR LE9 67 E1
Underwood Dr
RLEIW/BAR LE9 60 A5
Unicorn St *LEIN* LE4 12 B4
Unity Rd *LEIW* LE3 24 A2
University Cl
RLEINE/SYS LE7 13 F1
University Rd *LEI* LE1 35 G2
Upex Cl *RLEIS/BBY* LE8 63 H2
Upland Dr *COAL* LE67 6 B3
Uplands Rd *LEIS* LE2 43 F3
LEIS LE2 45 F2
Upper Brown St *LEI* LE1 2 E5
Upper Charnwood St
LEIS LE2 3 K3
Upper Church St
RLEINE/SYS LE7 4 D5
Upper George St *LEI* LE1 3 G1
Upper Green Pl
MKTHBORO LE16 74 D3
Upper Hall Cl *LEIE* LE5 28 C2
Upper Hall Gn *LEIE* LE5 28 C2
Upper King St *LEI* LE1 3 F7
Upper New Wk *LEI* LE1 3 J7
Upper Tichborne St *LEIS* LE2 3 K6
Upperton Ri *LEIW* LE3 34 B1
Upperton Rd *LEIW* LE3 34 D2
Uppingham Cl *LEIE* LE5 28 C5
Uppingham Dr
RLEIW/BAR LE9 68 B1
Uppingham Rd *LEIE* LE5 27 F3
RLEINE/SYS LE7 29 F5
RLEINE/SYS LE7 39 H1
Upton Dr *WGSTN* LE18 56 D1
Utah Cl *LEIW* LE3 24 A3
Uttoxeter Cl *LEIN* LE4 20 B2
Uxbridge Rd *LEIN* LE4 19 H3

V

Vale Cl *LEIE* LE5 28 C3
Valence Rd *LEIW* LE3 34 B1
Valentine Dr *LEIS* LE2 44 D2
Valentine Rd *LEIE* LE5 28 D5
Valiant Cl *LEIW* LE3 24 B3
Valjean Crs *RLEIW/BAR* LE9 32 A3
Valley Dr *LEIW* LE3 33 F3
Valley La *LUTT* LE17 81 F1
Valley Rd *COAL* LE67 6 C4
LEIN LE4 21 F3
Valley Wy *MKTHBORO* LE16 75 F5
Vancouver Rd *LEI* LE1 26 C3
Vandyke Rd *LEIS* LE2 45 F4
Vaughan Cl
MKTHBORO LE16 77 H4
Vaughan Rd *LEIS* LE2 43 E1
Vaughan St *LEIW* LE3 2 A3
Vaughan Wy *LEI* LE1 2 D4
Ventnor Rd *LEIS* LE2 44 B1
Ventnor Rd South
LEIS LE2 * 44 B2
Ventnor St *LEIE* LE5 27 F5
Verdale Av *LEIN* LE4 20 D2
Vernon Rd *LEIS* LE2 43 E1
Vernon St *LEIW* LE3 2 A2
Vestry St *LEI* LE1 3 G3
Vetch Cl *END/NAR* LE19 52 B3
Vicarage Cl *GBY/RBY* LE6 23 E4
RLEINE/SYS LE7 4 D5
Vicarage La *LEIE* LE5 28 B2
LEIN LE4 19 G4
RLEINE/SYS LE7 13 H4
RLEIS/BBY LE8 53 H3
Vicarage St *RLEIW/BAR* LE9 49 F3
Victoria Av *LEIS* LE2 3 J7
MKTHBORO LE16 74 B5
Victoria Dr *GBY/RBY* LE6 16 B5
Victoria Gdns *LEIS* LE2 36 A2
Victoria Pde *LEI* LE1 2 E3
Victoria Park Rd *LEIS* LE2 35 F3
Victoria Pas *LEIS* LE2 3 J7
Victoria Rd *RLEIS/BBY* LE8 53 H3
Victoria Rd East *LEIE* LE5 27 G2
LEIN LE4 20 D5
Victoria Rd North *LEIN* LE4 19 G4
Victoria St *END/NAR* LE19 53 E4
LEIN LE4 12 C4
RLEINE/SYS LE7 13 F1
RLEIS/BBY LE8 70 B4
WGSTN LE18 44 B5
Victor Rd *LEIW* LE3 24 B2
Victors Cl *LEIS* LE2 42 C4
Viking Rd *WGSTN* LE18 43 G4
Vincent Cl *LEIW* LE3 25 F4
Vinehouse Cl
RLEINE/SYS LE7 10 B1
The Vineries *RLEIS/BBY* LE8 64 D3
Vine St *LEI* LE1 2 D2
Vitruvius Wy *END/NAR* LE19 33 E5
Vostock Cl *LEIS* LE2 3 K4
Vulcan Rd *LEIE* LE5 3 K1
Vyner Cl *LEIW* LE3 33 E3

W

Wade St *LEIN* LE4 19 F4
Wadkins Wy
RLEINE/SYS LE7 29 G5
Wagtail Cl *RLEIS/BBY* LE8 70 C5
Wainwright Av *LEIE* LE5 21 G4
Wakefield Pl *LEIN* LE4 20 A5
Wakeley Cl *END/NAR* LE19 52 C4
Wakeling Cl *RLEIS/BBY* LE8 63 H1
Wakerley Rd *LEIE* LE5 36 D1
Wakes Rd *WGSTN* LE18 44 B5
Walcote Rd *LEIN* LE4 20 C5
Walcot Rd *MKTHBORO* LE16 77 H2
Waldale Dr *LEIS* LE2 36 A3
Waldron Dr *LEIS* LE2 45 G3
Wale Rd *RLEIS/BBY* LE8 53 H4
Walker Cl *RLEIW/BAR* LE9 * 69 E5
Walker Ct *LUTT* LE17 81 H3
Walker Rd *LEIN* LE4 19 F1
LEIN LE4 20 D1
Walkers Wy *RLEINE/SYS* LE7 4 D5
Wallace Dr *GBY/RBY* LE6 15 G2
Wallingford Rd *LEIN* LE4 19 F5
Wallis Cl *RLEINE/SYS* LE7 10 B1
Walnut Av *LEIN* LE4 11 F4
Walnut Cl *COAL* LE67 6 B4
LEIS LE2 45 E3
RLEIW/BAR LE9 68 D3
Walnut Gv *LEIS* LE2 42 B4
Walnut Leys *RLEIW/BAR* LE9 63 F4
Walnut St *LEIS* LE2 35 E2
Walnut Wy *RLEIS/BBY* LE8 54 B5
Walpole Ct *LEIW* LE3 24 D5
Walsgrave Av *LEIE* LE5 28 D5
Walshe Rd *LEIE* LE5 28 B4
Walsingham Crs *LEIW* LE3 32 D2
Waltham Av *LEIW* LE3 34 A3
Walton Cl *RLEIW/BAR* LE9 32 B1
Walton St *LEIW* LE3 34 C2
Wand St *LEIN* LE4 26 C1
Wanlip Av *LEIN* LE4 11 G5
Wanlip La *RLEINE/SYS* LE7 11 H2
Wanlip Rd *RLEINE/SYS* LE7 12 B1
Wanlip St *LEI* LE1 26 C3
Wansbeck Gdns *LEIE* LE5 28 C2
Wanstead Rd *LEIW* LE3 23 G5

Ward Cl LEIS LE2 42 C1
Wardens Wk LEIW LE3 32 D2
Wards Closes WGSTN LE18 56 C3
Wareham Rd RLEIS/BBY LE8 54 B5
Warmsley Av WGSTN LE18 44 A4
Warner Cl RLEIS/BBY LE8 64 A1
Warren Av LEIN LE4 21 E2
Warren Cl COAL LE67 6 C4
LEIE LE5 28 A2
Warren Dr LEIN LE4 21 E2
Warren La LEIW LE3 32 A3
Warren Park Wy
END/NAR LE19 40 C4
Warren Rd END/NAR LE19 53 F2
Warren St LEIW LE3 2 A3
The Warren RLEINE/SYS LE7 5 F2
Warren Vw LEIN LE4 21 E2
Warrington Dr
GBY/RBY LE6 16 A5
Wartnaby St
MKTHBORO LE16 77 F1
Warwick Cl
MKTHBORO LE16 74 D4
RLEIW/BAR LE9 30 A3
Warwick Rd END/NAR LE19 53 F5
RLEIS/BBY LE8 71 F3
RLEIW/BAR LE9 68 B1
WGSTN LE18 43 H5
Warwick St LEIW LE3 2 A3
Washbrook La
RLEIS/BBY LE8 59 G2
WGSTN LE18 44 D4
Washington Cl
RLEIW/BAR LE9 48 A5
Watchcrete Av
RLEINE/SYS LE7 5 F4
Waterfield Cl LEIE LE5 28 B5
Waterfield Pl
MKTHBORO LE16 * 74 D4
Waterfield Rd
RLEINE/SYS LE7 9 H2
Watergate RLEINE/SYS LE7 5 G2
Watergate La
END/NAR LE19 41 F1
Waterloo Crs RLEIS/BBY LE8 64 D3
WGSTN LE18 44 C4
Waterloo Wy LEI LE1 3 G7
Watermead Wy LEIN LE4 19 H3
Waterside Rd LEIN LE4 21 E4
Waterville Cl LEIW LE3 24 A4
Watery Gate La
RLEIW/BAR LE9 50 C3
Watling St LEI LE1 26 B3
Watson Av MKTHBORO LE16 77 F3
Watson Rd LEIN LE4 20 A5
Watts Cl LEIN LE4 18 A4
Waudby Cl END/NAR LE19 53 E5
Waveney Ri LEIS LE2 45 H2
Waverley Rd RLEIS/BBY LE8 54 C5
WGSTN LE18 55 F1
Wavertree Cl
RLEIW/BAR LE9 63 F2
Wavertree Dr LEIN LE4 19 H4
Wayfarer Dr RLEINE/SYS LE7 5 G1
The Wayne Wy LEIE LE5 27 H4
LEIN LE4 11 G5
Wayside Dr LEIN LE4 20 B1
LEIS LE2 45 G3
Weaver Rd LEIE LE5 28 D3
RLEIW/BAR LE9 49 F3
Webb Cl LEIW LE3 32 D3
Webbs Wy RLEIW/BAR LE9 60 B4
Webster Rd LEIW LE3 33 G1
Weir La RLEINE/SYS LE7 39 H1
Weir Rd RLEIS/BBY LE8 72 A4
Welbeck Av LEIN LE4 19 E5
Welbeck Cl RLEIS/BBY LE8 54 C5
Welcombe Av LEIW LE3 33 H4
Weldon Rd WGSTN LE18 44 B5
Welford Ct LEIS LE2 43 H1
Welford Pl LEI LE1 2 E5
Welford Rd LEI LE1 3 F6
LEIS LE2 35 G4
LEIS LE2 43 H2
RLEIS/BBY LE8 54 B3
WGSTN LE18 56 B2
Welham Rd
MKTHBORO LE16 75 E2
Welland Ct MKTHBORO LE16 75 E5
Welland Park Rd
MKTHBORO LE16 77 G2
Welland St LEIS LE2 3 K6
Welland Vale Rd LEIE LE5 37 H1
Wellesbourne Dr LEIW LE3 24 B1
Welles St LEI LE1 2 C4
Wellgate Av LEIN LE4 11 F4
Wellhouse Cl WGSTN LE18 56 A3
Wellinger Wy LEIW LE3 33 G1
Wellington Pkwy LUTT LE17 80 A2
Wellington St LEI LE1 3 F5
RLEINE/SYS LE7 13 E1
Well Spring Hl WGSTN LE18 56 C3
Welton Cl RLEIS/BBY LE8 72 A3
Wembley Rd LEIW LE3 23 H5
Wendys Cl LEIE LE5 28 D3
Wenlock Wy LEIN LE4 21 E4
Wensleydale Rd
WGSTN LE18 56 D2
Wensley Ri LEIS LE2 54 C1
Wentbridge Rd LEIN LE4 20 B4
Went Rd LEIN LE4 19 G1
Wentworth Cl
RLEIS/BBY LE8 72 B4
Wentworth Rd LEIW LE3 25 G4
RLEIS/BBY LE8 70 C4
Wesley Cl GBY/RBY LE6 22 C2
RLEIW/BAR LE9 67 E2
Wesley St LEIN LE4 19 F4
Wesley Wy COAL LE67 6 C4
Wessex Dr LEIW LE3 24 C5
West Av LEIS LE2 35 H3
WGSTN LE18 43 H5
Westbourne St LEIN LE4 26 C2
West Br LEIW LE3 2 C4
Westbridge Cl LEI LE1 2 C5
Westbury Rd LEIS LE2 35 G4
Westcotes Dr LEIW LE3 25 G5
Westdale Av LEIS LE2 54 A1
Westdown Dr LEIN LE4 20 C2
West Dr LEIE LE5 28 A2
Westerby Cl WGSTN LE18 44 B4
Westerby La RLEIS/BBY LE8 71 H5
Westerdale Rd WGSTN LE18 56 D1
Western Av
MKTHBORO LE16 77 G3
RLEIS/BBY LE8 70 B5
Western Bvd LEIS LE2 2 C7
Western Dr RLEIS/BBY LE8 54 B4
Westernhay Rd LEIS LE2 36 A4
Western Park Rd LEIW LE3 25 E5
Western Rd LEIW LE3 34 D2
Westfield Av RLEIS/BBY LE8 64 D2
WGSTN LE18 43 H4
Westfield Cl
MKTHBORO LE16 77 F1
RLEINE/SYS LE7 5 H1
Westfield Rd LEIW LE3 25 E5
Westgate Av LEIN LE4 11 E4
Westgate La
MKTHBORO LE16 76 B1
Westgate Rd LEIS LE2 43 H2
Westhill Rd LEIW LE3 25 E4
West Holme St LEIW LE3 2 A5
Westland Cl
MKTHBORO LE16 76 B1
West Langton Rd
RLEIS/BBY LE8 73 E4
Westleigh Av LEIW LE3 34 C2
Westleigh Rd LEIW LE3 34 C2
WGSTN LE18 55 E2
Westmeath Av LEIE LE5 28 B4
Westminster Dr LEIS LE2 54 D2
Westminster Rd LEIS LE2 36 C4
Westmorland Av LEIN LE4 20 A5
WGSTN LE18 55 F1
Weston Cl LEIS LE2 46 A4
Westover Rd LEIW LE3 33 F3
West St END/NAR LE19 52 C1
LEI LE1 3 F7
LEIW LE3 17 E5
RLEINE/SYS LE7 4 C5
RLEIS/BBY LE8 54 A2
RLEIW/BAR LE9 49 F2
West View Av LEIS LE2 42 B5
West Wk LEI LE1 3 H7
Wetherby Cl RLEINE/SYS LE7 5 F3
Wetherby Rd LEIN LE4 20 B4
Wexford Cl LEIS LE2 45 H4
Weymouth Cl WGSTN LE18 56 B3
Weymouth St LEIN LE4 26 D2
Wharf St LEIN LE4 12 B4
Wharf St North LEI LE1 3 G1
Wharf St South LEI LE1 3 G2
Wharf Wy LEIS LE2 54 B1
Wheatfield Cl LEIW LE3 24 A3
Wheatland Cl LEIS LE2 45 H3
Wheatland Rd LEIN LE4 18 D2
Wheatlands Dr
RLEIS/BBY LE8 64 D2
Wheatley Rd LEIN LE4 18 D3
Wheatley's Rd LEIN LE4 20 B1
Wheat St LEI LE1 3 G2
Wheeldale WGSTN LE18 56 D1
Wheeler Cl LUTT LE17 81 G4
Whetstone Gorse La
RLEIS/BBY LE8 64 A4
Whiles La LEIN LE4 11 H5
Whinchat Rd LEIE LE5 27 E4
Whinham Av
RLEIW/BAR LE9 68 B2
Whitby Cl RLEIW/BAR LE9 68 C1
Whitcroft Cl COAL LE67 6 C4
Whiteacres RLEIS/BBY LE8 63 G1
White Barn Dr
RLEIW/BAR LE9 63 F3
Whitebeam Cl
END/NAR LE19 52 C3
Whitebeam Rd LEIS LE2 45 E1
White Cl RLEIW/BAR LE9 69 E3
Whitefield Rd LEIN LE4 19 F4
Whitehall Rd LEIE LE5 37 F1
Whitehead Crs WGSTN LE18 43 H5
White Horse La LEIN LE4 19 H1
White House Cl
GBY/RBY LE6 16 A4
Whiteoaks Rd LEIS LE2 45 G5
Whitesand Cl LEIW LE3 24 B1
White St RLEIS/BBY LE8 71 H3
Whitley Cl LEIW LE3 25 F2
Whitman Cl LEIW LE3 24 B4
Whitteney Dr LEIS LE2 42 D4
Whittier Rd LEIS LE2 43 F1
Whittington Dr
GBY/RBY LE6 22 C1
Whittington Rd LEIW LE3 17 H4
Whittle Cl RLEIS/BBY LE8 53 H5
Whittle Rd LUTT LE17 81 F4
Whitwell Rw LEIS LE2 43 E3
Whitwick Wy LEIW LE3 25 G2
Wicken Ri WGSTN LE18 44 C4
Wickham Rd LEIS LE2 45 F4
Wicklow Dr LEIE LE5 28 A4
Wiclifway LUTT LE17 81 G2
Widford Cl LEIE LE5 28 A2
Wightman Cl
RLEIW/BAR LE9 60 B3
Wightman Rd
RLEIW/BAR LE9 48 C4
Wigley Rd LEIE LE5 28 C2
Wigston La LEIS LE2 42 D2
Wigston Rd LEIS LE2 45 E3
RLEIS/BBY LE8 54 B3
WGSTN LE18 44 D4
Wigston St LEI LE1 3 G4
RLEIS/BBY LE8 65 F2
Wilberforce Rd LEIW LE3 34 D2
Wileman's Cl
RLEIW/BAR LE9 49 E5
Wiley Wy LEI LE1 3 F7
Wilf Brown Cl
RLEIW/BAR LE9 49 H3
William Cl RLEINE/SYS LE7 5 G3
Williams Cl END/NAR LE19 52 D5
William St END/NAR LE19 52 D4
LEIE LE5 3 H3
Willoughby Gdns LEIW LE3 32 C2
Willoughby Rd
RLEIS/BBY LE8 64 C3
Willow Brook Cl LEIW LE3 17 E5
Willowbrook Cl
RLEIW/BAR LE9 68 D2
Willow Brook Rd LEIE LE5 27 E3
Willowbrook Vw LEIE LE5 29 E4
Willow Cl END/NAR LE19 53 E5
Willow Ct LEIS LE2 3 J5
Willow Crs MKTHBORO LE16 77 F2
Willowdene Wy
RLEIW/BAR LE9 48 B5
Willow Dr GBY/RBY LE6 23 E1
RLEIS/BBY LE8 65 E2
Willow Herb Cl LEIS LE2 46 A4
Willow Park Dr WGSTN LE18 44 A5
Willow Pl WGSTN LE18 56 B1
Willow Rd RLEIS/BBY LE8 54 B4
Willow St LEI LE1 26 C3
RLEIW/BAR LE9 30 A2
Willowtree Cl LEIE LE5 21 G5
Willow Tree Cl
RLEIW/BAR LE9 48 B3
Willow Tree Crs LUTT LE17 81 E3
Willow Wk RLEINE/SYS LE7 12 D1
Willsmer Cl RLEIW/BAR LE9 69 E4
Willson Cl MKTHBORO LE16 78 B1
Wilmington Rd LEIW LE3 34 B2
Wilmore Crs LEIW LE3 33 F2
Wilne St LEIS LE2 36 A1
Wilnicott Rd LEIW LE3 33 H4
Wilsford Cl WGSTN LE18 56 A3
Wilshere Cl RLEIW/BAR LE9 22 D5
Wilson Cl LEIW LE3 33 F3
Wilson Rd WGSTN LE18 55 E2
Wilson St LEIS LE2 27 E5
Wilton St LEI LE1 3 F1
Wiltshire Rd LEIN LE4 18 D5
WGSTN LE18 43 H5
Wimbledon St LEIE LE5 3 G3
Wimborne Cl WGSTN LE18 56 A2
Wimborne Rd LEIS LE2 44 B2
Winchendon Cl LEIE LE5 27 G3
Winchester Av LEIW LE3 34 B2
RLEIS/BBY LE8 54 A2
Winchester Rd
RLEIS/BBY LE8 54 C4
Winckley Cl
RLEINE/SYS LE7 39 H1
Windermere Cl
RLEIW/BAR LE9 49 F3
Windermere Dr
RLEIW/BAR LE9 61 H2
Windermere Rd
WGSTN LE18 44 D5
Windermere St LEIS LE2 35 E2
Winder's Wy LEIS LE2 42 D3
Windley Rd LEIS LE2 43 G3
Windmill Av LEIN LE4 11 H4
Windmill Bank WGSTN LE18 56 C2
Windmill Cl GBY/RBY LE6 22 D2
LEIN LE4 12 D4
Windmill Gdns
RLEIS/BBY LE8 72 A1
Windmill Ri GBY/RBY LE6 16 A4
Windrush Dr LEIS LE2 45 H3
Windsor Av GBY/RBY LE6 16 A5
LEIN LE4 19 H5
LEIS LE2 55 E2
Windsor Cl LEIS LE2 45 G5
Winforde Crs LEIW LE3 33 F1
Wingfield St LEIN LE4 19 H5
Winifred St LEIS LE2 2 D7
Winslow Dr WGSTN LE18 44 C4
Winslow Gn LEIE LE5 28 C2
Winstanley Dr LEIW LE3 33 H1
Winster Dr LEIN LE4 12 C4
Winston Av RLEIW/BAR LE9 61 H2
Winterburn Gdns
RLEIS/BBY LE8 53 H4
Winterfield Cl LEIW LE3 23 H3
Wintergreen Cl LEIE LE5 21 G4
Wintersdale Rd LEIE LE5 28 C4
Winterton Cl LEIN LE4 12 D4
Winton Av LEIW LE3 34 B3
Wistow Rd RLEIS/BBY LE8 57 H5
RLEIS/BBY LE8 71 F1
WGSTN LE18 56 B2
Withcote Av LEIE LE5 28 C5
Withens Cl LEIW LE3 25 E3
Witherdell LEIN LE4 18 A4
Withers Wy LEIW LE3 33 F4
Withington Cl LEIW LE3 33 F3
Woburn Cl LEIS LE2 42 C4
MKTHBORO LE16 78 B1
WGSTN LE18 56 C1
Wodehouse Rd LEIW LE3 34 A1
Wokingham Av LEIS LE2 54 D1
The Wolds RLEINE/SYS LE7 5 G1
Wollaton Cl LEIW LE3 23 H2
Wolsey Cl GBY/RBY LE6 16 A5
LEIW LE3 32 B3
RLEIS/BBY LE8 70 B3
Wolsey Dr GBY/RBY LE6 22 B1
Wolsey La RLEIS/BBY LE8 70 B3
Wolsey St LEIN LE4 26 A2
Wolsey Wy RLEINE/SYS LE7 12 D1
Wolverton Rd LEIW LE3 34 C3
Woodbank LEIS LE2 54 B1
Woodbank Rd GBY/RBY LE6 15 H4
WGSTN LE18 44 A2
Woodbine Av LEIS LE2 3 K7
Woodbine Crs LUTT LE17 81 G4
Woodborough Rd LEIE LE5 37 E1
Woodboy St LEI LE1 26 C3
Woodbreach Dr
MKTHBORO LE16 78 C1
Wood Br LUTT LE17 80 D4
Woodbridge Rd LEIN LE4 19 H4
Woodbury Ri
RLEIS/BBY LE8 59 E2
Woodby La LUTT LE17 80 D1
Woodcote Rd LEIW LE3 41 H1
Woodcroft Av LEIS LE2 43 G2
Wood End LEIW LE3 25 E3
Woodfield Cl END/NAR LE19 52 D3
Woodfield Rd LEIS LE2 45 F1
Woodford Cl WGSTN LE18 56 A3
Woodgate LEIW LE3 25 H3
Woodgate Cl
MKTHBORO LE16 78 C2
Woodgate Dr LEIN LE4 11 F4
Woodgon Rd
RLEINE/SYS LE7 17 F1
Woodgreen Rd LEIN LE4 27 F1
Woodgreen Wk LEIN LE4 27 F1
Woodhall Cl LEIW LE3 24 B5
Wood Hl LEIE LE5 27 E4
Woodhouse Cl COAL LE67 6 C3
Woodhouse Rd
END/NAR LE19 52 B4
Woodland Av
END/NAR LE19 52 D3
LEIS LE2 36 A4
Woodland Cl COAL LE67 6 C4
Woodland Dr LEIW LE3 33 F3
Woodland Rd LEIE LE5 27 F3
Woodlands Ct LEIS LE2 46 A4
Woodlands Dr GBY/RBY LE6 15 H3
Woodlands La
RLEIW/BAR LE9 23 E4
The Woodlands
MKTHBORO LE16 74 A5
RLEIS/BBY LE8 64 D2
WGSTN LE18 44 D4
Woodlea Av LUTT LE17 81 E3
Woodley Rd GBY/RBY LE6 22 C2
Woodman's Cha
RLEINE/SYS LE7 5 F2
Woodmarket LUTT LE17 81 G4
Woodnewton Dr LEIE LE5 37 H1
Woodpecker Cl LEIW LE3 32 A3
Woods Cl LEIS LE2 45 G2
Woodshawe Ri LEIW LE3 33 G3
Woodside Cl LEIN LE4 27 F1
RLEIW/BAR LE9 52 B3
Woodside Rd LEIS LE2 45 H5
Woodstock Cl LEIN LE4 19 E3
Woodstock Rd LEIN LE4 19 E3
Wood St LEI LE1 3 F1
RLEIW/BAR LE9 49 E3
Woodville Gdns
WGSTN LE18 44 A3
Woodville Rd LEIW LE3 25 G4
Woodway Rd LUTT LE17 81 F4
Woodyard La
RLEIS/BBY LE8 53 H3
Wooldale Cl RLEINE/SYS LE7 9 G5
Wootton Cl RLEIS/BBY LE8 53 H5
Wootton Ri LEIS LE2 42 D3
Worcester Av LEIN LE4 12 A4
RLEINE/SYS LE7 11 H3
Worcester Cl
RLEIW/BAR LE9 48 A4
Worcester Dr
MKTHBORO LE16 74 C4
WGSTN LE18 55 F1
Worcester Rd LEIS LE2 42 D1
Wordsworth Crs
END/NAR LE19 52 C2
Wordsworth Rd LEIS LE2 35 G4
Worrall Cl LEIW LE3 33 F1
Worrall Rd LEIW LE3 33 F1
Worsh Cl RLEIS/BBY LE8 63 H1
Worsley Wy RLEIS/BBY LE8 54 A5
Worthington St LEIS LE2 27 E5
The Wranglands
RLEIS/BBY LE8 70 C4
Wreake Rd RLEINE/SYS LE7 12 C4
Wreford Crs LEIE LE5 29 E3
Wren Cl LEIS LE2 43 E1
RLEINE/SYS LE7 4 A5
Wright Cl RLEIS/BBY LE8 63 H2
Wright La LEIS LE2 45 H4

Wroxall Wy *LEIW* LE3 25 G2
Wyatt Cl *LEIW* LE3 33 E1
Wych Elm Cl *RLEIS/BBY* LE8 58 D2
Wych Elm Rd *LEIS* LE2 45 E1
Wychwood Rd *RLEIS/BBY* LE8 64 A1
Wycliffe St *LEI* LE1 2 E4
Wycombe Rd *LEIE* LE5 27 G2
Wye Dean Dr *WGSTN* LE18 56 B1
Wykeham Cl *RLEIS/BBY* LE8 54 B5
Wylam Cl *LEIW* LE3 25 E2
Wymar Cl *LEIN* LE4 18 C4
Wyndale Dr *RLEINE/SYS* LE7 4 D4
Wyndale Rd *LEIS* LE2 43 H1
Wyndham Cl *LEIS* LE2 45 G1
Wynfield Rd *LEIW* LE3 25 F5
Wyngate Dr *LEIW* LE3 25 F5
Wynthorpe Ri *LEIW* LE3 34 A1
Wynton Cl *RLEIS/BBY* LE8 54 C5
Wyvern Av *LEIN* LE4 20 B5
Wyvern Cl *RLEIW/BAR* LE9 * 69 E4
Wyville Rw *LEIW* LE3 34 A4

Y

Yardley Dr *WGSTN* LE18 43 H3
Yarmouth St *LEI* LE1 3 F1
Yarrow Cl *LEIE* LE5 28 C1
Yarwell Dr *WGSTN* LE18 56 C1
Yaxley Cl *RLEINE/SYS* LE7 29 F4
Yeats Cl *LEIW* LE3 33 F4
Yelverton Av *LEIE* LE5 37 G2
Yeoman La *LEI* LE1 3 F3
Yeomanry Ct *MKTHBORO* LE16 77 H1
Yeoman's Dl *RLEINE/SYS* LE7 5 F1
Yeoman St *LEI* LE1 3 G3
Yew Cl *LEIW* LE3 32 B4
The Yews *LEIS* LE2 45 F2
Yew Tree Cl *LUTT* LE17 81 E3
RLEIW/BAR LE9 48 C3
Yew Tree Dr *LEIW* LE3 24 A4
York Cl *LEIS* LE2 55 E2
York Rd *LEI* LE1 2 E5
Yorkshire Rd *LEIN* LE4 27 E1
York St *LEI* LE1 3 F5
MKTHBORO LE16 78 A1
Yukon Wy *LEI* LE1 3 H1

Index - featured places

Abbey Business Park *LEI* LE1 26 A3
Abbey Community Primary School *LEIN* LE4 26 C1
Abbey Pumping Station *LEIN* LE4 19 F5
Abington High School *WGSTN* LE18 56 A1
Al aqsa Primary School *COAL* LE67 6 C5
LEIE LE5 27 G4
Alderman Richard Hallam Primary School *LEIN* LE4 25 G1
All Saints CE Primary School *RLEIW/BAR* LE9 66 D2
WGSTN LE18 56 A1
Anstey Nomads FC *RLEINE/SYS* LE7 9 H5
Ashfield School *LEIE* LE5 36 D1
Auster Industrial Estate *LEIN* LE4 20 D1
Avenue Junior School *LEIS* LE2 35 H4
Aylestone Leisure Centre *LEIS* LE2 35 F5
Babington Community Technology College *LEIN* LE4 18 B4
Badgerbrook Primary School *RLEIS/BBY* LE8 63 H1
Barley Croft Primary School *LEIN* LE4 18 C4
Barrington Park Industrial Estate *LEIN* LE4 18 B2
Barwell CE Junior School *RLEIW/BAR* LE9 48 A5
Barwell Infant School *RLEIW/BAR* LE9 48 A5
Barwell Medical Centre *RLEIW/BAR* LE9 48 A5
The Beauchamp College *LEIS* LE2 45 F5
Beaumont Leys Health Centre *LEIN* LE4 18 C4
Beaumont Leys School *LEIN* LE4 18 B5
Beaumont Lodge Primary School *LEIN* LE4 18 B1
Bede Island Business Park *LEIS* LE2 2 B6
Beedles Lake Golf Centre *RLEINE/SYS* LE7 5 E1
Belgrave & Birstall Station *LEIN* LE4 19 F2
Belgrave Cemetery *LEIN* LE4 19 F3
Belgrave Hall & Gardens *LEIN* LE4 19 G4
Belgrave Industrial Centre *LEIN* LE4 19 G5
Belgrave RFC *LEIN* LE4 19 F3
Belgrave St Peters CE Primary School *LEIN* LE4 19 F3
Belmont House Hotel *LEIS* LE2 3 H6
Bendbow Rise Infant School *LEIW* LE3 33 F2
Birkett House School & Hostel *WGSTN* LE18 56 A1
Birstall Golf Club *LEIN* LE4 19 F2
Bishop Ellis RC Primary School *RLEINE/SYS* LE7 12 D4
Blaby Industrial Park *RLEIS/BBY* LE8 54 A2
Bosworth Community College *RLEIW/BAR* LE9 30 C2
Bradgate Park Country Park *GBY/RBY* LE6 8 D1
Braunstone Frith Industrial Estate *LEIW* LE3 23 H5
LEIW LE3 24 B5
Braunstone Frith J & I School *LEIW* LE3 24 B4
Bridge Business Park *LEIN* LE4 12 B5
Bridge Junior School *LEIE* LE5 27 E3
Brockington College *END/NAR* LE19 53 E1
Brocks Hill Country Park *WGSTN* LE18 45 E5
Brocks Hill Primary School *LEIS* LE2 45 F5
Brooke House College *MKTHBORO* LE16 74 C5
Brookside Primary School *LEIS* LE2 45 H1
Brookvale High School *GBY/RBY* LE6 15 H5
Broomfield Primary School *RLEINE/SYS* LE7 5 G2
Bushloe High School *WGSTN* LE18 55 H1
BUSM Business Park *LEIN* LE4 26 C1
Buswells Lodge Primary School *LEIN* LE4 18 A4
Caldecote Community Primary School *LEIW* LE3 34 A4
Campanile Hotel *LEI* LE1 3 G1
Castle Hill Country Park *LEIN* LE4 10 A5
Castle Hotel *RLEIW/BAR* LE9 23 E4
Catherine Infant School *LEIN* LE4 26 D2
Catherine Junior School *LEIN* LE4 26 D2
Catherine Street Industrial Estate *LEIN* LE4 20 B5
Charnwood Health Centre *LEIE* LE5 27 E3
Charnwood Primary School *LEIS* LE2 3 K2
Chartwell Drive Industrial Estate *WGSTN* LE18 43 G5
Christ the King RC Primary School *LEIW* LE3 25 F4
Church Hill CE Junior School *LEIN* LE4 12 D5
City Gallery *LEI* LE1 3 G4
City of Leicester School *LEIE* LE5 37 H1
Clarendon Park Medical Centre *LEIS* LE2 35 G4
Clyde Street Medical Centre *LEI* LE1 3 H2
Cobden Street Industrial Estate *LEIN* LE4 27 E3
Coleman Primary School *LEIE* LE5 36 C1
Corus Hotel *RLEIS/BBY* LE8 54 B3
Cosby Golf Club *RLEIW/BAR* LE9 63 F5
Cosby Primary School *RLEIW/BAR* LE9 63 F2
Cossington Street Sports Centre *LEIN* LE4 26 D1
Cottage Lane Industrial Estate *RLEIW/BAR* LE9 69 E3
Countesthorpe College *RLEIS/BBY* LE8 64 C2
Crescent Junior School *LEIW* LE3 33 G1
The Croft Medical Centre *LEIS* LE2 45 G4
Crown Hills Community College *LEIE* LE5 36 D1
Darul Arqam Educational Institute *LEIE* LE5 27 F4
Darul Uloom School *LEIN* LE4 19 G5
Days Inn *LEI* LE1 3 F1
LEIW LE3 32 D3
De Montfort Hall *LEI* LE1 35 G2
De Montfort University *LEI* LE1 2 D5
Desford Primary School *RLEIW/BAR* LE9 30 A3
Dovelands Primary School *LEIW* LE3 25 F5
Dowry Furlong Wildlife Area *GBY/RBY* LE6 16 A3
Earls Close Industrial Estate *LEIN* LE4 12 C5
Eastfield Primary School *LEIN* LE4 12 D4
The Elizabeth Woodville Primary School *GBY/RBY* LE6 16 A5
Ellesmere College *LEIW* LE3 34 B3
Emily Fortey School *LEIW* LE3 24 D4
Enderby Danemill Primary School *END/NAR* LE19 52 D1
Enderby Leisure Centre & Golf Club *END/NAR* LE19 52 D1
Enderby Road Industrial Estate *RLEIS/BBY* LE8 53 G2
English Martyrs RC School *LEIW* LE3 25 F1
Euro Business Park *MKTHBORO* LE16 75 F5
Evington Pool *LEIE* LE5 37 G2
Evington Valley Primary School *LEIE* LE5 36 B2
Eyres Monsell Primary School *LEIS* LE2 42 D4
Faircharm Industrial Estate *LEIS* LE2 34 D3
Farmworld *LE15* LE2 37 F4
The Fairfield Primary School *WGSTN* LE18 43 G5
Farndon Fields Primary School *MKTHBORO* LE16 77 H4
Feilding Cottage Hospital *LUTT* LE17 81 H3
Fernvale Primary School *RLEINE/SYS* LE7 29 F4
Fleckney CE Primary School *RLEIS/BBY* LE8 70 A3
Fleckney Industrial Estate *RLEIS/BBY* LE8 70 C4
Fleckney Leisure Centre *RLEIS/BBY* LE8 70 B2
Folville Junior School *LEIW* LE3 34 A3
Forest Lodge Primary School *LEIW* LE3 24 C2
Fosse Medical Centre *LEIW* LE3 25 G4
Fosse Park Shopping Centre *END/NAR* LE19 41 H3
Fosse Primary School *LEIW* LE3 25 H3
Foxbank Industrial Estate *RLEIW/BAR* LE9 60 B3
Freemens Common Trading Estate *LEIS* LE2 35 F3
Friar Lane FC *LEIS* LE2 35 F5
Fullhurst Community College *LEIW* LE3 34 B2
Gartree High School *LEIS* LE2 45 F5
Gateway Sixth Form College *LEIS* LE2 2 D5
Gilbros Business Centre *LEI* LE1 3 G2
Gilroes Cemetery *LEIW* LE3 18 A5
Gilroes Crematorium *LEIW* LE3 18 A5
Glebelands Primary School *LEIN* LE4 10 C4
Glenfield Hospital *LEIW* LE3 17 G5
Glenfield Primary School *LEIW* LE3 23 H2
Glen Gorse Golf Club *WGSTN* LE18 45 H5
Glen Hills Primary School *LEIS* LE2 42 A5
Glenmere Primary School *WGSTN* LE18 44 D5
Gorse Hill Hospital *LEIW* LE3 17 H3
Granby Primary School *LEIS* LE2 42 D1
Grange Business Park *RLEIS/BBY* LE8 53 H2
Great Bowden CE Primary School *MKTHBORO* LE16 75 E3
Greenfield Primary School *RLEIS/BBY* LE8 65 E2
Greengate Medical Centre *LEIN* LE4 11 G4
Green Lane Infant School *LEIE* LE5 27 E3
The Green Surgery *COAL* LE67 6 B4
Greystoke Primary School *END/NAR* LE19 53 E3
Groby Community College *GBY/RBY* LE6 15 H5
Groby Trading Estate *GBY/RBY* LE6 16 A3
Guthlaxton College *WGSTN* LE18 55 H2
Hallbrook County Primary School *RLEIW/BAR* LE9 68 D5
The Hall Primary School *LEIW* LE3 24 C1
Hamilton Business Park *LEIE* LE5 21 F4
Haramead Business Centre *LEI* LE1 3 H1
Harborough Athletic Club *MKTHBORO* LE16 75 E5
Harborough Leisure Centre *MKTHBORO* LE16 78 A3
Harborough Theatre *MKTHBORO* LE16 77 H1
Haymarket Shopping Centre *LEI* LE1 3 F3
Haymarket Theatre *LEI* LE1 2 E2
Hazel Primary School *LEIS* LE2 35 F2
Heatherbrook Primary School *LEIN* LE4 17 H1

Heathfield High School *RLEIW/BAR* LE9 48 C4
Herrick Primary School *LEIN* LE4 20 B3
Highcliffe Primary School *LEIN* LE4 11 F5
Highfield Rangers FC *LEIN* LE4 20 C3
Highfields Primary School *LEIS* LE2 3 K5
Hill Lane Industrial Estate *COAL* LE67 6 B2
HM Prison *LEI* LE1 3 F7
HM Young Offenders Institution & Remand Centre (Glen Parva) *LEIS* LE2 54 D1
Holmfield Primary School *LEIW* LE3 32 D2
Holy Cross Catholic Primary School *LEIS* LE2 43 F4
Hotel Ibis *LEI* LE1 3 H4
Houghton on the Hill CE Primary School *RLEINE/SYS* LE7 39 H2
Humberstone Heights Golf Club *LEIE* LE5 28 A1
Humberstone Junior School *LEIE* LE5 28 B1
Huncote Cemetery *RLEIW/BAR* LE9 51 H3
Huncote Community Primary School *RLEIW/BAR* LE9 51 H3
Huncote Leisure Centre *RLEIW/BAR* LE9 51 G3
Hunters Lodge Medical Centre *LEIW* LE3 32 B3
Imperial Avenue Infant School *LEIW* LE3 34 B2
Inglehurst Infant School *LEIW* LE3 25 F3
Inglehurst Junior School *LEIW* LE3 25 F3
Inland Revenue *LEI* LE1 2 D2
Innkeeper's Lodge *RLEIW/BAR* LE9 32 B2
Irwin College *LEIS* LE2 3 K7
Islamic Girls School *LEIS* LE2 27 E5
Jewry Wall Museum & Site *LEIW* LE3 2 C4
John Doran Gas Museum *LEIS* LE2 35 E3
John Wycliffe Primary School *LUTT* LE17 81 F4
Judgemeadow Community College *LEIE* LE5 37 G2
Kestrels Field Primary School *LEIE* LE5 21 H5
Keyham Lodge School *LEIE* LE5 21 H5
Kibworth CE Primary School *RLEIS/BBY* LE8 71 H2
Kibworth Golf Club *RLEIS/BBY* LE8 72 B4
Kibworth High School *RLEIS/BBY* LE8 72 A4
Kibworth RUFC *MKTHBORO* LE16 78 A4
King Richard III Infant School *LEIW* LE3 2 A5
Kingsway Primary School *LEIW* LE3 33 G3
Kirby Muxloe Castle *RLEIW/BAR* LE9 23 E4
Kirby Muxloe Primary School *RLEIW/BAR* LE9 23 E5
Kirby Muxloe Sports Club *RLEIW/BAR* LE9 23 E4
Knighton Fields Primary School *LEIS* LE2 35 F5
Lady Jane Grey Primary School *GBY/RBY* LE6 16 A5
Lakeside Business Park *LEIN* LE4 12 B5
The Lancaster School *LEIS* LE2 43 G1
Langmoor Primary School *LEIS* LE2 44 D3
Latimer Primary School *RLEINE/SYS* LE7 17 G2
Launde Primary School *LEIS* LE2 45 F2
Leeson Clinic *LEIW* LE3 34 C2
Leicester Airport *LEIS* LE2 46 C1
Leicester Castle *LEI* LE1 2 C5
Leicester Cathedral *LEI* LE1 2 D4
Leicester College Abbey Park Campus *LEI* LE1 26 B2
Leicester College Bede Island Campus *LEIW* LE3 34 D2
Leicester College Freemen's Park Campus *LEIS* LE2 35 F2
Leicester College St Margaret's Campus *LEI* LE1 26 B3
Leicester Dyslexia Association *LEIE* LE5 37 F1
Leicester Exhibition Centre *LEI* LE1 3 G3
Leicester FC (Walkers Stadium) *LEIS* LE2 35 E3
Leicester Frith Hospital *LEIW* LE3 17 H5
Leicester General Hospital *LEIE* LE5 28 A5
Leicester Grammar Junior School *LEIE* LE5 37 G1
Leicester Grammar School *LEI* LE1 2 D4
Leicester High School Junior Department *LEIS* LE2 36 C5
Leicester Islamic Academy *LEIS* LE2 36 A3
Leicester Leys Leisure Centre *LEIN* LE4 18 A2
Leicester Montessori Grammar School *LEI* LE1 35 H2
Leicester Montessori School *LEIN* LE4 19 H5
LEIS LE2 36 B3
Leicester Montessori Sixth Form College *LEI* LE1 35 H2
Leicester Museum of Technology *LEIN* LE4 19 F5
Leicester Racecourse *LEIS* LE2 44 C2
Leicester Royal Infirmary *LEIS* LE2 2 E7
Leicestershire CCC (Grace Road) *LEIS* LE2 35 E5
Leicestershire Golf Club *LEIE* LE5 36 D3
Leicester Stage Hotel *WGSTN* LE18 44 A3
Leicester Tigers RFC (Welford Road Ground) *LEIS* LE2 35 F2
Leysland Clinic *RLEIS/BBY* LE8 64 C2
Leysland High School *RLEIS/BBY* LE8 64 B2
Lime Leigh Medical Centre *LEIW* LE3 34 C2
Linden Primary School *LEIE* LE5 37 E2
Little Bowden Primary School *MKTHBORO* LE16 78 A2
Little Hill Primary School *WGSTN* LE18 56 A2
The Little Theatre *LEI* LE1 3 G5
London Road Private Hospital *LEIS* LE2 36 B4
Longslade Community College *RLEINE/SYS* LE7 11 H3
Long Street Surgery *WGSTN* LE18 56 A1
Lubenham All Saints Primary School *MKTHBORO* LE16 76 C1
Lutterworth Golf Club *LUTT* LE17 81 G5
Lutterworth Grammar School & Community College *LUTT* LE17 81 F3
Lutterworth Health Centre *LUTT* LE17 81 H3
Lutterworth High School *LUTT* LE17 81 F4
Lutterworth Sports Centre *LUTT* LE17 81 F3
Magazine Gatehouse *LEIS* LE2 2 D5
Magna Park *LUTT* LE17 80 A3
Manorfield CE Primary School *RLEIW/BAR* LE9 60 B4
Manor High School *LEIS* LE2 45 H1
Market Harborough CE Primary School *MKTHBORO* LE16 74 B5
Market Harborough District Hospital *MKTHBORO* LE16 77 G1
Market Harborough Golf Club *MKTHBORO* LE16 77 H5
Market Harborough Medical Centre *MKTHBORO* LE16 77 H1
Marlow Road Industrial Estate *LEIS* LE2 34 D3
Marriott Primary School *LEIS* LE2 43 E2
Martin High School *RLEINE/SYS* LE7 9 F5
Martinshaw Primary School *GBY/RBY* LE6 15 H3
Mayflower Primary School *LEIE* LE5 36 D1
Meadowdale Primary School *MKTHBORO* LE16 75 F5
The Meadow Primary School *WGSTN* LE18 44 C5
Medway Community Primary School *LEIS* LE2 3 K6
Megabowl Bowling Alley *LEI* LE1 2 D2
Mellor Primary School *LEIN* LE4 19 H4
Memorial Hall *RLEINE/SYS* LE7 10 B2
Mercenfeld Primary School *COAL* LE67 6 B4
Meridian Business Park *END/NAR* LE19 33 F5
Meridian Leisure Park *LEIW* LE3 33 G4
Merridale Medical Centre *LEIW* LE3 34 B4
Merrydale Junior School *LEIE* LE5 27 G2
The Merton Primary School *RLEINE/SYS* LE7 13 F2
Millfield Community Primary School & Centre *END/NAR* LE19 33 G5
Millgate School *LEIS* LE2 35 G5
Mill Hill Industrial Estate *END/NAR* LE19 40 C4
Mill Lane Industrial Estate *GBY/RBY* LE6 23 G1
Moat Community College *LEIS* LE2 3 J4
Montrose Primary School *LEIS* LE2 42 D2
Mowmacre Community & Sports Centre *LEIN* LE4 19 E1
Mowmacre Hill Primary School *LEIN* LE4 18 D2
Narborough Health Centre *END/NAR* LE19 53 E3
National Space Centre *LEIN* LE4 19 F5
Nether Hall School *LEIE* LE5 28 D1
Newarke Houses Museum *LEIS* LE2 2 D5
New College Leicester *LEIW* LE3 24 D3
Newlands Primary School *RLEIW/BAR* LE9 48 C3
New Parks Leisure Centre *LEIW* LE3 24 C3
Newry Junior School *LEIS* LE2 43 F3
Newtown Linford Primary School *GBY/RBY* LE6 7 H4
New Walk Centre *LEI* LE1 2 E5
New Walk Museum & Art Gallery *LEI* LE1 3 G6
Northfield House Primary School *LEIN* LE4 27 G1
Nuffield Hospital *LEIE* LE5 28 B2
Oadby Golf Club *LEIS* LE2 44 C2
Oadby Health Centre *LEIS* LE2 45 E3
Oadby Industrial Estate *LEIS* LE2 44 D3
Oadby Town FC *WGSTN* LE18 44 D4
Oak & Ash Business Park *LEI* LE1 27 E3
Oakberry Road Industrial Estate *LUTT* LE17 81 H1
Oaklands School *LEIE* LE5 37 F1
Oaks Industrial Estate *END/NAR* LE19 52 C4
RLEIW/BAR LE9 49 E3
Odeon Multiplex *LEIS* LE2 35 F3
Old John Tower *GBY/RBY* LE6 8 B1
Old Mill County Primary School *RLEIW/BAR* LE9 68 D3
Old Wyggestonians Sports Club *WGSTN* LE18 44 D4
Orchard CE Primary School *RLEIW/BAR* LE9 68 B3
The Osiers Business Centre *LEIW* LE3 41 G2
Overdale J & I School *LEIS* LE2 44 A2
The Parkland Primary School *LEIS* LE2 55 F2
Parks Primary School *LEIW* LE3 25 E2
Pasley Road Health Centre *LEIS* LE2 42 D4
The Pastures Primary School *END/NAR* LE19 52 B1
Phoenix Arts Centre *LEI* LE1 2 E5
Piccadilly Cinema *LEI* LE1 3 F2
Picture House *LEI* LE1 2 E3
Piper Way School *LEIW* LE3 24 D4
Pochin Primary School *RLEINE/SYS* LE7 13 H4
Premier Travel Inn *END/NAR* LE19 33 F4
LEIW LE3 17 F5
LEIW LE3 25 E1
LEIW LE3 32 D2
RLEIS/BBY LE8 58 A2
Queensmead School *LEIW* LE3 34 A1
Queniborough CE Primary School *RLEINE/SYS* LE7 5 H4
Queniborough Industrial Estate *RLEINE/SYS* LE7 5 F4
Ramada Hotel *LEI* LE1 3 F4
Rana Academy *LEIN* LE4 19 G5
Ratby Primary School *GBY/RBY* LE6 22 C1
Ratby Sports Club *GBY/RBY* LE6 22 C2
Ravenhurst Primary School *LEIW* LE3 33 H5
The Record Office for Leicestershire *WGSTN* LE18 44 A5
Red Hill Field Primary School *END/NAR* LE19 52 C3
Regency Hotel *LEIS* LE2 36 B4
Regent College *LEI* LE1 35 G2
Regent Street Industrial Estate *END/NAR* LE19 53 F3
Richard Hill CE Primary School *RLEINE/SYS* LE7 10 B2
Ridgeway Primary School *MKTHBORO* LE16 74 D4
Riverside Community College *LEIW* LE3 34 B5
Riverside Community Primary School *LEIN* LE4 11 H5
The Robert Smyth School *MKTHBORO* LE16 74 C4
Rockingham Industrial Estate *MKTHBORO* LE16 75 E5
Rolleston Primary School *LEIS* LE2 54 D1
Roundhill Community College *RLEINE/SYS* LE7 12 D3
Rowlatts Hill Primary School *LEIE* LE5 28 A4
Rushey Mead Health Centre *LEIN* LE4 20 B3
Rushey Mead Primary School *LEIN* LE4 20 A5
Rushey Mead Recreation Centre *LEIN* LE4 20 A3
Rushey Mead School *LEIN* LE4 20 A3
Sacred Heart RC Primary School *LEIE* LE5 27 E4

Saffron Hill Cemetery *LEIS* LE2 43 F4
Saffron Lane Sports Centre *LEIS* LE2 35 F4
Saffron Lane Stadium *LEIS* LE2 35 F4
St Barnabas Primary School *LEIE* LE5 27 G3
St Crispins School *LEI* LE1 35 H3
St Cuthberts CE Primary School *RLEIS/BBY* LE8 59 E2
St George's Retail Park *LEIE* LE5 3 J3
St John Fisher Catholic Primary School *WGSTN* LE18 44 C4
St John the Baptist CE Primary School *LEIS* LE2 36 A3
St Josephs RC Primary School *LEIE* LE5 28 D2
MKTHBORO LE16 77 H1
St Lukes CE Primary School *RLEINE/SYS* LE7 29 F5
St Lukes Hospital *MKTHBORO* LE16 74 B4
St Margarets Baths *LEI* LE1 2 D2
St Margarets Business Centre *LEI* LE1 2 E1
St Margarets Bus Station *LEI* LE1 2 E2
St Margarets Sports Centre *LEI* LE1 26 A2
St Martins Shopping Centre *LEI* LE1 2 E4
St Mary de Castro Church *LEI* LE1 2 C5
St Marys Business Park *MKTHBORO* LE16 74 D5
St Marys CE Primary School *LUTT* LE17 81 E1
St Marys Fields Infant School *LEIW* LE3 34 C3
St Mathews Sports Hall *LEI* LE1 3 H1
St Matthews Business Centre *LEI* LE1 3 F1
St Patricks RC Primary School *LEIN* LE4 19 H5
St Pauls RC School *LEIE* LE5 37 G1
St Peter & St Paul CE Primary School *RLEINE/SYS* LE7 4 C4
St Peters CE Primary School *RLEIS/BBY* LE8 53 H4
St Peters Health Centre *LEIS* LE2 3 J5
St Peters RC Primary School *RLEIW/BAR* LE9 49 G2
St Thomas More Catholic School *LEIS* LE2 36 A5
Sandfield Close Primary School *LEIN* LE4 20 C2
Scraptoft Valley Primary School *LEIE* LE5 28 D2
Shaftesbury Junior School *LEIW* LE3 34 C1
Sharnford CE Primary School *HINC* LE10 66 C4
Shenton Primary School *LEIE* LE5 27 E3
The Sherrier Centre *LUTT* LE17 81 G3
Sherrier CE Primary School *LUTT* LE17 81 G2
Shires Shopping Centre *LEI* LE1 2 E3
Shonki Business Centre *LEI* LE1 26 B3
Sir Jonathan North Community College *LEIS* LE2 43 G1
Slater Primary School *LEIW* LE3 26 A3
Soar Valley College *LEIN* LE4 20 A4
Southfields Infant School *LEIS* LE2 43 F3
South Leicester RFC *WGSTN* LE18 56 B3
South Leicestershire College *WGSTN* LE18 55 H1
South Wigston Health Centre *WGSTN* LE18 55 G1
South Wigston High School *LEIS* LE2 55 E2
Sovereign Park Industrial Estate *MKTHBORO* LE16 77 H3
Sparkenhoe Community Primary School *LEIS* LE2 3 K5
Spence Street Sports Centre *LEIE* LE5 27 F3
Spinney Hill Primary School *LEIE* LE5 27 F5
Springfield Road Health Centre *LEIS* LE2 36 A3
Stafford Leys Primary School *LEIW* LE3 32 B3
Stokes Wood Primary School *LEIW* LE3 25 F2
Stonehill High School *RLEINE/SYS* LE7 11 G3
Stoneygate College *LEIS* LE2 36 B3
Stoneygate FC *RLEINE/SYS* LE7 29 G2
Stoneygate School *LEIS* LE2 36 A3
Stretton Hall (Hospital) *LEIS* LE2 46 C4
Sunningdale Industrial Park *LEIW* LE3 33 E1
Syston Health Centre *RLEINE/SYS* LE7 4 D5
Taylor Road Primary School *LEI* LE1 26 D3
Thistly Meadow Primary School *RLEIS/BBY* LE8 54 C4
Thomas Estley Community College *RLEIW/BAR* LE9 68 D3
Three Swans Hotel *MKTHBORO* LE16 77 H1
Thurmaston Cemetery *LEIN* LE4 12 C5
Thurnby Lodge Primary School *LEIE* LE5 28 D4
Thythorn Field Primary School *WGSTN* LE18 56 B4
The Towers Hospital *LEIE* LE5 27 H1
Townlands CE Primary School *RLEIW/BAR* LE9 49 F4
Travelodge *LEI* LE1 2 C3
Trinity Hospital *LEI* LE1 2 C5
Troon Industrial Estate *LEIN* LE4 21 E3
Troon Way Business Centre *LEIN* LE4 20 C3
Tropical Birdland *RLEIW/BAR* LE9 30 B1
University Exhibition Centre *LEI* LE1 2 C4
University of Leicester *LEI* LE1 3 H7
LEI LE1 35 G3
LEIS LE2 36 B5
University of Leicester Harold Martin Botanic Garden *LEIS* LE2 36 D5
University of Leicester Sports Ground *LEIS* LE2 37 E5
Uplands Junior School *LEIS* LE2 27 E5
Uppingham Road Health Centre *LEIE* LE5 27 G3
Victoria Clinic *LEIS* LE2 35 H3
Vulcan Business Centre *LEIE* LE5 3 K1
Walnut Street Medical Centre *LEIS* LE2 35 E2
Wanstead Industrial Park *LEIW* LE3 23 H5
Warner Village *LEIW* LE3 33 G4
Water Leys Primary School *WGSTN* LE18 43 H4
Watermead Country Park *RLEINE/SYS* LE7 12 B2
Weavers Close CE Primary School *RLEIW/BAR* LE9 49 F3
Welland Industrial Estate *MKTHBORO* LE16 75 F5
The Welland Park College *MKTHBORO* LE16 77 H2
Westbridge Industrial Park *LEIW* LE3 2 C4
Westcotes Health Centre *LEIW* LE3 34 C1
Western Golf Club *LEIW* LE3 23 H4
Western Park School *LEIW* LE3 24 D4
Westleigh Business Park *RLEIS/BBY* LE8 54 B2
Westleigh RFC *RLEIS/BBY* LE8 54 A4
RLEIS/BBY LE8 64 A1
Whetstone Golf Club *RLEIW/BAR* LE9 63 G2
Whitehall Primary School *LEIE* LE5 37 F1
Wigston Swimming Pool *WGSTN* LE18 55 H2
Wilberforce Road Surgery *LEIW* LE3 2 A7
William Bradford Community College *RLEIW/BAR* LE9 48 C3
Willowbrook Primary School *LEIE* LE5 29 E4
Winstanley High School *LEIW* LE3 33 G4
Wolsey House Primary School *LEIN* LE4 19 E4
Woodland Grange Primary School *LEIS* LE2 45 H4
Woodlands Day Hospital *END/NAR* LE19 52 D3
Woodstock Primary School *LEIN* LE4 19 E3
Woolden Hill CP School *RLEINE/SYS* LE7 9 G4
Wreake Valley Community College *RLEINE/SYS* LE7 5 E4
Wycliffe Industrial Estate *LUTT* LE17 81 H2
Wyggeston Hospital *LEIW* LE3 34 C1
Wyggeston & Queen Elizabeth I College *LEI* LE1 35 G3
Wygston's House Museum of Costume *LEI* LE1 2 D4
Wyvern County Primary School *LEIN* LE4 20 B5

Acknowledgements

The Post Office is a registered trademark of Post Office Ltd. in the UK and other countries.

Schools address data provided by Education Direct.

Petrol station information supplied by Johnsons

One-way street data provided by © Tele Atlas N.V. Tele Atlas

Garden centre information provided by:

Garden Centre Association Britains best garden centres

Wyevale Garden Centres

The statement on the front cover of this atlas is sourced, selected and quoted from a reader comment and feedback form received in 2004

Notes

Notes

Notes

Notes

Notes

AA Street by Street QUESTIONNAIRE

Dear Atlas User
Your comments, opinions and recommendations are very important to us. So please help us to improve our street atlases by taking a few minutes to complete this simple questionnaire.

You do not need a stamp (unless posted outside the UK). If you do not want to remove this page from your street atlas, then photocopy it or write your answers on a plain sheet of paper.

Send to: The Editor, AA Street by Street, FREEPOST SCE 4598, Basingstoke RG21 4GY

ABOUT THE ATLAS...

Which city/town/county did you buy?

____

Are there any features of the atlas or mapping that you find particularly useful?

____
____
____

Is there anything we could have done better?

____
____
____

Why did you choose an AA Street by Street atlas?

____
____
____

Did it meet your expectations?

Exceeded ☐ **Met all** ☐ **Met most** ☐ **Fell below** ☐

Please give your reasons

____
____
____
____
____

continued overleaf

Where did you buy it?

For what purpose? (please tick all applicable)

To use in your own local area ☐ **To use on business or at work** ☐

Visiting a strange place ☐ **In the car** ☐ **On foot** ☐

Other (please state)

LOCAL KNOWLEDGE...

Local knowledge is invaluable. Whilst every attempt has been made to make the information contained in this atlas as accurate as possible, should you notice any inaccuracies, please detail them below (if necessary, use a blank piece of paper) or e-mail us at *streetbystreet@theAA.com*

ABOUT YOU...

Name (Mr/Mrs/Ms)

Address

Postcode

Daytime tel no **Mobile tel no**

E-mail address

Please only give us your e-mail address and mobile phone number if you wish to hear from us about other products and services from the AA and partners by e-mail or text or mms.

Which age group are you in?

Under 25 ☐ **25-34** ☐ **35-44** ☐ **45-54** ☐ **55-64** ☐ **65+** ☐

Are you an AA member? **YES** ☐ **NO** ☐

Do you have Internet access? **YES** ☐ **NO** ☐

The information we hold about you will be used to provide the product(s) and service(s) requested and for identification, account administration, analysis, and fraud/loss prevention purposes. More details about how that information is used is in our Privacy Statement, which you will find under the heading "Personal information" in our Terms and Conditions and on our website. Copies are available from us by post, by contacting our Data Protection Manager at AA, Fanum House, Basing View, Hampshire, Basingstoke RG21 4EA.

We may want to contact you about other products and services provided by us or our partners but please tick the box if you DO NOT wish to hear about such products and services from us by mail or telephone. ☐

Thank you for taking the time to complete this questionnaire. Please send it to us as soon as possible, and remember, you do not need a stamp (unless posted outside the UK).

ML225